From The Trench of Mission Control to the Craters of The Moon

"The early years of America's human space program.
Stories from the men of NASA's Mission Control
Flight Dynamics group: The Trench"

**Dedicated to all those who worked on the historic
American Manned Spaceflight Program
and the projects that made real-time trajectory control
the reality it had to be to place men on the moon.**

Third Edition
Copyright © 2012

For additional information the reader can link to
the NASA History Portal at:

http://www.jsc.nasa.gov/history/

Praise for the 'TRENCH'

"From the Trench…" is a fascinating story of the formative years of the NASA Mission Control Center and Mission Operations team, written by those who guided the Mercury, Gemini and Apollo missions. These were amazing and dedicated people, and together they built the early MCC team that put Apollo on the Moon. Our nation is blessed that at a critical time in our history it could educate, recruit, and nourish such talent.

Today's leaders don't realize the power of space exploration in inspiring young people to become tomorrow's high-tech leaders. Space exploration draws them toward engineering and science careers, but also delivers intangible but real benefits to our national psyche. We need more visionary leaders, as in the years of Apollo, because our national lead in space technology is slowly dissipating from neglect. "From the Trench…" reminds us of just what this nation—and its people—can do when their energy is turned loose to achieve what others deem impossible. Leaders from the White House to NASA to those who work in flight control today will learn much from this book.

Thomas D. Jones, veteran NASA Astronaut

STS-59, STS-68, STS-80, STS-98

Author of:

"Sky Walking: An Astronaut's Memoir"

"Hell Hawks! The Untold Story of the American Fliers Who Savaged Hitler's Wehrmacht," with Robert F. Dorr

"Planetology: Unlocking the Secrets of the Solar System," with Ellen Stofan

Acknowledgements

We all owe a debt of gratitude to the vision, guidance and management mastery of Robert Gilruth, Christopher C. Kraft and Glynn S. Lunney.

Those of us who lived in the 50's and 60's and participated in the NASA Manned Spacecraft Program were beyond fortunate. We not only had the day to day experiences, but we also had a rare opportunity to be enveloped in the magic of working together as a very close team and family. Those learnings we have all carried with us into follow-on careers. We know the magic and the power of team and are fortunate to be able to carry that legacy to others in our personal and professional lives.

As we undertook this effort we were powered by the dedication of our consumate leader and mentor, Glynn Lunney and his framing of this biographical mcmoir project. To aid us in the process, Glynn contacted Dion McInnis, Associate Vice President of University Advancement for the University of Houston who instructed us in the methods of converting 'memories into memoirs'. His advice was critical to this entire effort.

We are grateful to the NASA History Office for their foresight in creating and conducting the Oral History Project that captured so many details from those who were involved in the NASA Houston experience. Many of the historical photos that are used throughout book were graciously provided by NASA and made the book so much richer in content. A compendium of specific interviews from members of the TRENCH are published under separate cover: *Oral Histories of NASA Flight Dynamics Controllers*

When we reached an obstacle of transcribing our initial recordings into text for this book we were fortunate to have the volunteer efforts of Maureen Bowen from NASA. In the course of piecing even more material together, we were joined in this transcription process by a fan of Mission Control, Todd Johnston of Waitsfield, VT, who volunteered to transcribe hours upon hours of recordings. This book could not have been as complete as it is without his unrelenting and timely help.

Nor would our efforts have been as complete without a special partner of our Flight Dynamics family, Ken Young, who was with us in the Staff-Support Room (SSR) throughout those magic years. His added recall was most helpful in the book editing process.

When it was all said and done, we look back at what we accomplished and realize that none of it could have been what it was without the round-the-clock support of our wives. They were our lynchpins not only in what we did in Houston, but in the writing of these memoirs.

Foreword

Dr. Christopher Columbus Kraft, Jr.

When asked to consider writing a foreword for those who call themselves "The Trench", I said I would first like to read what some of them had to say.

Reading the accounts of these men who gave so much of themselves to the success of NASA's manned space flight programs was not only worthwhile but very enlightening. Therefore, I am more than pleased to add my observations to the history these men have written about.

Jerry Bostick presenting Christopher Kraft
with an Honorary "Trench" membership
on behalf of Captain Refsmmat: "The Ideal Flight Controller"
1969

First, the word "trench" in the context of Mission Control. There are probably a number of definitions for the term, but mine is as follows:

The original control center was at Cape Canaveral. The Flight Dynamics Officer and his 'companion' Retro Fire Officer played a major role in the performance of flight control in Project Mercury. However, as this role required considerably more complex operations and analysis in the follow on programs of Gemini, and Apollo, the entire lower row of the mission control center in Houston was made up of engineers and scientists at an expanded number of consoles with multiple responsibilities. Their importance remained critical throughout every aspect of the mission.

As I came to hear about the "Trench", I saw it as a referral to the term as expressed in military usage. That is, it was a means of defense against any and all assaults on the safety and success of the mission to be conducted. These men and their tools certainly provided that assurance for all of the missions conducted in the Houston MCC (also known as the MOCR-Mission Operations Control Room).

There is a common thread which weaves itself through all of these memoirs. With few exceptions, they were a product of the culture born in the depression years of our country. As young boys, each was faced with the task of surviving an economic dilemma and having to fend for themselves. Attending college was almost unthinkable because of the lack of financial support from a struggling family. Yet, they all managed to make the unlikely happen and were responsible for building the team that took man to the Moon. The character they developed in their early years certainly became the dominating factor in their approach to what many believed in 1961 was an impossible undertaking.

As the manned spaceflight program began to develop in the late 50's, I was selected as one of the those who was given the task of putting man in space and eventually responding to the challenge made by President Kennedy of landing men on the Moon and returning them safely back on earth. The job was accomplished in a great part by the men in "The Trench."

Thank God for the ingenuity of these treasured Americans.

All who served in the Trench through Apollo 11
(in order of arrival at NASA)

Carl Huss*	Early 1958 to STG
Glynn Lunney	Mid 1958
John Llewellyn*	Late 1958
Tec Roberts*	4/59
George Guthrie	1/01/61
"Dutch" von Ehrenfried	6/1961 & 6/1966
Jerry Bostick	01/29/62
Cliff Charlesworth*	4/01/62
Bobby Spencer*	6/03/62
Charley Parker	6/03/63
Beverly Duncan	1963
Grady Meyer*	1963
Ken Russell	1/13/64
Ed Pavelka*	2/03/64
Dave Massaro	2/16/64
Phil Shaffer*	5/03/64
Liz Pieberhofer	1964
Dave Reed	6/22/64
Stewart Davis	7/16/64
Sandy Cassetti	1964/1965
Tom Weichel	6/22/64
Robert White	6/64
Will Fenner*	8/64
Chuck Deiterich	8/31/64
Granville Paules*	9/03/64
Will Presley*	10/19/64
Stephen Bales	12/64
Gary Renick	1/04/65
Tom Carter*	1964/65
Bill Gravett	1/11/65
Maurice Kennedy	2/08/65
Jim I'Anson*	3/03/65
Jay Greene	3/08/65
Bill Boone	6/15/67
Bill Stoval	7/03/67
Neil Hutchinson	2-3Q/1967
Jerry Mill	8/01/67
Walt Wells	1967
Ginny Engel	By 1967
Jim Payne	1967
Dean Toups*	1967
Jerry Elliott	1967-68
Ray Teague	1/07/68

*--deceased

I - Glynn S. Lunney 9

XI - Remembrances 381

Epilogue **417**

I - Glynn S. Lunney

THE FLIGHT DYNAMICS STORY

Prologue

It is daunting to try to do something like capturing history. In reading many of the books people have written about the space program, it is always impressive to realize the differences in the landscape that we each see. How it looks depends on our technical and emotional involvement in a particular set of events, and our place in the organization, which is a measure of how much scope we are exposed to. And then we have our own backgrounds, which are personal prisms for remembering and interpreting the events we were part of.

In a way, Apollo was a pivot point in history. This group of young men and their parents and grandparents came from a time before electricity, cars, planes, phones, indoor plumbing, charge cards and fast food restaurants. It was a world much more like the one people lived in during previous centuries. Our children, grand kids and subsequent generations live in an entirely different world – the modern one that came into being in the second half of the 20th century. This pivot coincided with the Apollo era, when all things suddenly seemed possible.

So we thought it worthwhile to capture the story of how a small group of young Americans, connected to those earlier times in many ways, prepared themselves and rallied to the challenge of Apollo. Our objective is not so much a recounting of space travel facts and figures. But rather, it is to leave, for our families and descendants, a sense of what it was like to be part of Apollo. Hopefully, some will be interested in what their grandfathers, uncles or even distant cousins did and how they felt being part of the first visit by human beings to another body in our solar system. We were a very small unit in the very large enterprise it took to get to the moon. And we were most fortunate and privileged to participate in this singular and historic achievement.

It was our grand adventure. We loved it.

The Flight Dynamics Branch

This is the story of a relatively small group of young men, all very early in their careers, most of them brand new college graduates. Each in their own way had been preparing themselves for their adult future when they came to NASA and human space flight. Our astronauts were selected in a national competition from the best of all of our test pilots and indeed they were. However, we ground operators (and all the other engineers at NASA) actually selected ourselves by showing up to participate in this grand adventure of going to the moon.

If it takes motivation and attitude to be successful, these young men were already there, even on a project that could easily seem impossible. We knew almost nothing about space flight. We certainly didn't know what it would take to land people on the moon and return them safely to Earth. But these young men came and they met the challenge. They had to invent it all - the control center, and all the tools of the trade such as orbital mechanics, propulsion and guidance systems, the integration with crew members, the procedures that were necessary, and then the mission rules that we learned to live by.

These young men had to master a very new and complicated discipline that we called "flight dynamics." And they had to prepare themselves to make decisions in the MCC on any and all of the flight dynamics matters relevant to the missions. As pioneers in the field, they faced decisions that had to be made in real time, without consultation or deferral, sometimes in seconds, and of the highest consequence. There was not much time to prepare.

In March 1962, I was named section head, a first level supervisor with all of two of us. In the summer 1964, I became the chief of the newly formed Flight Dynamics Branch with a total of thirteen of us. By this time, we had finished Mercury and were preparing for Gemini and Apollo. We had 7 men assigned to Gemini and needed at least nine -- three trained operators on three different shifts by 1965. Plus, more depth was still necessary to do the planning for the upcoming flights. Apollo had a mountain of work for the 5 assigned, with manned flights scheduled in 1967, less than three years away.

This growth came by March of 1968 - the branch had twenty-nine men to begin the final sprint to the moon landings. They were tested and tempered by ten manned Gemini flights, four unmanned Apollo flights and uncounted simulation exercises. They were ready for Apollo.

In reflecting on the branch, I am not sure how the interpersonal dynamics all came about but there was an extremely strong sense of unity, comradeship, and mutual dependence, united by a powerful commitment to make the program a success. They were also competitive about earning the choice—and most difficult—assignments. This was a "Band of Brothers" in the best tradition of that honored term.

'TRENCHMEN'

L-R: Will Fenner, Stu Davis, Steve Bales, Charlie Parker, Cliff Charlesworth, Ed Pavelka, Ken Russell, Jerry Bostick, Tom Carter, John Llewellyn, Bill Gravett, Dave Massaro.

Standing directly behind Ed Pavelka: Glynn Lunney

Some of this magic was the sense of coming together to do something really big, something that had never been done before. Some of it was in the mutual reliance of all of these men on each other. This was especially true and even necessary in the operations environment in the MCC. They had to come to an answer, sometimes very quickly, and they had to earn the trust that gave their answer credibility, and the answer had to be correct. They gradually learned what it took to prove their choices to their office supervisors, to their fellow flight controllers, to the best test pilots, to the flight directors and, most of all, to themselves. It was a magic time to see these twenty-something boisterous males come to grips with their new responsibility and embrace it. They even adopted a team identity for the three console positions which they manned and called their unit 'the Trench'. These 'Trenchmen' were amazing and inspiring. I have always felt privileged to have served with them.

The outstanding performance that these young men delivered will stay with them forever. They earned it. Today, looking back forty some years to the decade of the sixties, I am still extremely gratified that these men and I were granted this historic opportunity. We were not necessarily the best and brightest in the whole world. But we certainly were the most passionate and the most committed to making the program succeed. Today, we still gather up on various occasions where the same opinionated comradeship and hassling of each other is the order of the day.

ORIGINS

Early Times

My earliest memories were of the big yellow house on Main Street, in Old Forge Pennsylvania. It was the home of my mom's parents, but my grandfather Joseph Glynn had already died in May, about six months before I was born. My grandmother, Winifred Hennigan Glynn, was the lady of the house, and we lived upstairs. It was common in those times for 3 or more generations to live in the same house, at least for some time.

Glynn and Dad Bill

Life was simple, compared to later times—no cars, no phones, not much indoor plumbing and the only packaged entertainment was the movies on Saturday afternoon. Restaurants were also extremely scarce and very rarely visited. In an interview with our mom sometime in the late 90's, we asked how things were during the years of the depression before the war. She offered that "it was not so bad, we had enough to eat and, after all, everybody was in the same boat." And that was the way Mom looked at life.

In terms of recollections, some simple and sometimes vague things come to mind:
- All families had vegetable gardens in their yards.
- The horse drawn wagon carried large blocks of ice for the ice boxes. (There were no refrigerators)

- Outhouses were prevalent in all back yards.
- Doctors made house calls.
- We did not have a car until after the war. Hardly anyone did.
- The town was divided along ethnic walls, not ethnic lines.
- Everybody inside the Irish ethnic wall seemed related.
- Everybody in the house ate at the big table at the same time, except Aunt Bea who ate separately.
- The smell of baking bread.
- Mom singing.
- Mountains cradling the valley.
- Going to St. Lawrence Church on Sunday.
- The smell of grass in the summer.
- Terrible squeals as the next door neighbors slaughtered their hog.
- Deep snow in winter.
- Scary roots grew out of the potatoes in the cellar.
- Catching fireflies in a jar.
- Watermelon in the yard.
- Swings and rocking chairs on porches.

And that was the way it was.

By the time of the war, I had two brothers Bill and Jerry. (At my age, it was hard to figure what little brothers were good for—although I did later.) In all our early photos, we were far over on the skinny side of life and it looked like cameras must have scared us. Clearly, no movie talent there. Once the war started, we moved first to Bethlehem where Dad worked at US Steel. And soon, we moved to Philadelphia where Dad worked in the Navy shipyard, making submarines. We boys had a pretty good time in Philadelphia at 32nd and Pearl in a first floor apartment unit. The apartment was just a few blocks away from the University of Pennsylvania campus. There were a lot of kids on our block for kicking the can and playing stick ball with. The idea of the war did not penetrate much at our age.

We also enjoyed the neighbor couple upstairs, Mabel and Grady Jones and Mabel's mother, Floss. We thought Grady was cool. He was from North Carolina and had this drawl we tried to imitate. No matter how much Grady instructed us, we did not pass. Grady laughed at that a lot. He had a lot of funny, country sayings and was fun to be with. It was the first time that I ever met anybody from the South. Our parents always seemed to have a good time with Mabel and Grady and our folks continued to visit with the Jones's after we moved back to Scranton. Grady drove his 51 Ford sedan—a really cool car—up for a visit. He even let me drive it on the hill at the Old Forge home. It was the first time I ever saw an automatic transmission, let alone drive one. Also, it was on that visit that Grady bought me my first razor and showed me how to shave. They were great friends to our parents and us kids.

There was one group of outlaws on our block. Five kids lived on the second floor above our unit. We only knew them by their last name – Peppy. And we called them the Peppy kids. They had a chicken wire fence around their second-floor porch. This "cage" allowed them outside. But, it also allowed them to taunt us street dwellers, and throw ugly things down on us. The unforgivable insult was when they urinated on the clothes that mom hung out to dry in the yard. But, even worse, they managed to add their urine to our apple pie which mom had set out on our porch rail to cool. Needless to say, all of this inflamed us natives. Very occasionally, the Peppy kids would be out on the street by themselves. It might be by choice, by parent instructions or by God--we did not care. The cry went up "the Peppy kids are out" and we would find them and bang them up, appropriate for their offenses. It was good that they were as skinny as we were. The street fights were not always bloodless. I remember one battle against another neighborhood group of boys that was pretty intense. When I got home, I found that I was sweating profusely and, when I rubbed my hand through my hair, it came away covered in blood. Something heavy had pounded my head and split the skin open. I believe that it was my first time for stitches.

But our great adventures were mostly on the weekends when Dad was home. Everybody in the family except Jerry had a bike. Mine was a 24 inch one and Bill had a small wheel size of 20 inches. He had to peddle like the devil just to keep up with us. Jerry rode on the bar in front of dad's seat. This arrangement worked pretty well most of the time. Except once, Jerry held up our ride for about an hour because he could not find his pillow. By the time we got back from our couple of hours of biking, Jerry was in considerable discomfort and unable to sit. You can imagine the outpouring of sympathy for him. By my process of elimination, the pillow thief had to be Bill, but he did not own up. Bill was fairly stubborn about things. He could kneel down and bang his head on the sidewalk when he got mad or frustrated. He did turn out okay despite this affliction.

Many times, we biked down in the park and mom brought lunch in the basket attached to her bike. These were great times for the family. We liked to visit a park area called Lemon Hill. Many bike riding families showed up there on the weekends and enjoyed being out of the city streets and flying kites on the rolling green hills. For the parents, it had to be a welcome break from the work routine and the concern for relatives off in military service. Mom's brother, our uncle Steve, was out in the Pacific somewhere with the Seabees.

I started at St. Agatha's grade school on Spring Garden Street, about eight to ten blocks from our place. Bill followed in two years and Jerry did not start school until we moved back to Scranton after the war. Brother Bill and I walked to school every day and, with no school buses or parents to chauffeur us, we would collect a crowd by the time we got there. This gave us too much of a chance to visit with other classmates on the way home and sometimes we were late.

St. Agatha's grade school was run by the nuns. As anyone who went to school with the nuns back then will tell you, they were great for at least two things, one being the basics and the other being discipline. They were probably great human beings also, but in our station of life, it was all about the first two, with emphasis on the discipline part. Discipline came in the form of one of those three-sided rulers, about 3/4 inches on a side. They were designed by the devil, but the sisters used them anyway. And they were very good at it. They had our attention, so the basics could begin. And, if you got in trouble, your parents knew it was your fault, and no one else's.

On August 6, 1945, just eight days before the news of the unconditional surrender of Japan, Dad was inducted into the US Army and served in the Army Air Corps. Dad was stationed at a number of places around the country and I remember that Mom went to visit him one time when he was stationed in Georgia. This was during the winter and Mom expected the weather in such a warm southern state to be just like summer. It was not so.

Another problem followed Dad all of his service time. Somehow, the Army lost his papers, or at least the payroll papers. They still could ship him around to new assignments. But, the real downside was that he never got paid. Mom got a counter clerk job at the local drugstore. So, her paycheck had to support the home front and she also sent money to Dad for cigarettes and incidentals. The kids, of course, were never told any of this. It must have been about this time that Pop, my Dad's father, came to live with us. Our guess is that it was to watch us while Mom worked.

Dad spent his last time in service at Shepherd Field in Texas. He told us of the German POWs who were kept there. We were surprised to hear that they were relatively free to walk around the base, not in serious confinement during the day. And, they were very happy to be where they were rather than on any front, especially the Eastern one. I remember the celebrations when VE day and then VJ day occurred, people in the streets, car horns blasting, lots of cheering and weeping. I don't think I was aware that the next destination for Pvt. Lunney would have been the Pacific. When Dad finally got back home, he had this big duffel bag full of standard gear, all of which we thought was really cool. Uncle Steve of the Seabees brought home koala bear stuffed animals and a boomerang from Australia. It had been damaged some, but we loved throwing it out in the field. It did not work like we saw in the movies, but it was fun trying.

After the war, Dad bought a large truck, like you might see in the U-haul lot today. The cargo section was accessible from the cab and was good for traveling and camping. I don't know how Dad swung the money; maybe his Army pay finally caught up with him. Either way, Dad wanted to go into the moving business and tried to get a license to start the business but he was never successful. The story that I understood was that the local cab company blocked any approval. Whatever the reason, Dad was very disappointed and we did not forgive the yellow cab company.

With no more submarines to build in 'Philly, we moved back to Scranton. Dad was going back to the mines.

Years of Formation

When we moved back to Scranton, we rented the middle unit of a triplex in West Scranton at 1139 Eynon Street. This was probably in 1946 and we lived there for about five years. We went to school at St. Anne's, which was a very large parish with a twelve grade school. The nuns had different names than at St. Agatha's but they all went to the same training course. They looked the same and had the same three sided rulers. (I make fun of what has become a stereotype of the nuns, but they were selfless teachers of generations of young kids and the world is now a poorer place as they and their schools become more rare.)

At St. Anne's, I went in training to become an altar boy. The priest who led that instruction was Father John Mark. And he was a rigorous perfectionist and disciplinarian. But we really did learn the Mass and how to serve the priest who was conducting the service. Father John Mark drilled us on all the procedures and especially all the responses in Latin. Even today, I still find myself replying to myself in Latin to the prayers that the priest now says in English. And yes, I did get to try the wine.

Certainly, my early years were very strongly influenced by my family and the environment in which they lived. My Dad, my uncles Stanley and Steve, like so many others, worked in the mines of northeastern Pennsylvania. My two grandfathers also worked in the mines in their earlier times. My grandfather on my father's side was always called Pop by everyone, and he lived with us occasionally. My maternal grandfather also worked in the mines but he had died six months before I was born. We believe that all of the generations of men in our family who came over from Ireland beginning in the mid 1800's worked in the mines at some point in their lives. It was the primary industry in the region and there was not much other work available.

As a young boy, Dad started working in the breakers where the coal was separated from the slag by boys straddling the conveyor. He started this work when he was about twelve to fourteen years old, leaving school sometime in junior high. Being a coal miner was very difficult and dangerous work. It required the miner to quickly develop a wide range of skills. They had to be equipment operators, explosives experts, structural engineers, electricians, carpenters, and safety experts who were always conscious of the environment around them. They also had to be pretty tough. No, very tough.

These early years in the thirties before World War II were a time when people were not really recovered from the Great Depression. There were many aspects of life which were much more difficult than circumstances today. I never remember parents complaining about what had to be done. They simply did what was called for and conveyed those lessons to us by virtue of their example.

Everything that was done took considerably more effort than it did later. For example the simple act of heating the house required a regular routine of shoveling the ashes out of the stove, carrying the ashes to wherever we were dumping fill at the time, refilling the pails with coal from the garage and then replenishing the fire. In the Old Forge house on River Street, the coal stoves were on the first floor. One was for cooking and heat in the kitchen and another stove on the first floor added heat to the living area. This encouraged a very fast run downstairs in the morning to get near the stove. In the area of food, meals were pretty simple and basic. Meat and potatoes were a staple along with pasta and stews. I don't remember eating out at a restaurant until perhaps I was in high school and that was only on special occasions.

The River Street house was a family property on Mom's side with a deed dating back to 1860. When we first moved into the home on River Street, it did not have an inside bathroom. This was one of Dad's first major projects in the first home of which we were the owners and not renting. We were very willing and motivated workers on this project for obvious reasons. We had to add framing to create enough space for the extra room. And then Dad had to instruct us on lights and plumbing. Family transportation was never more than one car at a time and, at first, it was a 1930's something with a roll up front window for air conditioning. Later, Dad got a 1936 4 door Buick with a big straight eight engine and manual shift on the floor. This was the car I learned to drive on. Usually, there was no family ride available for us kids and the order of transportation was to walk, to bike, or to hitchhike.

When we did get that one car, they were generally in need of regular repair and maintenance. So, Dad was very sensitive to any driving faults causing a problem to his only car. And, God knows, we had them. Despite his caution, it seemed that we were always dealing with flat tires, failure to start or run and I even had a battery fall out of the car through a corroded case to the ground. Seeing it in the rear view mirror, I knew I was in trouble. A contributing factor to this failure was that I was driving through a field with lots of serious bumps; that fact was best left out of my accident report to Dad. Bill was pretty good about the driving. In addition to being a pretty good driver, my brother Bill became an expert on fixing cars. He usually had a carburetor on the kitchen table and he got pretty good at all kinds of repairs. Throughout our careers and into retirement, Bill is the Lunney go-to brother if you want something fixed. But, we all live 1000 miles apart. Jerry, on the other hand, came near to serious bodily harm from Dad for some of his driving antics, such as losing the car. That was a father/son "interrogation for the age" and it got even more memorable as Jerry "lost" the car several more times, each time he was out late with his buddies. Dad could not comprehend how one of his own flesh and blood could do this.

Our parents had a common division of roles for family administration. Dad was in charge of the big D for all around discipline; he was project management and operations for the work to keep our facilities - house, yard and cars - in order; he provided training and direction to our small work force; he certainly assured quality; he provided encouragement to our sports endeavors and our progress in school. And, he provided example constantly. When he left us with a job, he came back later with a clear idea about how much should have been accomplished. We either got a nod for ok, or a frown and a suggestion that meant "increase your productivity."

Dad also had a continuing series of projects at his work at Niverts where he worked, after the mines, from about 1951 on. Niverts was a company that gradually became a metal supply and fabrication company, from an early beginning in the junk car parts business. These projects ranged from taking down a high smokestack, building retainer walls, designing and constructing a warehouse and learning to weld aluminum before it was a common technique. Dad always displayed a sense of pride in doing any of these jobs well and he had little patience for fellow workers who could not organize an implementation as well as he did. He usually did things in his head and knew what would work and how strong to make it. Dad was also big on sports, loved his 'Phillies and Eagles. He always encouraged us to play ball and do well. When we were of the age, he came home one night with three different baseball gloves—fielder, first baseman and catcher—probably far more than he could afford. And those gloves smelled just the way I imagined a new leather glove would. We learned to "perform" on projects and to "play" with spirit.

Dad and Mom were always so proud of my opportunity to be part of the manned space program. They probably did not appreciate how much their example flowed through all of their children's accomplishments and would downplay it, when we pointed out that connection.

Two of Dad's projects stand out as examples. In the summer of 1951, we were newly living at the old family homestead on River Street in Old Forge. The house sat up on a hill—overlooking a cemetery on the East side and with an elevation drop of about thirty feet to River Street on the North side. Under a thin covering of soil barely enough for grass, the hill was made of layers of rock gradually sloping down from the house to the street. Dad wanted a garage down near the street and its location would be such that there would be a forty to fifty feet run of driveway, running east towards the cemetery, climbing about ten feet in elevation above River Street. Nearest to the street was the beginning of a driveway of about twenty feet in length. The job was to excavate a volume about twenty-five feet in length, twelve feet in width with a rock shelf about two feet high on the side where our house was and tapering to about the right elevation on the street side of the driveway. The tools were wedges and sledgehammers. The workers were three. There was plenty of room to dump the fill in the low spots. The job took all summer and Dad approved, and was probably even proud of us for the job.

Then, one Saturday, Dad came home with sections of a garage on a flat bed. It took a few more adult friends to wrestle the pieces into a garage, with a roof sloping front to back. With the heavy lifting done, Dad was able to package the completion into doable sized work packages for the three of us. During the driveway job, we began to call ourselves the Coolie Labor Union. Finishing the garage was easy for the Union. Now we had a garage with a lift up door and a storage area for coal.

Mom tended to the nurturing side of life. As Dad had projects, Mom had passions. She was committed to education, which she saw as a way to change the direction and prospects of one's life. She loved achievement and encouraged us to do well in school and all of our studies. She continued to write poetry throughout her life. We were consistently reminded, "You are not going to work in the mines, you will get an education and make something of yourself." This became an expectation that we tried very hard to satisfy. To do less would be to disappoint Mom and that was not anything we would choose.

Mom was God's steward of the Roman Catholic faith in our family. It was simply expected that we would attend Mass every Sunday, days of obligation and live in accordance with the teachings and precepts of our faith. No discussion. Even much later when we visited back home, Mom still preferred to get to church early by at least 30 minutes. It brought a smile to report the ritual to my siblings so that they knew it would be the same on their next visit. That faith was very much at the core of most of the people that we knew. It certainly was on display by the womenfolk, and perhaps less so by the men who did not say very much. But they did go to church every Sunday and they made sure that the kids did and that the kids behaved.

And in this time in March 1947, we gained a sister, Carol Ann, to complete our family picture. It took a while for brothers to grow to be fun. How long would it take a baby girl, I wondered. That too worked out in time.

In high school, Mom won a scholarship to Marywood College, a local school for girls. Graduating in 1934, she was not able to attend for reasons of supporting her parents. In her mind I'm sure, we had to take her place. She constantly reviewed our schoolwork and grades and was kind with praise for achievements.

Sometime in the eighth grade, I participated in a spelling contest. I was pretty good at the subject. However, I did not win but came in second. I do not know how it happened but I was offered a half-scholarship to the Scranton Prep high school. Looking back, there was more to this than I realized at the time. The spelling contest had no apparent connection to the Prep. Someone with authority or access to it had to have noticed and pushed my name forward. The Prep was (and is) the most highly regarded academic high school in our region and there was a tuition fee to attend. I never saw any hesitation on the part of my parents in urging me to accept. I wonder now what they had to do to swing the fee. But it was a decision firmly consistent with one of Mom's passions. It was decided that I could go. The Prep is a Jesuit school—Jesuits being one of the most notable teaching orders in the Church. At the time, it was not coed although it is now. And it was a life-changer and a new gateway.

It was not a large school. At the time of graduation in 1953, my class was forty-three young men. Most of my classmates were the sons of professional or business fathers. The Prep was the first time in my school life that I had to stretch to compete. I was behind on several fronts. I was only age twelve starting freshman year, about two years behind my peers. Physically, I was small in the extreme, perhaps a hundred pounds. And I had limited social experience in comparison. It was obvious I was in a new league. But, I have to give credit that everyone was fair to me, even welcoming. I never was made to feel like an outsider except for my own awareness that this was an impressive group from a different world than mine and with much academic talent and two years of maturity on me. I did fine on the academic side, participated in debate, the newspaper, track and enthusiastically in the outside basketball games even when the snow had to be often shoveled off the court to play. I never played inside on a real basketball court until I was at Langley field with the Space Task Group (STG), circa 1959. But basketball was a passion even if played outside. We had the blacktop court in the schoolyard where play went on throughout the school year. We had one rock surface court at home and the Old Forge kids that we played with had several. Lots of hoops, but some barely had nets. Another new insight on life came when I visited the home of a classmate, Rob Newton, and was surprised to discover that Rob actually had ice cream in the freezer at home. Ice cream in the freezer--that was a new thought and it seemed like a good idea.

The Prep had a very strong influence on me and I have a hard time explaining it to myself. I just know that it did. During my space career, I often found that I was aware that I was thinking through a problem in a way different from my colleagues around me. Not necessarily better, just different. My brother Bill went to Prep three years after me, and we have had current discussions about what we got from the Prep. Bill had the very same sense as I that it shaped him for life. And he had the same difficulty in justifying that judgment, but he knew it was so.

The teachers at Prep were a major change from the nuns. They were

Age 14

young men of college graduate age, some of whom had high school careers in football and other sports. They were smart, strong and athletic. They tolerated no out-of-line behavior and were physical about it. They were in training to become priests and we called them Mister Haske, Coll, Long, etc. It was hard to forget that they selected themselves to serve a higher purpose -- certainly impressive men. They pounded Latin, Greek, German, philosophy, logic, math and ethics into our heads and reinforced the subjects with a regular regimen of two-three hours of homework every night. The Jesuits prided themselves on providing a "classical education" and preparing young men for the priesthood or to become "Catholic gentlemen."

Great as it was, there still was the matter of tuition. And that brings me to another unexplained chain of events. Dad was in a new job by this time and it could not have paid as well as the mines. But he did get started on a new path that was eventually better for him and Mom and certainly safer than the mines. But there had to be less income for tuition. I wonder now if my folks talked to the Prep authorities about taking me out of school. And, if so, they were probably told to wait while other options were pursued. Here I am in my junior year, having just turned fifteen in November. During the next month, I found myself with a job opportunity perfectly fitted to my situation. The job was at the Diocesan Guild Studios, on the other end of the block from school. The store sold various kinds of religious articles to churches and individuals and was certainly tied into the organization of the Church and its workings. The job was close, part time and somehow that opportunity found me out of all the other possible candidates when I was not even actively pursuing a job. Tuition problem solved. Was all that a coincidence? Again, nobody said anything by way of explanation to me. But from the perspective of sixty years later, no, it was not a coincidence.

Somebody became aware of the problem and fixed it.

Part time was about fifteen to twenty hours per week and full time in the summer. I worked as a stock clerk, with the stock room being on the second floor. So, the stock team had to get everything up there, unpack and store it and bring it back down for sale. I was the only part timer in the store and at least five years younger than the next in age. Again, it was a stretch for me in many ways and fifty cents per hour became a lesson in earning money and seeing how far it might go. At one point, it was a shock to hear (unsubstantiated) that the boss, Mr. Maher, made $10,000 per year, an unimaginable sum. At my fifty cents an hour, I had a long way to go. I kept the job at full time in the summer and back to part time during my school term at the University of Scranton for my first two years of college studies. By the time I left, I was up to eighty-five cents per hour.

As another indicator of my standing in the social sphere and when it came time for this 16 year old to get a date for the senior prom, I actually did not know any girls of suitable qualifications. I had some cousins but that did not count. Eventually, one of the women at the Guild Studios arranged the date with her younger sister. And it worked out but was an indicator that I had some growing up to do.

In my senior year at Prep, I also began to focus on the pursuit of a college degree. I was pretty good at math and loved making model airplanes. I thought my choice was between accounting and engineering. My parents suggested that I talk to our local Doctor Marmo. He had been a long time doctor for our family who made house calls. He was only one of two people that we knew with a college degree. He listened patiently while I described my choices and he said, "Glynn, go for the engineering." It was a simple, short conversation and set my course for life. Thanks, Dr. Marmo and God bless your beloved Nittany Lions.

After graduation from the Prep, I knew I wanted to work on airplanes and the path became apparent. Two years were at the University of Scranton because it was so convenient and I could live at home. The University of Detroit offered an aeronautical B.S. through a co-op program. And, since it was also a Jesuit university like the one in Scranton, all my credits would transfer with a minimum of do-overs.

During my last summer at home in 1955, I had a state highway job near home before heading off to the University of Detroit for 3 years of their coop aeronautical engineering program. Looking back, I really don't know how I was offered that Prep scholarship. Somebody intervened and my guess is that it was a significant somebody from Prep. Likewise, how did the part time job at the Guild Studios come my way? Maybe someday, I will hear the whole story. I hope so.

On that path in 1953, I found myself repeating my early experience at Prep. I was sixteen and had filled out to a robust 120 pounds. This time, half of my class was comprised of Korean war vets back to get their degree. I was five to six years behind these guys and much more than that in terms of maturity. But, my study habits were current and sharp, so I had something valuable to offer. Many of them sought me out and I earned a place on the class roster.

There was another student from Old Forge in this pre-engineering class and his name was Tony Andreoni. Tony had a 1937 Chevy, which ran at least those two years at the University of Scranton and probably well beyond. We became close friends and did a lot of miles together. Tony had a year of chemistry in high school and I had none at Prep. College started in at least the second year of chemistry and Tony saved me. Our routine was something like this—Glynn worked until 5-6pm at the Guild, went home, did homework for 3 hours while eating and then we were off to meet our other classmates for an evening of shuffleboard, the shells and lots of laughs. My peers were a college degree in themselves and it was a grand time for two years. We went to class in old barracks buildings, which the University used to handle the surge in attendance after Korea. They were comfortable and did the job. This was the precursor to another lesson from my work in the space program. We had engineers from many schools and states but not the ' name' universities, and the young men did everything asked of them and more. This profession, as many others I would guess, is a matter of sound preparation, attitude and work ethic, not a school address.

Back to the family, we just absorbed the daily lessons of family and friends and took it as standard. Folks stopped by regularly for a visit or a glass of beer. Uncle Steve walked all of Old Forge every day on his regular daily visit to family and some of his friends, even if he only stayed ten minutes. Mom took on caretaker duties for my grandfather and both grandmothers as live-ins at various times. When our folks decided to tear down the old house on River Street and build a new one in 1968 after we had all left home, their cousins (Dot and Bernie Ostroski) immediately invited Mom and Dad to live with them for the construction duration in their home in Pittston. Our parents cemented their relationship with the three Ostroski kids that carried on the rest of their lives. Such was the way of family in the Lackawanna valley.

Relatively unspoken but pervasive at that time and in that place was the sense of patriotism for our country. It was very visible during the war years when so many went off to serve the country and the wives and mothers were left at home to care for the families. We did not have a lot of factories in the area where women went to work as in California in the aircraft factories, but there was plenty to do on the home front and women did it. And we never heard a complaint about it. Perhaps the last value that our parents worked hard to instill in us was something that I would call ambition. This was not the crass, self-involved ambition but rather a more noble desire for her children to be able to live a better life. In our family, even though I was going to a very difficult high-performance high school, the standard always was that you will learn; you will get an education and you will make something of yourself. It was considered mandatory that we do that and that we never even consider working in the mines.

Coal Miner

Christmas Eve, 1950. The men working in the Pagnotti coal mine in Pittston, Pennsylvania were beginning to think about enjoying Christmas day with their families and friends. And then, "Cave-in, chamber #2." The dreaded words ripped through the miners like a chain saw. Our Dad instantly remembered that his brother-in-law, Stanley Kulick, was working there with his buddy, Teddy. He took off for chamber #2, running as fast as he could. Dad was half way there before realizing that he was still carrying the jackhammer he had been fixing earlier. As he approached, he saw a few other miners scrambling into the shaft while struggling to see through the clouds of dust. This was a dangerous time because it was impossible to know how much more caving was imminent. The miners slowed their pace while calling out for the men in the chamber. Soon, a choking voice was heard, hard to understand but coming nearer. Then, the light from his helmet flickered through the dusty gloom and one of the miners emerged, so covered with black and dust that Bill was not sure who it was. And then he recognized Stanley's voice. "Teddy's still in there. The cave was on his side." One out, the other still unknown. More miners arrived, more lights to see with. Carefully, they advanced, calling for Teddy. No answer. More calls, still no answer. And there would not be an answer from Teddy on that Christmas Eve or any other time.

The feeling of having little control over one's fate had to be compounded for Stanley by the fact that he and Teddy switched sides of the coal car to shovel from on this particular night. Some of the other miners questioned that choice until Stanley explained that Teddy had asked to work on the side of the car where the roof later caved in. No matter, some measure of guilt must have attached to Stanley, although he never spoke of it. It was just one more burden that these brave and stoic men were accustomed to enduring, with never a complaint.

My Uncle Stanley left the mine that night and never set foot in the mines again. He moved his family to Connecticut, the closest place to our home in Scranton, Pennsylvania where he could find work. Stanley and his family did not move back for many years. Stanley never did return to the cold, dark, dangerous network of shafts and chambers under the valley, some only a few feet high and often with a foot of cold water.

Stanley did not return, but my Dad did and worked in the mines into 1951. I absorbed this experience without much discussion from either of our parents directly with us kids. This was a time when kids did not ask questions of their parents, especially when it was a serious matter. Much later in life, I learned more about the fear that gripped my Dad during his years as a coal miner. Mom told me how Dad hated to go to sleep at night. He knew that when he woke up, he would return to that fearful, dark place again. It never got any easier for him. But, he did it, like thousands of other men in Pennsylvania and other mining regions. He did it because it was the only way he had to take care of his wife and family. Now in my seventies, the more I reflect on those times, the more I appreciate the simple human dignity, even nobility, of these men and their wives. It was only later that they became known, also to others, as our "greatest generation." We already knew that.

The coal mines of the Lackawanna and Susquehanna valleys are gone now. Their demise can be traced to the Knox mine disaster in January 1959. At that time, mining operations were continually being extended to chase the coal seams, but got too close to the ice-swollen Susquehanna River. The subsequent cave-in of the river through the roof of the River Slope mine flooded a major part of the interconnected mines. The flooding could not be slowed even by dumping coal cars, truckloads of gravel and fill and some 800 rail road cars into the whirlpool. Sixty-two fortunate miners were able to escape, but twelve more were swept away by the deluge. After more than a century of commercial coal mining, mother nature finally ended this period in the history of our region.

But the mines continued to deliver more pain to the decent people of this area long after the mines were closed. The process of separating the coal from the useless slag resulted in large dumps of waste, but still containing some coal. It is believed that these dumps eventually caught fire and the fire spread by burning exposed coal near the surface and then beneath the surface. This burning emitted a foul smelling gas (hydrogen sulfide) strong enough to peel the paint from houses and making it appear that, in many places, the ground was burning. It also was responsible for the deaths of families as the gases leaked into basements at night and filled the home like a silent killer. Or the erosion collapsed the support for the structure of the house.

And, finally, many of the miners – some of the toughest stock you can find - died early because of the damage from coal dust to their lungs. This condition took my Dad in 1985 after years of fighting to breathe. We were told that his heart was like a marathon runner but his lungs were simply unable to perform.

This awareness in my early years left me with many feelings and convictions, some of which I can identify and some are just baked into who I am. However, there are at least two occasions which always trigger a response directly from the legacy of this experience:

First, any news report of a mine cave-in or trapped miners anywhere on the globe, immediately and with an emotional punch, causes me to stop, reflect and pray for their safe recovery and for their waiting families.

Second, much later in my life, and long after my time in MCC, I was occasionally confronted by employees who wanted to talk about the stress of the work in our comfortable offices. Stress? I could never muster any sympathy for the initiators of these discussions. I knew what my folks did for us. I could only guess what their parents and grandparents did for them. I wondered if they really understood and appreciated it.

University of Detroit: the NACA Co-op Experience

To finish my last three years, the University of Detroit Co-op program was a great way to earn the college degree. Besides the fine academic preparation, it was also a chance to experience the real world of aero engineering in the nation's pre-eminent aeronautical research organization. Besides that, the NACA (National Advisory Committee for Aeronautics) pay was just about enough to live on, and then pay for the upcoming school quarter of expenses. Based on the three-month rotation, I was only in Detroit in summer and winter. That was only three months during the regular University school year. As a result, we did not really attach to the University or its other institutions such as the sports teams or any other students outside of aero engineering.

In attending several of my wife's high school reunions, I was impressed by the closeness of so many of the men and women in her class. Also, Marilyn's classmates lived very close to each other at the time, and walked to school, which was all in the same neighborhood as their homes. As a group, they were closer to each other than my Prep class because the Prep students came from a radius of up to thirty miles around the region. There was no common "place" except for extracurricular activities. These were relatively limited and not like living next door. In retrospect, it was the same scene at the University of Detroit, not really connected on the emotional level. It was almost more of a business relationship. The University provided a service and we paid for it. That is not a criticism; it was just the circumstance at the time. Detroit was about a fifteen-hour drive from the Scranton area, subject to car breakdowns. The southern route went via the Pennsylvania and Ohio turnpikes. The northern passage was around the north side of Lake Erie through Canada, a long way to home. I never realized how relatively disconnected I was from high school and college until I witnessed first- hand Marilyn's class reunions and the experiences of our kids. All four of ours went to Texas A&M and rapidly developed far, far more of a lifelong emotional bond.

Most of the guys, from the Scranton area, and those we met in Detroit were all in the same financial boat, working 6 months of the year to pay for twelve months of expenses. Nobody else from Detroit co-oped at NACA in Cleveland, although there were a number of other University co-ops represented. Money was tight for all of us. I had two experiences that were memorable in that regard. In my first few weeks in Cleveland, I simply ran out of cash. I had no checking account. Such a thing as credit cards did not exist and it really wasn't much of an option to call home. So I went three days without eating any food, just lots of water. Finally, on the fourth day, my landlady may well have guessed the situation and invited me to dinner, the first real food in too many days. Whatever the menu was that night, it was the absolute best and got me over the hump.

In the last two quarters of school in the winter and spring of 1958, I had to stretch the funds to make it. It took a lot of dime hamburgers from the White Tower in Detroit for sustenance. I noticed that after that time, whenever I went close enough to smell the White Tower cooking, my stomach rolled over. People remember different things about college, and one of mine is about a few periods of hunger. While in Cleveland for some of my quarters, I also had a job at Seager's Sunoco gas station at night and on weekends. That helped too. Classwork and study in my last three years had all the charm of classwork and study. But it too passed. The grind of the study quarter was offset by the quarters of work at the Lewis Research Center. I worked in five different units there. One of them involved the study of the air cooling of a plugged nozzle used to vary exit area in the jet engine exhaust plane for optimum engine performance. One was jet engine testing in engineering cells. One was to investigate shock tubes and I had several tours in wind tunnels. The most advanced of these was a ten by ten foot test section capable of test speeds of up to mach 3.

College Graduation

'Co-oping' brought lasting rewards in beginning to understand technologies, analysis and testing. Jet engine testing relied on extensive pressure (and other) measurements throughout an engine. Today, you might marvel at how we took test points. Pressure sensors were fed to a very large vertical board with many manometer tubes, side by side, a room full of them, with a background grid to measure the various mercury levels. As a test point stabilized and was taken, the field of manometers was photographed. This film was then provided to a room full of women data technicians, where they manually read the manometer tube levels in the photos and eventually calculated a pressure for each sensor. This then provided a pressure distribution either inside an engine or over the surface of an engine inlet. This was a very far cry from automated IT systems of modern times, but the process taught rigor, discipline and working with people.

One of my assignments was the study of shock tubes to create a certain type of photograph, called "schleiren," of supersonic shock wave patterns.   Another was in various wind tunnels, including the ten by ten foot wind tunnel, which was unique in all the world.   Because of the amount of electrical energy used from the Cleveland grid, it was only operated at night.   I was the engineer on duty and did everything the technician, who knew all about facility, told me to do.   Respect the source of knowledge, especially when you don't know zip.   Whenever we finished in the morning, I hopped on the back of his motorcycle and went to the Airport bar on Brookpark road for beer and breakfast.

I really enjoyed my time as a co-op and the lessons lasted all my life.   I remember George Smolak, George Wise, Len Obery, Jim Connor, Nick Samanich and Jim Useller, all of whom tried to help this young co-op. So many of the engineers at Lewis were great at what they did and in providing guidance and advice to a young kid.   I thank them all.

Graduating to the NACA Lewis Research Center

My brief time at Lewis was fulfilling and a continuation of learning for later challenges.   Looking back on my brief time at Lewis after graduation, I see it now as the calm before the storm.   As a research center, there was a certain tempo and it was different from what the early manned spaceflight effort was.   Lewis had many brilliant engineers engaging the day-to-day problems of our aviation industry and trying to provide solutions, usually in the form of NACA technical reports.   They were also working subjects well before their time, such as long duration, low thrust engines for interplanetary trajectories.   This work was led by a man with the name of Wolfgang Moeckel.   I doubt he ever knew of me but I was impressed with him, his work and the foresight he brought to this subject, many decades before it was ever seriously considered for flight.   Lewis and the other NACA Centers, were intellectual property creators for the large and growing field of American aeronautics.   The Center had the feel of a well-endowed University research organization. But NACA people were seldom directly involved in the application of their research by US Industry.

At graduation, in June 1958, I joined a branch headed by George Low. At an early age, George caught the attention of NACA management, both in Cleveland and NASA headquarters in Washington, DC.   He was a very talented and highly respected engineer, who was comfortable with both technical and headquarters policy matters.   Later in the 60's, George became the Apollo spacecraft program manager after the Apollo fire on the pad, which killed three astronauts.   This turned out to be a relatively short but very intense period for George, who was one of the group of leaders who made Apollo a success.

In George's branch, my section head was John Disher whose hobby was to help with the race cars that ended up at the Indy 500 each year. John's section was exploring the new subject of the very high heat loads on entry vehicles into the earth's atmosphere at extreme speeds. In our small group, our testing was carried out by the air launch of multi-stage solid rocket propellant rockets with a small instrumented reentry model on top of the stack. The first stage was used to accelerate the stack to higher altitudes and then fire the rest of the stages to propel the model down towards entry conditions of very high speeds. The air launch was from under the wing of a B-57 and flew over the Wallop's Island test range off the coast of Virginia. There was another group from Langley exploring similar research and using ground launched solid propellant vehicles, one of which became the Scout launch vehicle. I co-authored a NACA technical report with Ken Weston on the heat transfer results on one of these flown models. Writing a NACA report was a rigorous and humbling process, with many reviews of the technical quality and one's use of the English language to capture the essence of the subject. All young engineers should go through this process at least once.

As a research center, there were always classes of new graduates coming to work at the Center. And the average age at the Center was on the young side. I roomed with two older hands in Lakewood. One was Jim Useller, older by twenty years and full of experience to pass on to me. Jim was a mentor in many ways, but especially in the lore of NACA and what it took to succeed there. He was also the chef in the house. Pete Wanhainen was the other roommate, and his passion was ice boat racing on frozen Lake Erie. He also liked regular sailing but that speed was tame compared to his ice boat.

There was a large group of younger folks still finding their niches. We had a great softball field on the Center grounds and it had a small truck size building, refrigerated and well stocked with beer and soft drinks, and a center of competition and fun during the summer months. There was an established softball league and we always had trouble beating the team from the rockets group. Bowling was the game for the colder months. Organized into leagues, bowling competition was a serious business. A few did not even have a beer untill after the frames were done. There were some good bowlers and then there were most of us who were not so good. One of the friends in our crowd was Pat O'Donnell who worked at Lewis in fuels and lubes. Her husband Wally owned the Fairview Park bowling alley. Pat and Wally hosted parties at their home. And, if you ever wondered what to do with damaged bowling pins, they made great fuel for the fireplace.

Into this sporting arena came one of the NACA nurses, Marilyn Kurtz. I had already met Marilyn during visits to the clinic and at lunch arranged by a friend. She was the junior nurse of the two at Lewis; the other, Ruth Elder, was more senior by a bunch. Marilyn was much prettier and more fun. Dr. Sharp, who was the center director and a very likable person, often asked Marilyn if the crop of young men was satisfactory to choose from or whether he should hire more. In the winter of 1959, a dozen or so of this intrepid band of bowlers went off to the mountains near Rome, New York to try their hand at snow skiing. Marilyn taught water skiing as a hobby on Lake Erie, and transferred some of that to snow skiing. Most of the rest of us were complete amateurs. Marilyn was more accomplished with her stem christies while we were still snow plowing and trying other poor imitations of skiing. On the "one more run" for the day, Marilyn fell, and when her bindings froze up, broke her ankle badly. Gino Bertolli and I found a rescue carrier and dragged Marilyn on it down the hills to the lift area.

At the clinic, the doctors found the break, set it and put on a cast. That evening we drove off on our return to Cleveland. Maybe as a portent that we could survive together, I was driving the car on the turnpike, with three passengers asleep in the rear seat and Marilyn in the front passenger seat. Hard to see it, but there were stretches of ice. The car started to slide and then to rotate slowly. There was nothing to do but wait and it seemed like a very long time of absolutely no control. The car finally came out of the spin, traveling in the original direction, still at 65 miles per hour and OK. Marilyn was in the front seat with her leg propped up on the dashboard. We looked at each other, smiled at our good fortune like co-conspirators and silently thanked our angels. The three folks in the back did not know until later that we had this turnpike ballet. On return to Cleveland and then a check with the hospital, the doctors decided that the break was not set well. They had to re-break it and pin it with a Rush nail.

This accident and recovery had two long-term effects. One is the consistent failure for Marilyn to pass the modern airport screening test and to be subject to special inspections. The other effect of my humanitarian visits to the hospital was the blooming of a flower which eventually became marriage and a full long life together with many wonderful fulfillments and joys. Some skiing accidents are for the best. This one certainly was for me.

At that time, something began that carried through my working career and even into retirement. And that was the association which I had with the pilots of the NASA aircraft division. Joe Algranti was a leader in the Cleveland aircraft operations and managed to get me back to Cleveland from Langley regularly. On one occasion, I was late getting from Goddard (GSFC) to Butler aviation, the private aircraft terminal at Washington National airport used by NASA. Then called National airport is now called the Ronald Reagan airport. Joe had already departed the terminal and was in line for takeoff. Butler dispatch called Joe, and Joe replied, "Bring him out but be quick about it." Whenever I travel through Reagan airport today, I wonder how this high security complex would react to a Jeep driver discharging a scrambling engineer and helping him and his bag to climb through the rear open door of a DC 3 while ready for takeoff on the runway. I expect they would not be happy.

Joe knew that there was a reason beyond work for me to return to Cleveland. By this time, Marilyn and I were seriously dating. Occasionally, Marilyn also had to travel to the new nuclear facility at Plumbrook in Sandusky, Ohio, seventy-five miles or so to the west. And this travel was sometimes by way of the Lewis Navion, a two seater which Eb Gough of Lewis Aircraft Operations loved to fly. Eventually all of this flying worked out. Both of us thank/blame Joe for keeping us together through those travel times. Afterwards, Joe moved to Houston and ran the MSC/JSC aircraft operations division for many years.

Marilyn and Glynn 1960

Over Christmas 1959, I worked up the courage to ask Dad Kurtz for permission to ask Marilyn to marry me. And we did on April 30, 1960. Marilyn loved her local church in Fairview Park, St. Angelas, in part because it was so beautiful. But our wedding turned out to be at the same time as a major repair and almost all of our photos included the scaffolds all over the sanctuary. So much for wedding planning.

The Space Task Group

Sputnik

In October 1957, Sputnik shattered American complacency and changed the world. The US political system responded with remarkable speed and cogency. As has so often been the case in American history, there were at least two men in critical leadership positions, President Eisenhower and Majority Leader of the Senate Lyndon Johnson, who were prepared to lead and did so most effectively. As the political process moved through the fact finding and the seeking of counsel, major legislation began which became the Space Act of 1958, forming NASA with its Space charter.

While the national policy deliberations were underway, the same emerging leadership process was occurring at the implementation level. NASA Headquarters tasked Bob Gilruth in May to plan a program to put a man in space. Max Faget had already proposed a concept in a conference in March, 1958. Building on that concept and with more leaders from the ranks of the Langley Center, such as Chuck Mathews, Chris Kraft and Caldwell Johnson, the leadership cadre of the newly formed Space Task Group (STG) rose and took command of the response to the Sputnik challenge. Their mission was to invent an American manned space program and to put it into flight safely and as quickly as possible.

In June of 1958, my first month after graduation, I saw the first line drawing of what became the Mercury spacecraft, prepared by Caldwell Johnson from the Langley Center in Hampton, Virginia, and I knew it was my future. (Later in the seventies, Caldwell and I would work closely on the Apollo/Soyuz project.) He was part of a group of engineers from the Pilotless Aircraft Research Division (PARD) and other units at the Langley Center. PARD had a similar research focus as the Lewis branch I was in. PARD testing was based on a ground launched solid rocket vehicle, known as the Scout. We both used the NACA range on the Virginia coast, centered on Wallops Island. As a result of this common focus, we were asked to begin some special studies in support of this emerging man-in-space effort, to be later named Project Mercury.

My Branch Chief was George Low, a highly respected engineer and manager. Within less than a year, George was also at NACA Hqs, as a key leader in the study of what to do after the Mercury project. Out of this and other work, came the core ideas for President Kennedy's later commitment to Apollo as a primary national goal. Looking back, I have to believe that the high regard which George had earned contributed to our being asked to join the Mercury team.

So our work started on Mercury, first on a part-time basis. But very soon, it became full-time and increasingly intense. At first in 1958, most of my time was spent in Cleveland with occasional trips to Langley. Then, I began to travel to Langley, spending most of the week there. The work was like a whirlpool, drawing me into the trajectory planning and plans for a control center. Eventually, I had a permanent change of station (PCS) to Langley.

The core of the Space Task Group (STG) was identified in a November 3, 1958 letter, requesting the transfer of thirty-six Langley personnel to the newly independent group. Not counting steno and file support and with the status of one person charged to remain with Langley, there were twenty-nine engineers and managers put in place to create and manage the human space flight program. In 1958, ten more engineers from the Lewis Research Center, who were already working on Mercury, joined the Space Task Group. I was one of those. Twelve more from Langley, including John Llewellyn, also transferred to STG.

The number and high caliber of transfers from Langley caused some problems. It was becoming increasingly difficult to transfer people from the existing centers to the new Space Task Group. And then, there was a major aerospace tragedy in Canada when the development of a new supersonic military airplane (CF-105) was canceled. This resulted in the loss of thousands of jobs in the Avro company and Canada. But it was like a gift from heaven for the STG.

Eventually, by April of 1959, twenty-five experienced and very savvy Avro engineers joined the US manned space flight program. This was perfect timing to complement the mix of talents and experience levels of the STG workforce. We already had a world-class set of leaders in place and the importation of the Avro engineers added a great deal of depth and capability to the growing organization. It also served to build out the management and supervisory structure which was then in place when STG began to hire a significant number of new college graduate engineers, especially in the early sixties after Apollo was started. And, most significant for me, it brought Tec Roberts, originally from Wales, who eventually became a strong influence in my early career.

This was another interesting coincidence in timing because it was the same time that 7 test pilots also joined STG and became known as the Mercury Seven. Their presence quickly became commonplace in the few buildings housing the fledgling Mercury team. There was a first-name-basis environment in STG. It was a heady time getting to know these new heroes and eventually traveling with some of them as the Atlas flight program began. As the group who would strap on these vehicles, it made the work more focused and personal for us.

In the middle of all this, I experienced another permanent change of status in my life when Marilyn agreed to be my wife. We were married on April 30, 1960 and moved into an 8x45 mobile home in Poquoson where many of the Air Force refueling crews and fighter pilots also lived. Marilyn and I started our marriage with 360 square feet of living space, soon to be shared with our first-born, Jennifer.

During the months before my PCS and up until March 1962, I worked in the Mission Analysis Branch of which John Mayer was the branch chief. John was a quiet spoken man, and very intense in getting the analysis and the numbers right. He taught us orbital mechanics in a formal course and in all of our daily interactions. It was the equivalent of a PhD in that subject, in all of its practical aspects, without overdoing the theory. John was a doer, a manager and a leader in the best tradition of NACA. He demanded the best from us and mentored us so that we would be able to deliver that best. In the late forties, he had also served at Muroc (later known as Edwards) in the X-1 days and he described his part in Chuck Yeager's X-1 flight, which first broke the sound barrier. John delivered the final proof of that achievement when he processed the tracking data and confirmed the onboard measurements. John was a link from the X-1 to MA-6 (Mercury-Atlas) in orbit.

As our work progressed from analytical studies to inventing how to monitor and protect the spacecraft during the launch phase and how to navigate on-orbit and to determine the precise time for the de-orbit maneuver, John was pushing the team through the theory stage and into the practical domain of assuring mission safety and success through all flight phases. One key step in this process was the decision to create a computer center with the appropriate software to provide the necessary flight information in real time. We determined the operational requirements and the software equations. They were then negotiated with the ground systems organization for implementation at the Goddard Space Flight center. Before that Center was fully open for business, their contractor, IBM, was using a computer system seen through the front windows of an office on Pennsylvania Avenue between the Capitol and the White House. Eventually, GSFC housed the computing system for all of the launch and orbital mechanics processing in support of the MCC at the Cape. And this was our beginning in learning how to use this new technology – computers - in our control center. And later, when the time came, John supported me for the flight dynamics officer position, first at Bermuda and later at the MCC at the Cape, even though it meant I would transfer to a different branch from his. Not all managers are so kindly disposed.

The mission analysis, or planning, function was an early incubator for the flight dynamics operator positions. John's deputy, Carl Huss, became the first console "RETRO." Carl worked that position for all the Redstone and Atlas flights and set the standards for that position, passing them on to John Llewellyn, starting with MA-7. And that was an interesting process to watch. Carl was Mr. Rigorous and John, for all his desire to pursue advanced degrees, was not. By the time preparations for Gemini began in earnest, Carl's duties as a manager of the mission analysis were such that he could not also serve as a console operator. John Llewellyn moved from a remote site capcom to a RETRO-in-training during the manned orbital Mercury flights.

The Mission Planning Team 1962

The reentry analysis I started with would lead to trajectory studies of the RETRO fire and entry phase of a mission as the spacecraft was returned from orbit to the earth. This return-to-earth function became an integral part of the two and, later, three console operator positions that supported the flight dynamics decision-making in MCC then, and to the present day. It used the call sign "RETRO." By this time, our studies included the launch phase of the Redstone and Atlas launch vehicles, which boosted the Mercury spacecraft into orbit. This brought me into the world of launch vehicle trajectory, reliability of our launch vehicles, launch phase monitoring as it might be done from a control center and the ground-based guidance system that was used for the Atlas vehicle.

John Llewellyn

John S. Llewellyn started with STG in about December 1958. I write these notes about John fully realizing that I can hardly do justice to his story. John is a larger-than-life character and the preeminent legend in the ranks of early (and probably all) of flight operations controllers. There are more John Llewellyn stories than any other ten guys combined. Just to give you an example of one of John's stories, it goes as follows. When John was going to William & Mary, he was married to Olga and had two daughters, Lane and Vivien. John was sent on assignment to the grocery store and, on the way, ran into his drinking buddies from school. They were headed to Florida where the sun was shining and they intended to spend several days there. They invited John to go along, and so he did. He did not think to call Olga at any time during this jaunt. He was just AWOL from the family for the next few days. Somehow he survived his return.

John was born and raised in the Tidewater region of Virginia, in the small town of Dare. He grew up boating on the Yorktown River, helping his dad with the farm and loving the game of football. His mom was a schoolteacher and emphasized that point of view on his upbringing.

Before college, John had volunteered to serve his country in the United States Marine Corps. His service put an indelible stamp on this big, strong, gung-ho soldier and, as the wheel of history turned, John found himself in far North Korea, and soon at a place called the Chosin reservoir. John never did talk at all about his experiences in Korea, but like the rest of the 1st Marine division, he was cutoff there when the Chinese army invaded across the Yalu River. For John, this became a battle that was up-close, personal, brutal and terrifying in the extreme. He did make it out and managed to bury the horrors of that ugly time. Ultimately, these memories came back with a vengeance fifty some years later. He had a very severe case of Post Traumatic Stress Disorder (PTSD) and learned more about it than he ever wanted to know. The treatment of this early trauma and its side effects over most of his adult life ultimately lead to profound changes in John, and all for his own good. He has earned an understanding of himself and sees his life much more clearly. He is also at peace with the past and with himself.

John and I came together in 1958. He had transferred to STG from the NACA center at Langley where he worked on high speed heat transfer problems as I did briefly at the Lewis Center in Cleveland. He began in the STG engineering organization, still working the heating problems. We were a very unlikely pairing of people and yet we are still close today after fifty years. John was big and physically strong; I was about 140 pounds. John was very macho and gung ho; I was small enough and probably sensible enough to not physically challenge anybody. John was married with two girls; I was just beginning to get a real prospect in Marilyn. John was a vocal atheist; I had twenty-one years of Catholic faith upbringing. John was interested in continuing his education and in earning advance degrees in physics; I had had enough of school and wanted to get on with the business of manned space flight. Other differences abound. It was impossible to get John to commit things to writing, while I had a knack for written explanations. John was the center of attention at gatherings. They were either robust when John arrived or he made them that way in short order. I was somewhat more careful and circumspect, preferring not to be at the center of a noisy crowd. John could win any ad-lib insult contest; I was not very good at the repartee.

Out of this background of almost complete opposites came a friendship that has endured for over fifty years, even though being John's boss was sometimes a challenge, probably for both of us. We only worked closely together for the first fifteen years. Our paths diverged at the time of the last few Apollo flights and there were long periods of no contact. And we each had many different experiences during those times. But our early work together made it easy to re-connect when we had the chance again.

To make up for some of my physical deficiencies, John took me to Judo class. Our instructor was a strong air police sergeant who worked on the Air Force side of the Langley base. I had been doing Judo at Langley for a year and learning some of the ropes. At that point, my folks came to visit us and Dad came to watch some judo. He saw John, at over two hundred pounds of solid muscle, throw me and then land on me, with his shoulder driving my solar plexus through my back and into the mat. It took me ten to fifteen minutes to be able to breathe. Dad reminded me that he had always advised me to be careful who I picked a fight with.

In our early times, John was not in the same flight dynamics analysis flow like I was. However, we did use personnel from the engineering function on a part time basis for flight support. John actually served as capcom and leader of a team that manned some of the remote stations in our network. He was the capcom for MA-4 at the Zanzibar station in September 1961 while the country was swept with some of the political volatility sweeping through Africa at that time.

John became something of an expert on the Mercury spacecraft clock, which was more complicated than just a clock.   It had lockouts, and other strange features and it was the primary reference for Retrofire. Because of that connection, Tec Roberts began steering John to learn the "RETRO" controller trade from Carl Huss, the original RETRO. Tec had his way at being persuasive about things like that, and coupled with some straight talk right at John, John saw the wisdom of Tec's idea.   It is easy to see why John loved the capcom line of work. He was a leader of a small, dedicated team, deployed to exotic locations all around the world, and well situated for more hell raising. But the role was being retired as the plans for a Houston-based Mission Control Center made the remote site teams obsolete.   Finally he was shanghaied into RETRO training for MA-6, John Glenn's flight in February 1962.   John loved to brief the astronauts on the clock and its arcane workings as it counted down to Retrofire. I think the astronauts admired his expertise and enthusiasm and they were probably aware of his military service record from Korea.

I tried hard to get John to document his briefing in a written report. This would be a one-time event which he could then use many times for his subsequent briefings.   Clearly this would be more efficient, but John loved the interactions that came with his free form briefing and that's the way it stayed. This was also the beginning of a long term attempt to inculcate "clear writing" into John's repertoire – another waste of time. John still grouses about times that Tec or I shipped him to clear writing class, always with negligible success.

There was one more thing John never liked. As we moved into Gemini, the console positions were Flight dynamics officer, now also a Guidance officer and still a RETRO controller. With the sensitivity of a Lance Corporal, John always wanted the title to be changed to RETRO Officer. His very passion on the subject caused us to procrastinate and deploy flaky reasons not to do it.

In Houston at the MSC, one of the notable stories concerning John had to do with his penchant for collecting parking tickets on-site. After a reasonable number with no correction in sight, Security talked to me as his direct boss (and probably John Hodge, our division chief). We temporarily pulled John's pass and sticker for driving onto the Center. I expected that John would park across the street and walk into the Center or get a ride from somebody else. That would be what most people would do. Not John. Ever resourceful, John trailered his horse to a shopping center across the street and rode into the Center for work. The Center did not have stickers for horses as the procedures did not anticipate this condition. And the mess from the all-day tie-up of the horse lead to more discussions and promises not to do that anymore. So, the saga of riding the horse to work was gradually absorbed into the always expanding legend of "John Star." John and his horse did make one more appearance that I know of in the Singing Wheel, one of our favorite watering stations in Webster. I'm sure it was a special occasion that prompted John to ride the horse up the steps and into the establishment. At least, I did not have to visit with MSC security for that one.

One of John's duties as a RETRO was to conduct the countdown to Retrofire over the net, 10-9-8-etc. In several sims, John did so but scrambled the numbers - 10, 9, 7, 6, 8, 4, 5, 3, 2, 1, mark. He always got to 'mark' at the correct time but he had to endure endless guffawing on his countdowns. As his boss (and friend), I did not want to see him embarrassed in front of his MCC peers. So, at night back in the motel, I made John practice the countdowns out loud. He was really ticked off about having to do that. In an angry, red-faced mood, he told me "Lunney, you SOB, you can't make me do that." But, I did and John got the counts correct from then on. I felt like I was pushing things a little close to John's edge on that and was glad when the problem receded.

John was one of a kind; nobody could make another mold like the one John came out of.

Mercury Redstone

All of this focus on the problem of creating a safe-flight-protection concept workable in the real world of tracking, computing and the control center lead to an early assignment for me which was a terrific learning experience. It was the need to understand the workings of the range safety function at the Cape. It was a similar discipline to the one we were beginning to invent but it was aimed at protecting the safety of people and facilities on the ground. Our focus was aimed at protecting the safety and return of the spacecraft and crew.

One of my early trips to the Cape

was in November 1960. At that time, we were trying to launch the first Mercury Redstone flight,
MR-1.

It was my assignment to observe the range safety officer in order to get a better understanding of what that position did to protect facilities and people from a wayward launch vehicle. I remember being impressed at how cool Captain Davis, the range safety officer, was. This was my first real countdown. My stomach was turning over at maximum RPM and yet he was so calm. When we had a hold in the countdown, he invited me to join him for breakfast. Captain Davis did a great job with the platter of eggs, bacon and all the trimmings. I was not able to do any more than a cup of coffee.

Range safety operations were a critical and important function. In a sense, it was similar to the job that we were beginning to invent for the flight dynamics officer. The RSO ensured that the vehicle would not deviate from its nominal path beyond a set of destruct limits designed to protect the people and the facilities on the ground. In those days, reliability of the launch vehicles was low enough that they had an average failure rate of about fifty percent. The RSO was often called on to destroy the launch vehicle before it did any damage. He had a number of systems that were used to aid him in that task. The first was a system of radars that displayed present position and projected impact location on plot boards in the range safety control room. There were also visual observers, located at strategic positions, who watched the launch vehicle through a template to detect deviations from the nominal path.

With this kind of information, the RSO could make a decision that the vehicle was approaching a destruct limit line. The RSO could then send the destruct command that would initiate the firing of a set of shaped charges usually running lengthwise along the tank or outer structure of the launch vehicle. These destruct systems were quite effective in splitting the stage open and spilling the propellants until the whole vehicle turned into a fireball. His action to destruct the vehicle was designed to protect property and people and, in a similar fashion, I was working on the problem of defining the limits of trajectory deviations which could imperil the safety of the astronauts.

The spacecraft had different abort modes, consider them escape routes for the crew, and our efforts turned towards assuring that those escape routes were not compromised by any trajectory deviation, hence some of our eventual limit lines. We also tried to control the location of the landing in case of a launch abort. Late in the launch phase, there was also some limited ability to vary the time of RETRO fire and control the landing point of the spacecraft to a designated recovery area in the Atlantic. Observing the RSO operation and knowing how often he had to take destruct action certainly underlined the importance and urgency of our efforts to develop a sound approach for limit lines that would protect the crew.

Eventually, the Mercury-Redstone countdown picked up and continued towards T-0. My stomach did not get any better. The countdown clock finally arrived at T-0 and there was considerable smoke on the launch pad. However, as the smoke cleared, it became clear that the Redstone rocket was still sitting on the pad and parachutes were being deployed from the Mercury spacecraft. This put the whole situation in a really high-risk condition. For unknown reasons, the Redstone had apparently begun to ignite its engines and then shut down. Although I didn't figure all this out at the time, the spacecraft reacted as it should have following a normal shutdown of the rocket at the end of its planned firing. This resulted in the jettisoning of the escape tower and, since the barostats sensed an altitude below 10,000 feet (the normal altitude for chute deployment), out went the parachutes.

So we ended up with a rocket that had been pressurized, armed, fired and released for flight and it was still sitting on the pad unconstrained by any hold-down device. On top of that precarious condition, the concern was that the parachutes would fill in the breeze and perhaps pull the vehicle over and cause it to collapse on the pad. The Redstone team in the blockhouse was scrambling to decide on a course of action to stabilize and "safe" this condition. I did not hear those conversations but I do know of one option that was being discussed with the range safety officer. Since all the ground umbilicals to the vehicle had been released for flight, there was really no way for the blockhouse to exercise any control. The option being discussed involved shooting a high-powered rifle at the Redstone tank and letting the fuel spill out.

I was completely new to this environment and knew nothing of "safing" techniques. But this did not sound like safety. My gut reaction to this rifle scheme was really negative. It was soon set aside.

The team in the blockhouse considered an option involving reconnecting the umbilicals. This approach involved sending some people, maybe only one, out to reconnect the umbilicals with a completely fueled vehicle precariously balanced on the pad. This was dropped soon also. Eventually, since the wind was very light and forecast to remain so, the concern about filling the parachutes and causing a tipover seemed less threatening. Finally it was decided to simply wait, let the launch vehicle batteries drain down and this would cause some of the valves to go to the safe position. There was risk with this path, but it was the one selected and resulted in the complete "safing" of the vehicle by the next day.

Up until this event, I had a rather constrained view of what my job as a Flight dynamics officer might entail. This experience drove home the fact that unplanned failures or events could really happen, and that the automatic system, or the crew, or some intervention by the ground crew could start another chain of events. All of a sudden, the preparation for effectively operating in the MCC took on several more dimensions than I had been imagining. This was much more of a lesson than I had expected on my very first day of limited operations involvement. From that day on, my thinking and that of my colleagues embraced the idea that the unexpected could happen and things could get even more complicated from there.

Back to Inventing the Discipline at STG

Besides these lessons from the RSO world, another important job on the ground was to make sure that the spacecraft was in a suitable and safe orbit. We spent considerable time deciding what conditions had to be met in order to consider the orbit safe and give it a "Go." The geometry of the launch phase was such that the point at which the launch vehicle was commanded to be shut down and the spacecraft was in orbit occurred halfway between the Cape and the station at Bermuda. These

MCC CAPE

and other trajectory-related conditions were the responsibility of the console operator known as Flight dynamics officer, call sign "FIDO."

By this time, the planning for control of the spacecraft in orbit had evolved to the concept of a Mercury Control Center, MCC, at the Cape and connected to multiple ground and ship-based stations around the world. The MCC - an acronym that worked equally well for the later Mission Control Center in Houston - was the command center at the hub of this network of facilities. It also received the telemetry and A/G voice from the local facilities at the Cape. The MCC was also supported by the Real Time Computing Center (RTCC) at the Goddard Space Flight Center (GSFC) in Greenbelt, Maryland. This computing center's primary function was to process raw radar data and provide position, velocity and other derived parameters to the MCC, in support of the 'FIDO' and 'RETRO' positions. The telemetry processing was not performed by the RTCC but was routed directly from the analog telemetry ground system to display devices, such as meters, strip charts or discrete events lights for review by the spacecraft systems controllers.

The implementation of the RTCC was a landmark case of multi-organizational cooperation. It involved the mission analysis people for the requirements for analytical tools and software formulations. Carl Huss and I represented the needs of the console operators for the definition of the content of displays, limit lines, abort mode actions, propulsion maneuver targets, mission events to sequence the programs and other operational parameters for MCC monitoring and control. Since the computers at the time were severely limited by memory capacity, balancing a useful requirement set within that constraint became a daily struggle. The management of the implementation was performed by Langley employees like Jim Donegan who eventually moved to GSFC to oversee the RTCC work. IBM won the contract for the hardware and software work. Lyn Dunseith, originally from Lewis like me, was the STG interface to the implementation team at GSFC and Lynn performed this role superbly well into the Shuttle flight program. Modern observers will be amused at the memory size constraint but the system was at the edge of the state of the art at the time. It was a regular cause for management review and a real test of the STG, GSFC and IBM team. But, the effective interaction of all the involved parties was driven by a uniform dedication to the same goals and was a tribute to the competence and professionalism of this team.

The network stations, referred to as remote sites, would be in contact with the spacecraft for a maximum of five minutes, often less, each time the spacecraft passed in their vicinity. The remote sites were capable of receiving telemetry, voice, sending commands and tracking the spacecraft by radar. The stations were also manned by a small cadre of operators whose job was to function like a mini MCC, for the time the spacecraft was in contact with their station. In effect, they were the eyes and ears and more of MCC as the spacecraft traced its ground path over the globe. The remote stations sent data back to MCC after the pass on a teletype system, but it was mostly a manual capture of a standard set of parameters plus news of any anomalies or significant items. It was tedious and slow but the guys made it work as well as it could. Voice quality between the MCC and the remote stations was mixed - some were good, but some had a habit of dropping out at inopportune times. The orbit was such that the spacecraft would traverse and flyover most of the globe in about twenty-four hours.

We had thirteen of these stations and the manning, training and logistics were major tasks in themselves. There were usually three to five operators called flight controllers at each one of these stations. The tasks were monitoring of the onboard systems, the health of the crew, a capcom and sometimes a designated leader of the team for sites involved in critical mission coverage such as Retrofire. This effort was a significant training and logistics problem to manage. Gene Kranz earned his spurs and more in the orchestration of this global infrastructure of intelligence gathering and real time response to the frequent problems of early space flight.

The Bermuda station was additionally configured with a set of plot boards driven by the local radar and identical to the plot boards at the Mercury Control Center at the Cape. These were the tools by which we were going to assure that the spacecraft was safely in orbit or to assist in a few specific abort conditions. With the support of John Mayer, I was selected to be the flight dynamics officer at Bermuda and served on three unmanned Atlas launches and on John Glenn's flight, designated MA-6. The station worked very well for this purpose and gave clear confirmation of safe orbit, which was also verified by the tracking displayed in MCC.

This was great operational experience for me and taught me how to get a station ready for its mission. All of our learning curves were very steep and I went on to be the flight dynamics officer in MCC at the Cape for the next three flights, MA-7, -8 and -9. The early opportunity to serve at Bermuda was a great assist to my knowledge and confidence. With all of the other stations around the world, it was also a great opportunity for STG to develop many of our young engineers into competent and confident operators ready to take their place in the MCC for Gemini and Apollo.

Christopher Kraft

No record of these times can be remotely complete without testimony to the pervasive influence that Christopher Columbus Kraft had on the programs, the organization, and especially all of us, his young followers. Whatever his various titles were during those years, he was our leader - "the" flight director - and our role model. His influence was always a lesson in leadership, and we strove mightily to emulate the same.

Over five decades, while he and I were sometimes in different organizations but still associated, Chris demonstrated over and over again that great leadership cannot be overrated. Chris had the skill of clarity in defining issues and solutions. In a world of many new and compounding complexities, Chris reduced problems to a crisp definition, to a few options and then a decision. He often left me wondering "Why didn't I think of that?" His calibration of his people at all levels seemed unerring and he located people where their talents were a match to the assignment. To others, he seemed to delight in stretching them to levels that they did not know they were capable of. Decisions were often quick and always crisp. "Yes, we'll do it that way." On personnel matters, he would ask "So you want to move to this job? Tell me why." Listening and then, "Fine, I agree, the discussion is over." And I never saw Chris avoid a difficult decision; he seemed to enjoy them and even to seek them out. Once made, everybody moved on. Things were not allowed to fester or to sit on hold.

Chris had real respect for his troops and it showed in how he dealt with subjects which might impinge on them. On one occasion after a scrub and a launch delay of several days, he decided that all of us at stations around the world would stay at our respective sites and forgo travel back home. We did have one higher level management person from a different organization who was in Bermuda to observe. He asked for an exception in his case, on the communication loop, essentially in front of the rest of us, and we all knew immediately how dumb that was. And, yes, he stayed deployed with all the rest of us. Perhaps the strongest demonstration of Chris's leadership was his trust in us. That trust actually empowered and challenged us. You did not want to be found unworthy.

The work itself forced us to strive for crisp, clear communications. This was best illustrated in our mission rule discussions of what level of failure would cause a major deviation to the plan. As most of us came to operations work, there was a natural tendency to avoid or stall on a decision. Usually this manifested itself as a discussion of symptoms or preliminary troubleshooting steps, but not the final decision on a failed or failing system. This learning stage was often made apparent by the admonition "Yes, but after all those preliminaries, what do you want me (or the crew) to do?" Since we had all been there, we recognized the clarity on the final recommendation being sought, and the implied rebuke to the stall tactic. By the way, this constant need for clarity in discussions, decisions, etc. probably inhibited the already meager poetic in us and, I would guess, frustrated the interviewers who were always trying, properly so, to evoke some expression of feeling and/or emotion from us.

The benefit of the impassioned debates over the mission rules was real and enduring. The discussions forced out all aspects of any applicable considerations and there were always champions for more or less risk or response to each of all the failures under consideration. It was not apparent at first but after months of this, we began to be able to generalize what was evolving. For example, we wanted enough redundancy so that we could still tolerate one more specific failure and still recover the crew safely. In the early days, these were aimed at deciding the redundancy levels necessary to continue on-orbit, or conversely to terminate the mission early. As these rules were tested in the integrated simulations with the crew in the simulator and the MCC, they eventually became, in essence, a code of ethics that defined the risk-reward trade-off. All of the operators and the crews gradually came together on a deep understanding of our compact with each other as to how we would manage risk. It was the process of going through each and every postulated condition and response, and testing of that framework in simulations that built the team confidence. The payoff is in invoking the familiar thought and judgment process when something outside the mission rules discussions occurs. And the unexamined conditions did happen. In those cases, we got to an answer consistent with our risk-reward framework.

The understanding that the team created was sometimes under-appreciated. There were several occasions in the future when a compulsion to manage and be the decision maker would infect people. This usually showed up as Headquarters people attempting to inject themselves into operational decisions. It is probably a common disease, but, in these cases, they skipped all the prior steps which created a common under-standing of the risk-reward trade. They probably viewed it as more of a prerogative matter and less as a culmination of the invention and train-ing process. The foray never lasted long enough before correction so that it never did any harm but it could have. Some incidents were testy and there will be more on some of those later.

Chris relished the give-and-take, the arguments, the new insights from our flight experience and all the other factors informing us of ways to improve the rules and the process. A favorite of Chris's was the simula-tion ordeal. After each sim, there was always a debriefing—what was done well or badly and why. These sims were a baptism by fire—the palms always got sweaty; any decision had to be justified, and one's honor was at stake, naked in front of his peers and the boss. And, most all of us spent some time in that naked position. But, it did raise one's determination to avoid screwing up. These screw ups were also the feedstock for ridicule afterward at every opportunity. Sympathy and propriety norms were uncommon.

We had adult leadership role models all around us. Another of those, mentioned earlier, was Tecwyn "Tec" Roberts. Tec came by way of Canada and the Avro windfall to STG. Originally from the country of Wales, he was raised in the small town of Trefnant Bach, Llanddan-iel. He was the branch chief and leader of the Mission Control Center branch. He was about 10 years older than the rest of us in the unit. But he patiently required our boisterous opinions to be backed up and rein-forced by well studied background, compelling logic and reasoning to support any positions we took. It was a maturity lesson that we all in-ternalized very well and enjoyed using to the fullest with our other col-leagues who did not have the benefit of Tec's coaching. He was a quiet spoken man, but did not shy away from pushing a discussion to what he thought was the correct conclusion. And he did it with grace, charm and a kind of impish style with which one could not be angry.

All twenty-two year olds should have an engaging, talented role model like Tec to start their career with. We would all be better off. When I went to meet with Tec at my request, he often started with "Well, Mr. Lunney what are you trying to sell to me today?" Guilty as charged. To whatever extent I was successful at the art of framing and selling ideas, Tec was the teacher who got me started. I sometimes am unhappy with and disagree with what I say or write, but looking back on my oral history interviews, I was happy with these comments about Tec, only slightly edited for clarity.

"So for a number of years, Tec was our leader and mentor and kind of a –not quite a father, but maybe an uncle figure- to a lot of us young fellows in the flight dynamics discipline and he was a tremendous help to Chris in putting together the Control Center concept in both of its locations. Tec was the original Flight dynamics officer at the Cape when they operated out of the Mercury Control Center. But he was such a gentle and yet demanding kind of guy—those two words don't go together, but he was that. He was kind of gentle with people and also demanding of their performance, and because of his talents, he evoked a tremendous amount of confidence that people had in him, management had in him, and it was like he was a perfect match for us."

"We were a random group of young engineers that arrived from all over America and a little brash and a little hasty at times and sometimes a little emotional and he would counsel us along. After Tec died a few years ago, I wrote a note to Doris expressing my appreciation for all that Tec had meant to me personally, and I told her how much I and the rest of the men who worked for him had learned from him and how I felt that I used a lot of what I learned from Tec in raising our family. So I wanted her to know that there was some of Tec Roberts floating around here in Houston in the next generation of Lunneys. Tec was one of a kind and I felt blessed because Tec was such a jewel and he got to be our boss. We had a wonderful time learning from him, and he had a hell of a time dealing with us, I'm sure."

In May, 1962, Chris Kraft was Chief of the Flight Operations Division (FOD). Tec ran the Mission Control Branch and I was head of one of his three sections with an overly complicated title of "Mission Logic and Computer Hardware." There were two of us - myself and Cliff Charlesworth. John Llewellyn was not yet a formal member of this section, but that happened soon thereafter. This unit was the precursor to the eventual Flight Dynamics Branch (FDB), formed later. Tec had to leave Texas for reasons of health before that August 1964 change. With his departure and the growing workload, a Division reorganization formed the Flight Dynamics Branch. Tec transferred to GSFC where he served in various management roles for the near-earth communication and tracking network that we used for manned flights. As expected, he was a great help to the network team and to us on the Houston end of the data lines. His example and teaching continued to make my life better long after he left us in Houston.

In 1964, the FDB had twelve men besides myself—seven assigned to the upcoming Gemini and five to Apollo—a very small staff indeed for the total effort. As another indicator of their task, I was also selected as a Flight Director in October 1964, joining Chris, John Hodge and Gene Kranz. Cliff Charlesworth, who was the FDB deputy Chief, was also selected as a Flight Director in January 1966 in the middle of the Gemini flight phase. We managed both jobs until March, 1968 when we were both transferred to a new Flight Director Office as Apollo approached. It is up to the FDBers to say whether this organization arrangement was a problem or an opportunity for them. With Cliff and I not available for assignment to any flight dynamics console positions, I would wager on opportunity. But, I get ahead of the story.

Moving Towards Operations

My assignment as the Flight dynamics officer at Bermuda was a great opportunity to gain experience in what flight operations was becoming. The Bermuda station was in an excellent location to evaluate trajectory conditions after engine cutoff. At this point, it will aid in understanding to review the general subject of the launch phase and the abort (escape) modes available to the operations team.

The Atlas launch vehicle was selected for the Mercury program on the basis of its stage of development and its lift capability. Probably, the most significant reason was that it was the only national system available to perform the mission on the planned schedule. I was amazed at the design of this launch vehicle. The structure of the vehicle was basically two compartments containing kerosene and liquid oxygen respectively, separated by a common bulkhead. The overall structure was a very thin sheet of aluminum fairly close to what we know as aluminum foil. The vehicle structure was so light that it had to be pressurized with a gas like nitrogen for most of its life on the ground. The internal pressure is what gave it shape, form and whatever rigidity it had. Yes, it was like a high-tech balloon. It was equipped with three engines in a horizontal row at the aft end. Like other rockets, it employed some degree of staging but it only dropped off the two outboard engines, no tankage. The vehicle continued under the thrust of the middle engine, called the sustainer engine, until commanded to be cut off by the guidance system. Unlike all successor orbital launch vehicles that have onboard inertial guidance systems, the guidance was performed by a ground based tracking and computing system at the Cape, known by its suppliers – GE (tracking) and Burroughs (computer for guidance).

Various factors combine to make the launch phase a very critical period of flight—booster reliability (about fifty percent in those years), short reaction times, high rates at which some failures develop, the catastrophic consequences of some malfunctions, limitations of the escape systems and techniques—to name some of the most obvious. I had the sobering experience of reviewing most of these films of launch vehicle failures. They stay with you for life, just like the Challenger videos do.

The function of range safety (i.e. the protection of personnel on the ground, property and facilities) is discussed elsewhere in the Mercury Redstone experience and was a good starting point to begin to conceptualize how to protect the spacecraft and crew. Range safety required an onboard destruct system, basically a shaped charge running the length of the tanks and on both sides of the vehicle. The concept was to stop the propulsion and disperse the propellants so they did not land in a concentrated mass. For staged vehicles, they required a hot wire type system between stages to fire the destruct system in case of the stages separating in an uncontrolled fashion.

In the case of Mercury, the spacecraft was equipped with an escape tower which was designed to separate the spacecraft from the launcher quickly enough and to a sufficient distance to survive the fireball created by the vehicle being destroyed by the range safety destruct system. There was a small delay of 3.5 seconds built into the system such that the command first alerted the crew and then delayed the actual destruct function to give the escape system opportunity to propel the spacecraft to a safe separation distance. By the time that the escape tower was jettisoned at about 2 minutes and thirty seconds, the vehicle was out of the zone of primary concern to the range safety officer. Then, escape was like a normal separation except that the crew action to separate also initiated an engine cutoff command to the Atlas engine. These were the onboard systems to separate the spacecraft.

Next came the techniques to decide to initiate an abort. Some vehicle failure modes, such as a hard over control signal or engine positioning system, could result in very rapid loss of control and vehicle breakup, especially during the first sixty to ninety seconds when the ship can be experiencing high dynamic pressures and resultant loads. Because of these possibilities, an automatic sensing and implementation system (ASIS) was designed to protect against this type of failure that exceeds the human ability to react quickly enough. This launch vehicle system would then trigger an abort sequence by the spacecraft. As in the destruct system, loss of electrical continuity between the spacecraft and Atlas would also trigger an abort. Operator intervention to initiate an abort was also available to the crew and to the flight director.

Unless we had the luxury of selecting a time to initiate an abort, the spacecraft would land anywhere in the Atlantic based on the trajectory conditions at the time. There was some possibility of landing point control for an abort in the last thirty seconds or so of Atlas flight. After separation at these velocities and altitude, the time of Retrofire could be varied from a minimum of thirty seconds to turn around to blunt end forward to a maximum of four minutes and still have coverage of the Retrofire sequence from Bermuda. The responsibility for selecting the fire time was assigned to the position of RETRO controller, consistent with his on-orbit responsibility for the calculation and orchestration of the RETRO fire maneuver. These two positions worked in very close coordination for the return to earth planning, with the FIDO assuring the best quality navigation solution for the RETRO calculation.

We spent a lot of time analyzing what combination of velocity and flight path angle would constitute an acceptable orbit. We finally ended up with a boundary of velocity and flight path angles that would provide the spacecraft with enough energy for a safe orbit. On the plot of velocity on the horizontal and flight path angle on the vertical, the go-no-go line looked like a slightly curved bow, as if the line representing a zero flight path angle was an arrow in the bow pointing towards a lower velocity than nominal. The boundary was about 100 feet per second below the nominal cutoff velocity to assure energy for at least one safe orbit before the drag would cause the spacecraft to reenter. This margin was a very small percentage (less than .5% of the required velocity of about 25,000 fps) and the evaluation required to assure an adequate margin could include the judgment of the operator since the random deviations of measured velocity could be a significant portion of the 100 feet per second margin.

I did not appreciate it enough at the time but the support of John Mayer was very important and gratifying to me in terms of the confidence he had in my ability to perform this job. For the position of Flight dynamics officer (FIDO) in the Mercury Control Center at the Cape, Chris selected Tec Roberts. This choice had been made sometime in 1960. Tec had arrived at STG in April of '59 with the Avro contingent and within one year had established himself as one of Chris Kraft's key managers and advisors. Although Tec did not have a detailed grounding in orbital mechanics, his common sense and good judgment made him the logical choice for this job. His performance in this role set the standard for the FIDO position and it remains so over four decades later. Probably about the same time, I became the candidate for the FIDO position at Bermuda. I remember a short and to-the-point discussion as John Mayer recommended my selection to Chris Kraft. I was twenty-four years of age.

We all were well aware of the criticality of this job. John Mayer was unequivocal "Chris, Glynn knows this as well as I do. I am completely confident he can handle this job." Chris listened and soon agreed. Without any dramatics or hesitation, Chris's ready confirmation of my selection was just another in a constant and daily delegation of responsibility to the people who worked for him. Looking back on this time, I have to be in awe at the level of trust and confidence that we were accorded. It was not cavalier. Both of these men had many opportunities to measure and test me before and after this decision because all of us worked in a very intense and open team fashion and were not constrained by organization position. All of us believed that Chris had a very accurate calibration of all of us and assigned us accordingly. But this willingness to trust us and give us the room to grow created an environment of can-do and will-do-no-matter-what which was the hallmark of the operations organization for decades and still is today. It drove us to an even higher level of performance to live up to Chris's confidence in us. In later years, I was exposed to many training sessions on leadership by national experts. My reaction always was, "Gee, I was living this lesson with Chris and others of STG when I was twenty-two. We just did not have the buzzword terminology."

This is a good time to underline the positive and demanding environment we worked in. I was too junior to see the relationships with other centers and NASA Headquarters in action, though I did see more of those interfaces when I became a Flight Director in 1964. Early on, the local scene was my daily reality. The tone was clearly set by Dr. Bob Gilruth. In all the notoriety, very strong personalities and press attention of the time, Dr. Gilruth seemed like the forgotten man. And yet he managed the direction of the work, the extremely strong management team of the STG and later, in Houston, the Manned Spacecraft Center. Neither I nor anybody else ever heard or felt anything but the utmost respect for our leader, Dr. Gilruth. He had as much to do with the ultimate success of the first decade of manned space flight as any other player on the scene.

You have no doubt heard of different management styles—management by: the numbers, consensus, goals, fear/ intimidation, ambiguity, among others. One of his direct reports who had also worked with him at Langley, before the space business began, described his style in a way that I have never heard of before or since. He called it "Management by Respect." Interpret that anyway you like, but I thought it was a real capture of his modus operandi. And it flowed through the STG and the MSC like the elixir of achievement. We saw it most often in the person of Chris Kraft, who lived this philosophy with a strong streak of trusting us with the job, and demanding that we get it right. What a fantastic opportunity for all of us to be part of this amazing team and charged with this national imperative of manned space and then, Apollo. We were truly blessed.

Working at the Bermuda station on TDY was a great experience and a smaller stage to learn on. John Hodge was the flight director of the team, which included a capcom, two systems flight controllers, a flight surgeon and the FIDO. We stayed at the BOQ at Kendall Air Force Base, which is where the station was. I served there for four flights, MA-3, -4, -5 and -6. MA-3 was planned to go into orbit but was destroyed by the range safety officer at forty-three seconds into the flight. The vehicle pitch and roll program failed to activate and the vehicle was climbing vertically. After the destruct command, the spacecraft sequenced just as it should have and was recovered. It actually flew on MA-4. The next three flights, MA-4, MA-5 and MA-6 were conducted with increasing orbital duration of one, two and three orbits before returning to earth. The flights also progressed in a biological sequence, from unmanned to the chimp Enos, and then to John Glenn's flight.

Besides the actual flights, we also deployed several times before scrubs and launch delays extended our stay or sent us home. This gave us time to explore the island. Our transportation was small motorbikes. The government of Bermuda severely restricted the number of cars and trucks allowed on the island and that was probably a good idea. We really enjoyed the motorbike mode of travel and it wasn't long before Al Shepard had us driving in a diamond formation. It was fun most of the time except that I got stuck once in the rear slot position when it started to rain. When we got to Hamilton, everybody else was a little wet but I had been sprayed with dirt for the entire drive. Al's comment was, "Lunney, you look like hell, but at least you kept formation."

The roads in Bermuda were cut out of the coral which is the basic structure of the island itself. One of our guys found out that coral is really not good for humans. He went over the handlebars of his motorbike and landed with his palms and arms outstretched. It didn't take long for the blood poisoning to show up. Jim was in the local Air Force hospital and the cure seemed a little barbaric. Every day, the nurse came in and scraped his hands and arms with a wire brush. We were able to make one medication contribution to his recovery. It was a bottle of Jack

Daniels delivered two hours before his scraping treatment and then self administered liberally.

I learned a few things about cards, rum, scuba diving and other matters from these trips but one travel story really stuck with me. Our team arrived at the Newport News airport for one of our excursions to Bermuda. The airplane was not available, some technical problem. We had a connection to make on Pan-Am out of Idlewild (now Kennedy in NYC) to get to Bermuda. Immediately, Gus Grissom went off to find a solution. He soon came back with one. He hired 2 local pilots, a local and his nephew, and an agreement to fly us to NYC. The flight in 2 separate small planes was uneventful and the uncle kept his nephew informed as to the details. I was in the nephew's plane. No problem. As we were pulling up to park the plane, one of the ground crew was guiding our pilot into the parking slot and was giving us the cut-the-engine hand signal. At about this time, the nephew decided that something was wrong—i.e. instead of Idlewild, he landed at La Guardia, the wrong airport. No hesitation on his part. He revved up the engine, and started to taxi back to the runway. Maybe he did but I never heard him talk to the tower. He knew he was at the wrong place, so he rolled out on the runway and took off. He was probably more afraid of his uncle than the other aircraft traffic or the FAA. We soon landed at Idlewild and parked by the other plane. Mission accomplished. We had a rousing time debriefing this bit of piloting in the Pan Am Clipper club.

On another trip, I ended up with a really severe cold – coughing, sneezing and feeling ugly. In this case, our flight surgeon Dr. Chuck Berry, came up with a civilized treatment. He got a humidifier and filled it with Drambuie and little water. I don't know how helpful it was for me but all of the guys enjoyed coming to my room and breathing in the Drambuie flavored air while they enjoyed their evening cocktail.

Besides Al Shepard, Gus Grissom was our capcom for one of the flights and Deke Slayton was capcom for MA-6. Back in Houston, Gus and Deke would occasionally drop by our home in Friendswood to drop off a load of fish from their day's excursion into the Gulf for king mackerel and sometimes red snapper. Even today, when I order red snapper that association comes flooding back. After John Glenn's flight of MA-6, Deke was looking forward to his assignment on MA-7. So we had several reasons to celebrate -- both the first manned orbital flight and the upcoming flight of Deke. And we did so.

When we got back to Langley, it was rather quickly announced that Deke had been taken off flight status and would not fly the next flight.

Only Deke can describe his disappointment with this turn, but all of us who knew him shared in the disappointment. Deke was a favorite of most people and we all knew how much the flight assignment meant to him. He finally did get his first space flight in 1975 on the Apollo/Soyuz test project. By that time, I was the Technical Director of Apollo/Soyuz. But in between 1962 and his assignment to Apollo/Soyuz, he served primarily as flight crew operations director for the rest of Mercury and all of Gemini and Apollo. NASA and the flight crews were fortunate to have such a highly respected and experienced pro steering and supporting the decisions during this historic era. Deke was always a voice of common sense and helped me a great deal on flights that I was serving as a flight director.

By this time, we knew that we were moving to Texas and building a new control center there. Communications around the world had become much improved since early Mercury and we would be able to remote the voice, telemetry, command and tracking reliably from the world wide sites back to the control center in Houston. Gemini was expected to fly in 1964, ie. within over two years. And Apollo was coming. Besides other personnel assignments, Chris wanted Tec to be in the middle of the action for the new MCC. So Tec retired from the FIDO position and I was assigned the role for MA7 and subsequent. The flight experience also allowed us to delete the FIDO function at Bermuda. I was delighted to be at MCC, the center of action for flight operations.

15 Months to John Glenn on MA-6

Most of 1959 and 1960 zipped by in a blur of putting theory into the practical reality of participating in the invention of a control center with a supporting computing center at the Goddard Space Flight Center (GSFC) and the world-wide network of remote sites to provide the infrastructure for a mission control function. All of these elements were being created simultaneously while the concept for operations evolved from a set of thoughts in the head of Chris Kraft to a compelling vision in the minds of his leadership team and especially his young believers. This was what we wanted to do. Invent, create, cover all the bases, master the complexities and reduce them to workable sized packages. As 1960 drew to a close, we were at the point of testing ourselves and our ideas in the unforgiving world of manned space operations.

On November 8, 1960, our fellow citizens elected our next President, a young senator from Massachusetts named John Fitzgerald Kennedy. It was a heady time, full of possibilities and promise. But none of us could imagine what this President, in a few short months, would ask us to do.

And so, we began the flight test campaign to put an American in space, on a mission designated MA-6.

MA-6 minus 15 months

November 19, 1960—As discussed earlier, this flight of the Redstone rocket with the Mercury spacecraft on the front end was a very short and low altitude flight of about four inches. After which time, the escape tower fired and the landing parachutes deployed. This was a very precarious condition—a fully fueled rocket with engine already fired and shut down, all systems armed for flight, standing free on the pad with no hold-down devices engaged, parachutes billowing in the wind and threatening to fill with air and topple the entire stack to a fiery death on the pad. After considering some risky alternatives to safe the situation, it was finally decided to wait, as long as the winds stayed low. Do not take precipitous action and let the batteries bleed down to the point where the propulsion system valves would go to the unpowered (closed) position. This course led to a safe condition by the next day.

In the space business, like many others, a failure (or near failure in this case) can lead to much more in terms of lessons learned than a nominal success. The lessons from this attempted flight are dramatic testimony to this truth. First, there has to be integrity in the allegiance of the organization. The booster engineer was from the Redstone organization at the Marshall Space Flight Center and spent his time after the incident speaking to the blockhouse in German and ignoring Kraft. You can imagine how that went down. Suffice to say, it never happened again. Second, all the thrashing about what to do reinforced the admonition to " do nothing if you don't know what to do." Third, we really needed better drawings and information on how the flight vehicles were configured. Fourth, I was amazed at how this situation escalated in complexity. It was nowhere near as straight forward as I assumed. It was like suddenly being able to see brand new dimensions to situations, when before, I only saw two. And it all can happen very quickly.

MA-6 minus 14 months

December 19, 1960—MR-1A flew a nominal flight.

MA-6 minus 13 months

January 31, 1961—The Mercury/Redstone, MR-2, was launched with the chimp Ham onboard. By this time, those of us not assigned to the

MCC or a downrange tracking ship, remained at Langley, getting ready for later Atlas launches. Again, the MR-2 events deviated from nominal because this Redstone burned its fuel at a higher rate than was planned. We therefore had an "early" shutdown, which triggered an escape tower abort, rather than a tower jettison from the spacecraft. This gave a very high 17 'g' kick to the occupant who was also being shocked despite his correct response to stimulus because of equipment failure. Events had not been kind to Ham, but he endured.

February 1, 1961—Our first child, Jennifer, arrived on this planet.

MA-6 minus 12 months

February 21, 1961—Mercury/Atlas, MA-2, was launched and proved that the STG design solution of a structural belly band between the Atlas and the spacecraft worked properly and was accepted as the definitive fix for the failure of MA-1 on July 29, 1960.

MA-6 minus 11 months

March 1961—The Redstone team at MSFC wanted one more test of the Redstone and it worked fine. The STG team thought the extra test was unnecessary and cost time and effort. But it was done and time to move on.

April 12, 1961—Yuri Gagarin flew one revolution around the earth. And, in the midst of so much progress in our program, the Soviet Union was back in the news with a really major step and we were still playing catch-up.

MA-6 minus 10 months

April 25, 1961—MA-3, slated for an orbital flight, had a launch vehicle failure in the planned pitch and roll program and was destroyed by the Range Safety Officer (RSO) at forty-three seconds into the flight. Thirteen days after the Gagarin success, the hole seemed even deeper.

MA-6 minus 9 months

May 05, 1961—Finally, the flight of Alan Shepard on MR-3 worked to perfection and America had its first manned space success. We were still behind—Yes. But, our stuff-- the spacecraft, the launch vehicle, the flight crew, the MCC team, the launch ops team, the network and the recovery team – was coming together. Yes. The national reaction of pride and joy at our success was a major lift to our spirits. We can do this. And Alan was his charming and effective self in the White House and the Rose Garden. Little did we know of the efforts of a small study team lead by George Low to chart a course for the space program that went far beyond bold and daring. Little did we know of the vision and determination of our young President.

May 25, 1961—What a speech—What a challenge. To go to the moon and to land there within the decade. My personal reaction was like many others of our brotherhood. Without knowing how such a thing could be done, it sounded way beyond any capability we would be able to achieve. Even today, I wonder if the President and his advisors really grasped the scale and difficulty of this endeavor. It sounded impossible. This may be how the big breakthroughs of history really happen. What a privilege to be part of it. And so we went back to work. The reaction of our fellow citizens to Al's flight was an incredible morale booster in itself. And then this unbelievable and unexpected demonstration of confidence dominated our lives for the next 10 years and beyond.

MA-6 minus 7 months

July 21, 1961—MR-4, piloted by Gus Grissom, roared off the pad to duplicate the performance of MR-3. And it did. But another unexpected event almost caused the drowning and death of Gus and did cause the loss of the spacecraft. Something caused the backup explosive system to fire and blow the hatch allowing seawater to flood into the ship. The proximity of, and the skill of, the helicopter crew saved Gus because his suit was not completely closed and was also filling with water. I never heard an official closeout of this problem—as to whether it fired as a result of an equipment failure or, as some suspected, that the crewman inadvertently hit the trigger. Either way, it hung over Gus's head for a while.

August 6, 1961—Again, a reminder of our position in the space race was emphasized by the seventeen revolutions of the earth by cosmonaut Gherman Titov.

MA-6 minus 5 months

September 13, 1961—The campaign to test the Mercury and Atlas vehicle moved into high gear with the preparations for MA-4. It was an unmanned spacecraft planned for a one revolution orbital flight. This was the first time for the spacecraft to perform in orbit and the first time that the Atlas would be used to lift the spacecraft to its intended orbit. And the first time that I had the opportunity to see the Atlas cutoff conditions in velocity and the flight path angle of the velocity vector. The solution was a little noisy but still clearly a "Go" for orbit. It felt a little strange to see the actual orbital conditions on the plotboard, rather than on a piece of paper, after so many discussions and speculation as to how good the processed data would be. It was a real pleasure to report to John Hodge, the Bermuda flight director " Flight / FIDO, we have a Go orbit." This was a continuum from the work that John Mayer did to reduce the actual radar tracking to confirm that the X-1 flight of Chuck Yeager at Muroc (Edwards) actually broke the sound barrier (one day after the fact) to one of his protégés confirming that the first Mercury spacecraft was really in orbit (and within a few seconds).

September 19, 1961—The awaited announcement came out. The STG was moving to Houston, Texas. This selection had been pending for some time and I was oblivious to the political process that arrived at that decision. Several factors came to my mind.

Several months previous, my wife Marilyn had been sending clothes and supplies to the people of Clear Lake who had been devastated by Hurricane Carla. Marilyn's questions ran to "Why are we going there? Isn't it flooded? How far away is Texas?" When our Dad returned from the Army Air Corps in 1946, he had been stationed at Shepherd Field in Wichita Falls, Texas. I remember him clearly announcing that he did not want to hear about Texas again, saying "All I ever saw was sand and rattlesnakes." And that was probably true for him.

Our experience was exactly the opposite of Dad's. We found a place where the people had the same attitude as President Kennedy, as in " Anything is possible. But you have to work at it to make it happen. Your future is what you make it." The Texans really loved the space program. They loved the astronauts and the idea of a grand challenge to visit our nearest neighbor in the solar system. This was in stark contrast to our neighbors near Hampton,VA. Many of whom referred to NACA (the predecessor to NASA) people as "NACA-Nuts." Our first impressions of local Texas support carried through a lifetime. We always felt most welcome and appreciated for what we brought to the State. Texas is home.

MA-6 minus 3 months

November 29, 1961—The last precursor to a manned flight was the MA-5 flight of a Mercury spacecraft for a three revolution mission carrying a chimp named Enos. It was only later as a Flight Director that I came to appreciate the situation the astronauts faced with the chimp flights. I should have been more empathetic. These guys came from a world of alpha males, fighter pilot squadrons and national test pilot schools for only the best in their profession. No room for chimps. And they heard the slurs from their fellow-jocks to their manhood when the description of space flight was "man-in-a-can," or "chimps were the first." I am sure they were happy to see the "long hairy line" of chimps at an end. The MA-5 launch was nominal and I got to see that beautiful radar tracking transformed on my plotboard into the clear display of a GO orbit. Things settled down for a while on orbit but conditions in the spacecraft deteriorated. We all followed the changes in the first two orbits. Finally, because of elevated cabin temperature and excessive firing of the control engines , Chris Kraft ordered the mission terminated after two orbits. The MCC team concept was maturing and gaining confidence.

December, 1961—The follow-on to the Mercury program was announced. It was named Gemini, a two-man spacecraft for the constellation of the twins. In my opinion, the Gemini program was the enabler of the rapid pace of the Apollo flights once we began the flight campaign in 1968. The design teams and the operations teams- planners, flight controllers and flight crews- profited immensely from the "boot camp" of ten manned Gemini flights to roar into Apollo with a competence and confidence that only "being there and doing it" can provide. The Gemini systems transitioned from analog to digital. We learned and tested rendezvous and docking under multiple conditions (prepping for the lunar rendezvous), docked propulsion maneuvers (as in the Apollo command ship CSM and the Lander LM), guidance controlled entries (as in Apollo reentries), long durations up to 2 weeks (the longest expected Apollo flight) and the space walk technology and techniques. To a man, the flight controllers and crews would testify that Gemini made Apollo possible in the time allowed. The experience gained avoided the need for an excessively long series of flights before the landing on the fifth manned Apollo. Imagine how history might look if Apollo XIII (the seventh manned Apollo) happened before the landing mission and with an operations team with less experience.

MA-6 Arrives

February 20, 1962—After multiple scrubs and delays, MA-6 lifted off

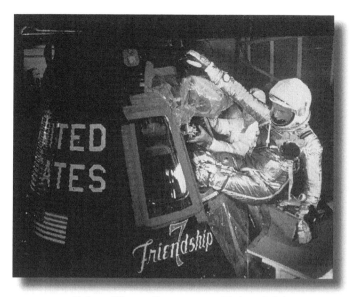

John Glenn Ingress to Friendship 7

on this date in February. Tens of thousands of Americans worked for this day and each can treasure the achievement and their role as a reward that they will always own. During the flight, a situation developed that was enough to try any man's fortitude. During the second orbit, an obscure telemetry signal was observed that indicated that the impact bag had deployed. It normally deploys in the landing sequence in order to cushion the landing in the water. The real significance was that the bag was behind the heat shield and this indication could mean that the heat shield was not firmly attached for reentry. This was an extremely difficult decision to grapple with. If the signal was not valid, the best and safest approach was to proceed nominally and jettison the spent RETRO package after the firing of the RETRO rockets. If the signal was valid, any assistance in keeping the heat shield in place (such as retaining the spent RETRO package after firing the rockets and reentering with the spent RETRO package in place) would serve to help keep the heat shield in place but the burning of the RETRO package could damage (or even destroy) the heat shield and/or change the vehicle aerodynamics to an unsafe condition. There were very competent advisors with strong opinions on both sides of the issue. It was ultimately decided to retain the RETRO package for reentry and John Glenn was so informed. He accepted the decision and it worked fine. The arrival of MA-6, coming through blackout, the parachute sequence and landing, was a special moment for this young space team. We had put our American in orbit and he is back home safely. But, again, we were forcefully reminded how quickly conditions could develop which can be a most serious threat to the survival of the astronaut and how we can be confronted with choices that have never been considered or studied.

The lessons learned from this experience still flow through the processes today. Much greater attention was (and is) paid to including redundant and/or complementary methods to absolutely confirm any indication of a threat by multiple paths. Gemini and Apollo quickly benefitted. In order to have a final authority, the mission rules now include an unequivocal statement defining the flight director as that final authority for any decision involving the safety of the crew and/or the success of the mission. Certain protocols were established to provide the program and engineering personnel with a communication path for answering questions or making inputs. This protocol evolved over the early programs to become a very well controlled, documented and powerful adjunct to the conduct of manned space operations, right up till today.

The significance to our country of this first big achievement in what had become known as the "space race" was manifested best by the outpouring of celebration and recognition of John Glenn across the country. One space flight and John went from a relative unknown to a national and international celebrity. And he carried it off with grace and dignity.

Completely absorbed at the time, we did not enjoy a lot of reflection time. But that period of fifteen months was a measure of what this country, and NASA in particular, can do. 6 Redstone flights, five Atlas flights with three of them to earth orbit, two new programs: Gemini to prepare for the future and Apollo to be the future, and a prospective move to Houston. It was a time to really enjoy the enthusiastic support of our fellow citizens.

During this fifteen month campaign, the Soviet Union flew two manned flights. Yuri Gagarin in Vostok one flew for one orbit on April 12, 1961. Gherman Titov launched in Vostok 2 on August 6, 1961 and flew for one day. The Soviets probably had other unsuccessful test flights during this time but they were not announced as elements of their manned program. We had not won, we were still behind but we certainly felt a lot better about our prospects.

MA-7

John Llewellyn got the prime RETRO assignment for MA-7 and Carl Huss, our across the street Friendswood neighbor, took on the mentoring role for John and later for Jerry Bostick. By this time, Carl's duties as John Mayer's deputy in the Mission Planning Branch were growing with the upbeat of Gemini and Apollo. It was interesting to watch this interaction between John and Carl. Carl was almost over the top rigorous and they could not have been more different in approach but they made it through.

John and I worked the MA-7 flight of Scott Carpenter together in the MCC at the Cape. From the beginning of the flight, there were problems with the spacecraft attitude reference. They were never really worked because Carpenter did not report that the instruments did not agree with the out the window view. He was also using an excessive amount of fuel trying to understand the source of "fireflies" around the spacecraft. John Glenn had reported on that phenomena, but Scott seemed determined to find out the source of the problem and solve the mystery of the fireflies. This caused a serious problem with the attitude control fuel that later ran out during reentry. The upshot of this distraction and the attitude reference problem was that, at Retrofire time, Carpenter was late getting in Retrofire attitude and still less than 100% focused on the RETRO sequence. At Retrofire, the spacecraft was still out of planned attitude in the yaw axis by a significant amount and the Retrofire impulse did not deliver all of the in-plane required braking velocity to land at the planned landing location. It wasn't long before the tracking data began to display an overshoot in the landing position. Llewellyn reported to Chris- "Flight this is RETRO, he's coming down about 250 miles long" and that's where the para-rescue team found Carpenter and Aurora 7 an hour later. When Carpenter was back on the carrier, he announced, "I didn't know where I was and they didn't either." John took this as a personal affront to his manhood and Chris Kraft took it as incompetence on Carpenter's part.

During the run-up to and conduct of any flight, the press corps shows up and press conferences and interviews abound. Sometime during the flight PAO was receiving a lot of press questions about trajectory subjects. This was understandable because all of this was brand new to them. At any rate, Walt Williams and Chris Kraft called me over and Chris said "Glynn, the press wants to understand more about ascending nodes and other trajectory stuff, why don't you go out there and start their education on your subjects." Both of them were chuckling to each other as my discomfort about this was obvious.

So, off I went to my first press conference, at age twenty-five to explain what the "longitude of the ascending node" was all about. It was the beginning of interaction with the press that carried throughout my career. These were testy at times because the press seemed to assume that we were not being truthful and/or accurate and they tried to catch us in mistakes. Over time, most of the press corps came to believe and even trust us. And we developed a better grasp of where the press fit in our American system and gave it its due. Many of the press regulars became life-long supporters of Manned Space Flight. Although in early times, we had a lot of laughs over how press reporting varied so far from the truth as we explained it. My wife, Marilyn, would be exasperated after listening to my press conference and then seeing the report either in print or on TV. "They never get it right, why do you guys bother?" was her recurring assessment.

Walt Williams joined the STG in September 1959 from the world of high-speed aircraft testing over the California desert at a facility known as the Muroc Army Air field and then later Edwards Air Force base. He went there in 1946 from the NACA Langley center and was involved in the testing of all of the historic and breakthrough aircraft of that period. He was named the first Chief of the NASA High Speed Flight Station at that location in 1949.

After over thirteen years in that crucible of modern aviation, he saw the beginnings of the reach to go beyond the atmosphere. This was done first by stretching aircraft beyond any current limits at the time and then joining the STG on a new path to "higher and faster." The new path envisioned propelling a manned vehicle on an ICBM class launch vehicle to speeds and altitudes beyond the reach of aircraft even today, fifty years later. Walt was titled as an Associate Director working for Bob Gilruth, the Director of STG. His role was to help define and oversee the operations of this new venture into space.

Walt brought three important strengths to the space theater: a wealth of flight experience, tremendous respect for the flying machines, and even greater respect for the men who flew them. His presence set the tone and the priorities with the operations elements at STG. He helped make the operations team – the astronauts, the flight crew support division and the flight operation division, that I was in, into a real force. He also brought an attitude, much like that of a middle linebacker.

**Walt Williams,
Chris Kraft
and John Hodge**

When you had a briefing for Walt, it was really necessary to prepare well and get it right. Walt had his own way of listening. He put feet on the desk, closed his eyes, and gave the appearance of napping. But after thirty minutes or an hour briefing, he would shrug himself to a standing position and summarize all of the essential points that were made. And then of course, he ruled on the issue that was being discussed. No games, nothing but the hard substance.

In both Mercury and Gemini, NASA bought the launch vehicle service from the Air Force and NASA dealt with the Aerospace Corp. (technical advisors to the AF) on all matters technical. I did not work with Walt much on the first program procurement, but I did on the Titan for Gemini. To my knowledge, Walt ran that activity with one technical helper, Bob Harrington. Bob kept the minutes and occasionally offered inputs, but Walt ran it as a one-man show. He must have had contracts and financial support but I never saw those functions in play. Maybe, Bob Harrington oversaw them. There were joint team efforts on the new abort sensing system for Mercury and its counterpart on Gemini, the malfunction detection system. These efforts involved additional NASA personnel, like Chris for the abort sensing system, on these specific subjects. But, Walt was the boss. When he walked in to run the meeting, the Aerospace Corp. team rose as one. The leader of that team was Ben Hohman, whom I understood to have worked at Peenemunde. It was probably my imagination but I could almost hear heels clicking at Walt's entrance. It was quite a performance for this twenty-five year old to witness.

Completing Mercury and Gemini

Cliff Charlesworth

In the first addition for what became the Flight Dynamics Branch two years later, I hired Cliff Charlesworth into the emerging Mission Logic Section in March 1962. If I had written a specification for my first hire and canvassed the country, I could not have selected better. Cliff was the first achiever in a long line of young men who joined the Flight dynamics team at the new Manned Spacecraft Center during the sixties. The solid majority of these young men, like Cliff, were exceptional and the work we were about to do offered them the opportunity to demonstrate their true potential.

Cliff was the start of that staffing process and he helped to frame what we were doing in so many ways-big and small. I don't credit any magical interviewing skill on my part. Cliff, and the rest, came because they wanted to participate and contribute to this historic program. *They selected themselves.*

Cliff brought a demeanor of calm, thoughtful competence with a no-nonsense attitude towards people's behavior, probably developed in his upbringing in Jackson, Mississippi and his couple of years service in the US Army. He had nicknames like 'Mississippi Fats' and the 'Riverboat Gambler' – all of which conveyed a man of reflection and action, an ability to assess situations and handle them. That was also the job description for a Flight Dynamics Officer, Flight Director, Program Manager, Head of a Directorate, Deputy Center Director – all of which were positions Cliff served in with distinction over his career.

Cliff had various quirks, like: "be on time, you are responsible for your work, take care of your hygiene duties before you come to work, get to the point and be clear in what you are saying and recommending." He also believed in supporting people, providing encouragement when folks screwed up, and helping them grow in their assignments. On visiting Cliff at home, I often found him in a lawn chair, having a beer and watering his lawn by hand. He claimed that he did his best thinking while watering.

He was a major contributor to the formation and leadership of the Flight dynamics team and in all his subsequent positions. Cliff was five years older than me, and although I was nominally the boss, he was always like the older brother I never had. He was always a good friend to me, and a trustworthy partner, in whatever we were doing. He tried to restrain my enthusiasm when appropriate by observing, "Lunney, you will never get an ulcer, you just give them to other people. You are a carrier." And, he did temper my passion occasionally with just the code-word "ulcer."

Cliff recommended and we hired Bobby Spencer a few months later. Bobby was a friend and colleague of Cliff's at his last job. Bobby joined the section in June, 1962 and was assigned to the Apollo group in the July 1964 organization of FDB. Bobby served as a RETRO throughout his FDB career and was the technical point man for the FDB command function of the Little Joe abort test at White Sands Missile Range, north of El Paso. Bobby sent the destruct command to the solid rocket when it got to the desired test conditions and that started the spacecraft abort sequence. We shared that project out at White Sands. When I was named as a Flight Director in August 1964, I was assigned as the over-all lead for the post-liftoff activities associated with these test flights, just like the handover between the MCC and the Launch Control Center. The White Sands Little Joe project was also my first opportunity to work with George Page of the Kennedy Space Center launch team. George went on to work Apollo, Skylab and Shuttle at KSC in various capacities, as did I.

Moving to Houston

We knew there was a site selection team formed to look for a permanent location for STG, as it was on its way to becoming the Manned Space-craft Center (MSC). I was happy that we were going to move from Virginia, because, although it was home to many of the men I worked with, I was not wild about it and looked forward to the change. The decision was made and announced in December 1961 that we were moving to Houston, Texas and to a particular area of Houston around Clear Lake, twenty miles south of Houston on I-45.

Immediately prior to this announcement, the area had been hit by Hurricane Carla. Marilyn was active in some of the volunteer efforts to collect and ship supplies to the "poor" people in Houston. Little did we know that we would soon be living there. We all had many questions about it and felt that we knew little about Texas except for the movie portrayals of the state.

After MA-7, I drove our '58 Chevy convertible, with no air conditioning, to Houston, while Marilyn and our daughter Jenny enjoyed their last visit for a while with her parents. As I was getting closer to Texas, I began to think of those movies, John Wayne – great big steaks and cold beer. And I couldn't wait to get to a Texas town to enjoy some of that fare. However, as I ordered my first steak in Texas, I found out about the dreaded "dry county." Yes, it meant you could not buy a beer to have with your steak, or anything else alcoholic for that matter. I wondered what John Wayne would think about that.

I went on to Houston, and eventually got to a rental home in Deer Park. Our friends, the Tindalls, had rented this home, and gave us the key to stay there until they arrived later. This was the last part of June, and was my first experience with the wonderful heat and humidity so well renowned in Houston. In due course, Marilyn and Jenny, now seventeen months, were due to arrive in Houston at Hobby Airport. At this time, Marilyn was almost eight months pregnant with our second child. She had made matching outfits for herself and Jenny for this auspicious trip. Airports in the sixties did not have long tunnels which now permit people to leave the plane and remain in at least some air conditioning. In those days, exit from the plane was accomplished with a set of stairs that are rolled over to the plane, secured in place, so that the plane door opens at the top of the stairs. Other people came off and I was just inside the door watching for Marilyn. It was about 3 pm and when she showed up at the door of the airplane holding Jenny's hand, the heat and humidity hit her "face-on." Marilyn staggered back into the airplane as if the wall of heat was assaulting her.

That was her welcoming moment to Houston, and I'm sure she wondered what she was doing here. Off we went, in our car without air conditioning, and we stayed in the Tindall rental house for a couple of weeks, which also had no A/C. When I got home from work, I often found Marilyn and Jenny in the tub, sometimes with ice cubes on special occasions.

Shortly after arrival, the city sponsored a welcoming event in the Houston Coliseum in downtown. This was the original site of what is now the Houston Rodeo currently housed in Reliant Center. This started with a parade, where the Mercury astronauts and much of the brass of MSC were paraded through town. It was a fantastic reception. In the Coliseum, there was all kind of entertainment including bands, and even a family version show by a well known stripper named Sally Rand. Houstonians were uniformly dressed in cowboy boots, big buckles, and cowboy hats. They were genuinely happy to have us here in Houston, and made sure that we had all the beer and barbecue that we could handle. This was an amazing change from the locals in Virginia. The people of Houston seemed to love everything about the idea of space and the fact that we were moving into their community. We could not have imagined a more friendly welcome.

As the time for the Tindall's move to Houston approached, we found an apartment, in a unit called the Chateau. It was South of 610 and a little west of the Gulf freeway. We moved in, just in time for the birth of our second child, Glynn, Jr. born August 14, 1962. Our offices were close by on the Gulf Freeway, and I started in the Houston Petroleum Center · at first. At about this time, there was some reorganizing and, in July of 1962, I became a section head in Tec's Mission Control Center branch, with one person in the section, Cliff Charlesworth.

Just days before Glynn, Jr. was born, the Russians launched another space first. Vostok 3 flew into orbit on August 11, followed by Vostok 4 on the next day. The two cosmonauts, Nikolayev and Popovich flew by each other, with the closest approach being 3.2 miles. At first, this was portrayed as a rendezvous and/or formation flying, but it was not quite that advanced. They just flew by within a close distance of each other. It was not a real rendezvous and certainly not a docking. But it was still a first. Both landed on August 15 within six minutes of each other.

News of the flight must have come to the U.S. on the weekend. We were still asleep and expecting a hospital baby run at any moment. Our morning rest was over when John Llewellyn showed up banging on our door. He was very upset that the Russians had pulled this off and re-minded me that we were still behind in this race. He wanted me to get up and go to work with him so we could "do something." John was very passionate about our space program. He did not want to lose any more time. But he did eventually settle for coffee and talk on that morning.

Completing Mercury

After a gap between MA-7 in May, MA-8 flew in October 3, 1962. This period allowed many of us to relocate and find our initial housing in Houston before the whirlpool of another flight. It also gave us time to welcome young Glynn, our first son, to the family born on August 14, 1962.

The astronauts must have been chagrined at the crew performance dur-ing the flight of MA-7. From the outside, it felt like a blood oath had been taken by the rest of the seven to deliver a textbook flight on MA-8. We all believed that Wally Schirra was the guy to do that. The flight was planned for six revolutions, nine plus hours and a big step along the way to a twenty-four plus hours flight on MA-9. We were still cau-tious about pushing the flight duration too quickly. On MA-8, our two consoles had a very nominal flight to monitor, as Wally ticked through the scheduled spacecraft tests. This performance was crowned by a

Pacific landing within sight of the carrier. Even by the name of his spacecraft, Sigma 7, Wally was promising a precise performance that would redeem the past and open the door to the future. He delivered on that pledge and we celebrated the flight. Our mission control act was continuing to improve.

MA-9 was scheduled first for a one day duration and, as launch date approached, increased to about thirty-four hours. The astronaut was Gordo Cooper, legendary for his stick and rudder skills, but sometimes used in buzzing the ground dwellers and ticking off his bosses. Because of the long duration, Cliff and I would share duties on the FIDO console, John and Carl on RETRO. Because of concern for running into some software "funny" under new conditions, we ran the GSFC computer complex and the flight dynamics consoles in MCC in a full up dress rehearsal of the thirty-four hour mission. All worked as it should and we proceeded to the countdown on May 15 with confidence, as did the whole MCC team.

Nominal was the flight until very late when an .05g light was reported by Gordo. This eliminated the automatic mode for Retrofire. Closer to Retrofire, the automatic control system inverter failed. Gordo would now do a manually controlled Retrofire and reentry. MA-9 landed within a few miles of the target ship, not bad for an astronaut uncompromised by thirty-four hours of zero g space travel. A great finish to our beginnings in space flight.

During the time from MA-7 until one month after MA-9, the Soviet Union conducted four manned missions. On Vostok 3, Nikolayev was launched into orbit on August 11, 1962 for what was announced as a longer duration flight. On the next day, Vostok 4 carried Popovich into orbit. The Vostok 4 launch was timed to accomplish a near- approach to Vostok 3. And it did with a closest approach of 3.2 miles between ships. Then, during June 1963 and a month after MA-9, the Soviet Union performed an "almost" repeat of Vostok 3 and 4. Bykovsky launched on June 14, 1963 in Vostok 5, followed two days later by Vostok 6 which carried the first woman, Valentina Tereshkova, on another near-approach flight. They also passed very close, 3.1 miles, to each other's ship. The flight durations were five and three days respectively.

These were not a rendezvous, nor a docking, nor even formation flying. But, it was a demonstration of four manned flights within a year, two on-time launches (necessary for this close approach) and a crew total of fifteen days in space with Bykovsky logging five of those days. Later reports indicated that Tereshkova had coping difficulties during and after the flight. Still, it was an impressive display of an up-tempo operation, even with the near-approaches accruing more credit than deserved. The Soviets played them straight and brief but western observers were disposed to overplay their significance.

And so Mercury closed out, six successful manned flights and a ton of experience and lessons. The team was also developing a strong sense of confidence in each other. We were not caught up with the Soviet Union but not as far behind as at the start.

Shawn Lunney joined the family on August 4, 1963.

Staffing Starts in Earnest in 1964

As a caveat, these staffing discussions are the best we can reconstruct of the populating of the FDB as the tempo of Gemini and Apollo really began to fire up during 1964. Our records are incomplete, fragmented and dates for arrival onto the FDB team for some people are not readily available. Up until the beginning of 1964, the team had eight people. We then added one per month during 1964, and five more during 1965. At the time of the July 1964 organization release, chartering the FDB, there were twelve engineers – seven in Gemini section and five in Apollo section – not counting myself as branch chief. And, I was about to be selected as the next flight director in August 1964. This took me out of any rotation for one of the console operator positions although I did continue to serve as chief of the unit for several more years.

Gemini flights were scheduled within the next year and actually occurred in April 1964 for GT-1, GT-2 in January 1965, and the first manned flight GT-3, in March 1965. The FDB Gemini section was headed by Cliff with John Llewellyn, Dave Massaro (another new RETRO), Charlie Parker (Guido), Ed Pavelka (FIDO), Ken Russell (Guido) and Robert White (RETRO). Although not listed on the July 1964 organization chart, Jerry Bostick was also assigned as a RETRO and soon as a FIDO, on detail from the John Mayer mission planning branch until March 1965 when he transferred into FDB. Grady Meyer was the head of the Apollo section, with George Guthrie (FIDO/ Guido), Dave Reed (FIDO), Phil Shaffer (FIDO), and Bobby Spencer (RETRO). All of these men performed admirably, and a solid majority of them went on to expand their contributions beyond their individual achievements by strong leadership and mentoring of the new engineers who were already there and those arriving over the next few years. As an example, Cliff was selected as a flight director in January, 1966, and Phil Shaffer along with Neil Hutchinson, a guidance officer, plus Chuck Lewis and Don

Puddy from 2 other branches were later selected as flight directors in 1971.

Jerry Bostick came to us by way of a three cushion bank shot. He seemed to know what he wanted and it took a little while for the tumblers of life to get to the "click" position. For his first cushion, he got the Army to assign him to the NACA Langley Research Center, and they put him in the Structures division, across the base from the STG. To his credit, it only took Jerry six weeks to start looking for another cushion. He did and joined John Mayer's mission planning branch, working for Carl Huss. This was a great opportunity for one of Carl's crash education programs and Jerry was helping with MA-7 Retrofire sensitivity analysis and then in the support room for the Cape MCC for MA-8. Carl later had a heart attack and Jerry was positioned to become a RETRO, joining John Llewellyn. This is where those cushions were steering him. By 1965, it was clear that Jerry was FIDO material and again, Chris agreed. Last cushion was completed. Cliff moved to the flight director role after GT-6 and Jerry was on for the GT-8 rendezvous and the first docking. He became the FIDO section head and, when Cliff and I moved to the Flight Director office in 1968, Jerry became the second chief of the FDB.

This staff of twelve in 1964, plus Jerry Bostick, nearly doubled over the next twelve months thru the first quarter of 1965. In order of arrival in FDB, there were: Stu Davis, Will Fenner, Chuck Deiterich, Gran Paules, Will Presley, Steve Bales, Gary Renick, Bill Gravett, Maurice Kennedy, Jim I'anson, and Jay Greene. These arrivals added to the strength and depth of the team and many continued in FDB or related work through their careers in NASA MSC (Manned Spacecraft Center) other government agencies, or in industry.

For those who remained with NASA, Ken Russell and Steve Bales went on to Associate Director roles in the Mission Operations Directorate. Jay Greene became a flight director, a Shuttle Orbiter Project manager, and performed as Chief Engineer for the International Space Station (ISS) when his tough-minded judgment carried the ISS through a very difficult period; some would say he saved the ISS. Others in the group had the potential to be flight directors or project managers, but opportunities did not always show up at the right time for them. Competition in the JSC Mission Operations Directorate has only intensified over the subsequent decades, primarily because the work continues to challenge people to be the best they can be - and they respond as these pioneers did, creating an abundance of talent.

In the hot months of 1963, we moved into our first home in Friendswood on Royal Court. A christening was in order for Shawn and seemed appropriate for our new home also. A hamburger and hot dog cookout in the yard with plenty of cold beer seemed like the way to start the house on the right track. It was also a lesson in the local "critter" kingdom. I never heard of chiggers before, but they knew about us. Charlie Parker, he of the zero- body fat body, sat in the yard amongst the sprigs of St. Augustine grass. It took a couple days for the chigger handiwork to show up. When it did, Charlie gave us a peek at the dozens of red welts encircling his waist at the beltline and around the top of the sock line, very itchy. I never understood how this happened to a native born Texan and yet they did not bother our kids in the yard. Maybe the kids moved too fast, or maybe Charlie was the bait for the whole herd of the hungry critters.

Grady Meyer was the Apollo section head. He was a very able engineer and augmented those skills with the experience of owning and operating his own airplane. When we got into the early unmanned Apollo, there was a capability to control the spacecraft attitude from the MCC with a hand controller and an eight-ball attitude reference display. Grady helped to make that capability operational but I still had real qualms over ever using it. Grady had an extra dose of confidence and it did not worry him. George Guthrie had a mission planning background also. George did not have the same aggressive attitude that most of the successful operators brought to the party. When guys questioned him about that, George allowed that he preferred to work in anonymity and not attract attention to himself. And he did a solid job on the early flights he worked.

Phil Shaffer was a welcome addition to our little band. Phil was the physically biggest of all of us and had a way of standing even taller and bigger when something was being debated or contested. He was called Jolly Red after the Green Giant ads for frozen vegetables. The red part was for the little bit of short hair left and for a very fair complexion, easily staying red in the Texas sun. Phil graduated from a university by the name of Panhandle A&M (a good school in Goodwell, Oklahoma) but a natural name for abuse. On occasion, I would kid Phil about his mail order degree in arithmetic. Phil had also worked at a Navy lab in Dahlgren, Virginia before joining us. He was a very quick study and would probably have excelled even without a degree. It was said that he belonged to the Mensa society for exceptional IQ individuals. And he assumed the role. He soon became the go-to guy in Grady's Apollo section, not only mastering the intricacies for himself but also as a mentor for the younger guys.

Jerry Bostick went into the Army after graduating from Mississippi State and somehow swung an assignment to NASA. Jerry joined STG in 1962 after realizing that the Structures division at Langley was not for him. And a good choice it was- good for him and good for us. Jerry has a story about his hiring into STG. He was being interviewed by Chris Critzos, an aide to Kraft. When his degree in Civil engineering came up as a question, Chris Kraft was asked and he said, "Hire him. Hell, we may need to build roads on the moon someday." When Kraft measured someone positively, the incidental of degree type did not matter. Jerry then started on a training path similar to my own. He worked for John Mayer and Carl Huss in the mission planning unit. It was not long before Jerry was working the same Retrofire analytics which started me on the path to become a flight dynamics officer. To make it official, he transferred to the FDB after GT-3 in April of 1965. When the yard parties at our home upscaled to oyster feasts, the Bosticks were the consistent champions with variations of an oyster Rockefeller creation, good enough to prevail over Hal Beck and his Jalapeno and Budweiser oyster dish.

We were really fortunate in our hiring results, since it is mostly a faith-based process for both parties. Ed Pavelka ('Fast Eddie') came to us from the University of Texas and was an immediate winner. Ed was a man of many talents. Besides his engineering aptitude, this smiling young man was a real artist, proficient at painting and drawing. We have a small Picasso reproduction in our home, compliments of Ed. It always draws a second look when people see it for the first time. After AS-501, the first unmanned Saturn V in 1967, Ed gave me a large painting of that ship in flight, also still in our home.

Ed was always whipping out a drawing or sketch to commemorate various events. His most famous rendering is of Captain Refsmatt (a concept best explained by a guidance officer) who became the model for an ideal flight controller- pocket protector, slide rule, uniform, among other things. Ed had an ever-ready wit for all occasions both verbal and pictorial. He was not, however, one of the verbal brawlers, but always more soft spoken. His love of cars and their repair and/or restoration was legendary and manifested itself in the largest and busiest car workshop in the branch. He was a family camping man and paired up with Chuck Deiterich and family regularly. To my knowledge, Ed never played any musical instrument, but, given his many talents, I would not be surprised if Joyce found some original symphonies in his papers someday.

That is the kind of guy Ed Pavelka was.

Speaking of Chuck Deiterich, he was a key addition to the RETRO group. Chuck brought a background of hands-on experience with home-made rockets and the understanding and repair of electrical simulation equipment. He was also the only guy besides myself who hailed from Pennsylvania. He became the expert on how the entry guidance system worked and why it worked that way. He also belonged to the car-repair group who passed in and out of Ed's workshop.

Dave Reed came along in the summer of 1964, graduating from the University of Wyoming that June. Dave was a weight lifter and looked the part. Cars seemed to run in this class of '64 arrivals. Dave had a classic Continental Mark II about 1956 vintage, which he kept and moved throughout all employment changes, although he didn't drive it much. He had another passion that he picked up here in Texas. His friend, Clyde Hesse, introduced him to sailing and Dave became quite adept at the tricks of sailboats. That came in handy shortly after our first boat, the Crackerjack, arrived in the family about 1965.

Dave spent a lot of time with us on the waters of Galveston Bay. We lost a lot of sunglasses, buckets, beer and kids gear, but we only lost the outboard engine once. Dave was resting a hand on it when the up motion lifted the engine off of its attachment structure and into the Bay. We learned a lot the hard way. Dave remembered one instruction on how to steer a course in case of a tiller failure by manipulating the sails. We got to try that one out for real when the tiller broke off.

Dave walked right into Apollo under the tutelage of Phil who was busy with the CSM. So when Dave asked about his assignment, Phil gave him the task of figuring out how to use the lunar module throughout all of its mission phases. As a result of that assignment and eventual use on Apollo XI, Dave is still, forty years later, in periodic discussions with Neil Armstrong on various subjects.

Four new RETROs joined the team - Dave Massaro, Robert White, Jim I'Anson and Bill Gravett. Jim I'Anson brought another connection with American history. He was a B-17 pilot during World War II. Bill Gravett is still playing his music and also teaching, including a class with our grandson, Drake. Dave Massaro's house in some isolated woods in Friendswood was also a gathering place for the RETROs. Robert White was quiet spoken and therefore somewhat of a balance function with that gang.

The ranks of the Guidance officers increased by four, also. Gran Paules came to us from the Navy and looked like the central casting model for a young officer, tall, blond smart and well spoken. Will Fenner always reminded me of my father, not in accent (Texan) but in how succinctly he expressed his thoughts: "I knew the dumb SOB would screw it up." He brimmed with reliability. Gary Renick and Will Presley rounded out a solid, dependable complement to the Guido team.

The FIDOs had gotten ahead on staff and only drew two more during this period. Stu Davis and another UT graduate, Maurice Kennedy, joined the group. Both were solid contributors. Stu left the group early and I believe that Maurice was one of the longest serving FIDOs.

As the decade went on, more young men joined this team. Jerry El-liot, Bill Boone from Mississippi, Bill Stoval and Jerry Mill added their talents to the mix. Arrivals contnued with transfers into the branch like Neil Hutchinson and Dutch von Ehrenfried. Dean Toups, Raymond Teague and Walt Wells joined at various times. Some stayed a while, some served a few years and moved on and the next wave began to appear and prepare for the later flights of Apollo. In the process of capturing these recollections, I feel disappointed in myself that I did not get to know everybody as ll as I could or should have. This is my fault, not anyone else's nose's. I can only offer in explanation that the times were busy and my other job demanded a lot.

Gemini: Low Earth Orbit Training for Apollo

In December 1961, NASA announced its plan for the Gemini program. It was to test as many as practical of the required spacecraft capabilities needed for Apollo in low earth orbit and in a two man spacecraft. Specific objectives for this intermediate step included:

- Long duration flight beyond the time required for Apollo
- Rendezvous, docking and docked maneuvers
- EVA experience
- Methods of controlled reentry and landing

Based on Mercury experience, Gemini was designed to be controlled by the astronauts. The design also incorporated easy access to remove and replace many spacecraft subsystems, as painfully learned during Mercury. Besides the entry module, it also had an adapter module for propellant systems, new fuel cells and other equipments. The design also had ejection seats instead of an escape tower and a paraglider for land-ing point control (a feature later cancelled). Gemini was to be launched on a two-stage Titan rocket that had been developed for the Air Force as an ICBM launcher. The Gemini/Titan also had new features and systems to enhance crew safety, like a malfunction detection system and redundancy in guidance, hydraulics, and electrical systems. Finally, a modified Agena-D was selected as the target vehicle for rendezvous and docking. The Agena was equipped with a docking system, on-orbit propulsion and a command link for the crew.

In the following five years, through 1966, the Gemini program flew two unmanned flights and then ten manned missions. In terms of the achievement of program objectives, the flight program was:

- A very effective follow-up to Mercury and was completed in five years.
- Highlighted by one mission of fourteen days, one of eight days, and five missions of three to four days with no apparent long-duration problems.
- A wealth of experience in rendezvous, docking and docked ma-neuvers, such as:
- ten sequences of rendezvous through station keeping
- seven dockings
- about ten docked propulsion maneuvers
- A substantial learning experience for how to do EVA. There were eleven hatch openings. But we did not master the subject until Gemini 12, the last flight.
- A complete success in automatic reentry and landing, with vari-ous degrees of closed-loop control and all with very accurate control of the landing point.
- Successful in zero g experience, both in terms of weightless ef-fects on humans, and crew performance of operational tasks

The performance record of the major flight elements was mostly suc-cessful with some notable problems. The Atlas Agena vehicle failed on two launch attempts. Before the first Gemini 6 rendezvous and docking attempt on October 25, 1965, the loss of the target vehicle resulted in a change of plan to rendezvous with the manned, long duration Gemini 7 flight two months later. The second failure of the Atlas Agena was before the planned launch of Gemini 9 on May 17, 1966. The Agena target vehicle was replaced by a simpler Augmented Target Docking Adapter configuration on top of the Atlas and launched successfully on June 1, 1966. This backup target vehicle was begun after the earlier Agena failure in the fall of 1965. Tom Stafford who was a crew member on both of these flights has good reason to believe that the Agena stage did not want to fly with him.

The Titan launch vehicle performed extremely well in its task of delivering the Gemini spacecraft to its planned conditions. As a measure of the Titan's dependability, it was the second vehicle launched after the target vehicle lift-off. It had to launch within very tight launch window constraints, now established by the target vehicle on orbit. The Titan team consistently met its launch window lift-off ninety minutes later.

The Gemini spacecraft accomplished all of its mission objectives except for some on Gemini 8. On that flight, a spacecraft thruster stuck open and caused the vehicle to roll with increasingly high rates. This condition forced the crew to undock and prematurely activate the entry control system to overcome the problem. Gemini 8 landed early in the Pacific, after only ten and a half hours of a planned four-day flight. There were other recurring failures mostly in the fuel cell systems and in the clogging of the attitude control adjusters. These failures were of continuing concern even thru Gemini 12, but they did not compromise the achievement of the flight objectives. Actually, the subsystems problems improved the trouble-shooting skills of the operation team members, both in the spacecraft and in MCC.

EVA presented us with surprises. From the experience of Gemini 4 in June 1965, EVA was not seen as exceptionally difficult. On that flight, Ed White egressed the spacecraft with a tether and an umbilical for all necessary services. He floated outside and moved around with a hand held thruster device, using pressurized nitrogen. It seemed relatively easy. However, one year later, the Gemini 9 EVA was an eye-opener in terms of how quickly events deteriorated to a life threatening condition facing Gene Cernan. The next EVA on Gemini 10 was relatively easy by comparison and then the Gemini 11 EVA was once again a very demanding chore for Dick Gordon. By Gemini 12, the provisioning of restraints for hands, feet, and body and water-tank training allowed Gemini to finish with a much better understanding of the necessary techniques for weightless EVAs.

The Flight Dynamics Team Tackles Gemini

The task confronting the Flight Dynamics Team as Gemini approached was immense. The question was how to use these flight vehicles to achieve orbit, rendezvous, docking, docked maneuvers, reentry, and accurate landings. These vehicles were a significant step up in technology and capability over the Mercury ship. The Trench had to understand the trajectory and orbital mechanics to master the necessary capabilities. They had to determine how to use the guidance and propulsion capabilities within the flight elements.   They had to figure how to turn all that understanding into an MCC capability that can direct and support these phases in real time.   They also had to smoothly fit their discipline into the operation of the overall MCC team and the flight crews.   Starting in early 1963, before the last Mercury flight flew, we began to grapple with these subjects.   As we did, the MCC Flight Dynamics team grew to include a third position, the guidance officer.

Expanding the Launch Phase Capabilities

Charlie Parker

The Titan launch vehicle had some major new capabilities compared to the Atlas used for Mercury.   There was the capability to switch-over to the backup guidance from the Gemini spacecraft and/or hydraulics within the Titan.   It would be reasonable to ask how we trained these young folks to perform this work.   Perhaps the best way to explain is by example.

Charlie Parker came to the group from a long line of Texans in June of 1963.   He was obviously observant.   When he asked, "Well, Glynn how much travel should I expect?"   My reply was, "Not very much."   My reply was based on the fact that things had changed since Mercury. The MCC was now in Houston and the Goddard computer complex was replaced by real time computing complex in the MCC.   Both of the facilities, MCC and the RTCC, were right here at home in Houston. However, Charlie was looking at my briefcase that had the remains of three years of airline baggage tickets on it.   As it turned out, travel did not turn out to be as big a burden for us as it was in Mercury.

When Charlie arrived, we were powering up for Gemini that brought a number of new features to manage.   Gemini had a digital computer – new to our spacecraft repertoire – and with a launch vehicle guidance capability.   A redundant set of hydraulics within the Titan launch vehicle and the ability to actually guide the launch vehicle thru the launch phase added to our complexity.   We also had to plan for rendezvous, docking, docked propulsion burns and reentry maneuvers.   We had already decided to add a guidance officer position to the other two positions.

Without knowing the strength of Charlie's capability, we had the guidance officer role as a blank sheet, and assigned the whole package to

Charlie.   For the first task of monitoring the Titan launch vehicle for either guidance or hydraulics switchover, we knew that we needed another console.   For it, we envisioned a bank of strip charts to evaluate the guidance signals and the hydraulics response of the engine actuators for each of the two first stage engines.   That was about as far as Cliff and I got in definition and turned it over to Charlie.

Charlie accepted that assignment with little or no comment and moved right into the definition of the specifics for the console.   He always seemed clear-headed and sure of what he was doing – always answering questions intelligently.   But, it was when he sat down at the console for his first simulation that he really impressed all of us.   Charlie was slender of build and he had the habit of sitting with the right knee over the left one and snaking his right leg around the left leg, as if it were made out of rubber.   Cigarette in hand, he was ready to go.

And he seemed to read the mind of that Titan launch vehicle.   Cliff accused him of "doing a mind-meld with the Titan." He read the vital signs of the rocket and could diagnose any guidance or control problems in very short order.   After our first day of simulations, Cliff and I looked at each other, and I observed, "Well, it looks like we got ourselves a real guidance officer."   Charlie was trained by taking on a big job and mastering it himself.   Somewhere in these early days, Cliff tagged Charlie as "the Fox," and it is still a favorite handle, even today.

Once the early Gemini flights were accomplished, Charlie turned to understanding how to use the on-board Gemini computer to control the attitude and propulsion capabilities.   These capabilities were targeted to accomplish the maneuvers calculated by FIDO, RETRO or in some cases by the onboard computer.   So, in answer to the valid question about how we trained him, the answer is: "We did not train him, he invented the position, prepared and trained himself."

We were always learning something from Chris that we could apply to our world.   By example, he taught us, "Give them a big job and any help they ask for – let them do it – test them and satisfy yourself about their abilities – and then trust them to perform."   Sounds simple, and this story repeated itself many times as young men stepped up to big challenges.   There were things like, how do we manage launch windows, rendezvous maneuvers, docking, maneuvers mated with the Agena target vehicle, and reentry for landing with the Gemini ship.   And in Apollo, how did we use the new Saturn V, the command service module, the Lunar module, their prime and backup computers, targeting for the injection maneuver to the moon, mid-course maneuvers, the placing of the vehicle into lunar orbit, the lunar landing challenge, lunar module ascent and rendezvous with the command ship, return to earth and eventually reentry and recovery. While all of the nominal missions were being examined, understood, and mastered, it was also necessary to maintain a return to earth and abort capabilities throughout the mission phases, even with various degrees of degraded onboard systems.

The experience of seeing Charlie blossom into a competent, trusted operator was repeated many times as our young men grappled with the unknowns of Gemini and Apollo.

Moving to Rendezvous

John Mayer's organization had developed its usual group of technical wizards for many of these subjects. People like Ed Lineberry, Ken Young, Bob Becker and Bob Regelbrugge stand out as aces on the rendezvous subject. Several people in the Gemini program office had also begun to explore this subject and were making progress. Jim Chamberlain from Avro was the program manager for Gemini, but, in our work, we dealt with Dick Carley, also of Avro, and Jim Rose from Langley. Both of these men worked in the Gemini program office (GPO) and had started on their own understanding of rendezvous.

We soon realized that the problem could best be understood in three separate segments. First, the two vehicles have to be in the same orbital plane. Think of the orbital plane as a flat surface and round like a plate. The spacecraft traverses the outer edge of the plate, but the plane is fixed in inertial space relative to the stars. Think of a plate inclined to the equator at about thirty degrees but the plane or plate stays fixed and the earth rotates underneath the plane. The spacecraft flies around the edge of the plate to traverse one orbit in about ninety minutes. If you plotted the geographical position of the spacecraft over time, it would look like a sine wave passing over the earth, but displaced to the West each time around by the distance the earth has turned in the ninety minutes of orbital traverse. Assume the launches are due east from the pads in Florida as that is the most fuel-efficient direction. Then the maximum latitude above and below the equator of the sine wave is essentially the latitude of the launch site. In one orbit or ninety minutes after launch of the target vehicle, a second spacecraft launch due east will come very close to being in the same plane as the original target spacecraft. The sine waves of each spacecraft would overlay each other. Because they are very close to the same plane, it takes only a relatively small amount of launch vehicle fuel to steer the second vehicle into the same plane as the target. Usually, because of inaccuracies and other difficulties, there is some small plane change correction yet to be made by either one of the spacecraft once in orbit to make the vehicles co-planar. And this became the approach for the first segment of the Gemini rendezvous problem. Actually, like all things in our business, there are often second or third order effects and there is one here which makes it a little more complicated than I just described. The earth's oblateness and the initial differences in altitudes between the target vehicle and the chasing spacecraft create small perturbations, resulting in differential nodal regression, to the inertial planes such that a correction must be made to the yaw steering of the launch vehicle to match the planes at the planned intercept rather than the initial insertion into orbit.

The second segment of the rendezvous is called phasing. At orbital insertion, the vehicles are now in about the same plane, but displaced from one another on the edge of the plate. Typically this might have the chase vehicle trailing the target vehicle by 500 to 1,000 miles. There are many sequences of maneuvers that can bring the two ships together and we examined many of them. The chase vehicle with lower altitudes than the target's is traveling faster and therefore catching up. The rate of catch-up can be controlled by altitude adjustments during this phasing period.

But, we were missing a part of the puzzle without knowing "the best way to bring the ships finally together." This was resolved when Buzz Aldrin arrived at JSC. He had just completed his PhD, and his dissertation treated how best to approach a target vehicle in order to facilitate a consistent approach for a crew member to monitor and provide visible cues as to how the closing part of the approach is going. To locate the final braking geometry, Buzz selected an approach in darkness, from below the target and slightly in front of it. This creates a line of sight to the target, which should be inertially fixed relative to the star field behind the target. Any relative motion of the target, against the star field indicates an error to be zeroed out by the approaching ship. The scale here is such that the distance to the target would be about ten miles when this condition applies. There is also a fore and aft correction that needs to be calculated or measured by radar. This amounts to a braking of about 30-40 feet per second as seen by the crew in the chase vehicle. Zeroing out this closing velocity occurs as the chase vehicle gets within a few miles or closer of the target vehicle. All nulling of relative motion is complete when the chase vehicle is within about the last hundred feet of the target. Manual crew control is then based on visual cues and is called station-keeping. The lighting is selected so that both vehicles are now out in the daylight for the station-keeping phase. The contribution of Buzz's work coupled with a clear understanding of the orbital mechanics developed by Ed Lineberry and his team completed the picture.

This approach with the third segment provides the end point for the phasing maneuvers in the second segment. Buzz recommended that the chase vehicle fly in a lower co-elliptic orbit than the target vehicle with an altitude differential of about ten to fifteen miles. The crew can track or see the target vehicle from this closing position and at a known elevation angle to the target, perform a small propulsion maneuver of about thirty to forty fps to create an intercept path that will meet the conditions described in segment three. So the early maneuvers are calculated to set up this ultimate braking geometry. This all seems so apparent now, but there were a lot of possibilities and mysteries to fathom before we got there.

And this technique continued to evolve. For Apollo, some plans were for a fairly rapid rendezvous sequence, completing on the first orbit. It continues to be modified today because of the scale of the Shuttle and Space Station vehicles. It is less of a fighter plane intercept and more of a berthing of a large ship to a larger ship. So, in modern rendezvous sequence, the final approach is set up to approach the space station from below and by traveling up the earth radius vector (called r-bar). The orbital mechanics are such that the shuttle is beginning to slow down relative to the ISS and falls to a condition of zero relative motion at the ISS, at which point the Shuttle would fall back down the earth radius vector away from the target if no further propulsive maneuver was performed. To match the ISS conditions, the Shuttle adds energy (versus braking) to achieve identical orbital conditions. This acceleration maneuver also directs the plume from the thrusters to the rear of the shuttle and away from the Space Station with its many appendages. This is a more benign approach scheme for avoiding any contamination damage or disruption from the thruster plumes on the ISS target vehicle.

This all came about four decades later as a more suitable variant for the final approach to the target. And, as in Gemini, the desired final conditions for intercept determine the intervening sequence of phasing maneuvers, although the time between launch and actual rendezvous is measured in days rather than a few hours in order to allow the crew to adjust to zero-g. We conducted a terminal phase similar to the Shuttle scheme on Gemini 11 with the first rendezvous and experimented with a variation to slow down the relative speeds on a re-rendezvous called the 'standoff' technique. These exercises were very helpful in tailoring the sequence to new conditions and constraints in the future.

And Using a Guided Reentry to Landing Point

Gemini did have a small Lift/Drag ratio (L/D), established by an offset of the center of gravity. This small amount of lift was then modulated by rolling the vehicle during reentry to provide the correct amount of lift in plane to reach the target. Once our team got comfortable with this guidance scheme and the control system to achieve it, they added some simulator time to see it all in action. This capability quickly became a known and comfortable staple for the RETROs and Guidos.

Early Gemini Flights

The first two Gemini flights were unmanned. The objectives of GT-1 on April 8, 1964 were to validate loads on a spacecraft shell and the combined structure of the spacecraft and launch vehicle. The vehicle was guided into a 100 x 200 mile orbit with a planned early reentry which occurred on sixty-fourth orbit. During its time on the pad, GT-2 was subject to some lightning strikes in the area that caused a delay. Then, there were two delays due to the threats of two hurricanes, Cleo and then Dora, resulting in a destack of the vehicle. Back on the pad on December, 9, there was a pad shutdown at T+ one second. After resolving the problem GT-2 finally launched on a short suborbital flight on January 19, 1965 with a duration of only nineteen minutes. These two flights were monitored by Cliff and me, John Llewellyn and Jerry Bostick as RETROs and the "fox," Charlie Parker.

As we prepared for GT-3 that flew on March 22, 1965, the first manned Gemini was crewed by Gus Grissom and John Young. Cliff, John and Charlie were the flight dynamics operators. It had been decided to "flight-follow" the MCC at the Cape with the new MCC in Houston. In my new role as a flight director in training, I and Jerry Bostick as FIDO and RETRO, and Arnie Aldrich as the Gemini systems expert were in the Houston MCC as backup. For the next flight GT-4 we reversed locations and were on backup duty at the Cape. We enjoyed making an occasional offer to take over for any problems at the other MCC.

The flight was such a technical success that the coverage degenerated into the "ham sandwich" crisis as John Young had smuggled an unauthorized sandwich in his suit pocket. Much ado about not much, except that the configuration system that controlled what was in the spacecraft was strengthened, but even then, not enough. This subject came back to bite NASA much later during the Apollo XV stamp cover fiasco, which was an acknowledged violation of common sense standards if not an actual legal transgression. At the time of Apollo XV, Chris Kraft was Center Director at JSC and spent the best part of a year dealing with the fallout from that issue.

Back to GT-3, we were all especially pleased that this flight went so well after the loss of the MR-4 spacecraft when Gus almost drowned. Most of us were very supportive and proud of Gus and happy in this success for him. As a measure of NASA and Deke Slayton's confidence in him, Gus flew the first Gemini and was scheduled to fly the first Apollo.

Gemini Titan Launch

Right after GT-3, Cliff informed me about the possibility of a space walk.The EVA activity was being considered for GT-4 but was still under wraps pending completion of certain certification tests. This was a big step for all of us even thought the Flight dynamics team was mostly an observer of EVA's. Mercury did not have an EVA capability and it was believed that we had to exercise EVA in Gemini before we got to the moon, where so much depended on a successful walk on the moon. The EVA was approved for flight only ten days before the mission, when the necessary tests on the EVA equipment were successfully completed. The four day mission was also a big step in flight duration from Mercury (one and a half days on MA-9) and three orbits on GT-3. GT-4 launched on June 3, 1965 with Jim McDivitt and Ed White as the crew. The orbit was nominal and, after separation, Jim attempted to station keep with the Titan second stage. As he came out of the night pass, he recommended the cessation of the station keeping exercise because it was causing excessive fuel usage. Chris at MCC agreed. This was an early indication that orbital mechanics played a big role in station keeping if the chase vehicle was very far away from the target, more than several hundreds of feet.

The EVA was next on the agenda and all preps were normal and GO's were given to depress the spacecraft. The EVA went for a short twenty three minutes from Hawaii to crossing the States. Ed White found it easy to use the nitrogen gun as propulsion to move himself and control his attitude. The crew had some difficulty with the umbilical hose and the pressurized suits when it came time to close the hatch. This equipment configuration is akin to wrestling a very large snake and capturing all of its body within the confines of a very small cockpit. Two crew members already took up quite a bit of the volume even before the umbilical, but the crew got the door closed and latched in due course.

In RETROspect, this experience probably misled us. We did not have any new or unexpected difficulty with EVA as it was conducted. We did not learn how difficult this kind of EVA was until a whole year later during the GT-9 EVA by Gene Cernan. Gordo Cooper and Pete Conrad crewed the Gemini 5 spacecraft on its eight-day mission, August 21 – 29, 1965. This was a three-shift operation for the MCC including the Flight Dynamics team. Jerry Bostick, Cliff Charlesworth, and Ed Pavelka were on the FIDO console – Tom Carter, Dave Massaro and John Llewellyn were on the RETRO console. Parker, Fenner, Russell and Bales handled the guidance officer position. This group handled all of the Gemini flights with a few changes. Cliff dropped out of rotation after Gemini 6 and Bostick and Pavelka rotated the prime FIDO role. Stu Davis joined to cover the Agena and Bill Gravett joined the RETROs on Gemini 7 and subsequent. Tom Carter was a new assignee out of John Mayer's Mission Planning branch.

After the usual simulation runs, they were all ready for GT-5, the longest mission yet flown in manned space of eight days, with a deployable pod for evaluating the rendezvous radar, and seventeen science experiments. Once on orbit, the new fuel cell system replacing the batteries had a problem with the cryogenic oxygen tank, in that the pressure fell from the range of 800-900 psi, to 70 psi and then leveled off. This was a real concern because the cryo tank pressure forced the oxygen into the fuel cell to generate electrical power. This somewhat precarious position resulted in a daily "GO-NO-GO" from MCC to continue each next day of the flight. The situation improved each day and the threat to the planned flight duration receded.

The rendezvous radar evaluation pod was deployed about two hours into the flight and successfully tracked by the Gemini radar. This radar testing was reduced in order to save electrical power but gave good results every time it was tested, including with an L-Band transponder, ground based at the Cape. For the rest of the flight, experiments and "living in space" activities dominated, as the crew adapted to this new environment.

It is worth mentioning some background on this eight day mission. Before Mercury flew, there were national level discussions and debates about the capabilities of men to survive in the weightless environment. It was said that they would become disoriented, confused and generally fail at piloting in this environment. These dramatic predictions turned out to be overdone and incorrect. We did find later in Apollo that a noticeable percentage of crew members could become ill if they were not careful to avoid rapid head movements in the first two or three days of space flight.   After which, they adapt and are generally fine and even with this condition, the crews have always been able to handle whatever was required. So there was some basis for concern but it was over played and not a show stopper.   It did not even manifest itself in Mercury or Gemini, but did in Apollo, where there was a significant volume in the cockpit to move around in and to induce this space sickness condition. Once recognized, this is a manageable situation, by avoiding head motions and not scheduling intensive operational activity until there has been one to two days to adapt.

We faced the same extremes in some of the other national Apollo debates, where it was claimed that the spacecraft would sink into the lunar surface. This was in contradiction to the experience with the early unmanned landers on the moon, which did not sink.

During this same period of 1964/1965, the Soviets introduced a newly named ship, the Voshkod and flew it three times. We found out later that it was the same one-man ship, Vostok, with barely volume accommodations for three unsuited crewmen and elimination of the ejection seat. Komarov, Feoktistov and Yegorov flew on October 12, 1964 for one day. Apparently seen as upstaging the two-man Gemini, it had to be a nightmare to cram into and stay for a day. The next Voshkod was an unmanned test ship and launched on February 22, 1965. On-orbit OK, the EVA airlock was deployed. However, signals from the ship were soon lost as was the ship. On March 18, 1965 before GT-3, Leonov and Belyayev were in space aboard Voshkod 2. The airlock was deployed and Leonov was outside for ten minutes when he started to ingress the airlock.

We later learned that the ballooning of the suit prevented him from fitting back into the airlock. He had to depress his suit a slight amount, inch back thru the airlock while the suit was repressurizing and then repeat the depress several times before clearing the airlock. At the time for automatic Retrofire sequence, there was no ignition of the rockets. This resulted in a ground decision to delay one rev and reenter manually. It was a real scramble for the crew and Retrofire was late and out of attitude. The vehicle landed 1200 miles long in a forest and the craft wedged in some trees. They egressed after the rescue team skied in to their location, and eventually returned after about two days in the forest. The world believed that the Soviets had a real 3-man ship and an EVA capability. And they did, of sorts.

Bill Tindall

Bill and Jane Tindall and their family of four first became close to us while still at Langley. The Tindalls were the first family in Virginia to invite us – Marilyn and I – for dinner with their family of three(at the time) kids - Dana, Mark and Amy. At the time, Marilyn was just pregnant with Jenny. I was working in the same organization as Bill at the time. Bill had a love of sailboats manifested in a 34' wooden hull sloop, which he was refurbishing in his barn. The Tindall property, from Jane's side of the family, was multiple acres with all sorts of equipment and out buildings. Bill used it all to get his required chores done so he would have time to work on his sailboat. Maybe it came from his time in the Navy, or maybe from his being raised on the water surrounding the family home on Cape Cod. However, the pace of the space program eventually caught up with Bill and he didn't even move the sailboat from Virginia to Texas.

Bill functioned as John Mayer's deputy and he was really fascinated with all of the new challenges facing the Mission Planning and Flight Dynamics teams. He was full of insight to help us new, younger guys cope with these orbital mechanics subjects and he was very good at both – the subjects and the mentoring. Bill always had a variety of jobs and usually was plugged into the point position on the most difficult subjects. He was the first to focus our attention on the possibility of dramatically simplifying the operations concept for Mercury, with a Mission control Center (MCC) in Florida and a dozen remote stations around the world with small flight control teams. He promoted the improvements in worldwide communications as being the enabler of a single control facility with all voice data, command and eventually video being routed to the MCC in Houston through the global network of receiving stations. Bill was the NASA lead for the software development by Draper labs and MIT for the Apollo computer. But, most dear to our hearts was his integration of the mission trajectory planners, the flight controllers, and the flight crews.

This meeting started out as something called "data priority," since one of the early issues was which source of navigation data to use in which phases and how to decide that choice in real time. At this level, the primary members of the MCC Flight Controller team to engage in these discussions with the mission planners, were the Flight dynamics operators. However, this activity quickly evolved into a more comprehensive process gradually including all of the systems flight controllers, flight software providers, the experts from flight crew operations division who devised the check list and the flight plans and then, most significantly, the flight crews enthusiastically engaged.   It was the forum in which we systematically talked through and vehemently argued about every step and decision in the process, precisely defining all of the "flight techniques" necessary to use the best of the spacecraft capabilities to accomplish back-up launch guidance, rendezvous, docking, docked propulsion burns, de-orbit and entry.   In later times, the name for this forum did become "flight techniques."

Bill was brilliant, enthusiastic, energetic, and he completely engaged all viewpoints in this process.   Bill's approach was to systematically start through all the mission phases and then on to the missions them-selves that exercised different rendezvous techniques. This process re-duced complexities to easy-to-understand building blocks. He would announce his subjects for upcoming meetings, for example "how much plane change correction to use from the launch vehicle", "what data source to use for each of the rendezvous burns," "what it is the most conservative rendezvous phasing sequence for the first mission attempt at rendezvous," among others. Like a court hearing with many repre-sentatives for all points of view, Bill would orchestrate the discussion and arguments surrounding each step along the way.   Since these deci-sions were often sketched out on a blackboard as the subject evolved, this was the root of the preferred method for winning, or at least control-ling, the debate - "Let me have the chalk now," or "He who has the chalk wins." Vigorous and spirited are the descriptors that begin to capture the rough and tumble arguments of the day as each participant pressed his case. Almost a miracle of competence combined with the sincere search for the "right" answer, this worked for us. Bill would record the result by dictating the same to Patsy Sauer, his secretary, who would then have the draft minutes available for team review within hours. These "Tin-dallgrams" became mandatory reading, study, and a widely recognized record of the progress of flight techniques.

Bill's enthusiasm was infectious. He was a master at blowing off some wild proposal without terribly offending the offerer, changing his mind as he came to accept another viewpoint, or strengthening his original position with new inputs from the team.   In this regime of resolving the details of flight operations for all of these mission activities, Bill has to get significant credit for enabling the success of Gemini. Again, as typical of those times, he was unheralded in the larger picture, and that was just fine with him.   The hundred plus participants went on to execute these plans and techniques superbly.   He truly was one of the MVP's for Gemini.

Not only did Bill contribute so much to the success of Gemini and later Apollo, with the same integration planning activity, but he was superb role model for accomplishment and leadership for our young engineers. And they soaked it up. You could see the growth in newcomers, like Ed Pavelka, Phil Shaffer, Dave Reed, Chuck Deiterich, Gran Paules, Steve Bales, and others as they lived this education. The FDBers who went on to the most success, consistently employed this Tindall model, much more useful than a theoretical course on leadership. They learned to take command, tackle the problems, enlist all the necessary help, test all the options, decide and build support to go forward.

Debriefing at the HofBrau Garden

If the preparations and the flights were intense, the traditional but informal debriefings were a raucous release of emotion by a group of men having just accomplished something big, very difficult, important to the country, and loaded with risk. Sometime in the immediate aftermath of the crew returning to Houston, we scheduled our unofficial debriefing at the HofBrau Garden in Dickinson, along I-45 and about ten miles south of Clear Lake. In the back of the property, the Hofbrau had an outside open area, with trellises and vines surrounding picnic tables and benches. The restaurant served German food – sausages, sauerkraut, potato salad, black bread and an unlimited supply of beer kegs. It seemed that we always had the place to ourselves and there were not any outsiders. The people at the HofBrau garden seemed to love having us there for these events, so they probably had closed off at the least the outside areas for us.

The only protocol was that there was no protocol. And the present concept of political correctness was nowhere in sight. With the first beer, the debriefing centered on any mistakes, slips, and character flaws of each of us. It was common to see our space heroes, standing on the table shouting insults at each other. Llewellyn and McDivitt were especially good at this. And whoever it was at any given moment that was leading the attack was either booed or goaded on to even louder and more extreme expressions of ridicule and insults. It was a great way to celebrate our work together.

The Clear Lake region was a much different place in those days - a lot fewer people, and much less traffic. Since these sessions ran past 9 PM, we were the only ones who were out. That made it easier for God to find us and look after us. My brother-in-law, George Kurtz, joined us for one session. Even with being a "people person" and a superb salesman, he was not sure how he would fit into this setting. It didn't take George long to claim a good niche for himself, as he sprang for the first keg of beer of the evening. From then on, George was an insider. George ran a sales organization with many sales people. He could not get over the dedication (almost obsession) that our people brought to their work. He asked how I managed that and wanted to transfer "it" to his staff. "It" just didn't travel that way.

Marilyn's dad, the first George Kurtz, also loved the HofBrau debriefings. When he and Mom Kurtz visited us, he was always excited to learn that we were having another debriefing. I gathered that Dad Kurtz did not have too much opportunity to float free like that in Cleveland. I used to make a point of telling my mother-in-law, Lillian, that NASA and the astronauts requested his attendance.   That was always sure to get us out of the house.   Besides the comradeship, George was from Pennsylvania Dutch country and he loved the food and beer at the HofBrau. We were always looked at a little suspiciously when we returned home. Later in life, George and young George always talked about these excursions with fondness and wonder.

Marilyn and Glynn at NASA picnic
1966

Family and the Trench

During these years, we had many occasions when members of the branch visited our home for food, drink and whatever frivolity was on for the day. Thanksgiving and New Year's Day were big football days and one of our gathering times. Many of the guys were still bachelors and so it became something of a tradition to gather at our house for these occasions. Not only was January first Marilyn's birthday, but on one of these New Year's days Marilyn was also twelve days away from giving birth to our fourth child, Bryan. Marilyn's description of these days was "the guys come early and leave late." Sometimes they even needed a little nudge when we got to the late side.

Bryan, Shawn, Glynn Sr, Glynn jr, and Jenny Lunney
Christmas 1968

I believe Marilyn must have kept watch for shock material that she could use to hasten the exit and to inject a little humility into our outspoken guests. This happened after a day where they all sat around drinking, watching the games, or knocking our little kids over by throwing a foot-ball at them so hard no one could catch it.

Jay Greene somehow became Marilyn's target on one of these January first holidays, just before Bryan's birth; maybe it was the long day of cooking, serving, and hostessing into the late side of the day. But she started to quote Redbook, which was a woman's magazine with presum-ably very accurate woman's viewpoint articles. And, so she confronted Mr. Greene, "Jay, I have been reading recent research which shows that plumbers are better lovers than engineers." I don't know if Jay had been bragging or just talking to bring down this indictment on his ego. But, his jury of peers obviously thought that he had and they piled on with glee. (They seemed to forget that they were engineers too.) Eventually, Jay surrendered the debate. We have revisited this story many times since with Jay and his supportive buddies.

I had hired Jay when he was working in the wire room at Downey, Cali-fornia, the home plant of the CSM. This recently graduated engineer from Brooklyn had moved to California to cut various types of wire in various lengths, and put them in a plastic bag for the manufacturing floor. To his credit, he did not see this job as the high point of his career and he joined the FDB. But that was the only time that Jay needed rescuing. Once here, he excelled at all of it.

At one point, Phil Shaffer brought live lobsters back from one of his trips to Boston on a visit to MIT Draper Labs of flight software fame. Everybody wagered various numbers of the house beers on the lobster races. I believe our kids enjoyed the races most and were unhappy when their favorite racer had to go in the boiling pot. I don't think they really cared for lobster eating at their age.

On football days, our boys took the most punishment. Football on television provokes the amateur observers to see how hard and far they can throw a football, especially at small moving targets. Our little boys enjoyed football and went out to innocently play with these men only to be blasted by their hard throws.

On a very hot humid day in the first days of July 1967, our family was driving on NASA Road 1 in front of the Center. Walking along the side of the road was a young man wearing heavy corduroy pants and a long sleeved wool shirt. I told Marilyn "This could be the kid I just hired from Wyoming. It looks like he doesn't know how to dress for Houston but we better pick him up before he melts."

Allegedly, Bill Stoval had a fiancée back in Wyoming. But it took so long for Ruth to show up in Houston that we began to suspect that this was just another Stoval story. But, there really was a Ruth and she was the complete antidote to Bill, delightful and charming. Later when we had the twins from Montana and Wyoming, Reed and Stoval, at the gatherings, we were able to send two each of our kids home with each couple for one night. Stoval found fruit loops in his beloved Corvette for a couple of weeks afterwards. Stoval always went out of his way to give his gracious hostess grief about over populating our corner of the world. (He and Ruth went on to contribute three of their own to our world once Bill caught on.) Although Bill left Houston in eight years to return home and take over the family business after his Dad died, our family had grown close to Bill during his short stay. Bill came as a bachelor and joined the regular gatherings. He was full of it and our kids - "rugrats" to him - loved to rally with him at the house. They liked Bill so much that he was their special target as they grew a little older for water balloons when he visited in his shiny Corvette. One day he showed up in brilliant yellow slacks and they did manage to get a couple of direct hits with eggs and water balloons on his slacks. He was not pleased, but he was thirsty and hungry so he stayed.

Bill became a protégé of Phil and he went on to be a FIDO for many launches up through 1975. We visited Bill, Ruth and their overpopulating three children when Jenny was in Vet School. Bill had arranged for an "internship" for Jenny at a clinic in Wyoming for a month during the summer. The "clinic" was an old place that couldn't even be called a barn, and it must have dated back to the early 1800's. They had a gigantic bull that looked like it weighed five tons tied up in a small pen. We guessed this was Jenny's first patient. Jenny's room was in the attic of the clinic with about four to five feet of clearance in the center of the sloping room. The place had all the amenities that you could imagine from the 1815's. Marilyn asked Stoval if there were any other college age kids around for Jenny to get to know. He knew that the clinic was on the edge of an Indian reservation which prompted him to comment: "The Indian boys would love to get to know her. They have never seen a redhead."

We actually left our girl-child there and Marilyn seriously cried almost the entire drive back to Texas. Jenny toughed it out, did fine and eventually escaped from that medieval place. As a reward, God gave her another internship in Kentucky. She had a friend at A&M who invited her to work on his Dad's ranch for the summer. What Jenny didn't know until she got there was that this was a fabled breeding ranch in Kentucky racehorse country. With neither the dad nor the son there, Jenny had a room in a Tara-like mansion that included a chef for all her meals, served in an opulent dining room, and a butler who drove her back and forth to the stable. Stud fees at this ranch were between $100,000-200,000 and all performed in a stable of rich paneling and chandeliers. Makes a regular male feel inadequate.

Our family, all of us, always felt a strong bond with Bill and then Bill and Ruth. We served as godparents for their oldest son and in 1987 our son Shawn invited Bill to be in his wedding party. I was always proud of how our kids bonded with many of the members of the branch.

The yard parties eventually moved on to become oyster feasts. Our boys were good at hosing off and cleaning the muddy shells, though they were not so wild about consuming the oysters. One of our bachelor sailing friends, Hal Beck, had a charming chuckle whenever he walked into one of our parties. He always carried a signature four foot wide ice chest from his sailboat, and his line always was "You never know when you might run aground." Hal was a North Carolina guy, and when STG was moving from Virginia to Texas, Hal decided he was not going to move that far away. He proclaimed his position for several weeks vowing that he would never see Texas. As move day approached, Chris called Hal in for a fifteen-minute discussion. Hal came out loving the idea of Texas and the big move.

I had considered taking flying lessons but that was outside the financial equation. So, sailing became a big part of our family leisure time. It was lot cheaper than flying and easily accommodated our whole family and friends besides. We spent a lot of time on Galveston Bay in our '19 sailing craft, Crackerjack. Bryan was sailing when he was just a few months old and this was before I learned how to get back through the channel in a big crosswind. Jenny and the boys learned quickly and were a big help with the sailing chores. In the seventies we had a real ship, a '30 Morgan, fiberglass hull, and it even had a head. This was stepping up to the high life. And later on, we had the Wednesday afternoon sailboat races, where the boys worked the sling for firing water balloons at the other boats. Hal Beck was on his boat "Sundance" which was designated as the committee boat, meaning that he did not race, but established the starting and finish line. Hal always had a bevy of bikini ladies to keep his boat clean and serve the beer and the food.

These were magic times for our kids and us. These were the years on the front end of the lifecycle when the primary world of the kids is family. That begins to change when their peer group moves towards more prominence, a natural part of growing up. We were lucky. Even moving into high school, there was a tight family circle until they went to college and then careers. Things changed, but we still remain very close and supportive of one another. Friendswood was a good choice for a place to live and raise a family. It seems like such a different world from today. We always left the keys in the cars, house unlocked and if the kids did something wrong, we usually heard about it before they got home.

From the time she was seven years old, Jenny constantly had a horse, and sometimes a couple of ponies in the mix. Her first horse pastured a half-mile down Melody Lane from our first home. Jenny regularly trooped off with a bucket of oats and a halter to go riding. Her riding progress around town was tracked by the "mom network" and the reports were called in as she made her way around town: "Jenny's doing fine." "She is by the rodeo park." Traffic was not much of a problem. Jenny used to compete in the July 4th celebration rodeo. She did the barrels and she always looked so small on top of her full sized paint.

She was and still is a very determined person and the horse had no choice but to behave.

Once, her horse "Jeep" contracted an ear infection. So Marilyn and Jenny explained to me how I had to put my arm around the horse's neck and hold him steady while they swabbed the medicine into the ear. We started into this procedure and in a flash, I flew into the air and then landed on my back as the horse reared up. Jeep went trotting off, unhappy with this treatment and heading back to his pasture. Marilyn's question was, "Glynn, what are you going to do now?" My answer involved getting a cold beer. Jenny and Marilyn went after Jeep and took him through the gate. Despite this lack of success, Jenny wanted to be a Veterinarian from the time she could talk, and so she is, a specialist in cardiology and internal medicine.

Glynn, Jr. was the quiet, studious type and with some aversion to attention. When we planned a family photo, Glynn hid out for the afternoon. He just didn't want his picture taken when he was young. He tried football in little league years and that was okay, but by the eighth grade, he had found other interests, like playing soccer.

Glynn could be very stoic and he did not go out of his way to let us know if he was hurt or felt bad. He was helping Father John at Mary Queen, at a Sunday morning mass, as an altar boy, when he threw up on the altar during Mass. He had cut his leg at Boy Scout camp earlier in the morning, but never told us, and wasn't feeling well. Father John just went on with the Mass. He was a whiz at debate and speech and was an original computer "geek." He used to spend evenings at the high school doing "whatever" on a mainframe computer system. He was very comfortable in the computer world and he could have easily made a career out of software and computing. He also played in the school band, and had a small group. We loved their "Glenn Miller" music. Glynn went to A&M on a scholarship, and became a petroleum engineer, trooped in the Chevron oil fields around LA for a year or two and followed that up by getting his Law degree from Stanford. He now teaches at Tulane Law School. Ever since his early college days he has run triathlons, and has since run marathons and a couple of Ironman races, designed for those who like ten to twelve continuous hours of strenuous exercise.

Shawn was the "leprechaun" and is a natural talker. Even today he can tell his mother the most preposterous story and her response is always to believe him: "Really, Shawn? I didn't know that." As another source of frustration for his mom, he had this thing of not liking to ride the bus from school. So he would get off at some early stop and go wandering. Folks would call and say, "Shawn got off the bus again and he is here."

Marilyn had to put Bryan on the back of her bike and go get him. He was always the kid that fell into the creek and ended up with croup every Christmas. Now we hear stories from Bryan and his friend of how Shawn and his sidekick Dean loved to terrorize and bully them. Bryan learned 'defensive' living at an early age. Shawn was the jock among the boys. On the little league football team, he was the kid who brought the plays in from the coach as he was the only kid who would remember the play from bench to huddle. Shawn's story is that he often counseled the coach with play selection. He was a good athlete and to this day is a "great salesman." He went on to play second base for the high school baseball team. While he was not a serious student at first, the light went on in college. A little late, but it was bright and it stayed on.

As the last and youngest of the clan, Bryan was always easy going and "his parents spoiled him and gave him everything" according to his siblings. Bryan gave up football after a serious hip injury and became a swimmer on the high school team. Bryan was a good swimmer and eventually served as a lifeguard at Astroworld. He really had to use a lot of Bullfrog sunscreen as his nose would get so sunburned. All the kids were good on the sailboat and could do anything required. Bryan was the lightest and the natural to be cranked up the mast as required on the boson chair. Marilyn was always afraid of that part.   Later in high school, Bryan was a friend to all. He never had a steady girlfriend in high school, but he got a lot of attention. The girl's moms often called to get Bryan to take their daughters to dances, proms, and other events. When he came home from college for a visit, and this was before cell phones, the girls would just arrive as he drove in. After all, somebody needed to carry his bags. When I was doing the Apollo-Soyuz project later, Bryan was a real buddy to Professor Konstantin Busheyev, my counterpart and Victor Blagov, one of the Russian flight directors. Twenty-five years later, he worked with Victor when Bryan was also a flight director, as Victor still was.

The boys always had a group of other boys around the house. Jenny hated having all these boys around and eating everything in sight. She tried to insult them into leaving, but that never worked. The boys and their friends still talk about the "sand-spreading" trap. I would order a truckload of sand for spreading around the yard and leveling the lawn. We took delivery on Monday, and they played in the pile all week. On Saturday, wheelbarrows and shovels came out with Dad, and we had a good workforce, six to eight strong young boys. Thirty-five years later and with their own families, they still laugh about the "sand spreading" and admit they were never surprised by my trap, only happy to play along with it. Wonderful times.

Back to Gemini Flights

Some time early in the operation of MCC in Houston, the unit of three flight dynamics consoles became known as "the Trench." John Llewellyn probably started it when a number of p-tube carriers piled up around his console, looking to John like artillery shells in a trench. Since the three consoles were also in the front row of MCC, the guys liked to think of themselves as the first line of defense for the crew and the mission. I liked it because the single name also captured the concept of a trio of consoles, all working together as one unit.

After the Agena failure for the original planned launch of GT-6, a very quick turn around plan emerged. It was decided to launch GT-7 first on its long duration flight of two weeks. During the GT-VII flight, GT-6 would launch to rendezvous with it. This would not permit a docking, but would get us started on real rendezvous experience. By this time, the Soviet Union had also tried formation flying. For this GT-7/5 combination, the trench had the same operators as GT-5. Frank Borman and Jim Lovell in Gemini-7 launched on December 4, 1965 and GT-6 attempted launch 8 days later on December 12,1965. However, GT-6 shut down on the pad, because one of the umbilicals pulled early. And as a very fortunate circumstance, during the recycle review, a dust cap was found post-firing in a main propellant line in the Titan which was already causing a decrease in thrust level. There was no lift off, the vehicle was still safe on the pad, and there was no ejection as there were not enough cues to warrant triggering an ejection. The commander, Wally Schirra, made a great decision to sit tight. With different timing of the umbilical release, we could have lifted off with a blocked main propulsion line. That would have lead to the need for a flight abort and a crew ejection, an escape none of us ever wanted to see. Instead, the vehicle was fixed on the pad, the count recycled and Gemini 6 launched on December 15, 1965.

The rendezvous of GT-6 followed a perfect choreography and resulted in Gemini 6 station-keeping with Gemini 7 six hours after liftoff. What a celebration for the whole team especially the Trench. It was a wonderful experience to watch our new operators calmly and professionally execute the rendezvous process so close to the nominal plan.

There were some changes after the first of the year:
- Bryan Lunney was born on January 12, 1966.
- Chris Kraft removed himself as the Gemini flight director in order to focus on Apollo.
- Cliff Charlesworth was selected as a new flight director.

John Hodge and Gene Kranz were the two flight directors for Gemini 8 as they planned to head a two shift operation in MCC for what was planned to be a four day mission on GT-8   The launch of the Atlas Agena worked fine and Agena 8 was on orbit as a target vehicle for the rendezvous. The crew of Neil Armstrong and Dave Scott launched in Gemini 8 on March 16, 1966. The same Trench team managed the same rendezvous choreography to a station-keeping position and then docking six and a half hours after lift-off.

Not long after that, the docked vehicle began to have rates and deviations in attitude. At first, it was believed that the Agena control system was causing the problem and the crew disabled the Agena attitude control system. For a short time that seemed to help, but then the unexpected rates returned and began to roll the vehicle. The crew tried the Agena attitude control again. When that didn't work, Neil Armstrong decided to separate by undocking from the Agena. Since the configuration was now lighter, it started to roll faster. This had to be arrested and brought under control quickly. Neil brought the entry control system on line and shut off the power to the primary control system used for on-orbit operations. The entry control system was actually two completely redundant propulsion systems but with limited fuel supplies. It was the "get-home" system as opposed to the much larger propulsion system used on-orbit but jettisoned with the adapter section prior to reentry. Because of its use to regain control, a significant portion of the entry control system fuel had been used up.

John Hodge, the flight director on duty, correctly found this situation to be very serious: primary control system off, the entry control system activated and now low on fuel, and the spacecraft heading onto ground tracks which would provide significantly reduced coverage of the spacecraft for the next ten to twelve hours. Faced with all that, John decided to land Gemini 8 early and in the Pacific with a flight duration of slightly less than eleven hours. The recovery was successful. And, clearly, it was another example of superb emergency decision-making by the crew commanders - Wally on six and now, Neil on eight.

Another management change occurred after Gemini 8. John Hodge joined Chris getting ready for Apollo. Gene, Cliff and I were to take up Gemini. After Gemini 9 with Gene as lead, it was expected that Gene would go back to Apollo. He did, but he returned for Gemini 12, as we were not as happy with the two-shift operation as we expected.

By this time also, I had been the flight director on the first unmanned Saturn 1B launch of the new Apollo command and service module (201) on February 26, 1966. This was a test of not only the active systems in the vehicles but also a test of the heat shield for reentry. It also had some significant challenges for the MCC operators, with a capability to control attitude by ground command if the automatic control system failed. I was very relieved that we never had to exercise that option. The countdown produced one space-first but it was not a pretty one. The launch had been scrubbed by the LCC at the Cape. The flight team in MCC was milling about, getting ready to leave but waiting to see if recycle estimates for the next countdown were coming in yet. After a number of minutes, Kurt Debus, the Launch Director at KSC called and asked, "Flight, can you unscrub the scrub?" This was a new term for me and everybody else, but the meaning was crystal clear. A check with our controllers, the M&O for the MCC and Network for the remote stations and data support resulted in a scramble. It all came back positive so our GO went back to Dr. Debus promptly. The flight was a nominal and excellent success. But as a result of the first scrub, our boss Chris had left to catch a plane for an out of town meeting and missed the flight, probably the only one he ever missed. He never said anything, as in happy, mad or raging. So I assume happy.

Gemini 9 was planned as a rendezvous and docking mission, with re-rendezvous sequences and a very extensive EVA. The EVA centered around a major new system mounted on the back end of the Gemini spacecraft adapter and called the Auxiliary Maneuvering Unit (AMU). This was a considerably more complicated EVA than any we had attempted so far, because Gene Cernan was actually going to don this back pack device by backing into it and "strapping" it on. After release from the Gemini, Gene would pilot the AMU through its paces, although with a tether. We still felt the tether was prudent. In talks with Tom and Gene before the flight, it was the first time that I came to really appreciate the physical demands of EVA. As a preparation for that, both of them were doing weight training, especially upper body. Wrestling that umbilical into the cockpit and getting the hatch closed were not optional.

Gene Kranz was the lead flight director for this flight. And so we came to launch day on the Gemini 9 mission, and on April 17, 1966, the Atlas Agena was launched first as a target vehicle and ended up in the Atlantic right off the coast of Florida. Because of the failure of the target vehicle last fall, a back-up stage was conceived and implemented as an alternative to the Agena stage. It was called an augmented target and docking adapter (ATDA). It was put on top of another Atlas and launched on June 1, 1966. The Gemini spacecraft was planned to follow one revolution, about ninety minutes later, but it was scrubbed when ground equipment failed to properly load the azimuth signal for the guidance computer. Quickly, this was resolved and Gemini 9 went into orbit on June 3, 1966.

In the meantime, the Agena systems flight controllers had been observing high fuel usage on the ATDA stage since it got on-orbit. There was also no confirming telemetry signal indicating shroud separation. This set off some rapid response in trying to understand the shroud a lot better than we did. Some astronauts on travel on the West Coast (McDivitt and Scott) went by the factory and looked at flight hardware first hand. After review at the Cape, the launch crew reported the most likely cause of the hangup as a configuration error in attaching a lanyard. This explanation still left us with a dangerous condition.

The rendezvous went like clockwork and more of the new trench operators got to try their skills at orchestrating this new technique (Ed Pavelka and Bill Gravett). Tom Stafford had just flown GT-6 and the GT-9sequence went smooth as glass. When the crew was station keeping, they reported that the shroud covering the docking system on one end of the ATDA was not fully deployed. It appeared to be still held together by the metal band and the partial opening made it look to Tom Stafford like an "angry alligator." And the name stuck. Commands were sent to

Gemini 9 "Angry Alligator"

cause vehicle motions in an attempt to free the shroud. As expected, that did not improve the situation. We were left with an incomplete opening and two halves of a shroud with some amount of stored spring energy still sitting there.

Instead of the planned docking, we waved off and did a separation maneuver to buy a little time. This maneuver was designed to create an equi-period Gemini orbit that would return to the ATDA in one revolution. When the crew returned, there were no changes or any new ideas. "Don't intervene if you don't know what to do" was a guiding principle that had served us well over the years. And we stuck to it.

There had been another planned re-rendezvous scheduled for this mission to simulate a lunar module abort scenario. We decided to embark on that exercise at this point because we could not dock and to continue station keeping just expends fuel. That would also give us time to consider what if anything to do next. In MCC, we were opposed to going any further with crew EVA actions to attempt release of the shroud. But, we now had time if anybody came up with a different and workable idea. Assuming there would not be any such breakthrough, the crew could then get a solid sleep period before the demanding umbilical EVA to operate the AMU on the next flight day.

All was under control, until I was summoned to a special management meeting. On arrival, there was ongoing discussion about how to do an EVA to free the shroud. Most of the management of MSC was there: Dr. Gilruth, Chris, Deke and Chuck Mathews, the MSC Gemini program manager, and George Mueller, the Associate Administrator of manned flight and other NASA HQ people. Buzz was presenting and I wondered if this was his idea. Dr. Gilruth had been cross-examining Buzz and was negative on what he was hearing. The idea of trying to "do something" to release the shroud took on an air of unreality. We had been through this with the MCC teams and it was unanimous that the risks outweighed the gains by a clear margin: lack of EVA experience, lack of a real approach to fix the problem, and not the right balance of risk-reward. Long discussion and a good summary by Gene Kranz on the shroud and mechanisms did not seem to register. There was a sense of being enamored with the idea of successfully "doing something" on the part of some people there, especially those from HQ and two parties from MSC, Buzz Aldrin and Chuck Mathews, the MSC program manager. Chuck spoke in favor of doing an EVA to fix the problem and there was no more objection voiced - Gene's was already noted. I learned later that Chris and Dr. Gilruth felt that it was so obvious that this was a bad idea that it would be refused by the crew (or MCC team) later. It still seemed to me like an idea worthy of a resounding 'Hell no' right up front.

My observation was: In decades of dealing with flight problems before and long after GT-9, this stood out as a bad idea deserving of firm rejection. Maybe, there was something else at work that we operators were not aware of. There was an easy way to handle that by just telling us. But we never learned of extenuating circumstances. Nevertheless, it goes down as an anomaly in our flight decision-making history.

There was an undercurrent of another ongoing dispute. We had a history of HQ attempts to inject themselves into operational decisions, at least the "big" ones. In early Gemini, HQ sent us a person (can't remember his name), new to all of us and to this business, to make the "big" decisions in MCC. On his first countdown, Chris and the LV test conductor scrubbed the launch for good reason. But this fellow considered it his prerogative. His only problem was that he could not enter the discussion because he did not know how to work his intercom. Some boss. Later in that day, I inadvertently walked into a conference room, deserted except for Chris and this guy. In the silence, I could immediately feel that the temperature in the room was in the 30's. Chris was in one of his towering "angries." I turned right around, left and never saw that guy again.

To tie this 'compulsion--to--intervene' and the EVA decision on GT-9 into a package, I noticed later (by GT-10) that there was a pronounced change in attitude about the role of the HQ mission director. From then on, their only request was that we inform them of any change in plans so that they could keep headquarters appraised. No harm, perfectly fair. No one talked to us about this shift to a more sensible role by headquarters and it took a while to believe that it was real. But, it is easy to imagine their horror when they realized that they almost made a colossal mistake in overruling MCC and ordering this decision on the Gemini 9 EVA. (There could not have been more dramatic evidence of what a bad decision it was than the results of the upcoming planned EVA within twenty-four hours.) They apparently and wisely decided to stay out of operational decisions and to support the flight team in the future. To their credit, they did.

Some of this urge to assert derived from the fact there were many people in our industry who participated in space hardware development programs and it is somewhat natural to assume that one's experience applies to this new field of space operations. However, it did not. I have tried to convey the time and effort spent on mission rules (our code of ethics for risk/reward decisions), flight techniques, simulations, actual operations and years of immersion. These are the prerequisite experiences, much more so than design.

While this management dispute played out, Tom and Gene in Gemini 9, were doing the re-rendezvous to test the approach by the chase vehicle from a position above the target. In this approach, the crew is approaching the target from above and the features of the earth below are behind the target vehicle. The combination of ocean and desert background made it difficult to have a good continuous visual of the target vehicle during the whole time. Nevertheless, it was successful and the crew flew up close to the ATDA, within inches, and took more photos. By that time, the crew had been up a long time with the intensity required for three rendezvous sequences and Tom requested that any EVA to work on the shroud be postponed to the next day because of crew fatigue. This was essentially a NO-GO for the shroud EVA because we did not have the fuel to park and re-rendezvous again. We were delighted with Tom's assessment and agreed.

On the next flight day for the planned EVA, preps were nominal and the hatch opened at 49:22 elapsed time. The crew reported difficulty with the umbilical, much stiffer now as it was pressurized. This was followed by almost two hours of scary reports from our friends in Gemini 9. On the trip to the rear of the Gemini spacecraft where the AMU was located, Gene reported serious fogging on his visor. When he arrived at the AMU station, he reported that any work took four to five times the effort he expended in training. Gene had difficulty deploying the arms on the AMU and began to rest periodically to attempt to clear up the visor fogging. Only marginal improvement in vision resulted. This was becoming very serious and we could not do anything to really help. Tom, the decision maker on the spot, called off this excursion. Gene wrestled his way back into the cockpit. He and Tom got the umbilical pulled in and closed the hatch in a little short of two hours. It wasn't until post-flight that suit inspection revealed a tear in several layers of Gene's suit, caused by contact with an antenna. That's closer than anybody wants to get. And another good call by the commander. Gemini 9 landed and we truly celebrated their return.

And soon, Gemini 10 readied for launch on July 18, 1966. John Young and Mike Collins were the crew. The objectives were: to rendezvous and dock with Agena X, to use the docked Agena 10 and Gemini 10 to rendezvous with the Agena 8 stage, to conduct EVA operations, to conduct docking practices and experiments. This was a fairly complex flight schedule, as demonstrated by having three vehicles lined up in the same plane, after orbital insertion. Gemini 10 was trailing the

Agena 10 by 850 miles and leading the Agena 8 vehicle by 500 miles. Rendezvous choreography had advanced to three active vehicles being managed in earth orbit. I was the lead flight director.

Because of the number of maneuvers, spacecraft fuel was a critical resource and Tom Holloway, the flight activities officer (FAO), developed a clever set of mission options whose choice depended on the level of Gemini fuel remaining at various mission points.   Often, this type of "what if" analysis is not used, but it was a lifesaver on Gemini 10.   During the initial terminal phase of the Gemini-Agena 10 rendezvous, there was a surprisingly high level of Gemini fuel usage due to deviations in the braking phase.   This triggered a major mission change, which had been carefully thought out and extensively discussed in finalizing Tom's contingency planning set of options. It was easy to decide to select the option to remain docked to the Agena X stage for an extended time of about thirty-nine hours.   In this option, the necessary maneuvers for rendezvousing with the Agena VIII were made with the propulsion of the Agena X docked vehicle.

Once at the Agena 8 stage, the crew had already undocked from Agena X and intiated preparations for the second EVA which was an umbilical based excursion by Mike Collins to retrieve an equipment package mounted on the Agena8.   The EVA was limited to forty minutes (one daylight pass) because of the need to conserve fuel and not spend any more on station-keeping with the Agena 8.   It went OK but the sample package slipped away on Mike Collins return to the hatch The Trench team was the same one as GT-9 and they were getting very good at this rendezvous game.

Because of the complex set of mission options that Tom Holloway developed and coordinated with the rest of the team, his contribution and understanding were seen as vital to the execution of the flight.   Therefore, I had decided preflight to move Tom Holloway into the front room of MCC, and it was the first time we ever had a FAO serving on console in the front room of MCC. (And, it has remained that way ever since.)

We had spent time over several months perfecting this set of mission options and I wanted Tommy's expertise available to the flight director and his team.   That caused some problem in the Astronaut corps, because the checklist and flight plan activities had been located in a back room and in direct support of the capcom.   This was an organizational accident of sorts due to the fact that the astronauts and the FAO people worked in Deke's flight crew directorate which was parallel to Chris Kraft's flight operations directorate.   Two of our astronauts complained to Chris Kraft that this move of the FAO to the front room was a bad idea. Chris referred their complaint to me and Cliff. We were exceedingly ticked that they had gone to Chris directly without asking us for the rationale. Cliff and I went to see them in their office and after some discussion, the conclusions were: yes, the FAO position belongs in the front room reporting to the flight director and if they had any other problems, they would take them up with us first.

Cliff was the lead flight director for Gemini 11, and it flew on September 12, 1966 with Pete Conrad and Dick Gordon. Cliff was the lead flight director and I was in support. In this context, the "lead" role mostly affected pre-flight choices. The "lead" was the primary interface for coordination with the crew, mostly on scheduling activities and selected subjects. He also selected the rest of the flight directors and made their assignments as to mission phases covered. In this case it was easy, Cliff did the prime crew wake shift and I did some of that and all the rest. The Trench team carried over from Gemini 9 & 10.

Bill Tindall had been stretching the team to even more of a rendezvous challenge. One lunar rendezvous scenario envisioned an accelerated sequence with station-keeping at the first apogee, or in about one-half of an orbit. So we needed to develop techniques to achieve this very fast paced rendezvous. Bill had managed the planning team through all the arguments and difficulties and by flight time, had an enthusiastic crew on board and in the MCC, ready to rendezvous in less than one orbit.

The third launch attempt was a charm. Gemini 11 made a small plane change correction after insertion, then a terminal intercept maneuver, and then a few mid-courses and braking had the crew station-keeping by an hour and twenty minutes. Docked burns and docking practice added to program experience and on the second day another umbilical EVA commenced. After hatch opening, Dick Gordon proceeded to the nose of the spacecraft and attached a tether from the Agena to the Gemini docking bar. Again, like Gene Cernan, all of this proved very difficult for Dick and his labored breathing, coming to us over the air- to- ground loop underscored his difficulty. The EVA was terminated early after about one-half hour, but the tether had been secured. The crew difficulty was clear evidence that we still could not execute an EVA successfully with reasonable crew workload and that we had more to learn.

One of the highlights of Gemini 11 is the series of iconic photos over the Indian subcontinent, taken from an altitude of 750 miles. Gemini 11 flew in this kind of orbit for two revs after a docked burn by the Agena 11 stage. Once returned to the usual 160-mile orbit, the crew did a stand up EVA, and later undocked from the Agena for tether operations.

As Gemini 11 backed away from the Agena and the tether played out, the crew began the first experiments in tether dynamics. The crew was able to spin up the two vehicles attached by the tether and it seemed to be easier to control than we expected. We didn't have a planned use of this capability but the sponsors of the tether test thought it might serve someday as a way to keep vehicles together in orbit when they weren't able to dock. It was also thought that this might be a form of inducing a minor G field on the vehicles.

Because of the high fuel usage during the terminal phase of Gemini 10, my intuition led us to try a modified terminal phase approach that slowed down the relative motion, as the chase vehicle approached the target. We were only going to try this re-rendezvous if we had sufficient fuel and the crew was okay with an early wakeup. Even before MCC called, the crew was up and powering up the guidance equipment for the test. As usual, the crew wanted to learn as much as we could about this new world whenever we had an opportunity. We called this a standoff rendezvous because we positioned the Gemini chase vehicle in exactly the same orbit as the target, but displaced behind so that it trailed the target by twenty-five miles. The rendezvous worked fine. And as late as the ninth manned Gemini flight (GT-9), we were still adding to our inventory of knowledge and experience at every opportunity. Some of this experience probably helped when the Shuttle/Station approaches were being adjusted from fighter pilot intercepts to the berthing of very large vehicles, which do not permit a lot of braking plume impingements on appendages.

Gemini 12 was crewed by Jim Lovell and Buzz Aldrin. It was the last of the Gemini flights and we were still looking for a solid EVA success. All other program goals had already been exceeded. Lift-off was on November 11, 1966 at 3:46:30. By three hours and fifty minutes GET (ground elapsed time), the crew was docked to the Agena. The rendezvous radar did not work for the last phases of rendezvous, but the experienced Trench team vectored Gemini 12 to its terminal phase conditions. Once on the intercept, Buzz Aldrin was the class expert on terminal phase without a rendezvous radar and lived out his PhD dissertation.

There were three EVA's – an extended standup EVA with hatch open for two and one half hours, a planned umbilical EVA that was the big test of new EVA restraint provisions and a later stand-up EVA to eject unneeded equipment from the cockpit. There was a continued set of Gemini system problems besides the radar loss – oxygen to water warning lights in the fuel cell system, some degradation in fuel cell performance, little or no thrust from several thrusters, and an increase in regulated pressure in one of the two entry control systems. The team of flight controllers and flight crew were quick to stabilize all these problems.

The EVA went very well. One significant improvement was a set of handrails for the crew to use in traversing to the rear of the spacecraft. Other handholds were in the rear of the ship where Buzz slipped his boots into very large slippers that restrained him at this workstation. Gemini XII training for EVA also initiated the first time use of a large water tank to simulate some aspects of the EVA environment. This combination of aids and new training method coupled with scheduled rest periods led to a very controlled and successful EVA.

I have often wondered whether the Gemini EVA planning would have been more successful if it had been done in the same fashion as the Bill Tindall model that galvanized the attention of the total community on the rendezvous subject. The EVA planning was more of a closed shop exercise, totally within the flight crew directorate, where the leadership changed on each flight to the EVA astronauts themselves.

The Gemini flight program concluded with the return of Gemini 12, but the benefits cascaded down through the Apollo program and all subsequent manned flight programs. As the Gemini program finished, the operations team, comprised of mission planners, MCC flight controllers, and the flight crews, was ready to roar into Apollo, with the hard earned portfolio of solid competence, wide experience and strong self-confidence in the ability of this team to do the Apollo job well.

Since the Voshkod flight featuring Leonov's EVA immediately before our first manned GT-3, the Soviets did not fly a manned spacecraft that we knew of during the ten manned flights of Gemini.

Apollo

Apollo Was Coming on Fast

President Kennedy announced in May 1961:

> *"First, I believe that this nation should commit itself to achieving the goal of before this decade is out of landing a man on the moon and returning him safely to earth."*

In fourteen months, NASA announced the selection of the Apollo mission mode of lunar orbit rendezvous (LOR), a dark horse and latecomer to the competition of ideas for how Apollo should be done. There were already two other options: All-on-one launch or earth orbit rendezvous (EOR). LOR became the mission framework for deriving the necessary flight hardware elements that then set the stage for the definition of new facilities, especially at the launch site. NASA had also contractually engaged American industry in the design and building of these major equipments.

By the start of 1967, five and one half years after President Kennedy's speech, many Apollo growing pains had already been experienced, overcome, rendered acceptable or were still pending:

- Most of the development work of the vehicles was well along, engaging ninety percent of the total workforce of more than 300,000 people.

- NASA assessment and critique of contractor progress was ongoing and shaking up some of the major companies, especially North American aviation, the builder of the Command snd Service Modules (CSM). The progress at North American was the subject of the critical Phillip's report, written before the Apollo fire.

- Many personnel and organization changes had already occurred during this early period.

By this time, the Apollo effort felt like a national mobilization, consistent with the fact that the peak NASA budget in the middle sixties was about 4.5% of the annual federal budget. (This compares to 0.5% in the last decade or so.) There had been significant growth in the NASA ranks of the manned spaceflight team and the NASA organization structure. This process evolved from 1961 on and there were various regimes in NASA headquarters, plus the new roles for the Marshall Space Flight Center (MSFC) in Huntsville, Al and the launch team in Florida (now named the Kennedy Space Center, KSC). The new roles for these organizations were reasonably well established by the start of 1967.

In NASA Headquarters, a strong central program management function had been formed lead by George Mueller, previously of TRW, with General Sam Phillips of the Air Force as the Headquarters level program manager. There was considerable staff at NASA HQ and a special contract for Bellcom to assist headquarters as an integration contractor. Almost all of the new Headquarters executives had different background than NASA or NACA. With the new players and cultures came tension, some conflict, but also new ideas. Perhaps most significantly, George Mueller forced the concept of "all – up testing", rather than "one component at a time," an approach that was favored by the Von Braun team at MSFC, primarily for engines. Sam Phillips brought a wealth of program management experience from running the Minuteman ICBM development, and as vice commander of the Air Force Ballistic Missile Division. General Phillips established a formal design review process that became the core model for all of the subsequent NASA developments, with modifications as appropriate for new conditions. But NASA HQ was a major new player and it took some adjustment, especially at MSC that had been the singular leader of manned space until this shift. To the credit of all the management parties at Headquarters and the Centers, they gradually, and sometimes painfully, worked their way through this "newness" and made it work, sometimes bending the rules to local culture.

For MSC, in Mercury and the early Gemini, the headquarters interface was much simpler and more in the tradition of NACA. STG/MSC managed the spacecraft contractor and the procurement of the Air Force launch vehicles in the "Walt Williams" mode. The original Mercury launch site team was mostly staffed by STG engineers from the Lewis aircraft organization and some Langley engineers. They were a detached field site group from STG and then MSC.

MSFC had the Apollo job of developing two new launch vehicles, Saturn 1B and the Saturn V. KSC had the job of developing the new facilities and processing capabilities with the largest launch vehicle ever built in the US.

By this time, Apollo also had a flight history of four little Joe tests of the escape system plus two pad abort tests, three Saturn 1B test flights, with two command and service modules on those test flights, designated 201 and 202.

Most would agree that the Apollo program had achieved considerable momentum, yet there were still concerns for the reliability and maturity of the flight vehicle development and, many of the necessary relationships in this new management complex were still being smoothed out.

The Apollo Fire

All of this progress and momentum came to a wrenching stop on the evening of January 27, 1967. The crew of Gus Grissom, Ed White and Roger Chaffee were in the Apollo command module on the pad, struggling with a "plugs out" test, where the spacecraft would be unplugged from ground power and go on internal spacecraft power. The first manned flight was a month away. As with other tests in those days, there were frustrations with the general rate of progress of the test and the crew/ground communications in particular. It was a struggle, with interruptions to troubleshoot the problem. With irritation, Gus commented, "How do you expect to communicate with us in orbit if you can't even talk to us on the pad?."....More waiting.

This test was being conducted in the same way as previous Mercury and Gemini pad tests where the cabin pressure was two psi greater than the 14.7 psi of the external ambient pressure, a cabin total pressure of 16.7 psi of pure oxygen. Soon and in rapid succession came the chilling report from Gus, "There is a fire in here" and then, "Get us out of here" from Roger. Reports of flames and smoke in the white room came from the ground team. A rush of technicians charged to get the spacecraft hatch open. Time stood still. And finally, the report on the net was, "The crew is dead." It happened so fast, and three of ours were gone. How could this be?

Chris was on duty in MCC where the test was being monitored like an actual countdown. Despite his own pain and an overwhelming sense of "We put them in this trap", his presence helped stabilize the mostly young operators through the immediate shock, some still crying quietly in disbelief. I was not on duty. Marilyn and I were expecting Val and Bill Anders and Linda and Jerry Bostick for a Friday dinner. Instead, I was now meeting Jerry at the Control Center. In the parking lot, Dutch von Ehrenfried, a guidance officer on duty for the test, kept repeating, "Horrible, horrible." Buck Willoughby was an Apollo GNC flight controller and a former AF pilot agonizing over the events, "I remember pilot buddies going out on patrol and not coming back. But, I never had to listen to such a loss happen right in front of me."

The mood was one of devastation and shock. And another reality was forming. No, we were not in charge of the vehicle design but we had many opportunities to challenge the conditions of this test and the whole idea of the oxygen/fire risks and a satisfactory escape path for the crew. Like so many others, we had gotten used to the idea of this pure oxygen cabin and the many previous tests in the earlier programs gave us the false basis for acceptance. A sense of guilt took hold and it does not go away.

And so, the immediate events unfolded: funerals, the formation of an Accident Board, the search for causes, the fresh examination of other risks, the deliberations for changes in hardware, methods, processes, people, and organizations. The review was systematic and ruthless as it laid bare the shortcomings, which gave the appearance of rapid progress. And gradually the necessary changes were made. George Low was assigned as the spacecraft program manager and he quickly moved to harness all of the MSC management talent directly to the recovery of the Apollo program and they relished the opportunity. George also assigned Frank Borman as his man in the North American plant in Downey, California to oversee and expedite the necessary changes. It wasn't long before George was flying this entire group plus his project managers to both major spacecraft contractors, North American Aviation and Grumman for the Lunar Module. George was an artful leader and manager and focused all of the resources at his command on the same goal. He also smoothed many of the rough spots in the interface with Headquarters. Gen. Phillips and George were formidable together. In the opinion of the many, George was the orchestrator of the success of Apollo from this point on to the landing.

External to NASA, there was considerable attention to the accident review. There were some who questioned whether we should proceed at all. Some of this came at NASA in the congressional hearings. And uncertainty hung in the air. In May, Frank Borman was testifying. Frank is a very straightforward, intelligent and forceful man. In one of these sessions, his limit was reached and he said respectfully, "We are trying to tell you that we are confident in our management, in our engineers and in ourselves. I think the question is really: Are you confident in us?" Expressed clearly in "Congress Speak," this was the street version of put up or shut up. It also seemed to be the turning point. Apollo was soon back on track with support and a green light from our Congress.

Other changes occurred in Flight Operations:

> George Mueller prevailed upon Chris to give up his flight director role and focus on the management of his total Apollo effort. Chris hated to give it up, but it was time.

*Chris named three new flight directors for Apollo: Gerry Grif-
fin, a GNC flight controller for the CSM, Milt Windler from
Recovery operations and Pete Frank from the mission planning unit. This was the first flight director selection of two
from ranks other than MCC flight controllers. All 3 of these
men were pilots or aircrew members. Gerry had flown back
seat with Bill Anders in the AF. Pete was a Marine fighter pilot
and Milt was an Air Force fighter pilot.*

During this period, the Soviet Union first flew its version of a real three
man ship, called the Soyuz. Launched on April 5, 1967, the sole cosmonaut, Vladimir Komarov, was killed when the parachute system failed
on landing.

Even today, we still carry the scars of guilt over the fire and how we
missed it.

Coming Back

1967 moved on with increasing focus and clarity on the job ahead. There
was a sense of determination and resolution that the spacecraft would
be properly fixed and the program would get back on track, stronger
than ever. We owed that to the crew of Apollo I. In early 1969, George
Low was reflecting on the program and referred to the fire as the turning
point, saying, "It required us to build a different Apollo spacecraft and it
created an entirely different atmosphere among ourselves, our contractors and within MSC."

In our Division, a big challenge fell to the CSM branch of Arnie Aldrich. These were the systems operators in MCC who watched over
the CSM, now in a process of being significantly upgraded. They were
in this period of modification full time and the rest of us involved on
a part time basis. We also had to follow the requirements for and the
progress of the flight software and the MCC software. In his evaluation of the MIT software deliveries, George Low felt that the deliveries
were lagging and not reliable. As a result he assigned the flight software
responsibilities to Chris Kraft and Chris then delegated it to Bill Tindall.
Within a month Chris set the ground rules to forcefully control changes.

The MIT effort on flight software quickly began to yield results and
reliable deliveries of software. We also began to prepare for three more
unmanned flights. I was assigned the first Saturn V launch of an unmanned CSM. Gene Kranz had the flight of an unmanned lunar module

in earth orbit and Cliff drew the second Saturn V/CSM flight.   These were now labeled Apollo IV, V, and VI, although we also referred to the Saturn V flights as 501 & 502.   This assignment continued me on the path of studying the CSM and resulted in a week-long CSM training session in Downey, California during the summer.

There was a large group, probably 20 from the MCC team attending and about five of us who brought families along on this trip. This was the first time for our family to see California, Disneyland, and the Pacific and on a clear day to see Catalina and the mountains around LA. We drove our station wagon over I-10 to the LA area, and broke the trip into three days of driving. Bryan was about eighteen months and really impressed us all. He was able to chew up a big portion of a styrofoam ice chest during the three day drive west. I think the other boys were feeding him.

We rented a small cottage down by one of the beaches, about a block off the ocean.   We also found out that we could not walk barefoot on the sand without torching our feet.   But the pain was worth it to get into that beautiful blue ocean. We all went in and came bouncing back out as fast as we could. I had no idea the Pacific was that cold. If you look around the beach in southern California, most people are there on the beach with towels under them, but not in the water.   Those who are in the water are usually wearing some type of wetsuit or they are just there to cool off and get out fast.   The family did enjoy their time on the beach while I spent most of the week looking at 2000 viewgraphs of spacecraft schematics and trying to fathom their mysteries.

Disneyland was also a real treat for the kids and us. None of us had ever seen the place and it was enchanting. A day of "Small, small world," Magic Mountain, more rides and long lines before we eventually wore out.

On our return to Houston, it was time to start preparations for 501. The CSM spacecraft was very familiar to me and the mission would be conducted primarily in earth orbit. The Saturn V would be launched, first two stages would be fired and discarded, the third stage called the S-IVB stage would propel the CSM into earth orbit. A few revolutions later, the S-1VB would relight and push the CSM to a high apogee orbit of 10,000 miles. Once on the way down from that maximum altitude, the service propulsion system (SPS) would fire to accelerate the spacecraft to the same velocities that would be experienced in a worse case return from the moon. (This was a big step up from the Wallops Island days of doing the same type of testing but on a far smaller scale.) This was a great test of the thermal protection system and all the guidance, flight control and propulsion systems. It was also time to fly the Saturn V, which was a giant monster of a rocket about 365' tall. Five F-1 engines powered the first stage, delivering one and a half million pounds thrust per engine. That was seven and a half million pounds of thrust, lifting a six million pound vehicle off the pad. The second stage had five J-2 engines of 230 thousand pounds of thrust each. The third stage propulsion is used to achieve earth orbit and then the single J-2 engine is fired again to achieve escape velocity when the mission is to go to the Moon. The entire vehicle is steered by guidance equipment in the instrument unit at the top of the three Saturn stages and below the CSM, LM and protective shroud.

The whole machine is an exercise in "big." Everything about it was big and the Vertical Assembly Building (VAB), where the Saturn V was stacked for launch, is 525 feet tall. The vehicle assembled on the launch platform and then the platform with the Saturn V on top is transported to the pad by a crawler that also weighs about six million pounds. At liftoff, the five engines are generating the equivalent of 180 million horsepower with one percent of that energy converted into noise. It is no wonder that Walter Cronkite had to duck to safety in his TV booth a couple of miles from the pad with the ceiling tiles falling down and the entire building and windows rattling violently.

In preparations for the launch, the MCC participated in a three-day count-down test at the Cape. This was about a month before the launch and it was really a struggle for the KSC launch team. There were so many new systems with a new vehicle, a new pad, a new launch facility. It took two weeks to complete this three-day test. This was a real learning chore for that team at the Cape. We felt sorry for them at times, as they struggled to get their arms around this massive set of equipment and the people trying to master them.

Finally we were ready for launch. Grady Meyer had already left NASA and George Guthrie was at the FIDO console. John Llewellyn was at RETRO, breaking in Jim Payne. Gran Paules and Neil Hutchinson were the guidance officers along with Steve Bales. There were some back up operators for this nine-hour mission and this was a first for Neil Hutchinson who had spent his early years in the NASA computer division overseeing the RTCC. Neil ascended quickly through the ranks to be the computer supervisor, for all the computers in MCC, and was now on the receiving end.

The flight was as nominal as they get and we were very impressed with the performance of the Saturn V. The Saturn V was going to be our ride to the moon and it was a joy to see that it worked just great.

Next up, on January 22, 1968, was another unmanned flight this time of the LM. Gene Kranz was the flight director for this mission, designated Apollo V. These unmanned flights were always more complicated for us in MCC. With the crew onboard, we did not have to program the whole flight sequence and could change things or respond to anomalies more quickly and easily. We already had three unmanned CSM flights by this time, but this was the first for the Lunar Module. The flight objectives approximated the accomplishment of the propulsion burns on a typical lunar landing mission. There were a number of propulsion burns with the descent stage. Then a fire- in-the-hole maneuver to separate the ascent from the descent stage was conducted and the ascent stage was then sequenced to simulate the rendezvous maneuvers.

This was the first flight for the new LM team of flight controllers in MCC. The systems GNC controllers were Jack Craven and Bob Carlton and others plus the trench team of Dave Reed and Gary Renick. New FIDOs were Maurice Kennedy, Bill Stoval and Bill Boone. At Guidance, Russell and Fenner moved over from Gemini. The first descent stage burn only continued for a very short time. Because the engine did not rise to the thrust level within the time constraint that the onboard computer was expecting, it commanded an engine shutdown. Recovery from these conditions resulted in a profile where some of the individual steps, like firing and shutting off the engine had to be commanded from MCC. This became more constraining because the commands sometimes had to be repeated four or five times before the communications worked. Apollo V was a baptism by fire for a new LM team of MCC controllers and they prevailed.

We had one more unmanned flight to accomplish, Apollo VI on April 4, 1968. It was essentially a repeat of Apollo IV from last November. It was very important to get a good repeat test, especially of the new Saturn V, and we all knew it. Same trench manning as Apollo IV was in effect except Jay Greene was prime, with George Guthrie as backup and Neil Hutchinson was prime at Guidance. Soon this monster Saturn V lifted off. And then bad things started to happen. The first stage had a severe case of POGO that almost caused a vehicle level structural failure. Once through the first stage, our expectation for return to nominal was shattered again. One of the five J-2 engines shut down and then another one also shut down. Only three of the five engines continued to run and the guidance system tried to get to the target conditions by burning all the fuel through three engines instead of five. The third stage took over and it got to the best orbit that it could. Cliff and the trench team thought that they could recover and get close to the preplanned mission with the second burn of the S-IVB. The 'gremlin party' in the Saturn was not finished yet. The S-IVB stage did not ignite to perform the next planned firing. This would have propelled the CSM to a 10,000-mile apogee orbit. On a lunar mission, this second burn of the S-IVB is the one that would inject the two spacecraft on an escape trajectory to the moon. The team used the SPS engine to get as high an apogee as they could, and still performed the later burn that would accelerate the spacecraft to the desired entry conditions. The achieved conditions were adequate for a good thermal test, but not exactly what had been planned.

Apollo VII

When I was assigned to the first manned flight designated Apollo VII, I was happy to know that Wally Schirra was the CDR. I had not worked yet with Walt Cunningham or Don Eisele, but I clearly remembered and respected Wally's performance on MA-8 and GT-6. He had done a great job on these early flights and I was looking forward to this maiden Apollo flight, along with Gene Kranz and a new flight director Gerry Griffin, fresh from the ranks of the Gemini GNC operator position. It was also the first 'prime' role for Phil Shaffer at FIDO and Will Presley at Guidance. Apollo VII was the first flight test of the newly designed CSM and a very important step in the Apollo flight sequence and of ten days in duration.

As something of a premonition, I was listening to the launch team loop from KSC in one of their early tests of the spacecraft. Wally jumped all over the test conductor for something that bothered him in the handling of the vehicle. I was not able to tell what the basic issue was but they were on opposite sides of it. I had never heard this kind of challenge on the loop before, expressed with gruff hostility, and no opening for discussion. The event passed and I thought it was just a bad day for the parties. Little did I know.

We were getting ready for the beginning of simulations with the crew in the simulator and the flight control team in MCC. These simulations were designed to test our plans and procedural reactions to various problems and were the final steps in training for a flight. We took them very seriously. The first run turned into a circus when the first couple of malfunctions were inserted by the training team. From the crew came "Whoop de doo, this case is crazy and not worth our time." A continuing diatribe for several minutes rolled out of the crew cabin. As the run finished, we gathered on the communication loop to debrief this simulation.

Before the complaining started up again, I announced, "This training is important for the flight, we must have your cooperation with what we are trying to accomplish here. We can't have this circus routine, so unless you cooperate with what we are trying to accomplish, we will not continue." More contention and finally, I said, "Okay, let's go see Chris and Deke, we will take the tape over and let them listen to it to settle this dispute." From the CDR came, "tape, tape, what tape?" I told them it was standard practice to help us with the debrief and reconstruction if necessary. All of a sudden, the tone changed and confrontation melted into cooperation. This change in attitude was fine by me and we went through the next two months or so with no disputes and again I thought it was behind us.

On October 11, 1968, the countdown culminated in a perfect launch and a brand new Apollo spacecraft in a nominal orbit with a crew of three ready for ten days of wringing out our new Apollo CSM ship. By the next day, Wally had come down with a bad head cold. Lot of flight surgeon talk back and forth and by the 2 am press conference, we had a big audience of "newsies" looking for the "head cold" story. This interest in the head cold continued for the rest of the flight, but things got worse. In the meantime, we had a lot of work to do and a lot to learn about this new vehicle. We had preplanned tests and a longstanding approach to follow up on those tests results to learn all that we could.

We soon had a problem with the first time use of an onboard television camera to connect the country with what was going on in our spacecraft. Wally had been against this idea of an onboard TV from the beginning and refused to use it in the first scheduled slot. This led to more discussions/arguments with Deke. Finally, the CDR was willing to use it later and we soon listened to the "Wally, Walt, and Don show" for ten to fifteen minutes every day. It's amazing what being on TV will do for your disposition. He still had an outburst about "going to be an onboard flight director for these updates," which are computed on the ground to get to the desired conditions and often vary from the preplanned nominals. This griping was really starting to get to me. About half way through the flight, my wife, Marilyn was walking me around our street every night to let off steam. This was done out of the earshot of our children, because my reaction was becoming bluer in tone. Wally had his final argument with Deke prior to entry. Wally refused to wear his helmet because he was concerned about clearing his passages during entry and having his hands free to get to his nose. On the other side, the risk was losing cabin pressure that would result in the loss of the crew.

Wally did what he wanted.

This had to be really hurtful to Deke also, who was always a great defender of crew prerogatives and choices and a long time friend of Wally.
It was a very rare occasion when Deke communicated personally with
the crew during the flight. And Deke must have had more than his fill
of arguing in public and rebukes from his Commander.   He was done
with these fun and games. Apollo VII landed.

Flight Directors

Gene Kranz, Glynn Lunney, Gerald Griffin

None of the crew ever flew again, either by their choice or other circumstances. Wally had already announced his decision to retire before the
flight. However, his crew mates, Walt and Don, had been in a 'no-win'
box and seemed to get more uncomfortable with it as the flight progressed. Allegiance, in this case to their Commander, should be a two
way street with a balanced set of reciprocal obligations. The example of
the leadership of Chris Kraft illustrates how he gave opportunity, wise
direction, support and trust to us. In return, we gave him our loyalty,
respect and very best efforts. The result was in perfect harmony for all
of us and with the purpose and mission of the larger manned space team.
Everything fit and the net balance for all parties overflowed with mutual
satisfaction. In the case of the crew, the Commander received the allegiance of his crew mates. But, what did the Commander provide in
return to his crew and the entire Apollo team? Did his actions support
the interests of himself, his crew mates, the MCC team and the larger
manned space team? Did they lead to benefits which were appropriately
balanced for all parties? The answer is No. As a case study of real-
world leadership, this had to grade as a sorry failure. The actions did
not even support his own interests and resulted in a sad way to the end

an otherwise great career.

I was often asked what the other astronaut reactions were to the Apollo VII fiasco. Although I never said this publicly, I privately pointed, not to any verbal comments by members of the astronaut corps, but to the FACT of complete cooperation from the crews of Apollo VIII, IX, X, XI, etc. They were the testaments that said it all.

Somewhat overshadowed by the circus environment, Apollo VII made an absolutely vital contribution to qualifying the new CSM to support the upcoming flights. I did not know what the next step was until my friend Cliff Charlesworth, who was assigned as lead flight director of Apollo VIII, laid the plan out for me before I even left the MCC building. He told me there was good chance of going to the moon on the next flight. My first reaction was, "that's crazy, we are not ready yet and that's a big change to the planned sequence." But, by the time Cliff and I left the control center, twenty to thirty minutes later, I was smiling, no, *grinning*, about what was to come.

In the aftermath of Apollo VII, Chris and I and others were invited to a visit at President Johnson's ranch. And, that was quite a show. Chris was included in a driving tour of the ranch, with the President driving through the pastures in a Lincoln convertible at a brisk speed, as he introduced his herd to the NASA officials. The President impressed me as a big, strong, forceful man very accustomed to getting things his way. He was much more impressive in person than the schoolteacher image he conveyed on TV. And Lady Bird Johnson was as gracious a lady as I have ever met. She saw to it that we were well attended while her husband was touring. She was far more gracious and engaging than the media portrayals of her at the time. Not the first or last time that the media should be ashamed.

Apollo VIII

Unbeknownst to me, Chris had discussions with some of his immediate staff in April of 1968 that blossomed later. He was thinking out loud and brainstorming with the staff about the current state of problems – schedule delays of the LM and its software. He was insistent that each mission should make a real contribution to clearing the hurdles to the earliest possible lunar landing. I was told later that the concept of a lunar flyby or a lunar orbit mission was mentioned in that context. John Mayer jumped on these ideas enthusiastically and Chris told him to continue to develop such options.   I'm sure that John went had his lunar wizards at full speed within the hour. Ideas for lunar alternatives were in play. This raises another dimension of the Kraft/Mayer synergism.

Whenever we moved into a new field such as rendezvous, lunar trajectories, LM landings, or navigation around the moon—Chris always seemed very proud to ask John Mayer to illuminate this new territory for all of us. And John was the coach who always seemed to have whatever was needed in development. I called them the mission planning wizards – Ed Lineberry, Hal Beck, Emil Scheisser, Dave Alexander, Ken Young, Bob Becker, Bob Regelbrugge, dozens more and they showed up when needed, always with answers.

By late July, George Low was discouraged about the rate of LM progress. Shortly thereafter, he introduced the idea of flying to the moon on Apollo VIII without the LM. Bob Gilruth, Chris and Deke all soon agreed. I expect that they had the same reaction as I did when I found out about the plan. And then the idea sinks in. We have the CSM ready after Apollo VII, Marshall knows how to fix the Saturn V, we have an "open" flight slot. We can go to the Moon and we can fill in one big hole in our experience. When Cliff had told me about it, after Apollo VII, I went in minutes from "crazy" to "brilliant, breakthrough, and why didn't I think of that?" And this is where the earlier staff work paid off. John Mayer and Bill Tindall were aware of the difficulty of lunar orbit navigation from the earlier unmanned probes, so their approach was to go for a lunar orbit with the same geography as the landing mission planned. This would map all the specific mass concentration anomalies in the gravity field. With that work as background, Chris quickly persuaded the MSC brain trust. Lunar orbit was a bigger step with more risk than a lunar flyby, but we had to do it soon anyway. To state the obvious, we can't land on the moon until we go in orbit around the moon. On that same day, the MSC management, immediately flew to Huntsville, Alabama to describe the concept and enlist Von Braun's team to become part of the solution.

It would take further study, but Von Braun and Sam Phillips thought it was great, the best idea they heard yet. And so, the marketing of a beautiful idea started, to the rest of NASA Headquarters, to the industry leadership, and the rest of Washington external to NASA. NASA did an amazing job keeping this plan close to the vest, until all the reviews were made, all the necessary approvals were reached and Apollo VII was successful. It is easy for me to imagine the excitement that was growing and then leaping across this Apollo team. This is what we came for. And in early November, the news went public with six weeks to launch.

1968 had been a year of turmoil for the American public. It started with the TET offensive in Vietnam, a US military victory turned into an advertised defeat by the media, the hippie movement, the drug scene, the assassinations of Martin Luther King and Robert Kennedy, civil rights marches, President Johnson's refusal to run for another term and ended with the Democratic convention in Chicago with protest and mayhem in the streets. America had to be ready for some good news.

Cliff was the lead flight director joined by Milt Windler and me on the other shifts. This was a mission made for the trench team. It was all about navigation, guidance, and new lunar propulsion requirements for going into and leaving from lunar orbit. Jay Greene, Chuck Deiterich, and Gran Paules were on the launch shift with Cliff. The other shifts would be manned by Ed Pavelka, first time as Apollo prime, Phil Shaffer, and George Guthrie at FIDO, Jerry Bostick, John Llewellyn at RETRO, Charlie Parker, Ken Russell, and Raymond Teague at Guidance. This was a very strong team and we still had an equally strong trench team supporting Gene's preparations for Apollo IX. That mission was planning a work out with the command service module and LM manned vehicles in earth orbit. We would also add additional guidance operators to cover both of the ships.

The Marshall (MFSC) team did a superb job in quickly understanding and fixing the problems of Apollo VI. The entire Saturn stack was in countdown on the morning of December 19, 1968. After liftoff, the crew of Frank Borman, Jim Lovell, and Bill Anders were in orbit in about twelve minutes and on an escape trajectory in a few short hours, aimed at orbit around the moon. Once on the coast phase, my team came on duty and we became involved in resolving an anomaly during the first SPS burn. There was an excess of helium in the propulsion system from the loading process at the launch site. The engine passed this non-combustible gas during the burn. The MCC operators analysis was confirmed by Harry Galenas of North American Aviation. He was able to match the anomaly to the helium loading process and restored full confidence in the SPS. At the time I was dealing with this anomaly, all of the MSC and Headquarters management were off listening to an onboard recorder that had just been dumped to the ground (this meant that the contents did not go out over the normal air to ground loop). On the tape, the crew reported the first motion type sickness in one of our astronauts, Frank Borman. This event made for much conversation with management and the flight surgeons, but in the end the crew had a three day coast period out to the moon with light housekeeping duties. Before arrival at the moon, the symptoms had sufficiently abated.

Another peculiarity of the trajectory and the lighting was that the crew never did see the moon as they approached.   My team was on for the lunar orbit insertion (LOI) burn.   There was universal awareness that, once in lunar orbit, the SPS propulsion system was the only system that had enough energy to boost the CSM out of lunar orbit and on the way back to earth. NASA had become famous for redundancy, but here there was no backup to the SPS.   Our mission rules said we had to have an essentially perfect system to proceed with LOI. We did and the capcom relayed the "go for LOI."   Soon the spacecraft would go behind the moon and lose all communication with earth.   The LOI burn would oc-cur in the middle of the pass on the back side of the moon.   In MCC, we would have an early indicator that the burn had started and then that it was close to nominal.   One clock was set up to count down to the acquisition of signal of the communications system assuming there was no burn at all.   This condition meant that the spacecraft would still be flying at much higher speeds and would arrive back in view of the earth about two minutes earlier than the nominal time line would be. We had a clock also counting down to the nominal arrival of the spacecraft within our communication coverage.

Waiting was something we had become used to, but this wait had a distinct edge to it. Most of the flight controllers sat quietly, eyes on the two clocks listening and probably offering a prayer. In due course, the first clock reached zero and there was no communication from the ship.

The second clock continued to count, reached zero and almost at the same time, the crew re-ported that the spacecraft was in lu-nar orbit. It was lu-nar orbit on Christ-mas Eve 1968. Playing to an Ameri-can audience, which was overdue for a reason to celebrate, it choked up all of us.   Misty eyes, nods all around, and touches on shoul-ders and backs were

Earth Rise

the shared signs of a decade of work together by the MCC team.

The crew had a good time picking out craters and landmarks and matching their visuals to their lunar maps. They were the first humans ever to look at the moon this close up, and to contrast it with their view of earth, a beautiful blue planet in the blackness of space. What a time, what a Christmas Eve. And then on the next to last orbit, the crew conducted a TV tour looking inside and outside the windows. It seemed to me to have an undercurrent of reverence for what we were seeing, and then Bill Anders started and they each contributed to the reading of passages from Genesis. "In the beginning, God created the heaven and the earth." And the familiar voices of our friends softly recounted the biblical story of creation. And as one, all of us in MCC felt the power and awe of the moment. We could only look at each other.

In another revolution, the spacecraft was on the way home – a nominal return, and a perfect splashdown in the blue Pacific. Apollo VIII was recovered by the Navy crew of the USS Yorktown, who gave up their Christmas holiday time to retrieve the spacecraft and three American astronauts. Many citizens today remember mostly the lunar landing mission as the symbol of Apollo. For us, Apollo VIII was the opening of the gates to the lunar landing mission. It was the breakthrough that made our path to the landing much less uphill, maybe even downhill. We even got a telegram from a citizen, who thanked NASA for "saving 1968."

1968 and the second half of the sixties were a traumatic time in our country. Many people, even today, are defined by what they were experiencing and even participating in during those times. Certainly, we were. But ours was a markedly different experience, very strongly felt and limited to a small fraction of the population. For us, although we were aware of all the divisions and changes tearing at our country, it was as if we lived on an offshore island. The mainland was suffering through these turmoils and upsets. We felt the pain of our countrymen but we had a mission to perform. Our life was on the island and we were completely focused on the challenge of the space race. This was our Camelot, our special place where our work was our life. We lived, and were marked by, a far different view of the sixties than the vast majority of our people who were on the mainland.

The Remaining Steps Before Landing

By virtue of the preparations for Apollo VIII, we had captured the mission mechanization in our people, the RTCC computers, our procedures, and the mission rules. The following phases were now added to our portfolio of building blocks for Apollo:

- *Launch windows to meet Lunar target conditions.*

- *The translunar injection (TLI) from earth orbit by the S-IVB.*

- *The Coast Phase with mid –courses, passive thermal control and abort plans*

- *Lunar orbit insertion (LOI)*

- *Lunar orbit operations*

- *Transearth injection for return to earth*

- *Coast phase home with mid-courses to meet entry conditions.*

Short of the actual landing and EVA, we were now planning to demonstrate the lunar landing sequence of propulsion maneuvers of both LM stages and the CSM. These would be performed first in earth orbit on Apollo IX and then in lunar orbit on Apollo X. This was a simple, logical plan to capture all of the requisite experience short of landing and EVA.

Apollo IX

The crew of Apollo IX was Jim McDivitt, Rusty Schwieckart, and Dave Scott. Jim and Dave were Gemini veterans and this was the first flight for Rusty. Gene Kranz was the lead flight director for Apollo IX. The LM team, trench operators and systems flight controllers were ready while another set prepared Apollo X. Dave Reed was the experienced hand at the Lunar Module, and the leader of the Trench team at FIDO. Greene, Boone, Kennedy and Pavelka rounded out the FIDO team. Fenner, Renick, Paules and Wells were at Guidance with Jim I'Anson, prime at RETRO, and Spencer, Deiterich, Elliot and Llewellyn on the other shifts. The crew and the MCC team put the vehicles through their scheduled paces and all of the new equipment worked just fine.

This was a tribute to another of the major Apollo contractors, Grumman and their sub-contractor team. The only threat to the timeline was not hardware but a human one. Rusty came down with the same kind of motion sickness which affected Frank Borman on Apollo VIII. The Apollo spacecraft was different from Mercury and Gemini because it was a bigger cabin and enabled the crew to move around, much more so than the strapped in the seat configuration of Mercury and Gemini. This resulted in a scrub of an EVA backpack test and a space walk by Rusty from the LM to the CSM. All in all, Apollo IX was a great test of the LM and the team was beginning to feel the lunar landing within reach. Next up was Apollo X on May 18, 1969.

Apollo X

Tom Stafford was the commander of Apollo X with a crew of Gene Cernan and John Young and a combined total of five Gemini flights in experience. Tom and Gene had flown Gemini 9 together and with John Young, they were very well versed in the rendezvous sequences as was the MCC team. This Apollo X crew was the only one which carried three crewmembers, all of whom served as commanders of Apollo flights. I was the lead flight director with Gerry Griffin, Pete Frank, and Milt Windler. Bill Stoval was the prime FIDO after less than two years with us, with Shaffer, Greene, Kennedy and Guthrie each on-console for some of the critical phases. Russell was the prime for a Guidance team of Paules, Renick, Bales and Teague. Tom Weichel was the prime RETRO with Deiterich, I'Anson and Elliott. We had considerable depth in the Trench by this time, with a cast of solid operators at all positions.

The mission was planned to provide as much Apollo XI specific information as possible. Once in lunar orbit at sixty miles altitude, the timeline called for the descent orbit initiation maneuver that put the low point of the orbit about 50,000 feet or eight miles above the moon surface where the powered descent to the moon would take place for the landing mission. This was the first time at this low altitude and it had to feel like the LM was clipping the mountains. Gene Cernan relayed that sentiment to the world with "We is GO – we is down amongst them." And later, "That one looked like it was coming inside." Tom was known for some salty language of his own. Picking out a crater, he remarked "there's old Censorinus, bigger than shit." Gene affectionately called Tom "mumbles" because it was hard to understand him sometimes. Tom's annunciation always seemed to clear up just when he was compelled to observe something with a salty remark. No harm done, just men working. Gene Cernan added a "SOB" later when the spacecraft control system put in a rapid attitude change when Gene was not expecting it. A big descent stage maneuver and later separation of the ascent stage with the crew cabin set up the rendezvous chase by the LM ascent stage just as it would be two months later. Rendezvous was completed, and they docked with the command ship and after almost sixty-two hours in Lunar orbit, the crew was on its way home. One minor problem with fuel cell 1 caused it to be taken off line while in Lunar Orbit. The fuel cell was put back on line for TEI and then kept in reserve off line during the flight back home.

The LM worked to perfection. Our last set of questions and uncertainties, those which could be answered were, and we and the world started counting the days to Apollo XI.

Apollo XI

After the years of anticipation, the time for landing on the moon was at hand. Two choices remained open until fairly close to launch. The first was: which crew man would climb down the ladder first and into the history books. The second choice was when to do the moonwalk after landing (relatively soon or after a sleep period). The landing crew was Neil Armstrong and Buzz Aldrin while Mike Collins flew the CSM solo in lunar orbit. Each had flown one Gemini flight.

Probably of equal or greater significance to Gemini experience, Neil had strongly supported the use of the lunar landing training vehicle (LLTV) at Ellington and flew it when he could. The LLTV was an ungainly contraption that looked like a metal bed frame with a throttle-able engine to simulate the descent propulsion system and an attitude control system with small thrusters. There was an ongoing discussion between the crew office and some of the MSC management, Chris and Bob Gilruth in particular, about the wisdom of continuing to fly this machine. Neil had ejected from it once during 1968. A new version was produced to fix previous problems and the chief of the aircraft pilots, Joe Algranti, ran a test flight. He also had to eject. The crew office, especially Neil, insisted that it provided the necessary link in training for the final minute of selecting a landing spot and putting the vehicle down safely. Much discussion ensued but still Neil and Buzz separately flew this training vehicle on different days in the month immediately before their launch. I believe that Neil was one of, if not the only, pilot who could have convinced management to continue to fly it. Such was the respect earned and accorded to Neil and his piloting judgment.

When the decision of which crewman would be first down the ladder, the initial deliberations revolved around the unspoken assessment of the respective qualifications of the two men. At this stage of consideration, the choice leaned heavily to Neil. Eventually, it was observed that the path of opening the LM hatch swung the edge of the door inward and from left to the right side of the cabin, making it conclusive that the crewman on the left side of the cabin, Neil, was clear to go out first. In my view, this supplied a technical rationale for what the choice would have been anyway.

Returning to the subject of whether to do the moon walk soon after landing or schedule a sleep period, we flew with the latter timeline as the baseline plan with the understanding that circumstances might well lead to the early moon walk. After the actual landing, the early EVA won out, as in, "how could anybody just go to sleep while the long sought prize was there for the taking?"

The Trench team had many tough phases to prepare and train for and more than enough talent to cover them all. Greene, Reed, Shaffer, Boone and Bostick were the FIDOs. Deiterich, I'Anson, Spencer, Elliot, Weichel and Llewellyn manned the RETRO position. Guidance assignments were Presley, Paules, Bales, Russell, Renick, Fenner, Mill and Wells. Certainly, the Guidance officer was about to earn his pay.

Another late development found in the landing simulations was the appearance of computer program alarms during the powered decent to the surface. To Gene Kranz's landing team this was a brand new problem to be understood and defensed. It fell to the guidance team to orchestrate the solution technically with advice from the onboard software team at MIT and Houston. The program alarms were an indication that the computer was being asked to do more then it could within the computing cycle and this is what the alarm was trying to tell us. More was learned and understood about program alarms in these last few weeks than we ever knew about them in the years leading up to the flight. With that in our tool kits, the team was "GO" for the moon.

Apollo XI lifted off on July 16, 1969 to the rapt attention of the entire world and especially the hundreds of thousands who would see and feel it at the launch site. Man's first big step in reaching for the stars was underway. The mission events occurred as nominal - a term we had learned to dearly love. We are often asked how it feels to be in MCC. Most of the time is a relaxed but guarded diligence. But, for the big mission phases, it is like an electric field is raising the hair on the body and stimulating the synapses firings inside ones' brain. I love that feeling of readiness and concentration.

The MCC team - the Trench, the systems controllers for the CSM and LM, the communications controllers, the planning positions and the flight directors - was an average age of twenty-eight and ready for the biggest events of their young lives. And, no matter what shifts we were assigned, we were all plugged in at the consoles for landing and the expected moonwalk.

But during descent, computer program alarms started. Neil reported "program alarm 1202, 1202." Our young guidance officer Steve Bales, with his staff support team led by Jack Garman, responded "We are Go on that alarm, Flight." Three more program alarms showed up on the way down. Steve and his team assessed them all as "GO." And then it was "60 seconds" called up from the MCC, alerting the crew they had only that much more fuel before having to land or abort. Buzz reported "60 feet, down 2.5 fps, 2 forward." Neil was searching for a landing spot. Then "30 seconds" was called up. Buzz called "40 feet, picking up some dust, 30 feet. 2 1/2 down" Landing was close and then we heard: "Contact light. Shutdown. OK, engine stop." *Landed.* Soon Neil came on to tell us and the world, "Houston, Tranquility base here, the Eagle has landed." Capcom Charlie Duke replied, "Roger, Tranquility. We copy you on the ground. You got a bunch of guys about to turn blue. We're breathing again. Thanks a lot." And it was true. The last stages of landing seemed to be the longest seconds in our flight history.

Cliff was the lead flight director and was on duty for the Moon Walk. From "one small step for man, a giant leap for mankind" to back inside the cabin, the grainy images captured us and the world for a short time of absolute wonder. Soon it was time for the ascent and rendezvous with Mike Collins in orbit and my black team was on duty. For most of the MCC shifts, we were always mindful of the possible mission conditions that would lead to terminating a phase and downgrading to a reduced mission. Once the phases began that were "coming home," there was no "NO-GO," only "GO" and whatever it might take to keep it that way. LM ascent was the start of the only "GO" stage of the mission. Some events might be delayed but only temporarily. After LM liftoff, we experienced more of that wonderful "nominal" stuff - docking, LM jettison, TEI, mid courses, entry and splashdown.

The recovery carrier carried a new trailer onboard, which looked much like one of those Airstream travel trailers. This would be home to our astronauts for an evaluation period as a precaution against bringing back to earth some alien biological agents. They smiled through the window and through this process, perhaps knowing that these were their last few days of privacy and calm. We stood around the control center, flags in hand, cigars all lit, congratulating each other and not wanting the moment to pass. My mind turned to what it took to get to this point and the people who made it happen- the work, the good times, the tough times, the sacrifices, the fire, our leaders and this MCC team of mostly '20 somethings' all of it came flooding in. We did something that started out as impossible. And it was accomplished in eight years and two months from the day of President Kennedy's speech in May, 1961, less than 100 months. Good job, guys.

First Men on The Moon July 20, 1969

On the Soviet side, since the first flight of Soyuz 1 in April of 1967 that ended in the death of Vladimir Komarov, their program was going through a recovery of its own. In 1968, Soyuz 3 flew with one crewman, Georgy Beregovoy. On January 14, 1969, Soyuz 4, commanded by Vladimir Shatalov, lifted off. Three cosmonauts, Krunov, Yeliseyev and Volynov followed the next day in Soyuz 5. The mission was a real rendezvous and their first manned docking. Two of the Soyuz 5 cosmonauts transferred into and returned in Shatalov's Soyuz 4 spacecraft. And that was the last manned mission for our competition before the moon landing. Unknown to us at the time, the giant heavy lift, Russian N-1 rocket failed and blew up on the pad in July, 1969. An unmanned probe, Luna 15, crashed on the moon on July 21, 1969 *during* the Apollo XI mission.

Apollo started as part of the US-Soviet Union global confrontation known as the Cold War. The Cold War began shortly after the end of WW II and was the global state of affairs until the Soviet Union dissolved in 1989. While it was ongoing, this confrontation was competed in many theaters and at various levels of hostilities, some conducted by proxies. It lasted for about forty-four years. The "space race" began with Sputnik in 1957, approximately the start of the second quarter of the Cold War. By the halfway point in 1969, the "space race" had been won. Within fifteen months of Apollo XI and after Apollos XII and XIII, I would travel with a 5 person delegation headed by Dr. Gilruth to Moscow in October, 1970 to discuss the possibility of establishing requirements for the technical systems for rendezvous and docking in order to make possible the rescue of astronauts or cosmonauts by space-ships of the other countries. From a competitive condition to a limited but admirable cooperative effort was the next step. This eventually led to the test flight of all these equipments. It was also a test of the mutual trust and commitment of both countries to this humanitarian purpose. During this effort, I met many of the cosmonauts from the sixties flights and some of the men behind the Soviet programs. The Apollo Soyuz flight experience also was the foundation for the decision in the nineties to invite the Russians to join the existing international partnership on what is now the International Space Station- a global effort involving sixteen countries and expanding.

As Apollo recedes in time and becomes more historical then contempo-rary, the significance of Apollo will draw more discussion and debate. Eventually, in the long sweep of history to come, it will be seen as a starting point. We might ask ourselves what else happened in the 1400's besides Christopher Columbus in 1492.

In the immediate aftermath of Apollo XI, I remember somebody inter-viewing many of us in NASA and soliciting our views as to the signifi-cance of Apollo. Many answers were in the geo- political, security and technology realms. You could classify mine as more a view as to how far and fast this human race has come- the first time we humans left the planet and visited our nearest neighbor in the solar system- 200,000 years since homo sapiens appeared and about a million of our genera-tions. And of all of those humans, we were the fortunate few who were given the opportunity to work the Apollo program. What a gift. I will forever be proud of this operations team- planners, MCC operators and astronauts and especially the young men of the Trench. And to our leadership, thank you for your trust in us. It has been the greatest of pleasures to serve with all of you. God bless you all.

Epilogue --Family

Mom and Dad gave us our start in the small coal-mining town of Old Forge, Pennsylvania. Their faith in God and life was reflected in the birth of three boys, Glynn, Bill and Jerry, in the continuing depression of the thirties and our sister Carol after the war. Their faith in us was always evident in the high expectations they set for us, and the quiet encouragement that was ever present. From the present perspective of my own lifetime, I have a much sharper appreciation for what they did and what it must have taken. Thank you Mom and Dad - you set us all on different but satisfying courses, even if we then moved away from home and raised our families that you loved in distant places.

It is amazing how two decisions we make early in life have such long-standing consequences for us. Before we are mature enough to know much, we choose a career path and a spouse. Profession choices usually work out and, with an education, can be adjusted. But, this choice of spouse is a first order determinant to our wellbeing, state of mind and happiness. Marilyn and I recently celebrated our fiftieth anniversary with family and friends. We are on the other side of life from those choices now. And I treasure all the good times and joys with our loving family and I have to wince at my shortcomings.

With four kids, Marilyn served on every child-related activity in Friendswood. As a first, she initiated the start of the Catholic Church in town when baptism for Shawn was two towns away. Then came swimming, cub scouts, brownies, and boy scouts, little leagues for every sport, horse lessons, PTO, PTA, and others I probably never knew of. Eventually, the school board and then president of the school board were guided by her "close to the kids" insights. The community drafted her for a new justice of the peace position in recognition of her service and an election with four contending lawyers could only have one outcome. For the Trench, there was a magic time in the sixties and early seventies when our home was their home and gathering place, even after they married. It was part of the bonding of this band of brothers that has lasted a lifetime and full credit goes to Marilyn for her patience and caring.

It goes without saying but must be proclaimed—Marilyn made it possible for me to participate fully in this grand adventure. She managed the daily press and crises of family life and did so with caring, competence and common sense. It was comforting for me to know that all would be well with the Lunney unit while I contributed what I could to our Nation's space program.

Our kids went on to professional careers. Jenny is a veterinary specialist in cardiology and internal medicine, and runs her own business with husband Kyle of the same credentials. Their three girls are Erin, Caitlin Shea and Daira. Glynn graduated with a BS in Petroleum engineering, worked a few years in the 'Oil patch', went back to Stanford Law and now teaches Law at Tulane University in New Orleans. His three boys are Connor, Bryce and Grant. Shawn took his marketing degree and grew to become a business strategist VP and head of various departments for several small medical device companies. Shawn and his wife Becky have three girls: Abbey, Kendall and Jordan. Bryan is a flight director in MCC, first for the space station and now for the shuttle. We are the first family to have two generations serve in that position. His wife, Amori, works in the school system as a substitue teacher and they have three children also: Christopher, Macy and Drake. All of ours graduated from Texas A&M and are Aggies to the core.

When I look back on our family times especially early with the young men of the Trench, it is with a sense of joy and wonder. Being a husband, father and now grandfather is a wonderful gift. I confess that I have received far more than I may have deserved. It is true that the space work was an obsession for me, like so many others at the time. I missed a lot of kid activities and I never made time to coach one of the teams. However, I did try but failed (according to Marilyn and her girls) at umpiring some of Coach Marilyn's girls' softball games. The credit for bridging this gap in our family activities belongs one hundred percent to Marilyn. She was the glue that held us together and kept all of our aspirations supported and encouraged. Some years ago and somewhat accidentally, the subject of dad's missing time and its effect on our kids came up for family discussion. Our kids, old enough then to be our teachers, felt that they did get a life lesson out of those times. They did not attach much significance to dad's missing time from their games or events. Rather they saw the larger lesson. Living life with a commitment to a noble cause and the dedication to serve it well was the lesson they took away and internalized for themselves. I would add that they have improved on the lesson by a better balancing of their life's priorities.

And now to close and respectfully acknowledge:

The gift of values and formation from Mom and Dad.

The gift of such wonderful children and grandchildren.

The gift of and by Marilyn to create and sustain this
envelope of love to encompass all of us.

You have blessed me beyond measure.

Thank you.

II - Jerry C. Bostick

TRENCH MEMORIES

Copyright © 2010

By Jerry Creel Bostick
329 Meadowlakes Drive
Marble Falls, TX 78654-7105

(From the beginning through achieving President Kennedy's goal)

Growing up in rural Northeast Mississippi was a blessing which I did not realize at the time. All I wanted then was "out!" I remember working in the cotton fields watching cars pass by on the nearby road. I wondered what kind of occupation the people in the car had that allowed them not to be in my position. Where are they going? What are their jobs? How much does a car like that cost? Will I ever be able to afford a car of my own?

Even though eight generations of my ancestors, on both my Father and Mother sides, had been farmers since arriving in the United States, I definitely did not want to continue that tradition. Early on I thought there must be a better, easier way to make a living. Until I was twelve years old we did not have indoor plumbing. When we finally got it, I thought we must be rich because a lot of my friends still did not have it.

I worked with my Dad on the farm almost every day from sunup to sunset. What I did not appreciate until much later was that I was learning a work ethic which would serve me well for the rest of my life. My parents, of English, Scottish and Irish descent, were teaching me valuable lessons, like "Nobody owes you anything. You have to earn everything for yourself. Any job worth doing is worth doing right. You can accomplish anything you want, but it's up to you to work hard for it. If you want to earn the respect of others, always tell the truth, even if it hurts."

At age 13 I began to seek outside employment. My folks said that would be okay as long as it did not interfere with my home chores, which mostly involved helping my Dad with farming. We raised cotton and corn and had a few dairy cows that had to be fed and milked. At first I got a job delivering newspapers. This involved getting up early to pick up the papers by 6:00 am, then riding my bicycle to deliver them, which took about an hour. I also got a job selling magazine subscriptions. This also involved a lot of bike riding. My parents restricted my sales route to a two mile radius of home, so in a rural community, that limited my prospects.

My first real paying job was pumping gas at the grand opening of a new service station. I told the owner that I would work for free at the grand opening and that if he liked my work, he could then pay me for

Age 14

weekend work. He must have thought I did okay, because I then started working 12 hours each Saturday. I soon graduated from just pumping gas to doing lube jobs, changing oil and washing cars. My mother's specific advice was "Do any job that you have better than anyone else."

I continued working at the gas station on Saturdays and also got a job at the local theater selling popcorn at night. The projectionist suddenly quit, so I moved up to that job. I saved enough money to buy my first car when I was 15. I bought a 1950 Ford for $300. At that time in Mississippi you could get a driver's license at age 15.

Working at the theater five nights a week and at the gas station on Saturdays interfered with my school homework, but I continued to make good grades. Based on those grades, I was offered a job for one month as a Page in the State legislature. By luck, I was assigned to the Lieutenant Governor who told me he thought I should go to Washington as a Page. He contacted my Congressman who offered to hire me as a Page for a month. My parents bought me my first suit, a navy blue one, as that was the required uniform. So, at age 15 I boarded a train and headed for Washington D.C.

In those days (1955) Congress was only in session from 12 noon to about 2 pm each day. I figured I was there to work for my Congressman, so I showed up at his office each morning at 8 and asked if there was anything I could do. After Congress adjourned each day, I went back to his office and continued to work on anything else they wanted me to do. I had no idea that this was not expected and that I was the first Page who had ever done that. I just figured I was supposed to work whether the House was in session or not. So I was in his office every day hand addressing envelopes, running a mimeograph machine, or anything else they needed done. When the time was approaching for me to go back to Mississippi, the Congressman told me that "the girls in the office tell me they can't get along without you, so would you like to stay longer?"

He said that his patronage appointments were already committed for the rest of the year, but that he had spoken to the other Congressmen and Senators from Mississippi and that they could pool their patronage and allow me to stay. I was thrilled, so after clearing it with my parents, I stayed on for the next two months, rotating on a daily basis from one office to the next. Since I was missing school back in Mississippi, the school agreed to continue sending me homework assignments as they had been for the planned one month.

To my great surprise, my Congressman called the next Fall and asked if I would like to go back to Washington and work full time as a Doorman in the House of Representatives. That would require that I enroll in the Capitol Page School, which met each weekday from 6:30 until 10:30 am. I would have to find my own apartment, mentor his Pages who he would continue to have on a monthly basis, and to work in his office when not on duty as a Doorman. I was thrilled to accept. At last, a job other than farming!

So I worked as a Doorman in the House for the next two years and attended Capitol Page School. I graduated as Valedictorian.

VP Nixon presenting my CPS Diploma

Nearing graduation time I begin to think a lot about what I would do next. My Congressman though I should go to the University of Mississippi and major in law, as he had. I didn't really want to be a lawyer and I didn't want to go to Ole Miss. My Mother, an elementary school teacher, was a graduate of Mississippi State and that's where I wanted to go.

I took an aptitude test which said I should either be an engineer or a funeral director! I certainly did not want to be a funeral director, so I started thinking about majoring in engineering. I checked a book out of the Library of Congress titled "What Engineers Do." After reading it, I was convinced that I wanted to be an engineer. The only question being what kind? By my senior year in college I still had not settled on exactly what type of engineer I wanted to be, so I figured out which branch of engineering would be the quickest in which to get a degree. That turned out to be Civil, with emphasis on structures. I thought I was destined to design and build structures (buildings, bridges or whatever) and was very comfortable with that choice.

During my college years I had several jobs to pay for tuition and expenses. I washed dishes in the cafeteria, scooped ice cream in the "Dairy Products Grill" (called the DP), and delivered newspapers on campus. During the summers I initially measured cotton land for the US Department of Agriculture. Farmers were given an acreage figure for cotton and the government sent people out with aerial photographs to actually measure and make sure the farmer wasn't planting more than his allotment. I was not usually greeted with open arms and even occasionally was forced to leave by farmers with shotguns! However, I enjoyed the job because it involved "technology" I had never been exposed to before: aerial photo maps and a wonderful instrument called a planimeter, which you ran around the perimeter of a field on the map and it automatically calculated the acreage.

The last two summers of college I got a job with the Mississippi Highway Department surveying for new roads and overseeing construction of roads and bridges. I loved that job also because it too, involved technology new to me. My favorite was testing concrete samples (pigs, they were called) in the lab. I thought it was neat to put pressure on a concrete cylinder until it cracked.

When interviewing for jobs before graduation I had choices between several state highway departments, oil and gas refineries, and a couple of aircraft companies. I decided to accept an offer from Boeing in Seattle in the weights and balances department. I would be doing things I had never dreamed of, like reviewing the design of aircraft structures and calculating the center of gravity. Plus, Seattle was about as far away as I could get from the cotton fields of Mississippi. I was very happy!

Soon after accepting Boeing's offer, I was walking across the campus one day with a friend who needed to go by the Placement Office, so I went with him. The Placement Director saw me and said "I know you've already accepted a job with Boeing in Seattle, but I've been trying to get NASA to come here for interviews and they have now agreed to come, but I don't really have any good people for them to talk to. Would you please sign up for an interview and act interested?" As a favor to him I signed up. I unfortunately cannot remember the name of the NASA guy who did the interview, but he convinced me that there was no better place for a Civil/Structural Engineer than the Structures Division at the NASA Langley Research Center in Hampton, Virginia. I received a firm offer from NASA the next week, so I called Boeing and told them I wasn't coming.

In my last semester at Mississippi State, I had a GPA which exempted me from final exams. This meant I could leave early and start working at Langley. However, the ROTC commissioning date was after final exams, so I was faced with hanging around for two weeks just to get sworn into the Army. I visited with the Professor of Military Science and Tactics, (PMS&T), the head Army guy on campus to discuss my dilemma. He pulled out Army regulations and read to me: "ROTC cadets must be commissioned on the campus where they received instruction, except by permission of the Commander in Chief."

So, it appeared I was doomed to delay the beginning of my NASA career in order to receive my Army commission. When I told my wife Linda about what the PMS&T said, she asked, "Who is the Commander In Chief?" While explaining to her that he was the President of the United States, it occurred to me that while working in my Congressman's office, I had dealt with many requests for favors from constituents. There was a network of people in Washington who handled such special requests without ever getting the principals involved. So, I called my Congressman's secretary and explained my situation. The next day she called to tell me she had a letter signed by the Commander in Chief saying I could be commissioned by any officer at any U.S. military base and that she had already spoken to the Base Commander at Langley Air Force Base and that he would be happy to swear me into the Army. This meant we could leave immediately for Virginia and start to work.

Once at Langley I was assigned to the Erectable Structures Section, Space Structures Branch, Structures Division. I was assigned a research project to design, build and test an antenna that could be folded up into a very small package, launched into space and then unfurled to be used as a communications satellite antenna. At first I was really excited. What a challenge and what an opportunity! I would have use of all the wonderful facilities at Langley: test stands, vacuum chambers, etc. However, I soon began asking questions of my Section Head about who needed such an antenna, to what specific use it would be put, and what would become of my project after the one year in which I was expected to complete it. He could not give me satisfactory answers, so he sent me to the Branch Chief. Same result. So I ended up visiting with the Division Chief, Mr. Heldenfels. The real answer was that I would write a NASA Tech Note which would go out to all NASA libraries. Then "people will call you and ask questions, and most likely, ask you to help them build one." My question then was "What if nobody calls?" The answer was that I would be assigned to another research project.

This made me very uncomfortable and led me to the conclusion that I was not a research person. I would much rather work on solving known problems.

At about this time I noticed that my office mate, Jim Martin, was disappearing at lunch time almost every day without explanation. At Langley, everyone usually "brown bagged" and ate at their desk. After a few days of this, I asked him what was going on. He whispered for me to follow him out into the lab. There he told me that the Space Task Group, on the other side of Langley field, was interviewing for people to work on the manned space program, and he was trying to get a job with them. This really excited me. There was a group that probably really had some problems needing a solution. Some of my college friends had gone to work for NASA's manned space program, most in Huntsville, Alabama, but they all had degrees in Aeronautical Engineering, so I never had considered that as an option. I asked my friend if he could set up an interview for me. Anything other than research was attractive, and it was rumored that they were moving to Houston, Texas, which I though would be a much better place to live than Hampton, Virginia.

My interview at the Space Task Group was with Chris Critzos, who was an Executive Assistant to Chris Kraft. Just the association with

Chris Kraft excited me. I had read about him and seen him on TV several times, and he had become a hero of mine. He was so articulate and always very nicely dressed. He was the Flight Director of the early Mercury missions. (How much more important can one get?)

When Critzos explained to me that they were looking primarily for Aeronautical, Mechanical and Electrical Engineers, not Civil Engineers, I felt instantly as if I was doomed to research at Langley for the rest of my life. As I was dejectedly leaving his office, in walks the man himself, Chris Kraft! Critzos introduced me to him saying, "This young man is a Civil Engineer now working in the Structures Division at Langley. I explained to him that we are not looking for Civil Engineers." Kraft looked at me and asked why I wanted to come to work on the manned space program. I explained my dissatisfaction with research and I that I really wanted to work on solving real, more immediate problems. Without any more questions or comments, Kraft turned to Critzos and said, "Hell, hire him. We may need somebody to survey the moon."

So, in late March, 1962, after only doing research at Langley for 6-7 weeks, I was hired by the new NASA Manned Spacecraft Center. The first people I met were Glynn Lunney and Lyn Dunseith. They were both very nice and receptive. I knew immediately that I was going to like this new job a lot.

In the middle of all this, my wife Linda was expecting our first child. Son Michael Tiffin Bostick was born March 26, 1962, in Hampton, Virginia. Linda knew I was trying to get a job with the manned space program and that it would require a move, but she was a little surprised when she was still in the hospital and I asked how soon she would be able to move to Houston, Texas. Her reply was, "I can leave as soon as you need." She knew that I really wanted this new job, and neither of us really liked living in Hampton/Newport News, so she was as ready to go as I was.

There was only one small problem. While in college I was in Army ROTC, which meant I was facing a two year commitment in the Army. I was a little nervous about explaining this to Chris Critzos, afraid that it might blow the whole deal. However, he said that was no problem and that I needed to talk to Bob Ernull, who worked there and was serving out his Army time. Ernull explained to me the entire process: when called to active duty by the Army I would have to go to

Army school for 6-9 weeks, but that upon completion of that, I could get assigned back to NASA. I would continue to be officially in the Army and receive Army pay, but I would work at NASA just like all the regular NASA employees. What a relief! I really was going to have a job as a Steely Eyed Space Scientist! Not bad for a kid from the cotton fields of Mississippi.

My new assignment was to the Trajectory Analysis Section in the Mission Analysis Branch. My immediate boss was Carl Huss, who also served as the Retrofire Controller in the Mercury Control Center at Cape Canaveral. Pretty exciting stuff! Carl was at the time already heavily involved in preparations for Scott Carpenter's flight and was at the Cape most of the time.

He told me to follow Clay Hicks and Charlie Allen around for a few days and they would train me to do the trajectory design for upcoming missions. Within a week I was doing analysis of reentry trajectories, varying the time and spacecraft attitude of retrofire, to determine the change in landing position. If retrofire is late by 1, 2, 3, etc. seconds, how far downrange does the spacecraft land? If the spacecraft is out of the correct attitude in yaw, pitch, and roll by X degrees, how does that affect the landing point? The plots I generated from these trajectory runs ended up in Carpenter's on-board Flight Plan! Something I had created was actually going to fly in space and if the astronaut used the data, he would land closer to his intended splashdown point. How much better can life get than this?

In early April we were off to Houston. I dropped wife Linda and son Mike off in Mississippi with her parents, which was hard to do, but I had a job to do and was excited about it. In the meantime, I had received my call to active duty and was required to report to Fort Bliss in El Paso for nine weeks of Artillery training, beginning in early May. Specifics would come later

What was then called the Manned Spacecraft Center was spread all over Houston in temporary offices while the new facilities were being built in Clear Lake. The Flight Operations people were in the Houston Petroleum Center (HPC) on the Gulf Freeway. I got a room in a motel on South Main, where several other Flight Ops people were staying. Marty Jenness, a mission planning co-worker, was staying there, so we carpooled to work each day. I continued to work with Clay Hicks and Charlie Allen, mostly in planning the MA-8 mission of Wally

Schirra. Carl Huss, by phone from the Cape, still had us doing some special studies for Carpenter's MA-7 flight, but I spent most of my time on MA-8 launch abort studies which would end up in a formal publication prior to the flight. I still had a hard time believing I was doing stuff that Flight Controllers and astronauts would actually use. What an exciting job!

Just after arriving in Houston I learned that my Army report date would be May 5, 1962. I would be going to Fort Bliss in El Paso, Texas, for Artillery School. I really wanted to see my newborn son before leaving, but had not worked at NASA long enough to accumulate any leave time. I told Carl Huss about my situation and he said I should just take time off without pay and go see my son. Since Kraft was at the Cape, Huss suggested I go see Sig Sjoberg, Kraft's Deputy, and tell him I needed to take leave without pay. Huss said he would call Sjoberg and tell him I was going to make such a request and he didn't think there would be any problem. When I saw Sjoberg, he seemed to fully understand and said to give him a day or so to work on it and he would let me know.

The next day I got a call to his office. I wondered why the secretary couldn't just tell me yes or no over the phone, but if Sjoberg wanted to see me, I would surely go to his office. He asked me again where in Mississippi I was going and how far it was from the Marshall Space Flight Center in Huntsville, Alabama. I told him it was only 1 ½ hours away. He said that he was supposed to go to a meeting in Huntsville, but couldn't make it, so could I go and sit in for him? I said sure, so travel orders were cut for me to fly to Huntsville for a meeting on a Friday morning, but not return to Houston until the following Monday. Sig explained that he would expect a written report of the meeting and that if I were to use my rental car for any personal business, I would have to pay for it myself.

If I had ever doubted I was now working with a bunch of wonderful people, this proved that I certainly was. Sig had not only allowed for me to go see my new-born son, but had arranged it so that I didn't have to take time off without pay. I did write a report of the meeting which I attended on his behalf in Huntsville, and sent it to him. He called and said he would like to talk to me about it. I figured he had more questions about the meeting, but when we met he only had questions about how my son was doing.

In early May I reported to Fort Bliss for the beginning of my Army tour. The drive from Houston to El Paso was a long desolate one. It was pretty hot for that time of year, and my Chevy convertible did not have air conditioning! For nine weeks I attended Artillery school, learning about Nike Ajax and Nike Hercules missiles. The last week of school involved going to the White Sands New Mexico missile range and actually firing a couple of each. My last Hercules shot actually hit and destroyed a drone target. This was not planned, as a proximity fuse was supposed to explode the warhead a "safe" distance from the drone and only knock it down, not destroy it. I figured I would get into trouble, but it was determined that the fuse had been set properly but malfunctioned. I graduated number one in the class of about 30.

I found out later that I had been used in ROTC classes at Mississippi State as an example of how one does not do things in the military. "You do not pull strings to get around regulations. This guy has done an unpardonable thing. He got the Commander In Chief to allow him to receive his Army commission at an Air Force Base, of all places."

However, after I graduated from Artillery School as number one in

U.S. Army Air Defense Artillery Fort Bliss, Texas,
June, 1962

the class, they put my picture up in the ROTC building since I was the first cadet from Mississippi State to ever do that. I went from goat to hero in only a few months!

While at Fort Bliss, Scott Carpenter's Mercury Atlas Seven flight took place. I listened on the radio and was dismayed that he was out of attitude at retrofire and landed several hundred miles long. I said out loud to the radio, "Why didn't you use my charts? They were in your Flight Plan!" It turned out he got carried away with the scenery and did not pay attention to his attitude. He just wanted to enjoy the view from space!

Upon completion of the Artillery School, I was assigned back to NASA in Houston. I would return to the same job I left nine weeks before, but I would receive Army pay. It was a struggle for the next two years living on $238/month with no overtime pay and no Army Commissary closer than Fort Sam Houston in San Antonio, which was my official base. My Branch Chief, Carl Huss, did allow me to keep track of the overtime I worked (which routinely was 3-4 hours per day) and use it as compensatory time-off rather than use any of my Army leave. The plan was that by not taking any of my leave, I would get reimbursed for it upon completion of my two year tour.

Upon return to Houston, I heard from my good friend Tom Carter, who was then working for the Tennessee Valley Authority. Tom and I had met at Mississippi State. We had a lot of classes together and lived in adjoining apartments our senior year. Another classmate of ours was the son of the pool hall owner in Starkville, so the three of us spent more time playing pool than we did hitting the books.

Tom called to ask if there was any chance I could help him get a job in Houston with NASA. He sent in an application, and I recommended to Carl Huss that he be hired. So within a few weeks, old friend Tom and I were sharing an office in HPC. Soon after I became a Retro, Tom followed. There were now two flight controllers with Civil Engineering degrees from Mississippi State.

In 1964, about six weeks before the end of my tour of duty, the Army pulled one of its favorite tricks and reassigned me to Fort Polk, Louisiana, which was the nearest Army base to my "Home of Record" in Mississippi. The Army pays you for returning to your home upon tour completion, so by the reassignment, they would have to pay me less money for the trip.

In the notification of the change, I was ordered to report for duty at Fort Polk, Louisiana. I reported as ordered, but in civilian clothes rather than Army uniform. That caused a bit of an uproar at Fort Polk. "Where is your uniform?" In fact, I did not own an Army uniform because I wasn't required to wear one at NASA! They started asking me about my MOS...Military Occupational Specialty. What was I qualified to do? They told me I would have to buy a uniform and return for duty for the next month before my dismissal date. I ended up having to use all my military leave in order to return to Houston to work! So much for the plan for getting paid for my unused military leave.

While I was on active Army duty, Carl had gotten me promotions "in absentia." So much to my surprise, I went back on the NASA payroll as a GS-11. From Army pay to a GS-11 level at NASA was one of the biggest raises I ever received, plus I could now get paid for overtime.

During my two years as a military detailee at NASA, I worked on mission planning for Wally Schirra's and Gordon Cooper's flights. For both of these missions I got to go to the Cape for simulations and the actual missions. I don't think I was ever happier. Here I was in the middle of the most exciting thing going on in the world (or at least I thought so). Along with Charlie Allen and Tom Carter, I worked in a "back room" supporting Huss, the Retrofire Controller. This concept later became the Staff Support Room activity we had in the new Houston MCC.

Cooper's was the last Mercury flight scheduled, but I did a lot of work on a possible MA-10 flight, which would conduct a water ejection experiment from the rim of the heat shield during entry and hopefully alleviate "blackout." The blackout period during entry is caused by ionization of the atmosphere which blocks out communications for a few minutes. The water ejection was believed to be a solution to this problem, in that it would break up the ionization.

I prepared a presentation on the proposed mission and went over to the Farnsworth/Chambers building to present it to Walt Williams, who was the Deputy Director at the time. This was my first presentation to such a high-up official and I was a little nervous about it. None of my bosses, Huss, John Mayer, nor Kraft went along (which was typical of their management style), so I really was on my own. A couple of minutes into the presentation, Williams closed his eyes and I would have sworn that he was sound asleep! This made me even more nervous. I didn't know whether to continue the presentation or stop and try to wake him. I continued. Once I had concluded, he opened his eyes and asked several questions which revealed that he had not been asleep, but in fact had heard every word. He thanked me, said it was a good presentation and said he thought the water injection scheme would work. Unfortunately, the mission was not approved, so we never found out.

Shortly after MA-9, the last Mercury flight, Carl Huss suffered a heart attack. It was not life threatening, but he would not be able to continue as a RETRO. John Llewellyn moved up to the prime RETRO position and I was asked to be his understudy. Now I was going to be a FLIGHT CONTROLLER, not just a "back room" guy!! How good can life get?? I continued mission planning work for the upcoming Gemini missions, but beginning with GT-1, an unmanned test flight in April, 1964, I was a Retrofire Officer. Llewellyn had questioned why the RETRO was only a "Controller" while everyone else was an "Officer", so the name was changed.

Cape MCC
Gemini 1
April, 1964

We continued to fly missions from the Cape through Gemini 3, the first manned Gemini flight. One of the changes in the Cape Control

Center between Mercury and Gemini was the addition of a Guidance Officer position. The "GUIDO" was the third member of the Flight Dynamics team. I did not fully understand the specific contributions of the Guidance Officer until we began simulations. Charley Parker, the original GUIDO, had developed all the displays to monitor and compare the on-board and ground based guidance systems. It immediately became clear why the Guidance Officer was there and how valuable he could be to the Trench team. During the first day of simulations, Charley would tell us things during the launch phase like, "You may see a little deviation in flight path angle coming up in about 10 seconds, but don't be alarmed. The guidance system is just taking a long time to converge." To the amazement of both the RETRO and FIDO, the launch plot boards would reflect exactly what Charley had said. Lunney, Cliff Charlesworth, Llewellyn and I would just look at each other and say "How does he know all this?" Early on, Cliff started calling Charley "The Fox", not because he was sly or conniving, but because he was so quick, clever, skillful and shrewd! I began to wonder how we had ever flown the Mercury missions without a GUIDO.

GT-3 was the first manned Gemini flight, with Gus Grissom and John Young as the crewmen. After two unmanned flights and a week-long Network Simulation, I was beginning to feel comfortable as a RETRO. Of course I fully realized the difference in having two humans on-board. This was the real thing. Actions, or inactions, by the Flight Controllers could have severe consequences.

The crew simulator was in the same building at the Cape as the control center, so this made simulation de-briefings much more realistic. The crew would come into the control room and we debriefed eye-to-eye. After a long day of sims with the crew, at the conclusion of the last debriefing, I heard Grissom say "Okay, I'm headed for the Mousetrap. Anyone want to ride with me?" Nobody else said anything, so I finally said "Yea, I would like to." Gus had the coolest Corvette I had ever seen, so I was excited about getting to ride in it. Little did I know that the more experienced Flight Controllers had ridden with him before and didn't really care to ever do it again. Once we got in his car, he did a couple of tailspins in the parking lot and then headed for the main road to the gate. I looked at the speedometer as we passed the Air Force gate and we were doing 120 mph! The guard had apparently experienced this before, because he only saluted as we passed by. Gus turned into the parking lot at the Mousetrap, one of our favorite watering holes, doing about 80 mph and began doing tailspins again. Somehow, he ended up parked by the front door, with the front of the Corvette pointed toward the street, just as if he had easily backed into the spot. When we got out, I could hardly stand, much less walk. Gus just looked at me and said "You okay?" Never again did I volunteer to ride with him.

Staying at the Cape during Mercury and early Gemini flights was an experience. We scrubbed missions a lot, so we usually ended up staying there much longer than planned. This was hard on our families back in Houston, who in general thought we were off just having a good time. We did have some pretty good meals. Chris had some favorite steak houses and Glynn liked an Italian place in Merritt Island, which is where I learned to like Chianti. My favorite was Ramon's, which had wonderful prime rib. It was there that I had my first margarita. Across the street from Ramon's was Jack Bishop's Gulf station, where a guy by the name of Chuck Miller worked. We usually filled up our GSA cars there. When Chuck found out that the Mission Control Center was going to move to Clear Lake, Texas, he loaded up his whole family and everything they owned in an old station wagon and went to Clear Lake. He bought a corner lot in Nassau Bay and put in the first service station, a Texaco, there. He ran the first wrecker service from there also and made enough money to become the local Ford dealer.

If we had any spare time in the daylight, we played volleyball at the motel. Carl Huss was given the name "Dancing Bear" for the way he continually jumped around on the court (before he had his heart attack). Almost every night we would play some kind of card game, usually poker. Never being any good at the game, I usually just watched. Mostly, however, it was long days and hard work. We didn't complain, but it was <u>not</u> a vacation.

Between GT-3 and GT-4, Cliff and Glynn came to me and asked if I would like to switch from RETRO to FIDO. Cliff was going to leave the FIDO position and join Glynn as a Flight Director. They pointed out that if I chose to do so, I would have to move from the Mission Planning and Analysis Division to the Flight Control Division. I said yes, I would like to do that. John Mayer, my Division Chief at the time, had a fit. He said he would not consent to the transfer. Lyn Dunseith, a Branch Chief in MPAD, advised me to <u>not</u> do it, his rationale being that "the real work takes place in MPAD." That's the only time in my career that I did not follow Lyn's advice. I respected him greatly, but I knew what I wanted to do. Mayer, John Hodge (Flight Control Division Chief) and I ended up in Kraft's office to resolve the issue. Chris started the meeting by asking me if I wanted to transfer and why. He must have liked my answer, because he immediately said "So be it, the transfer is approved."

Several months after the transfer, Mayer offered me a job as Section Head in MPAD if I would transfer back. It would be a promotion to a supervisory job and a pay increase, so after thinking about it for a couple of days, I said yes. Mayer said he would start the paperwork. Soon thereafter, Chris showed up in the control center during a simulation. He came to my console and asked why I wanted to transfer back to MPAD. I explained the supervisory aspect and the pay increase. He asked how many people I supervised as a FIDO. When I said none, he pointed out that the FIDO position was the lead position in the Trench and that I not only supervised the RETRO and GUIDO, but also the Flight Dynamics people in the RTCC and the MPAD people in the SSR. Then he shifted to the pay increase. He said that he understood that, but that in his experience "Your needs always grow to meet your income."

He departed by saying that he would not interfere either way, it was entirely up to me. Within a few seconds after he left I concluded that he thought I should stay, so that was my final decision. If Chris Kraft took the time to talk to me about it and really gave the impression that I should stay, I wasn't about to do otherwise.

GT-4 was to be the first flight controlled from Houston. Because the control center there was brand new and we didn't want to take any chances, a skeleton crew of Flight Controllers was deployed to the Cape for the launch phase. Glynn was the Flight Director, Arnie Aldrich was the combined EECOM and GNC, and I was the combined RETRO, FDO, and GUIDO. Alan Shepard was the assigned CAPCOM, but he didn't show up for the 3-4 days of simulations we had prior to launch. At the Cape, all the switches which controlled the ground computers were on the CAPCOM console, so for the sims, I had to serve as CAPCOM as well as all three Trench positions. On launch day, Shepard showed up. As he was unpacking his head set, I went over to him and started explaining the changes in the switches on his console from what they were during the Mercury program. He never even looked up at me, but finally said "Do you know who I am?" I replied "Yes sir, I know who you are and I know you have worked this console during the Mercury program, but there have been a lot of changes for Gemini and if you don't do it right, you'll f..k the whole thing up." He looked shocked and said, "Well in that case I guess you had better show me what I'm supposed to do."

During the launch phase, the Houston MCC lost power but did not hand over to us at the Cape. Thankfully, they came back up after less than a minute, but we gave John Hodge, the Houston Flight Director, and Cliff, the FIDO, a hard time for not handing control over to the Cape like they were supposed to. Shepard operated the computer switches on his console just as I had instructed. When we built the MCC in Houston, this problem was solved by putting all the computer switches and the Abort switch on the FDO console, where they should have been all along. After launch, Glynn, Arnie and I went to the Cape Skid Strip and boarded the Gulfstream for Houston, where we would pull shifts during the rest of the mission.

We were flying Gemini missions about once every two months, so these were busy times. We also had to get used to the new control center in Houston. The capability existed to display a lot more data than we had at the Cape. We had console call-up displays, a huge rear-projection screen in the center of the room, and large TV displays on

MCC Houston with old style plotboards
Gemini 5

either side of the big screen. One new thing was the pneumatic tube system which allowed us to send messages to the RTCC, our staff support room and to all the other controllers in the MOCR. For the first two flights, we brought in the old style plot boards, like we had at the Cape, and placed them in front of the big center screen, because we were not sure the new-fangled displays would work. For those of us who had worked at the Cape, the whirring of the plot boards make us feel more comfortable.

During the launch phase of Gemini 5, Dr. Chuck Berry, the chief doctor, or "Surgeon" as he was called in the MOCR, wired me, Chris Kraft, and himself with ECG monitors. He wanted to compare our heart rates with Cooper and Conrad in the spacecraft. When he reported that Cooper had gone to sleep during the pre-launch countdown, I knew that I probably would not win the $10 bet for who would have the lowest heart rate.

About three minutes into the launch, doctors from the Surgeon's staff support room came running into the MOCR to see if I was alright. Once the crew got into orbit, they removed my monitors and told me that I had a highly irregular heart beat which I should have checked out.

I was diagnosed with Wolff-Parkinson-White syndrome, which was described to me as "a perfectly normal abnormality." In a normal heart, there is only one path for electrical signals to flow from the atria to the ventricles, causing the heart to beat. With W-P-W, there are two paths, causing the signal to get to the ventricles too soon, resulting in irregular and high heart rates. It doesn't happen all the time and I am not even aware when it is occurring. I just considered it as having redundant paths and never did worry about it. It did cost me $40; $10 each to Conrad, Cooper, Kraft and Berry.

The next Gemini flight, was even more eventful. We were to launch an Agena target vehicle and then launch the Gemini spacecraft which would rendezvous and dock with the Agena. However, the Agena exploded during launch, so an alternate plan was developed to go ahead and launch Gemini 7 on its planned date, then launch Gemini 6 which would perform the planned rendezvous, but no docking.

Cliff was the prime FIDO and did the launch and rendezvous. Of course, I was there to watch it all because I knew that if we did rendezvous, it would be a first in space flight history. The Russians had beaten us on first satellite, first person in orbit, and first EVA. If we could successfully pull off the rendezvous, it would mean we finally had beaten the Russians on something! Feeling that we should somehow celebrate this accomplishment, I asked Kraft if it would be okay if I could get some American flags, hand them out at the end of the rendezvous and ask everyone to wave them. He said he thought that was a wonderful idea, so I called Ginny Engle, the FDB secretary and asked her to find as many small American flags as she could. It turned out that her husband worked at a funeral home where they had several such flags on hand which they put on vehicles for military funerals. So, at the conclusion of the first space rendezvous, everyone in the control center waved their flags and showed how proud we were to be Americans. I believe this was the first, and last, time we ever celebrated during a mission. Tradition was that we would only celebrate once the missions was successfully concluded, demonstrated by the astronauts being safely on the recovery ship. We did continue to fly our flags on each subsequent mission.

Another flag waving event during the mission was the birth of my daughter, Kristi Anne, on December 17, 1965.

Gemini 8 was the first time we rendezvoused and docked. I was the prime FIDO, Tom Carter was the prime RETRO, and "The Fox", Charley Parker, was the GUIDO. The launch phase went well, until Charley said to me, "FIDO, you're looking good coming onto the third scale, but it's going to be a little noisier than you have ever seen before." When the Velocity vs. Flight Path Angle plot did go to the third scale (approaching the final couple of minutes of powered flight), the Titan onboard guidance system was all over the place. When Charley first warned me, I thought "Why the hell is he telling me that?", but when it happened, I probably would have had a heart attack if he had not warned me. Once again, I felt it sure was a nice thing to have a Guidance Officer sitting next to me.

We made it into orbit just fine and the rendezvous phase went great. We were pretty happy upon completion of the successful docking and were thinking about going to have a cool one. Then the crew came over a tracking station and reported that they were spinning out of control and had to undock from the Agena, thinking it was the culprit. My first thought was "Damn Agena! What a sorry piece of trash!" In order to stop the spinning, the crew had to use one of the spacecraft backup attitude control rings. The Mission Rules said that if this happened, we had to reenter at the next opportunity. So Tom and I did not hand over to the oncoming shift but started planning for a contingency area landing, which was in the North Pacific, in the dark. As far as the retrofire, entry and landing, everything went fine. Once the recovery helicopter got there and dropped two swimmers, we heard almost immediately that a third swimmer was being dropped into the water. This usually meant that something was wrong with the crew, because the third swimmer was a doctor. It turned out that the doctor was dropped because the first two swimmers were sick and throwing up. The flight crew, Neil Armstrong and Dave Scott, were fine. The contingency recovery forces had been in a bar, drinking more than they should, when called to duty for crew rescue in the North Pacific. They thought it was just another simulation and didn't take it seriously until they were over the spacecraft. Somehow, they got the astronauts onboard the helicopter just fine and then headed for the recovery ship. Armstrong told me years later that on the helicopter ride, all the recovery forces

Celebrating Gemini 8
successful recovery

were passed out on the floor. He woke up one of the guys and said "I think you're supposed to be checking us out medically. Didn't NASA send you a big box with thermometers, blood pressure cuffs, etc.?" So they found the box, opened it and started reading the instructions. Neil and Dave finally told them what to do and how to do it. Dave verified this story and added that once they were in the Admiral's quarters on the ship, a recovery guy came to him and whispered "Sir, do you know how to open the hatch and get into the capsule?" Dave replied that he did and asked why they needed to get into it. Turns out that after they got the capsule on deck, they had closed the hatch not realizing that one of their guys was still inside!

When the Agena target vehicle for Gemini 9 was lost in another Agena launch failure, the Augmented Target Docking Adapter (ATDA) was launched (on an Atlas booster) to serve as a docking target. Once again, anything having to do with Gemini docking targets had a problem. One of the lanyards on the shroud enclosing the docking adapter got hung up, not fully exposing the docking port. Telemetry signals indicated that the shroud had separated, but not jettisoned. A couple of days later when Tom Stafford and Gene Cernan completed the rendezvous, the telemetry was confirmed. Stafford said it looked like "an angry alligator." So, not being able to dock, the Gemini 9 crew conducted two more rendezvous exercises with the ATDA. Cernan set an EVA time record of over 2 hours, but his visor became fogged, and he was therefore unable to test the astronaut maneuvering unit. We were getting the rendezvous down, but successful demonstration of docking and EVA seemed to be problematic.

On Gemini 10, with John Young and Mike Collins aboard, we finally had a good rendezvous <u>and</u> docking. The rendezvous, due to some on-board navigation problems used a lot more fuel than planned, so rather than separating and practicing more docking maneuvers, they stayed docked with the Agena until it was fired to take them up to over 400 miles to rendezvous with the Agena from Gemini 8. So we set an altitude record and rendezvoused with two different targets. The EVA experience was better than Gemini 9, but still had problems. Collins, like Cernan on 9, found it difficult and tiring to move around. He got tangled in the umbilical several times.

Gemini 11 was a challenge for the Trench. We were to attempt a first orbit rendezvous (M=1, we called it), which took a lot of precision in target vehicle launch time, chase vehicle launch time and maneuver execution. This was a demonstration of the capability needed on Apollo for Lunar Module launch and rendezvous with the CSM. Ed Pavelka and Steve Bales as the Prime FIDO and GUIDO, respectively, spent many months in preparation for this dicey rendezvous and (with a little help from Pete Conrad and Dick Gordon) pulled it off perfectly.

In between Gemini 11 and 12, we conducted a Network Simulation, NS-2, to work out the kinks in the Apollo network, Phil Shaffer had done most of the work in preparation for this exercise. I sat in most of the time just to learn more about Apollo, since I had spent most of my time on Gemini, plus Grady Meyer had left and I was the new Flight Dynamics Officer Section Head.

MCC During Gemini 12

With only one more Gemini flight to go, we still had some EVA procedures to perfect. As far as the Trench was concerned, rendezvous and docking was becoming routine, and that part of the mission went off without a hitch. Much to the pleasure of everyone involved, the EVAs also went very well. Hand restraints had been added to the outside of the spacecraft to facilitate moving around and a new water tank in Clear Lake had been used for the EVA preflight training.

So now the lead-in programs, Mercury and Gemini, were complete and it was time to get on with our new National objective...landing a man on the moon by the end of the decade. We only had three years remaining, so that goal seemed like a big challenge, but one we were more than willing to take on. We felt like we were finally catching up to the USSR, if not ahead of them. We rarely talked about it, but we all wanted to "beat the Commies!"

By the end of Gemini, we had already completed three unmanned Saturn 1B/Apollo test flights, so most of the Trench Apollo guys felt pretty comfortable with the vehicle, the network and the Control Center. Now it was time for the good stuff...manned flights!

AS-204 was to be the first manned flight of Apollo. Most people now refer to it as Apollo1, which it later was named, but at the time, to us it was AS-204. AS, of course stood for Apollo Saturn. The number 204 meant that the booster was a Saturn 1B and it was the 4th flight of the

Apollo hardware. The January 27, 1967, launch simulation, officially considered not hazardous because the Saturn 1B was not loaded with fuel, was a "plugs-out" test to determine whether the spacecraft would operate nominally on internal power while detached from all ground cables and umbilicals. There previously had been a lot of problems with the Block 1 CSM and Gus Grissom, the flight Commander, had even hung a lemon inside the spacecraft.

There wasn't much for people in the Trench to do on such a pad test, other than make sure all of our countdown procedures were correct and carry out our usual interface with the Range Safety Officer at the Cape. I had been in the Control Center during the day and it seemed the test was going fairly well, even with a long list of technical problems. So, at around 4:30 PM, I left for home. Linda and I were scheduled to have dinner that night with Glynn and Marilyn Lunney and Bill and Valerie Anders. While showering, I got a call from Glynn. Linda said that he wanted to talk to me even though he realized I was in the shower. He told me that dinner was off and that he would meet me in the Control Center. "Something has happened", was all he said. Figuring that it must be something pretty big to call off dinner, I hurredly dressed and drove to the Control Center.

As soon as I got out of my car, I saw Dutch VonEhrenfried, who had been on duty as the Guidance Officer, walking toward me and openly weeping. "They're all dead" he said. That's all I could get out of him, so I dashed upstairs to the MOCR. Not much time had elapsed since "something" had happened, so the room was not yet sealed. I quickly learned that there had been a fire inside the Command Module and that all three crewmen, Gus Grissom, Ed White and Roger Chaffee, were dead. It was one of the lowest moments of my life. The astronauts were not only co-workers, they were friends.

I had a general acquaintance with Gus and knew his wife Betty and their kids. Ed White and I attended Seabrook Methodist Church together and our wives and children were friends. He and I served as co-lectors once, where we jointly read the Scripture lesson for that Sunday, alternating verses. The Chaffees lived in Nassau Bay where we lived and we had a good relationship with both Roger and Martha. That was my first thought, "I have lost my friends." It was made even worse by learning that they had been trapped inside the spacecraft and had burned. The whole thing had been recorded on the voice loops and several console auxilary recorders, but I refused to listen. It took me years to get that vision out of my mind.

This was NASAs lowest point. Many years later, people referred to Apollo 13 as "NASAs finest hour" because we were able to snatch success out of the jaws of defeat, and it is hard for me to argue against that characterization, but I firmly believe that the NASA response to the AS-204 fire was its finest hour. Before the end of the day of the accident, NASA appointed an investigation committee, called the Apollo 204 Review Board, headed by Langley Research Center Director, Dr. Floyd Thompson. The Board met the very next day at the Kennedy Space Center. Within two days, the Flight Dynamics Branch, which was located in JSC Building 45, had vacated our office space to make room for the Board when they came there. Frank Borman, who had flown on Gemini 7 with Jim Lovell, played a key role in the investigation.

One event which has received a lot of attention after the accident, was the assembly of all Flight Controllers, by the then Head of the Flight Director's Office, Gene Kranz. In the Building 30 auditorium he told us all that the accident was our fault because we had observed all the problems with the Block 1 CSM, but had not adequately spoken out. We accepted that. Near the end of his speech however, he directed all of us to go back to our offices and write "Tough and Competent" on our blackboards, because that's what we were going to be from that day forward. Some of us from the Trench just kind of looked at each other and frowned. On the way out of the auditorium Cliff Charlesworth remarked, "If you are really tough and competent, you don't need to advertise it." I did not write those words on my blackboard and I don't think anyone else in the Flight Dynamics Branch did. We mostly all agreed with Cliff.

I know Gene was sincere in his remarks and agreed with his assessment that we could all do more; but most of us, if not all, did not agree that we should adopt some new public relations campaign to show the world we would do better.

Within 21 months, NASA and North American Aviation determined the cause of the fire, redesigned the CSM to hopefully preclude a reoccurance, and launched the first manned Apollo mission, Apollo 7.

In the meantime, we flew three unmanned test flights, AS-501, -204, and -502. AS-501 (Apollo 4) was the first flight of the Saturn V and the first flight of its S-IC and S-II stages, as well as the first restart of the S-IVB stage. It was an "all up" test, a bold philosophy developed by Dr. George Mueller, the NASA Associate Administrator for Manned

Space Flight.

This cut down the total number of tests, as needed to accomplish President Kennedy's stated goal of a manned lunar landing by 1970, but it meant that everything had to work properly the first time. This was also the first time that the Apollo spacecraft reentered the Earth's atmosphere at speeds approaching those of a lunar return trajectory. To a lot of people's surprise, the mission went very well, achieving most major objectives.

AS-204 (now Apollo 5) was the first flight carrying a real Lunar Module, although as I recall, they left the landing legs off to save weight! The primary goal of the mission was to test out the ascent and descent engines and to perform a "fire-in-the-hole" test where the ascent stage of the LM would initiate firing while still attached to the descent stage. This would simulate a lunar descent abort and a normal launch from the lunar surface. All did not go well in the first attempt to fire the descent engine. After about four seconds of firing, the guidance computer shut off the engine, thinking that the thrust was not building up fast enough. Dave Reed, the Prime FIDO, and other controllers came up with a technique to start the burn manually, which worked without a hitch. The descent engine was ignited twice in this fashion and performed as planned. Then the "fire-in-the hole" burn also worked like a charm. After one more burn of the ascent engine, all major test objectives were met. This crazy looking Lunar Module, the first true spacecraft, because it could only operate in a vacuum, really did look like it would work. Dave Reed, who had spent most of his NASA career on the Lunar Module, had a good day.

AS-502 (Apollo 6) was the final unmanned Apollo/Saturn flight and only the second test of the Saturn V. Since AS-501 had gone so well, we figured this flight to be a piece of cake. Not so. During the first stage of launch, the S-IC experienced "pogo," a severe oscillating up and down movement of the whole stack. Once we got through the first stage, we figured that the worst was over and we could press on with no more anomalies. Not so, again. One of the five S-II stage engines developed performance problems and finally shut down. A few seconds later, a second engine also shut down. The Saturn Instrumentation Unit computer was able to compensate and burn the remaining three engines much longer than usual. After S-II shutdown however, the S-IVB stage also experienced thrust problems and realizing the altitude was too high, started pitching down, approaching the abort limit lines. Jay Greene, the Prime FIDO, earned his money that day, keeping his hand close to the abort switch, but remaining calm.

We finally got into orbit, albeit a rather peculiar ellipical one. Then, the S-IVB stage failed to restart, which was to be a test of the Translunar Injection. That planned burn would also have allowed another test of reentry, achieving a velocity approximating that of a lunar return. It was finally decided to burn the Service Propulsion System engine to achieve an altitude and an entry speed as high as possible. It was a good unplanned test of the SPS, but most mission objectives were not met. It was always interesting to me that even with all the Saturn V problems on this final test flight, the system was certified for manned flight without any further tests.

In 1968 I was appointed to be the JSC Range Safety Representative, responsible for coordinating the launch range safety aspects of the Apollo, Skylab, and Space Shuttle Programs with other NASA Centers and the Range Safety Office of the U.S. Air Force Eastern Test Range. Glynn Lunney had been the Rep up until then, but he and Chris Kraft felt it appropriate that an active FIDO, who had the primary interface with Range Safety during flights, be made the official Rep. The Range Safety Officer monitored the launch phase much as the FIDO did, but had different limit lines. His responsibility was to protect people and facilities on the ground, and he had the capability to terminate thrust and initiate destruction of the launch vehicle if his limit lines showed that an impact was going to be over land in the Cape area. Obviously, all FIDOS and Range Safety Officers coordinated very closely and had procedures to be used during launch to ensure that each knew what the other was thinking and doing. This close coordination became even more important on Apollo, because the Lunar Modules destined to land on the moon would carry Radioisotope Thermoelectric Generators (RTGs), which would power various experiments to be left on the moon. In case of an Apollo launch abort, the Range Safety Officer was concerned that the radioactive device could cause a lot of damage in the launch area, so we had to conduct several drop tests of the containment device for the RTG to ensure that it would survive, without breaking open, in such an abort.

Progress was being made at North American Aviation on the redesigned Command and Service Modules and the Trench turned it's attention to this critical first manned Apollo flight, Apollo 7. The computers in the RTCC had now been upgraded to IBM 360-75s, giving us much more computer power and display capability than we had previously had. There were five of these computers, each with the unheard of memory capacity of 1 megabyte! These were the latest and greatest computers that Government money could buy. We got serial number 1. Only one was used for real time support, with another serving as a back-up. The other three were used for software development.

When I became Chief of the Flight Dynamics Branch, Gene Kranz, the then Acting Flight Control Division Chief, called me into his office to explain his new rules for how the FDB would submit their requirements to the Flight Support Division (FSD) for implementation in the control center.

Historically, all Flight Control Division requirements were collected by Dick Hoover's Branch, packaged into Flight Control Data Acquisition Requirements (FCDAR), and then submitted to FSD. The one exception was the Flight Dynamics Branch. Much to the dismay of John Hodge, Gene Kranz and the other Branch Chiefs, we always worked directly with MPAD and FSD to implement our requirements. This was a tradition established by Glynn Lunney, going back to the Mercury days, when the computers and the implementors were at the Goddard Space Flight Center.

MPAD developed most of the trajectory processors, and the FSD personnel liked working directly with us to develop displays. Others in FCD, especially John Hodge and Gene Kranz, always felt we got more than our share of RTCC computer capability with this arrangement, and now Gene was going to put an end to that. He told me that if I would not submit FDB requirements through Hoover, he would find a new Branch Chief who would. My answer was that we could not operate that way and that he might as well start looking for a new Branch Chief. When I got back to my office I called Jim Stokes, the FSD Chief, and told him about my conversation with Gene. He immediately called Gene and told him that he would not accept any FDB requirements through Hoover, so if he wanted any trajectory and guidance capability in the Control Center, he had better leave it the way it was. I didn't hear any more from Gene and I got to keep my job.

Phil Shaffer was the lead FIDO for Apollo 7 and took much of the load in FDB preparation. It was a jam-packed timeline. Many spacecraft systems and flight techniques had to be tested on this flight if there was any hope in maintaining the goal of landing on the moon by the end of the decade.

On Friday, August 9, 1968, only a month prior to the planned Apollo 7 launch, things got a little more hectic. I received a call from Gene Kranz, now the Flight Control Division Chief, asking me to join him in a meeting with Chris Kraft. Arnie Aldrich was also invited; so the three of us showed up in Chris's office.

Chris, as usual, was brief and succinct. He said that George Low, the Apollo Program Manager since the fire, wanted to go to the moon before the end of the year. Assuming that the Apollo 7 flight went well, the very next one would be a lunar orbit flight, without the Lunar Module. The LM was still behind schedule, and Low saw this as the only way to maintain the lunar landing schedule. Chris said that he would need an answer as to whether we could support such a flight by the following Monday morning.

Chris said that he and Low were going to Huntsville that afternoon to see if they could have the Saturn V ready by December, and that he would let us know that night how the meeting went. He called me, and I assume Gene and Arnie, that night and said that the Huntsville folks thought he and Low were crazy, but would take a serious look at it. I then told Chris that in order to do a thorough assessment of our capability, I needed to bring in Bob Ernull from Mission Planning, and Jim Stokes from the Flight Support Division. There were just too many questions about the mission planning and the MOCR/RTCC for me to answer alone by Monday morning. Chris said he understood and said that he would call them himself, just to make sure they understood that this was an important exercise. He said he wanted to have another meeting the next morning, Saturday, with me, Gene and Arnie and that he would invite Ernull and Stokes to that meeting.

In the Saturday morning meeting, Chris expanded a little on the Huntsville meeting, and said he thought they would give a "go" because they didn't want to be the Center which said no. Ernull said that he would need complete access to both the Building 12 and the MCC computers 24 hours a day between then and Monday morning. Jim Stokes said he would need to bring in some IBM and Philco guys to help him access the readiness. Chris okayed both, but told Stokes to not tell the IBM and Philco people any more than he had to. "Bring in whomever you need, but you don't have to explain the details of the plan." I asked Chris if I could bring in Chuck Deiterich, Ed Pavelka, and Charley Parker. He said "Okay, but make sure they know this is not to be revealed to anyone else." Almost as an afterthought, Chris then said that since this would be the first time we would be using the Return to Earth software in the Control Center, and since I used to be a RETRO, he wanted me to be a RETRO again if the mission was approved. I just responded "Whatever you say."

When I got back to my office, I called Deiterich, Pavelka, and Parker and asked for them to come in as soon as they could. They all showed up within a half hour. I explained to them what was going on, who was involved, and what I needed them to do. Ernull was doing the basic mission planning, Stokes was assessing the ability to implement all the MCC software and displays required. What I needed each of them to do was look at the minimum software and displays they could live with, assess the console procedures and come up with the training requirements. I told each of them that they would be the lead operators at their positions, but explained to Chuck that Chris had asked that I be a RETRO once again. This came as a shock to Chuck, because he had not been a lead operator on a manned flight, and he realized that the team he would be leading consisted of his Section Head, John Llewellyn, and me, his Branch Chief. He did not hesitate, however, to take the assignment.

By Monday morning we were able to report to Chris that there was no valid reason we could not fly the mission in December. We could have all our procedures ready and get in the training time needed. We still had some work to do with Jim Stokes on the mimimum MOCR displays we could live with, but were confident we could work that out.

Stokes said he could have the essential software ready (Translunar Injection, mid-course corrections, Lunar Orbit Insertion, Transearth Injection, etc.) and the telemetry data that Arnie said the systems controllers would need. Ernull recommended a December 20 launch date. He also said that MPAD could support the mission with the Auxilary Computing Room (ACR) to back-up the MCC calculations as required.

Chris told all of us that a final decision would not be made for another few days, but for us to proceed as if the mission would happen, just continue to keep it under wraps. About a week later it was announced that the December mission, Apollo 8, would be commanded by Frank Borman and that it would be an earth orbit mission with a "lunar option." It did not take long for people to figure out that something strange was going on, and most suspected it was a lunar flyby, without going into lunar orbit. It was not until after the successful completion of the Apollo 7 mission that the full Apollo 8 plans could be revealed.

But before we could embark on this bold mission, we had to fly the first earth orbit flight. Apollo 7 was launched October 11, 1968.

Commander Wally Schirra was a very close friend of Gus Grissom and felt a deep personal responsibility to make sure the necessary spacecraft changes were made after the fire, and then fully tested during the mission. This, plus the NASA management's desire to test the hardware as quickly as possible, resulted in probably the most ambitious flight plan we had ever flown.

Each day was jam-packed with tests, with very little, if any, free time. One of the activities which Schirra did not want in the flight plan was live TV. He thought this was unnecessary and took up valuabe test time. He lost that argument, but never liked the idea of doing "public relations stunts" on a hardware test flight. This attitude of Schirra's, along with a very full flight plan, plus a head cold he contracted in orbit, lead to some tension between the flight crew and Mission Control.

I was not personally involved in this tension during the flight, so am not qualifed to talk about it. I do know that after the flight, both Don Eisele, the CM Pilot, and Walt Cunningham, the LM Pilot, told me they were sorry if they caused us any problems, but they were just following the lead of their Commander, Wally.

From a technical point, the flight was a huge success. The newly redesigned CSM worked really well, and everyone involved was pleased with the results. It cleared the way for the bold Apollo 8 flight to the moon which was officially announced soon afterward. One interesting note about this flight: after clearing the launch tower, Eisele said, "I vonder vere Guenter Vendt?", referring to Guenter Wendt, the long time Pad Leader, who was the last person the flight crews saw before launch. This line was later used in the movie *Apollo 13*.

With the sucessful completion of Apollo 7, the Apollo 8 lunar orbit flight was offically announced and we began an intense preparation period to get ready for this bold and exciting flight. This would be one of the toughest missions we had ever flown. The prep time was short and we would not have all the MOCR computing capability and displays we had originally planned, but nobody complained. Finally, we were going to the moon! The Flight Directors would be Cliff Charlesworth, Glynn Lunney and Milt Windler, with Cliff as lead. Obviously, everyone in the Trench was very happy to have two ex-FIDOs being the FDs on all the critical phases.

The crew assigned to Apollo 8 was one we all liked and respected; Frank Borman as Commander, Jim Lovell as Command Module Pilot, and Bill Anders as Lunar Module Pilot (even though there would be no LM on this flight). Borman had done an outstanding job in overseeing the changes to the CSM after the fire, Lovell was considered by most people in the Trench to be the best rendezvous pilot you could have, and Anders, although he had not flown before, had proven to be a very smart and easy guy with whom to work. As a CAPCOM, he had gone out of his way to learn as much as he could about the Trench and had picked it up quickly. We would be flying a dream mission with a dream team as the crew.

The launch phase went smoothly, even though we had experienced all the problems with the last unmanned Saturn V flight, AS-502. There was a little "pogo" during the second stage, but nothing like before. We spent a couple of revolutions in earth orbit and then gave a "Go" for TLI, Translunar Injection. Even though we had done this numerous times in simulations, this one was for real. In the Trench, we all kind of looked at each other and without words said "We're really going to the moon!"

TLI, transposition and docking all went well also. On the way to the moon, Charley Parker and I entertained each other with a discussion about how much we could speed up computer processing if we could come up with a decimal based time system. Pretty crazy, but a reflection of how well things were going. Early in the third mission day, we entertained ourselves with discussions of what would happen when we got to the lunar sphere of influence, a point at which the gravitational pull of the earth and moon would be equal on the spacecraft. Of course, we knew that nothing would happen, but it was entertaining to have this discussion. This would be the first time that a manned spacecraft had ever escaped the gravitational pull of the earth.

Targeting for the moon is somewhat like duck hunting. You don't shoot at the duck, you shoot ahead of its flight path and let it fly into the shot. So we were shooting (targeting) for a spot out in front of the moon's path (left side as you look up at the moon) and trusting God that the moon would get there at the right time. We wanted to miss the moon by about 60 miles, which seems like a lot, but when compared to how far we were from Earth, almost a quarter million miles, it was miniscule.

Now it was time to get ready for the Lunar Orbit Insertion (LOI) burn.

We did one more small mid-course correction burn and then started running the final calculations. I remember thinking, "Okay, this is serious business!" Not that everything we did in the Control Center was not serious, but we were getting ready to pass a maneuver to the flight crew that would put them in an orbit about the moon. Ed Pavelka, who was the FIDO on duty for this, calculated the final LOI burn numbers, wrote them on the PAD to be given to CAPCOM for his read-up to the flight crew, and then went over them about three times to make sure he had written them down correctly. Without saying anything, I knew Ed was having the same thought: "This is serious business."

Once the maneuver numbers were passed up to the crew, I really felt helpless. There was nothing else we could do. We would soon have loss of signal with the crew as they went behind the moon, where the LOI maneuver would be performed. For about 20 minutes we would have no contact with them. Never before had I experienced such a "hand wringing" time. We set the clocks on the RETRO console, one to count down to spacecraft acquisition time if no burn occurred, and one for a nominal burn. There were too many options for partial burns, so these two times would frame the situation.

Just after loss of signal, Lunney, who was the FD on duty then, said over his loop "Okay, all Flight Controllers, this is a good time to take a break." My initial reaction was, "Has he lost his mind? We have astronauts behind the moon and he wants us to take a break?" I quickly realized, however, that he was, as Glynn usually was, exactly right. There was nothing we could do for the next 15-20 minutes to help the crew and this was an excellent opportunity to go to the restroom and then come back to wait for acquisition of signal from the spacecraft.

We all got back into the MOCR well before the time of spacecraft acquisition if no LOI burn had occured. That time came with no signal, which was somewhat comforting, yet we still could have had a partial burn, which would have not been good. Finally, the time of acquisition reflecting a nominal burn came, and almost exactly on time, we heard the crew report "Houston, this is Apollo 8. Burn complete." What a relief and what an experience.

For me it was an assurance that, indeed, there was a God and He was, among other things, a good navigator. He had gotten the moon to exactly the right spot at exactly the right time! We actually had American men in orbit around the moon! About four hours later, we had the crew do a small burn to put them into a circular lunar orbit.

Earth Rising

On Christmas Eve, the crew caught all of us by surprise by reading from the Book of Genesis about the creation of Heaven and Earth. I was totally overwhelmed, and tears came to my eyes How more appropriate than a Bible reading about creation, coming from the first people to ever leave the influence of Earth, on Christmas Eve?

But now it was time to get ready for another critical burn, Transearth Injection, TEI. The Service Module engine, SPS, would have to do another perfect burn to start the crew on their way back home. We were all apprehensive once again when the spacecraft went behind the moon for the last time before the burn.

Waiting, when there is absolutley nothing you can do, is a helpless feeling. When we heard Lovell report "Houston, there is a Santa Claus," the MOCR let out another collective sigh of relief.

Apollo 8 was certainly my favorite flight up until then, and still is. It was bold, it was exciting, it was historical, and it was successful. We had finally demonstrated that we had the hardware, the techniques and the people to pull off such an awesome adventure. We also demonstrated that we were clearly ahead of the Soviets. President Kennedy's goal now really felt achievable. Of course, we had not landed, but I felt like Apollo 8 had "baked the cake," and the landing would just be putting the icing on that cake.

The next flight, Apollo 9, would start applying that icing. The Lunar Module was finally declared ready and we would test it thoroughly in earth orbit. In my mind, Apollo 9 was Dave Reed's flight. Dave had been working on the LM since he first arrived at NASA. He had made many trips to Grumman, the manufacturer, in Bethpage, New York, and to the MIT Draper Labs, and made a lot of inputs into the propulsion and guidance systems. We all kidded him about "his" flimsy, funny looking spacecraft, and he became very defensive of the LM. "It will work great. Just wait and see." Of course, many other Trenchmen had invested a lot of time and effort in the LM, but Dave was the easiest target for our "ridicule" of the LM.

As I stated earlier, Apollo 7 had been a very ambitious test flight with a jam-packed flight plan. Apollo 9 was even more jam-packed. This would be the first manned LM flight. Not only did we have to completely test the LM propulsion and guidance systems, but also a few little things like rendezvous and docking with the new Apollo hardware, and EVA. We had done all this during Gemini, but not with the much different and hopefully better, Apollo systems. The Apollo V unmanned LM flight had been a pretty good test of the propulsion systems, but now we had to test them the way they would be used on a lunar landing mission, with astronauts aboard. One of the big differences was that the LM would separate from the CSM, with rendezvous and docking absolutely critical to the survival of the LM astronauts, because that was their only way of getting back to earth.

The mission went very well, and all of us felt better about being able to reach President Kennedy's goal, now only nine months away.

A more extensive test of the whole Apollo system, including the LM was scheduled for a couple of months later. Apollo 10 would be a manned simulation of the real thing, a "dry run" of the lunar landing mission with everything except an actual landing on the moon. They would even target a landing at the site planned for the upcoming Apollo 11 flight. This flight crew was another one in which all the guys in the Trench had a lot of confidence and trust. Tom Stafford was Commander, with Gene Cernan, LM Pilot, and John Young, CM Pilot.

The Apollo 10 flight was another huge success. All the hardware, the Manned Space Flight Network (MSFN) and flight and ground crews performed as designed and expected, with few problems. Stafford and Cernan came within about 8 miles of the lunar surface, causing Stafford to say, "We're down here amongst 'em." The total system, including the Trench, was now ready for the real thing, Apollo 11, which was scheduled for July, only two months away.

The crew for Apollo 11 was yet another one with which the Trench was familiar and very comfortable. Neil Armstrong, the Commander, was

"Mr. Cool." None of us had ever seen him get ruffled. On Gemini 8, when his spacecraft went into a wild tumbling mode, he was as calm and casual as a test pilot can get, and by all accounts, did exactly the right thing. Buzz Aldrin, the LM Pilot, was a rendezvous expert and had been the guy to show that EVA was easy, if you prepare right and have the right body support, like hand and foot holds. Mike Collins, the CM Pilot, was in the "cool" class with Armstrong. He just always did a great job and took everything in stride. The Trench assignments came about by pure rotation. I would have been comfortable with a number of controllers, and we had at least two or three people who could have been lead for the new critical phases: powered descent/landing and ascent/lunar orbit rendezvous.

Prior to lift-off on July, 16, I think most of us had a similiar feeling to that which we had prior to Apollo 8, "Okay, this is real." This is what we and the Country have been waiting for. The Trench approached the flight with confidence. Even though we were confident, and this was the third time we had gone through things like translunar injection and lunar orbit insertion, we all realized that this was not a test flight. It was not a dry run. This was the mission that most of us had spent our entire careers preparing for.

The mission went extremely well until we got to powered descent. About 5 minutes into descent, the LM guidance computer started issuing a series of 1202 and 1201 alarms. Computer alarms are not what you want to get during such a critical phase. After Armstrong reported the first one, I immediately looked at Steve Bales, the GUIDO on duty. Steve, with confirmation from our SSR, reported to Flight what we were "go" with that alarm. Shortly thereafter, the second one was reported by Armstrong. Again, Steve told Flight "We are go on that one. Same thing." We determined later that the alarms were just a report that the primary computer was getting behind on its tasks and needed to terminate some non-essential calculations. A few years before, a Draper Lab software programmer had written a program that prioritized the calculations the computer had to do and would terminate the one at the end of the list if the computer became overloaded. This was somewhat revolutionary in computer programming. It turns out that the alarms were occurring because the rendezvous radar as well as the landing radar was operating. The rendezvous radar, which was tracking the CSM in lunar orbit so that it would be ready if we had to abort the landing, was obviously at that point less important than the landing radar, so the computer was just announcing that it was becoming overloaded and was going to terminate the lowest priority job.

Then it became obvious from crew reports that they were going long and could not find a nice smooth spot to land. The last few seconds before landing were very tense, as we were approaching running out of fuel. We all started breathing again when Aldrin reported they were "kicking up dust", indicating they were low enough that the descent engine exhaust was impinging on the lunar surface. Then finally, Armstrong's report: "Houston, Tranquility Base here. The Eagle has landed." WE HAD DONE IT!

It came as no great surprise that Armstrong and Aldrin decided they would start preparations for the first EVA, rather than waiting until after their scheduled sleep period. Every astronaut and flight controller descended on the MOCR. Everyone wanted to be there and witness the first step on the moon.

Each console had four places (jacks) to plug in ear phones, and these places soon filled up. Pete Conrad, who was scheduled to be Commander on the next lunar flight, could not find an open jack at the CAPCOM console, so I invited him to plug in to the last jack available at the FIDO console.

Pete and I were sitting on the small ledge behind the FIDO console when Neil stepped onto the lunar surface and said, "That's one small step for man, one giant leap for mankind." Pete turned to me and asked "What did he say?" I told him that Neil had said something about "a giant leap for mankind." Pete thought about that for a couple of seconds and said "That's just like Armstrong to say something profound like that. If it had been me I probably would have said 'Jesus Christ, that shit is slippery!'"

When I left the Control Center, I went to a local liquor store and bought a bottle of Scotch for Steve Bales and left it in his car in the Building 30 parking lot. I was convinced then, and still am now, that had it not been for Steve's knowledge and skill, we would not have been successful in landing on the moon that day. Unfortunately, I found out years later that the bottle was not there when Steve headed for home. I still owe him one.

The rest of the Apollo 11 mission went very well. After splashdown, I left for Mississippi to see my parents. When I arrived, my dad said that I had received a call from Phil Shaffer and that I was to call him back, no matter what time of day or night. When I called, Phil said that President Nixon was going to issue the Presidential Medal of Freedom to the Apollo 11 Flight Operations Team, and that Kraft thought it should be received by someone from the Trench. Phil's question to me was, "Who should it be?" My answer was Steve Bales, whereupon Phil said "Good. That's what I already told Chris."

EPILOGUE

I cannot conclude these memories without acknowledging a group of people and two individuals.

The group is the Flight Dynamics Branch, the Trench. I have been extremely fortunate in my lifetime to have experienced many interesting and exciting jobs. Of all the jobs and all the groups of people, the 1960s and the FDB folks stand alone as the very, very best. In no other job have I had the trust and respect for my co-workers like I had then. For most of us, it was our first job and there were no textbooks or previous experiences to guide us. Even though we were Government workers and had to have a hierarchy on paper, we always worked as a team. Everyone just accepted assignments and went off to accomplish them, knowing that their teammates were relying on them to do it right. Unfortunately, in later years and different jobs, I would discover that this was not the norm. We had a unique environment with a unique group of people. We all participated in making history. That environment, most likely will never be repeated. Yes, we were confident, sometimes bordering on arrogance. We were a proud bunch and rightly so.

The first individual I want to single out is Chris Kraft. Much has been written and said about him, but we were fortunate enough to have worked with and for him. As I mentioned earlier, when I was in college I saw Chris on TV and he became my hero. Here was a man who was in charge of our manned space flights and he was so succinct and articulate. Besides that, he also was a handsome man and dressed very nicely. Never did I dream that one day I would meet him, much less work with him. I certainly never dreamed that one day he would chew out Carl Huss because Carl was making fun of me for always wearing a suit jacket.

I always found Chris to be extremely intelligent and not one to waste time on trivial matters. He always got directly to the point. He had an unusual ability to look at a pile of crap and find a pony. While others were wringing their hands trying to figure out what to do, Chris would quickly analyze the situation and come to a conclusion that others would immediately see as the correct one.

Some have said that Chris was "unforgiving," saying if you ever screwed up, he wouldn't give you a second chance. I am a living testament to that not being true. He <u>was</u> intolerant of incompetence, but mostly, he was intolerant of people who didn't level with him. If anyone ever tried to pull the wool over his eyes or lie to him, then he was very intolerant. He was just as intolerant of people who would not admit they had made a mistake, or try to talk their way out of failure. Many, many times throughout my career around Chris, I made many mistakes. The first one I recall was my first simulation as a RETRO in the Mercury Control Center. I royally screwed up a launch abort sim…my very first one! In the debriefing, when it came my turn, I just told him that I had screwed up and I would try not to let it happen again. Two other new controllers that day tried to talk their way out of mistakes. They were never seen in the Control Center again. Yes, Chris could be "unforgiving," but only if you were not honest and straightforward with him.

Throughout my career, I have tried to emulate Chris. He taught us all, by example, to delegate decision making to the lowest possible level. He made sure that people knew that he trusted them and that he expected them to accomplish their assignment without minute-by-minute guidance from above. When people working for him did an outstanding job, he recognized them and praised them. He always gave credit to the people actually doing the work, and never tried to take any of the credit himself.

Chris is even more of a hero to me now than he was before I ever met him. I feel truly fortunate to have had the opportunity to work with such a giant.

The other individual I want to recognize is Glynn Lunney. Many of the characteristics I attributed above to Chris Kraft can also be said of Glynn. From the first day I met him, I liked him. He was personable and carried on a conversation that convinced me that he really cared how I was doing. When I started working with and for him, his intellect and savvy became very obvious. Not only was he smart and a very quick learner, he had more common sense than most people.

Glynn, like Chris, could be intolerant of incompetence, but he also, like Chris, was forgiving. He taught me to use mistakes as a learning tool. He preached to me that if you don't make any mistakes, you aren't stretching yourself.

I, like others in the Trench, was always happy when Glynn was the Flight Director on my shift. I was well aware that he knew as much about my job as I did, but this was comforting rather than threatening. I knew that he would understand what I was doing, not ask a lot of dumb questions, and that he trusted me. How could you ask for a better leader?

When I think of Glynn, beyond his expertise and savvy, I also think of his kindness and generosity. He genuinely cared about the people with whom he worked. It was not a casual question when he asked "How are you doing?" He really cared. Throughout the '60s, Glynn and Marilyn went out of their way to feed and entertain us in the little free time that we had. They always invited those in the FDB who did not have families or could not go home for the holidays, to share that time with their family. They treated all of us as if we _were_ a part of their family. These times were a great contributor to the comradery which developed in the Trench.

I was fortunate to work with and for Glynn in many different jobs, for many years after Apollo. Our paths seemed to cross many times and I always thanked my lucky stars when they did.

I will be eternally grateful to Glynn for his guidance, his tolerance and most of all, his friendship.

III - H. David Reed

LOOKING BACK

Copyright © 2010

By H. David Reed
90 Page Brook Road
Carlisle, MA 01741

As long as I can remember I always had a certain curiosity as to how things worked. I also like to build things. One of the first model cars I built…I actually carved from scratch out of a block of balsa wood. I designed it and then proceeded to whittle away. It had doors that opened and headlights that worked. I don't think I was much older than 12 at the time.

Not sure where all that curiosity and creative drive came from. I do recall that the last time I ever saw my father (1964) he took us (then wife Vicki) for a ride in his car. He instructed us to put on the shoulder harness he had installed. He had designed them for the CA Highway Patrol. They were in all their cars. A patent??? NOT!!

I do know that my heritage can be traced to George Lewis in Brenchley, Kent England in 1575. Descendents from this point later came over on the Mayflower. John Howland married another passenger Elizabeth Tilley, and their genealogy traces directly to my Grandfather, Oscar Lewis. Oscar married my Grandmother, Nettie Plato whose heritage traces to John Alden and Priscilla Mullin, also on the Mayflower.

We know that my great-great Grandfather had the wanderlust. He was making a good living in New York (Oneonta) when he decided he wanted to start up again "out west." He built a raft with a "modest" cabin on it, packed up his family of *nine* children, wife and dog and floated the Allegheny River to the Ohio River and on to the Mississippi. He started over in Middleton, Iowa and was again successful. The wanderlust also struck one of his boys who left in 1852 in a wagon train to make his fortune in the West. His exploits are all recorded in our family genealogy files and include the record of his return to Iowa 14 years later. He took a steamer from San Francisco to Nicaragua and rode horseback across the isthmus to reach the gulf. From there he traveled on another steamer to New York. There he continued his journey on a new invention that appeared in his absence (called a steam train) and returned to Middleton, Iowa.

I was born in Nebraska and still an infant, was taken to Billings, Montana where I grew up in the "west." I was raised by my grandparents a good bit of the time as my Mom was single and worked four different jobs to keep bread on the table for my sister and me. I had an older sister, a dog and a red wagon. What else did one need? I used to make that comment/observation to people and tell them that I had those and my friend Karl had a dad. Seemed equal to me. People seem compelled to add however…"poor child." Strange!!! I really never knew my Dad and to this day it doesn't bother me. I think it bothers them though.

I also know that I was raised in the company of three VERY strong-willed women. That gave me something in my makeup that served me well from then on.

My maternal Grandfather was my male role model. I was blessed with his caring and osmotic learning as he never lectured. He just set the example of what was expected. He ran a lunber yard in Billings and when I was maybe 14, he let me work there. He explained however, that the pay would only be a dollar a day because he wanted me to learn the value of money. It was a valuable lesson and I slowly started saving my money as I had found a "car"[1].

As a teenager in those days, I was fascinated with model airplanes and of course rockets which was made indelible by the launch of Sputnik.

I began building rockets at 15. I made my own black powder for fuel using ingredients described in a book on Chinese rocketry. We had a VERY small library in Billings and I was ecstatic at finding that book.

You could purchase the ingredients (potassium nitrate, sulphur, charcoal) at a drug store in those days. But try that today and you'd be arrested. I got better and better at creating "hot" mixes and my rockets went higher and higher as I evolved my designs and fuel formulas.

Like all rocketeers of then I suppose, I did run into a few problems. I recall one rocket that I fired from my backyard climbing to about 15 feet and then laying over horizontal heading toward the neighbors' yard (shades of a scene from the movie 'October Sky'). Why was (is) it that every neighborhood had one old 'biddy'? And wouldn't you know that my errant creation would slam into HER back porch and start a small smoke scare. Needless to say, she called the Police. Fortunately when they arrived my grandfather spoke to them and all was washed over, though I could no longer launch from my backyard.

So if I had to find the wide open spaces then I might as well increase the range of what I would test. The result of that escalation in difficulty was a "liquid" fuel rocket that was actually powered by a pulse jet engine. It had a second stage and a parachute that would deploy at fuel depletion.

---

1 *I had purchased my first car, a 1929 Model-A at age 14 for $35. At that age I couldn't get a driver's license (at 16 though I could get a learner's permit). I spent the intervening time tearing that car apart and learning how it worked. I rebuilt it, repainted it and finally I was 16. It would transport me and my rockets to the wide-open spaces..*

My first and last
"liquid fueled" rocket

All set.???!!!
The maiden launch wasn't what I had hoped for. I took the rocket up to the airport. Why not ? Wide open spaces...yes? My friend's father had a hanger up there and I drove in behind it and set up the rocket.

All was proceeding smoothly until I hit the spark. The fuel had dribbled down the nozzle/throat and instead of the compressed air and fuel getting it 'together' and causing the pulsed ignition to take place, it just caught fire.

There was my creation engulfed in flames. So I did the "logical" thing, grabbed it and moved it away from the fuel spill and associated fire. I then proceeded to lay the rocket over on the ground. Oops! It was still armed and I had cleverly included three mercury cell tilt switches that triggered an "abort" sequence complete with engine fuel cutoff and chute deploy if the nose tipped more that 30 degrees from vertical! As designed, the fuel cutoff valve actuated, the second stage fired and then the parachute deployed. I would have to be content at that moment with small successes!

Suffice it to say I was hooked on rocketry and in 1957 when Sputnik went up I was determined that I wanted to fly rockets in some capacity or another. One year later in 1958, NASA was formed. I was still in high school but from that point on, I would then focus on a path to make my dreams come true. I looked for nearby colleges that had any form of aerospace courses in their catalogue. The closest I could find was the University of Wyoming where they offered a mechanical engineering degree with an aeronautical option. They had two courses directly relevant to rocketry. One in keplerian (orbital) mechanics and the other in rocket chemistry. Between them, as I recall, they were only 4 semester hours out of 144 needed for a Mechanical Engineering (ME) degree. But that was more than any college in Montana offered.

While working at my degree I managed to secure lab space for exper-imentation with the pulse jet. Not content wit the size of the one I brought with me, I researched the German V-1 and built a working 1/2 scale copy. Either of these would be installed in a test cell I had built complete with a high pressure air source that was from a compressor on an old Navy ship, The USS Wyoming."

Pulse jets make noise. Lots of noise. It was so loud that it would totally disrupt classes in the engineering buiding. The college laid the law down and said I could only "fire those things" during the lunch hour.

How I stumbled into my job at NASA

I plodded on through four years including summer school, so that my last semester of my senior year would have very little class load and I could concentrate on job searches (and sleeping in). I went to cam-pus interviews for Boeing and Dupont. I was flown to Seattle and also to North Carolina for follow-up interviews and was offered jobs from both companIes. But all I really wanted was an offer from NASA. At last, a recruiter from NASA showed up. His name I recall was George Struhall…from the thermodynamics engineering side of the house in Houston.

I was living off campus my senior year in a small house with a fraternity brother. One groggy morning the phone rang and it was George Struhall from NASA in Houston wanting to know if I would be interested in a job in thermodynamics, designing heat shields. Hell, it didn't matter what they wanted me to do really…it was NASA calling. What I did next I will never know why. I told him of all things *"I'd have to think about it."* DUMB! My roommate agreed. As he scolded me "the very place you wanted to be and you said 'you'd have to think about it???'"

The very next morning another call awoke me. Again the voice intro-duced himself from NASA and he began to talk about a job. Before he could finish (thinking it was the man from the previous day) I blurted out "I'll take it." Only it wasn't the same caller. On the other end of the phone was Glynn Lunney who was a bit dumbfounded at my response and asked "Don't you want to hear about the job?" I said "yes" but that I would still take the job. "OK" responded Glynn, "I'll send you the paperwork."

And the rest is history. Glynn was a protégé to Chris Kraft and I became a flight controller in Mission Control just like that. I was to be on the ground floor of the Apollo Lunar Landing program! In 1964 I graduated, got married and drove to Houston. Just a short of five years later I would be a 28 year old flight dynamics officer for the first lunar anding, Apollo XI.

Most of us hired in those days were young and inexperienced. But then there *wasn't* anyone who had experience in what we were about to do. But the real visionary behind insisting that college graduates be given equal consideration came from Bob Gilruth who headed the Manned Spacecraft Center who so instructed his staff.

There were a number of visionaries behind what NASA was about to do. Years after Apollo, I asked Dr Kraft if he knew who it was that made the decision to land on the moon. He recalled that that Gilruth had attended a meeting at the White House to brief President Kennedy on a circumlunar flight possibility and that it was President Kennedy himself who asked: "why not land?"

Those were such rapid fire times that it's a wonder we have any memories of what we did. I was assigned to focus on the lunar module (LM) as the team that was in place was heavily into knowing and working with the Command and Service Module (CSM). The time for the lunar module flights was far enough away to keep me out of their hair and occupied. I still trained with those in the office, sitting in as an observer on Gemini launches and actually had a minor role in the first launch of an Apollo unmanned spacecraft.

I had great mentors in Glynn and Phil Shaffer. They encouraged me (I really didn't need much). When Phil suggested that I watch over the needs we would have as driven by the Lunar Module, I grabbed the LEM like a dog with a bone and "shook it." I traveled to MIT in Cambridge, MA (MIT Instrumentation Labs) and at 24 or 25 actually stood at a chalkboard with Norm Sears of MIT looking on while I scribbled out logic flow charts for the lunar module computer. He was so patient with us "kids." He managed to politely NOT shake his head!

I learned a lot from Chris Kraft as well. To watch him cut through the chaff was a lesson in itself. One of the memorable lessons I learned from him occurred during the preparations for Apollo 204. We were in a final mission rules review with White, Chaffe and Grissom. I was going over the procedures I was to follow to test the abort switch on my console to the spacecraft. I was to inform tha CapCom that I was sending the command and he then was to inform the crew that the command was being sent. Kraft interjected and said "that's too complicated. Why don't you [FIDO] have a direct loop to the spacecraft?" I thought that was a no no but Kraft had said it! Next countdown test, that loop was on my console and I dutifully used it.

After the simulation Kraft opened the debriefing saying,"who the hell was talking to the crew!?" I timidly raised my hand and recounted our previous discussion the day before. He then said: "Young man, some day you will learn that great men, like women, often change their mind. Now get that loop off your console!"

Wasn't ALL work and no play however. The experiences we had often had an element of comic relief in them as revealed in the NASA oral histories in John Llewellyn's interviews.

When we were in the fervor of the Gemini missions Manned Space Flight was now a National interest. So NASA decided to commission the Kingston Trio to record "These 7 men." The recording session took place at the center under the watchful eye of Paul Haney, the head of Public Affairs.

That afternoon when I returned home after work I got a phone call from Paul who lived in the apartment directly across the pool from my apartment. He explained that the Kingston had finished the recording and he was having a couple of folks over for cocktails to meet them. Took me all of two seconds to accept the invitation and show up at his door. There I met Bob Shane, Nick Reynolds and Dave Guard. As the cocktails flowed, the Trio popped out their instruments and the few of us (maybe 4 or 5) who were there were treated to a number of songs truly "up close and personal." We heard a couple of "spicey" songs that they told us would never be recorded. It was quite an evening, especially for someone who was a big fan already.

And the Apollo story would not be complete if it didn't mention the brilliant but light hearted consummate counselor to Apollo, Bill Tindall. Bill ran what was known as the Data Priority or Mission Techniques panel. He produced over 1,100 meeting memos typed by his ever patient secretary Jane Wyatt. These "Tindall Grams" as they were called, documented key decisions for Apollo Operations. As Chris Kraft observed: "those meetings were the hardened core of Apollo as far as operations planning was concerned. That's where the famous 'Tindallgram' name came from." He continued, "It would be difficult for me to find anyone who individually contributed more to the success of Apollo than Bill Tindall."

To illustrate his keen insight, years later I visited with Bill and wife Jane at their cottage on Cape Cod. A sparrow perched nearby flew off and right through a nearby bush and a maze of branches. Bill pointed at the bird and said to me: "We've got a long way to go with guidance computers. The bird's brain is no bigger than a grain of rice and came into existence fully loaded and ready for flight control, complete with collision avoidance."

Not that I didn't have enough to do learning my job, but in my spare time I began to restore another Model A. That car would be with me for the duration of my time in Houston, transporting me to and from the Manned Spacecraft center for work. It seemed somehow ironically appropriate.

The time was fast approaching when I would get my "bath by fire" as Cliff Charlesworth phrased it. My first real flight was Apollo V, an unmanned flight of the Lunar Module. It was essential to know if it's two rocket engines would perform as intended in a complete vacuum as there was no possible way to duplicate that environment on earth. The mission had a serious setback on the very first burn over Australia. The ultimate result was we didn't get to use the computer we had worked so hard on at MIT. However, using a backup system we were able to meet the primary mission objectives of firing those rocket engines to measure their performance in a vacuum.

My next flight would be Apollo IX, a full up dress rehearsal for a lunar landing. It too was to be completed in earth orbit. We were to duplicate the entire lunar landing time-line. It was tricky at best and all in all it was the toughest mission I would ever fly, Apollo XIII not withstanding.

I trained closely with the crew on Apollo IX. Rusty and Jim became my working partners in mission rules development and mission execution planning. One afternoon we three were at the Cape running rendezvous simulations in the LEM trainer. It was cramped in there but there was room for me if I sat on the ascent engine cover behind the crew. Simulations had rigged a long box with chain driven model of the CSM inside. They placed a camera on one end and the model would move in sync with induced LEM motions for terminal phase. At some point I got a call from the "simsupe" saying that they had a visitor and would give up my seat for a few minutes. Glad to...it was kinda uncomfortable so I could jump out and stretch my legs. I opened the door and started down the stairs when the guest passed me to take my seat. I could watch the same visuals tha the crew was being presented on a monitor at the sim console. The crew started another closing sequence but to my surprise they were not seeing the CSM. They were seeing the "Enterprise" from Star Trek. I don't recall asking why but I did think it was curious. Momentarily the simsupe said OK, you can go back onboard. As I started up the stairs the guest blew by me and down the stairs on his tour of the facilities. As I approached the simulator door Rusty bounded out saying, "I forgot to get his autograph. My sons will kill me." I went inside the LEM trainer to await Rusty's return. "Who was that?", I asked Jim. "That was William Shatner, Captain Kirk of the TV series Star Trek!"

Apollo IX was as noted the most compex mission I ever flew. The rendezvous was of particular concern as Jim and Rusty would be away from the CSM in a vehicle that had no re-entry capability. We had simulated the CSM going after the LEM for rendezvous should that contingency arise. The turning point in the rendezvous sequence would be the CSI (Coelliptic Sequence Initiate) maneuver which would place the LEM on a path of return to the CSM. The thrust for that maneuver would come from the Descent engine. it would be the first time it had been used in a manned spacecraft. If we got passed that critical event we would know that we had a working engine and plenty of maneuvering capability to pull this off. The burn took place over the Canary Island tracking station (CYI). I could see it happen in real-time on my displays and the trajectory begin to close. While still over CYI Jim McDivitt called over the loop saying, "Is Dave Reed smiling yet?" Indeed I was. We finished the rendezvous as planned and then went into the rest of the mission objectives.

One of these objectives would be to have the Lunar Module perform a docked burn pushing the CSM. It went fine. Little did we dream that test would be as critical as it was in our plans to save Apollo XIII.

Next up for me was Apollo XI which would be "nominal" (except for the lunar launch). We realized then, that if we could get through simulations we could get through anything. Still, we were all no doubt scared to death as we stepped up to that ultimate mission. I was assigned to "launch" XI and to setup the lunar lift-off targeting.

Lunar Lift-Off Apollo XI

The origins of pin-point landing techniques

I had literally trained hundreds of hours (220 logged) simulating Saturn launches. A FIDO's job was tracking and maneuver calculations. Each of us had begun to accumulate many, many hours in training in various specialty areas and mine was turning out to be launch phase, launching at least 5 Saturn vehicles.

Looking back, it is difficult to comprehend that adding up all the on-board guidance systems capabilities (including the cameras that were launched) that a cell phone today far exceeds them in total. Equally hard to believe was what we were able to do with our Real Time Computer Complex (RTCC) IBM 360's with only 8MB of memory operating at 600 hz. A wonder that we had the patience to wait for the calculations to finish!

We had two key people supporting us. One was known as 'DYNAMICS' who was my I/O link to the computer. Usually it was a fellow named Pete Williams. He was a brilliant thinker and a cool, collected individual. I was MOST fortunate to have him on shift with me that early morning as Apollo XI was preparing to lift off from the moon. In those days Pete used a teletype keyboard to insert our maneuver inputs for calculation. Another key computer position was SELECT. His job was that of selecting the best tracking source for these calculations. During launch he/she (we had both) had C-band and S-band radar, as well as multiple telemetry sources.

As I recall all went super smooth for America's first flight to the surface of the moon, Apollo XI (except for the 1201 and 1202 alarms)[2]. No lightning (as we were to experience on Apollo XII); no floating solder particles in abort switches (as were waiting for us on Apollo XIV) and no cranky capture latches (Apollo-XIV also). Just pucker time during touchdown!

After Apollo XI landed, as the World celebrated and sipped champagne, I slept in preparation for my shift prior to lunar launch. I would work with SELECT and DYNAMICS to get all the relative geometry down and work out the correct ignition (Lunar Module lift-off) time for return to the CSM. Piece of cake really. All we needed was the touchdown landing "site" vector and a solid ephemeris on the CSM.

I sat down at the console for that prelaunch shift and was debriefed by the previous team to complete hand-off. I probably had my second cup of coffee by then and got on the loop to SELECT to get the best landing site vector. I remember asking SELECT what he had for touchdown. I'll never forget his answer when he said, "take your pick FIDO!" I also remember not reacting too positively to his offer.

He explained that we had five different "sites." He said "we have [inertial vectors] MSFN (tracking radars), PNGS (primary LM guidance computer), AGS (backup LM guidance computer), the targeted land-

---

2   *Neil had this to say about the call "GO on that alarm" by Stephen Bales: "I was reassured. Atitude indicators, velocities, etc. were all looking correct. I was definitely going to continue until something from you guys indicated we had a major problem or I could see evidence of that myself."*

ing site and, oh yes, the geologist have determined yet another location based upon the crew's description of the landscape and correlating that with orbiter photos."

With the uncertainty presented by these "multiple choices," we needed to be confident that our choice was a correct one. It was the COMPUT-ER DYNAMICS computer controller, Pete Williams who reminded us that current rendezvous radar tracking data from the LM on the CSM

Splashdown Apollo 11

I am at center left in the White Sportcoat facing the camera, looking for key people to sign the original launch plotboard

would provide the relative position information we could use to work the problem backward. This was an option in the flight plan (P22) but was not scheduled. We knew where the CSM was and the problem was a relative one between the CSM and the LM, not requiring a geographically defined latitude and longitude but inertial vectors. To do this we would need to have the rendezvous radar (RR) turned on in the LM one revolution earlier than planned. Only two more passes of the CSM remained before Ascent ignition, before we had to have a solution to this problem.

I remember taking my headset off and walking up to the Flight Director, Milt Windler to explain the situation. We only used that kind of face to face communication when we had a serious problem such as this. I detailed the problem as best we knew it and the process that we'd have to follow to get the data we needed, and why we had to start a rev early to finish the calculations and then find the critical lift-off time for lunar launch. I recall the CapCom instructing Buzz Aldrin that we needed him to perform the RR check early but I don't believe that CapCom explained why, just another check was all. Shaft & trunnion angles were passed up to aid acquisition. Right on time as the CSM cleared the horizon we began seeing data. We counted the agonizing minutes as the telemetry came flowing in. Now we had the vector data we needed to run the problem (a rendezvous problem in reverse) and get the correct liftoff time[3]. And that's what we used. Later we would find out just where were we on the surface. We were actually around 25,000 feet from at least one of the other choices we had! At 5,000-fps orbital velocity of the CSM that could have been up to a ten second error in liftoff. This was a metric we were concerned which results from site errors. That would have meant we'd need a LOT of RCS (reaction control system fuel) to play catch up or slow down in a rather abnormal rendezvous situation.

We had done what we had all accepted as a National objective. We saw to it that President Kennedy's goal for America was achieved.

The plot board shown above was signed by all who were there that day including John Glen and of course later, by Neil, Buzz and Mike. The original copy of that signature "board" was sent to the Smithsonian where it was on display for a year or so following Apollo X.

Then came Apollo XII. The prime objective would be to do a pin-point landing next to an unmanned spacecrat (Surveyor III) that had landed three years earlier. By so doing, this would allow us to bring back components of the Surveyor that had been exposed to years of intense cold

---

3 *This technique, would be used in subsequent flights as a standard procedure until MPAD had confidence in the high speed descent trajectory processing software (Lear filter).*

and heat soak conditions which would be most helpful in understanding any deterioration to electrical and mechanic systems that might result.

Pete Conrad trained on a duplicate Surveyor at Hughes Aircraft and reported back during a meeting that was chaired by Dr. Low (Apollo Program mgr). Pete pointed out that there was not enough time to unscrew and disconnect the parts the flight plan called for. Pete said he needed something like bolt cutters. Immediately someone from flight crew offered that they could get a specification out for bid and test within a month. Dr. Low asked that the doors to the room be closed. He then reminded this individual that we were launching in three weeks! He instructed this same flight crew rep to "go to Sears, purchase two bolt cutters, and stamp them flight qualified. Next item on the agenda!" That solved that problem but what about making sure we landed next to the Surveyor?

I had been assigned the descent phase for Apollo XII and we worked on methods to ensure that we did touchdown at the Surveyor site. I wasn't about to go through another landing site search again.

Ultimately *"WE"* found a solution to the problem experienced on Apollo XI. *"WE"* in this case is pronounced E-M-I-L [Scheisser] when it's spelled out. He was the soft-spoken genius in MPAD (Mission Planning and Analysis Division) behind the solution.

In the end, the simplicity of his solution was the ultimate testimony to his genius. Emil reasoned that if the descent orbit insertion (DOI) burn was perfect, then the resultant elliptic orbit would be oriented with it's major axis in exactly the right position relative to the powered descent ignition point, which itself was relative to the landing site. The LM in that orbit would have a radial rate that would be predictable as well as observable with MSFN doppler radar. If however, its rate of change was off, i.e., if the doppler shift was different than the desired orbit, then the actual orbit was incorrectly oriented or shifted by a measurableamount which would translate into a downrange error[4].

Pete Conrad (Commander) thought in the end that we wouldn't really be able to get him within the 600 feet Emil would quote. So just before launch on Twelve, Pete told me "You can't hit it anyhow. Target me for the center of the surveyor crater." His full account of our dialogue is

---

4 *The doppler measurements were so sensitive that during flight these radars could "see" any spacecraft movement instantly. We used to chuckle that the radars knew who was up before the telemetry readings saw the exhaust heat of their urine dump. Like Newton said: "for every action there is an equal and opposite reaction."*

accurately recorded in Andrew Chaikin's book. "A Man on the Moon" (pp 257-58).

During the actual descent you can hear the crew exclaim, "Hey, those boys on the ground do pretty good work" as they spotted the surveyor directly in front and below. Knowing he had asked me to target him directly on top of it, Pete grabbed the stick and maneuvered around to the opposite side of the crater. I don't think he had any real worries. We were probably only good to about 1,000 feet. Much better than 5 miles!

All in all, Apollo XII went pretty close to perfect just as Apollo XI had. Other than the rocket being struck twice by lightning during launch (which took the Apollo Command Module computer off-line) Apollo-XII was 'nominal' from start to finish.

Pete Conrad and Al Bean (Apollo XII lunar landing crew) had a few American Flags with them on that Flight and they gave me one when they returned. From that mission on, pin-point landing was assured. Without it we never could have done the exploration that we needed to accomplish on subsequent flights.

Then of course there was Apollo XIII. Much of what myself and the other controllers contributed is explained in some detail in many different books including Jim Lovell's book "Apollo 13."

While there have been many books written and movies made about these events and individuals involved. One needs to read them to get a complete and *accurate* picture of who all the players were and to separate fact from fiction in some of the associated biographies.

We Followed In Footsteps Made By Pioneers

Lawrence Cutler Mansur

The last of Goddard's original team.

It was in the mid seventies and we were living in Carlisle, MA when a good friend, Bill Brown introduced me to a Mr. Mansur. It was on the occasion of an "Old Home Day" town celebration and though I was in charge of some aspect of the day, I immediately forgot all that after I heard his story and learned just who I was speaking to.

I would guess that 'Larry' was in his late 80's. He was bubbling over with curiosity about the moon program and was asking numerous questions about landing on the moon. I'm sure I was giving him answers to as many as I could but they had to be interspersed with all my questions about what he had done. A true pioneer and I had an audience with history. He explained that he worked with Robert Goddard as his machinist in Framingham, MA!! (My jaw must have dropped noticeably!)

As we jabbered on, he told me a story that is now cast in history and became a part of all rocketeering jargon. He went on to explain that "In the early days"….their first rockets were simple in that the engine was mounted atop a framework that suspended the fuel and oxidizer tanks below the engine nozzle. This gave the rocket a rudimentary pendulous stability system. Rudimentary perhaps but the oxidizer they used was liquid oxygen (LOX)!

The whole rig was placed inside an old claw footed bathtub that served as a flame bucket for launch. The fuel and oxidizer were introduced sequentially using remotely controlled valves. The team was positioned a short distance away behind a berm should anything go awry.

All was set and the kerosene valve switch was activated to open the flow of fuel. Next the LOX valve was cycled open, followed by the depression of the ignition switch which he said was nothing but a model-T coil for spark. But when it was pressed nothing happened. Being "good engineers" as he phrased it, they did what any good engineer would do and repeated the sequence. This time the kerosene valve opened and fuel was flowing to and through the rocket engine. The LOX flow was started again and then the ignition switch pushed.

"After the explosion" he said, "there was nothing left of that bathtub that was any bigger than an inch across!"

What had happened? During the first cycle the kerosene valve had stuck and no fuel was introduced. However the LOX valve did open and LOX flowed to and through the engine then down to the bottom of the tub where it began to accumulate. The spark did not cause ignition as there was no fuel. But the next cycle DID introduce kerosene which now flowed down to the pool of LOX in the bottom of the tub from the previous LOX valve opening. The subsequent spark of ignition set it all off.

"After that," he said, "we purchased cinder *blocks* and built a place to hide behind to protect ourselves." He looked right at me and wryly added, "I believe you now call that a *blockhouse*!"

Leaving Houston

Leaving NASA/Houston was a tough decision. But bureaucratic creep was all around us and it was ominously clear that no longer could we be as "tight" in making decisions using our own interactive wits. From here on in it was to become rule by committee. I wanted my memories of the Space Program to always be at their crest. It was time to go.

I had made arrangements to leave Houston after Apollo XIII and join a another startup government agency in Cambridge, MA. My hope was that the idea of building a new adventure from the ground up would be possible again. With that thought pushed to the background I focused on Apollo XIII. Launch went smoothly and my shift was over. I was home asleep when the explosion occured. A friend called me that night and wanted to know what had happened. Being at home I knew nothing. I returned to bed but shortly the phone rang again. Another friend with the same question.

Now I was *wide* awake! I turned on the TV for in those days the local and national coverage was often focused on NASA. I looked at the image on the TV of the interior of the contol room. There, standing together dealing with the problem were most of my TRENCH colleagues. Obviously I would be of more help if I didn't join the crowd but instead got some sleep. I recall taking three aspirin and getting some needed sleep. When I arrived at the center in the morning I was "bright eyed and bushy tailed" and was selected to be the FIDO on the prime control team.

We did what we had to do to get the crew home. Chuck Deiterich (RETRO) and I pushed for a trajectory around the moon as we had plenty of propulsive power. We had tested the docked burn of the LM on Apollo IX so it was a viable option. Chuck and I rehearsed and rehearsed using off-line computers running the final mid-course maneuvers and setting up the delicate S/C orientation for LM jettison and reentry. There were many close calls on that mission and the ultimate manner in which we all pulled together is legend. Many books have been written about Apollo XIII. To sort out any rewriting of history, the reader is encourage to read further to understand who the true heros were.

At splashdown of Apollo-XIII, I placed a call to Cambridge (U.S.DoT) and informed them that I would not leave Houston with Apollo-XIII being my last flight. I would stay for Apollo-XIV and if all went well, then I would come to Cambridge. With the exception of a floating solder ball in the Lunar Module Abort switch, Apollo-XIV did go smoothly, although we did our first wave off of a lunar descent while we created a work-around for the switch problem.

All of us who worked for Glynn and Chris were carefully trained and watched over at the same time. Our efforts did not go unnoticed by them and numerous awards were bestowed on us for our accomplishments. Beyond internal NASA recognition, I was also a joint recipient of the Presidential Medal of Freedom for my contributions in the safe return of Apollo XIII.

Equally humbling was the gift the crew of Apollo XIV presented to me upon their return: a named crater on the moon.

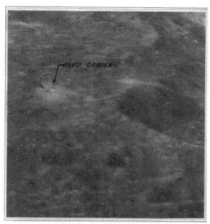

THE BRIGHT CRATER PICTURED ABOVE IS LOCATED ON THE LUNAR FARSIDE AT APPROXIMATELY 110°E LONG 3°S LAT.

USING MY PREROGATIVE AS AN EXPLORER TO NEW TERRITORY I NAME THIS CRATER <u>REED CRATER</u>

APOLLO 14

After Houston, my learnings from NASA stayed with me. I will always be grateful for the exposure to cool headed management that I witnessed and was guided by each and every day. As best I could, I carried those lessons with me in my career.

In multiple projects around the world, working on behalf of many different government agencies, including the State Department, The United Nations, U.S. Air Force, U.S. Army, the Drug Enforcement Agency, and the Coast Guard, I kept those management methods alive and passed them on to those who worked for me.

I was most fortunate again to have another opportunity to start something new and to build and work with teams of people invested in 'can do' in the same spirit as NASA. To this day they are as grateful for my learning as I was. For as we still do in our Flight Dynamics Family, "The TRENCH", the group that I assembled in Cambridge in a project called "INTRANSIT" continues to this day to get together for the holidays and often a summer BBQ.

I lived a chance of a lifetime.

I am eternally grateful.

IV - Charles Franklin Deiterich III

MY PATH TO THE TRENCH AND BEYOND

Charles Franklin Deiterich III

Looking to the sky, wearing a helmet and glasses belonging to Joe Gillespie, a WWII B-24 pilot and next door neighbor.

Please note, of the topics, that I will discuss below, there is no good way to logically group them. Many of the activities overlap or occur in parallel (we might call this multitasking today). Thus, as it seems appropriate to me, I will just put forth the descriptions.

The "DIETRICH" family

The Dieterich family originated in Germany. The castle Hirshengen situated in Swabia, near Michaelbach, near Stutgart, built about 1253, was the seat of the German Family of "DIETRICH." Johann Peter Von Dietrich was the last to own the castle, losing it during the thirty-year-war (1618–1648). His son Wilhelm Emanuel Dietrich was born in 1680 in Dresden; he had many sons and from these I am descended. The name "DIETRICH" in the German language means "skeleton key." The original spelling of the family name was "DIETRICH." It has been spelled Deitrich, Deiterich and Deitterick.

My Great Grandfather, Peter Dietrich, was born in 1820 in Kubelberg, Bavaria, Germany. In 1841, he immigrated to the United States and first settled in Pottsville, PA along with a brother, Adam, and a sister, Louisa. In 1863, Peter and Adam Dietrich, stone masons, helped to build the Immaculate Conception Church at Bastress, PA. Peter Dietrich was a member of the Catholic Church until after working on the church at Bastress. He then broke from the church because he was never paid for his labor. After Peter's wife's (Rebecca) death, he returned to the Catholic Church. He died November 23, 1900 and is buried at the side of his wife in the old Rosemont Cemetery in Bloomsburg, Pennsylvania.

I was born in Mahoning Township, PA, but lived in Bloomsburg, PA. I was named for my Grandfather and Uncle; thus I am Charles Franklin Deiterich III (a.k.a. Chuck). My Grandfather was born before the civil war in 1860. He was a public school truant officer and janitor. Even though he was the truant officer, all of the youngsters liked him. He was married to Sarah Coleman in 1884. He was a great humanitarian, but even with 13 children of his own, he managed to help the underprivileged students in his school. Mechanically minded, he was an excellent handyman and passed this trait on to his heirs.

Some pocket watch history: Charles Deiterich Sr. owned a Hampden key wound pocket watch dating from about 1877. Before he passed away in 1940, he gave the watch to my Uncle Charlie, who later presented it to me. Long, long ago, Charles Sr. was polling a boat along the mill race near Irondale (which is now part of Bloomsburg). The water in mill race, which generated about 200 horse power, was fed from a dam on Fishing Creek to an Irondale mill. As my Dad told me, Charles Sr. accidentally dropped the watch into the race. Fearing he may have lost it for good, he quickly stuck his pole into the bottom of the race to hopefully mark the location. Returning a little later, he went swimming, dove for the watch and, by golly, he recovered it. Subsequently, this watch had many years of service as the engraving on the silver cover has been almost worn away.

Charles Deiterich Sr. Family Plus 5 Grandchildren

My Dad, Harry Franklin (far left above) was born in 1901, and was very mechanically inclined. During WWII he worked at the local airport as an aircraft mechanic. In fact, my first airplane ride, at the age of 5, was from the Bloomsburg airport in a Stinson Voyager. Later, he was employed as a machinist. His 1931 Ford was a bit cantankerous in the wintertime. As Third Street was downhill for about 4 blocks, Dad would park facing downhill hoping he could use gravity to start his car.

In our back yard, he had a chicken coop for hens. Somewhere he heard that when the winter days seemed longer to the hens, they would lay more eggs. Always improvising and when electrical wire was hard to get, he ran a single 110 volt wire to the coop and driving a metal rod into the ground he completed the circuit to a light. A bit dim, the extra light seemed to do the trick, or so he related.

My Mom, Mary born in 1904 (one of 9 children), had roots in county Waterford, Ireland with parents Richard Dowd, 1864, and Agnes Treas, 1868. She graduated from Bloomsburg Normal School and taught school in rural West Virginia, all 4 feet 11 inches of her. As for the rest of my immediate family, I am the youngest of a brother, Dick, and two sisters, Molly and Ruthie.

Richard Dowd's Family minus 1 (My Mom is far left)

Two blocks away from my home in Bloomsburg was the Bloomsburg State Teachers College (previously Bloomsburg Normal School and now Bloomsburg University). Starting in 1942, BSTC was one of only five colleges in the nation that served as a Naval Flight Instructor School under the Navy's V-5 cadet training program. Classes were held on the campus while flight training took place at the Bloomsburg airport. I went to Ben Franklin elementary school on the campus, where the BSTC college students would practice teaching.

During WWII, I remember the air raid warning sirens and the blackouts where everybody had to turn out all of their lights. At that time, my brother was in the Civil Air Patrol and had hung warplane silhouettes in his room. These were a teaching aid for ground observers to recognize enemy warplanes. These and my first airplane ride kindled my interest in aviation. Additionally, my Dad would draw an instrument panel on a small blackboard, and with a stick, I could pretend to be a pilot. I also had my share of Jim Walker balsa gliders and even a rubber powered AJ Hornet or two (25 cents in 1948).

The only car I remember in Bloomsburg (through 1951) was that same 1931 Model A Ford. As a second job, my Dad called square dances. Late one cold Saturday night on the way home from a dance, I was sharing the back seat with a speaker system. All of a sudden the bottom dropped out. As I looked out the window I could see one of the rear wheels rolling into a field. Dad stopped, retrieved the wheel, took a lug nut from each of the other wheels, mounted the wheel and we were on our way. He always seemed to have a solution to most problems.

When I was about 8, I received a Lionel train set for Christmas. Shortly thereafter, I could put the train layout together: wiring the switches, the lights for the houses, and the other operating equipment. From this activity, I gained much insight into electrical matters. I always enjoyed doing things from riding wagons, bicycles, skis, and the Flexible Flyer sled I inherited from my brother after he joined the army. Wood Street, a half a block away, was too steep for cars when it snowed, so the police would block it off for the kids to sled.

Although not too cool, I learned to ride on my sisters' 24 inch girls bicycle. However, when I was about 10, I received a new Western Auto bicycle for Christmas. My buddies and I would ride all over town and it was always a challenge to ride straight up my street without zigzagging (remember back then bicycles had fat tires and only one speed). Later in Texas, I can remember riding to the bottom of Lake Houston before it filled up. Although small, I played football in the seventh grade and attended junior high dance nights at the community center.

After arriving in Houston, Texas in early 1952, I initially lived with my brother so I could get back into school. Since Dick had won $100 in a Chronicle football contest and opened a model shop in his garage, I started building and flying powered models. In the spring of 1952, Ed Pavelka and I attended Burbank Jr. High School. Ed was a much better builder than I. During the summer of 1952, I moved to Galena Park, however in 1954, Ed and I traveled with my brother to Beaumont, Texas to attend a model airplane contest. As a teenager, I went to many contests from Ellington AFB to the Dallas Naval Air Station.

My years as a Boy Scout added to my interest in things from camping to maps and navigation. Boys' Life Magazine, published for Boy Scouts, often contained science fiction stories about space travel written by Robert Heinein. These writings just further fueled my interest in reaching out beyond current boundaries. I achieved Scout's second highest rank, Life Scout.

I attended Galena Park schools from the ninth grade through graduation in 1956. Although I was not in the top two of my class, I was somehow selected as "Most Intelligent" by the high school teachers for the senior class "Who's Who." Taking chemistry in my junior year, I decided to be a chemist, however, the next year, physics became my goal. A long time in coming, but, and while I was in high school, I got my second airplane ride from a classmate, Charles Lang, in an Aeronca Champ at Clover Field near Friendswood, Texas. Years later, my sister and I were discussing our years at home and decided that our family was not even close to being "well off", however, we never even considered that things could be lacking, let alone being poor.

Luckily for me, I became acquainted with Father Vincent Guinan, who would come to celebrate mass at Our Lady of Fatima Church in Galena Park. Since he was the founding president of Houston's University of Saint Thomas (UST), I had a powerful benefactor who obtained a scholarship for me.

For four intense years, I commuted between Galena Park and UST in the Montrose area. Initially, I rode to class with my good friend Fred Young. One day in Fred's new shiny black 1957 Chevrolet, an eighteen wheeler decided it wanted to be in our space. The contact between the truck's tire and Fred's fender occurred on Ritchey Street between Shaw and LaPorte Road (now Texas highway 225). At the red light and fleet of foot, Fred leaped from the Chevy and mounting the truck's running board he finally got the attention of the driver and the issue was resolved. As our schedules diverged, I had to take a Texas Bus Lines bus to downtown Houston and then board a Houston Transit bus to get to college. On June 8, 1958, I bought my first car, a 1950 4 door Studebaker Champion for $295. Finally freedom of movement.

During the summers and part time during school, I had many jobs. They ranged from, digging ditches, painting 16 inch oil pipes, pulling electrical cables at Brown and Root Marine Yard, working in a print shop, painting dorm rooms, selling shoes at Easter time, delivering newspaper bundles, repairing electronics, instructing physics lab, to grading math papers. Later on and while at JSC, I taught instrument ground school at Alvin Jr. College and then sophomore physics at San Jacinto College.

Sputnik was launched while I was attending the University of St. Thomas. With our physics professor (Father Braden), several of us decided to try our hand at launching a rocket. Starting from a small CO_2 cartridge and progressing to a CO_2 cylinder (about 2 feet long by 3 inches diameter) we were able to reach heights of about 1000 feet. Being "thorough rocket scientists" and even though having a "small program", we had our test requirements.

**Lee Butler, Fr. Braden and Me
2010**

To determine if we had enough thrust on the large rocket, we made a test set-up consisting of a spring scale, a pen on a rotating paper recording drum, and our launch rail. Attaching the anchored spring scale to the rocket on the rail and with the pen on the paper, we were ready to go. We had a "C" clamp at the top of the rail, and Lee Butler of our team, put an extra turn on the clamp to assure that the rocket could not leave the rail. Oh, I failed to mention that the test location was inside the UST's physics lab. The members of the test team, about 4 in number, and for safety, crawled under the several tables in the lab. When the lanyard was pulled rupturing the diaphragm inside the nozzle, there was a loud whoosh, CO_2 filled the lab, the hook on the end of the scale straightened, and along with the rocket's ascent, the pen went vertically up the recording drum. All that saved the lab ceiling and perhaps the roof was the extra turn on the clamp, which did move, but held fast against the thrust of the rocket. After the test we knew it could fly.

Rocket and Launch Rail

A launch

Our first launch was on the north side of Westheimer Road in west Houston. It was a pasture then, but is now Briargrove subdivision. Although aerodynamically stable, we did not realize a fixed finned vehicle would weather vane into the wind. A southerly breeze altered our flight path towards the Westheimer traffic. Obviously, this scared the daylights out of us. Luckily, we were far enough away that the highway was not reached. However, the rocket did bury itself in a mud puddle and it took a mine detector to find it.

After college in 1960, I worked at Transport Flight Systems/Vecto Instrument Corporation. I was responsible for the sustaining engineering on two aircraft simulators. Both the single engine and twin engine trainers were used for corporate pilot training. It is interesting how I got this job. I was looking through the "Yellow Pages" and found a small aviation oriented company near what was then "Houston International Airport" (now Hobby Airport). After a short interview, the owner, Fred Burger, showed me a console to test aircraft instruments. He said if I could get it working he would hire me. A few hours later, I was gainfully employed. While there, I managed to get several more airplane rides.

I moved on to Dresser Electronics as a junior electronics engineer and later in 1963, to Test Equipment Corporation (TEQUIPCO). In addition to transistor testing equipment, TEQUIPCO made foghorns for offshore oil platforms. Simple in concept, the foghorn consisted of a four inch speaker element centered in a 4 foot parabolic reflector. In the design area, one of these units was tied to an FM radio that was tuned to KQUE. Everyone remembers where he or she was when they first heard of John Kennedy's assassination. When I first heard, I was listening to the foghorn.

By now I was married to Betty Tumlinson and with three kids (Billy, Carol and Gini). Betty is a native Texan. Both sets of her grandparents had farms dating back to the late 1800's. These, north of Houston, were a favorite target on weekends, especially before the kids started school.

Going to NASA

When NASA moved to Houston, I applied to the MSC engineering area but was rejected as my degree was only in physics not electrical engineering. My second NASA application got to the operations area and the Flight Dynamics Branch. So in 1964, Glynn Lunney and Grady Meyer (who liked my aircraft simulator experience) decided I should be hired. The week before I was to start at MSC in August, we decided to take a vacation. Leaving the baby with grandparents and the two preschoolers in tow, we headed for Big Bend National Park. When we got to the desert, but typical for us, it was raining. With the cooler, higher elevation camp sites full we had to stay down where the temperatures reached 100° F. Of course back then, protective car seats were still unknown. Thus the kids could snooze in the back of the station wagon (no air conditioner then either) as we drove around sightseeing. Driving through the Texas hill country, we were making our way back home. Since Betty had gotten a toothache about midnight, we were looking for a dentist. We arrived in Burnet, Texas about 7:00 AM and found one walking to his office. Since then, we bought a lot on nearby Lake Buchanan and built a cabin. Later, we bought 26 acres and built our retirement home. Both places are near Burnet. It is interesting how little things can shape your life.

Since most of us in Glynn's branch were young and certainly new to space flight, training became a large part of our lives. As we prepared for mission support, we participated in integrated simulations, classroom courses, 'part task' spacecraft mockup training, spacecraft system design reviews, etc. To expose the untried Trenchmen to an operations environment, Glynn would send us to monitor simulations at the Cape or operations at White Sands Missile Range (WSMR). Bobby Spencer, our point of contact for the Little Joe II project and the folks at WSMR, was a FIDO for the Launch Escape Tower test flights. With us under Bobby's wing, most of the new hires in 1964 had a chance to monitor the activities at White Sands. Staying in El Paso, with evening excursions to Juarez, became a prescription for many bottles of Bacardi rum to make it back to Houston. Speaking of Bobby, we all remember his used car dealings. In fact, two of my second but reliable cars came through him.

In March of 1966, I was sent to North American Aviation in Downey, California to participate in the critical design review of the Apollo Entry Monitoring System. I decided to take some annual leave and drive our 1965 Chevy. Leaving our girls with their grandparents, Betty, Billy, and I headed out. Arriving in El Paso the first day, I felt we had it made. However, deciding to get the oil changed in Las Cruces, we found that we had significant tire breakdown. Buying 4 tires at a service station on a Sunday morning is not all that pleasant. We planned to camp along the way thus saving money to pay for our new sleeping bags. Two days later we were in Downey. As I rode to NAA with Claude Graves, Betty was free to cruise about in our car. Wanting to see the Pacific Ocean, she headed west on the Imperial Highway, nearing Watts she started thinking she had gotten too far from the hotel, so she backtracked to Downey. It turns out that on that very day (March 15), the second of the Watts riots erupted (the first occurred in August 1965). Another bullet dodged.

One time Bill Stoval and I were in the crew procedures dynamic simulator (CPDS) executing a CSM launch abort using the SPS. This simulator used cockpit movement to simulate launch accelerations. At liftoff, the cabin rotated back so as one goes to lying on his back there is a sensation of launch forces. At cutoff the cabin would pitch forward, giving the sensation of free-fall. For our run, we lit the SPS engine and felt the g's from the SPS thrust. While the maneuver progressed, Bill decided to clean up the switch positions on the instrument panel. Two of the switches he flipped turned off the SPS. As we lost the sensation of acceleration, I managed to hit the "Direct SPS Thrust On" button which restarted the SPS and completed the abort to orbit maneuver.

Starting out in the Apollo section, I worked just about all of the Apollo flights, beginning with AS-201. Mostly as the lead Retrofire Officer, but for Skylab and later, as a Flight Dynamics Officer, as the duties of the two positions were then combined. Halfway through the Gemini program, the Flight Dynamics Branch was reorganized into 3 sections including the Retrofire Officer section under John Llewellyn. Apollo I (first designated as AS-204), Apollo VIII, Apollo XI, and Apollo XIII are clearly the most indelible missions in my memory.

Air Force Major Walt Wells, of the branch, was assigned to support AS-201 at the Cape. His job was to send the abort command if the launch director said "Launch Requests Abort" prior to the Saturn rising above the launch tower, a.k.a. "Tower Clear." Otherwise, the launch director was to remain quiet. Wells later told me he almost sent the abort command because he misheard the words when the launch director said "Lost Television." But not being sure, he did nothing, hmmmmmmmm.

Still flying models, I reconnected with my old friend, Ed Pavelka, also in the Flight Dynamics Branch. Both living in Friendswood, we would fly models, and not unforeseen, he was still a better craftsman than I. One time, while flying my radio controlled model in the very large field behind his house, it got away. We chased it through weeds and mud. Exhausted when we finally got to it, we had to call one of our wives to come get us. Scouts, softball, and little league baseball occupied a good bit of my non-working hours. With lots of family camping, our interest in the outdoors led us to buy the lake front property near Burnet, Texas. Many, many long weekends and summer vacations were spent there. Occasionally, Ed and his family would come up and spend some time with us, as well as many others from JSC. Ed was always into cars; he would buy an old Corvette, Mercedes or Mustang and restore it. At one time, his bug bit me and I picked up a 1960 Austin Healey 3000, which was adorned with a Chevy V8 engine. I painted it, got it running, and drove it for several years (carefully).

After working hours, there were lots of activities for the folks at JSC. Softball seemed to be the favorite, but there were touch football, basketball, model airplanes, canoe trips, and more. One of my most exciting adventures was a hike when I trekked 50 miles across the Grand Canyon and back with Mike Collins and Chirold Epp.

Then there was a planned canoe trip. Will Presley, Dean Toups, Will Fenner and I were going to try the Guadalupe River below IH-10. For practice we made a trial run on Clear Creek. Toups and Presley were in one canoe, Fenner, his daughter (Joanie) and I were in another. Coasting along on our way to the park in League City, Toups and Presley decided to go for rapid acceleration with what they dubbed a "power stroke." Basically a reasonable plan except that they both dipped their paddles on the same side of the canoe. Their power stroke definitely was that, but instead of moving forward, there was instant rotation of the craft with both of them ending up under water. After we righted their canoe, they climbed aboard. The only things lost were Presley's sunglasses and their pride.

Due to high water on the Guadalupe, we elected to go to Canyon Lake instead. Fenner had to bow out, so Jerry Mill became my canoe partner. Our Memorial Day excursion went without incident, even our trip to Bandera's Silver Dollar Saloon where Mill got carded by the sheriff (who sounded a lot like Rocky Stone).

Unlike most mothers today, Betty stayed at home with the kids. After school, Betty was a Cub Scout den mother and helped with Gini's Blue Birds (part of the Camp Fire Girls). Supper was always a time when we all would be together. Although, over time, the post supper activities might differ, as there was always something happening. Ed and I helped coach little league baseball for our boys, Bruce and Bill. Also, and for several years, I helped coach Carol's softball team while Betty was the scorekeeper. Sometimes, I would give the umpires heartburn, as I knew the rules better than they did.

Jim Elk, also a JSC engineer, was the Scout Master of Bill's Boy Scout troop. He really believed in letting the boys do the planning and organizing for their functions such as canoe trips, campouts, hikes, and training sessions. Leaders were in place mainly for safety. I was an assistant scout master in the troop. Although there were monthly campouts, which Bill always attended, I was only able to take part in about 50%. Both Bill and Bruce received their Eagle rank at the very same Court of Honor.

Bill, although not too big on academics, liked to delve into the way things were put together and worked, from clocks to cars. His first car was a Volkswagen bug, which he pushed home from a neighbor's house, except for the engine, which he brought home in a wheelbarrow. After much tinkering, disassembly and reassembly he got it running. So practiced, he could extract the engine in about 30 minutes. He continues today to rely on and to add to his self taught and practical knowledge.

Carol liked school and was adventuresome. One day while catching bees in a glass jar, she fell, the jar broke, and she severed some tendons in her left hand. Quickly, Betty took her to the family doctor who sent her on to an orthopedic surgeon. Eventually, she regained full use of her hand and, perhaps, partly because I insisted she could only use a manual typewriter in typing class.

Gini was a bit more cautious. Never too excited about sports, but she always attended the other's games with Betty and me. One time at the lake, she managed to get up on water skies behind our 1958 forty HP outboard boat. After going about 100 yards she realized where she was, that is, going 25 mph over the water, she dropped the tow rope. Slightly undersized and delicate as a youngster, she is strong in heart and mind.

Side stepping a bit, the flight dynamics folks spent much of our time supporting "Data Priority" meetings (a.k.a. Mission Techniques) chaired by Bill Tindall. This forum drove the integration of the onboard crew procedures and the flight dynamics procedures and operations. The onboard guidance and control system operations were a significant focus of these meetings. It was in this forum, that the crew and ground operators formulated data exchanges for trajectory control and monitoring procedures.

The mission rules, those real time decision trees, reflected the vehicle abilities, limitations, and failure modes as discussed in the Data Priority meetings. The mission rules had a wide swath of review, from management to informal discussions between the crew and flight controllers. At one such meeting in the Flight Dynamics Staff Support Room, we were reviewing our mission rules with Gus Grissom and the other crewmembers of Apollo I. Charlie Duke was a member of the support crew for that mission, thus he was not very high on the food chain. During the meeting, poor old Charlie spilled a cup of coffee. So here a fellow, who one day will walk on the moon, is down on his hands and knees wiping up the floor with paper towels. As fate would have it, I was supporting the plugs out pad test on the evening of Jan 27, 1967, when fire within the command module took the lives of the Apollo I crew.

Since I was assigned to Apollo VII, I was highly involved in several key preflight activities: trajectory planning, developing requirements for the real time mission computer, developing mission rules, console procedures, etc. However, in August (just a month or so before Apollo VII), Jerry Bostick, my branch chief, called Ed Pavelka (the FIDO section head), Charley Parker (the Guido section head) and me to his office. He told us that we would be prime for the Apollo VIII mission which, by the way, would be going to the moon in five months. The other two Retros were to be Bostick, and John Llewellyn, my section head. It turns out that even though I had been the prime Retro on two unmanned missions, I was going to be prime on my first manned mission. Although we could not say that Apollo VIII was headed to the moon, everyone not associated with the mission knew the plan.

During one of the Apollo VIII simulations, Cliff Charlesworth, the lead flight director, could not read my writing of "8." I would write it in one motion. He called me to his console and demonstrated how to make two little circles, one above the other. After this, my "8's" were legible and I still make them that way to this very day.

The Retro primary duties (for both nominal and abort situations) were to determine the return to earth trajectory maneuvers and subsequent atmospheric entry. Key to this activity was the aerodynamic configuration of the spacecraft for entry and the weight and center of gravity of the vehicle. A component of the planning was the assured separation of the entry vehicle from the remaining elements. Expanding on the idea of safe separation is the planning to avoid any potential recontact with other vehicle elements after undocking or vehicle element separation. To this end, John Llewellyn instructed his section to develop a comprehensive "Separation Handbook" and procedures to cover all nominal and abort situations: all trajectories including launch, earth orbit, cislunar, lunar orbit, and vehicle configurations. It could have been a premonition or just good insight by John, but this book was instrumental during Apollo XIII real time planning.

On Apollo VIII, Jay Greene and I were on duty starting before launch through TLI. After separating from the SIVB, the crew felt that they were not moving away from the spent booster. The Trench then generated a midcourse correction, which definitely resulted in positive separation. Although Jay and I started out with Charlesworth for launch (the lead flight director always flew the launch phase), we changed flight directors and moved to the maroon team with Milt Windler for the transearth injection (TEI) and entry phases. Whereas the systems flight controllers stayed with a given flight director and team color, the Trench team would focus more on the trajectory activities and move from flight director team to flight director team.

At an Apollo X Data Priority meeting, the Trench pushed for a definite separation sequence for CSM separation from the LM ascent stage. However, the crew felt that they could just maneuver away from the LM after its release. As it turned out, the separation attitude had the LM toward the sun. Additionally, since the docking tunnel was left pressurized, the LM popped off into the sun when the separation bolts were fired and was lost to the view of the crew. In itself, this would not be a big deal, but the ascent stage engine was about to send the LM into a solar orbit. It can be a bit unnerving when the exact location of near-by thrusting vehicle is unknown.

After the lunar module ascent from the moon on Apollo XI, Jay and I were on the console preparing for TEI in a few hours. As the vehicle came from behind the moon, the crew had already closed out the LM, but 2 hours early. Not wanting to stay attached to the LM for 2 more hours, the Trench was tasked to generate a separation plan. Again the issue of separation arose but adequately put to bed.

With the safe return of Apollo XI, it was time for another road trip. After packing the 65 Chevy, we aimed for Colorado with camping along the way. Even with three young grade schoolers and long distances, everything was fine. While trekking along in Carlsbad Caverns, Betty noticed that going up hill tended to be a bit tiring. That is, until, she noticed Gini hanging on the back pockets of her jeans. You have to remember this child, small at birth and a bit delicate, started talking long before she decided to walk. The water in Vallecito Lake, where we had camped, sure was cold, but the kids didn't notice, I did. On our way home to Texas, we had a flat tire at Wolf Creek Pass. Being as it was time for lunch and we were near the crystal clear headwaters of the Rio Grande, I dipped out some water and Betty made chicken noodle soup and sandwiches while I changed the tire.

During the Apollo XI celebration parade in downtown Houston, and as noted in the Houston Chronicle, an "elderly" man (not so elderly in my view now) stepped from the Main Street curb and handed Neil Armstrong a small American flag. It turns out that this was my father. Later Neil asked if I would want this flag, but, like an idiot, I declined.

It seems that Jay and I always managed to be on duty for some of the more exciting times: the first manned Saturn V launch, the first manned

TLI, the first TEI, the first manned lunar entry, the first lunar landing, and the first lightning strike of a manned launch vehicle. During the Apollo XII launch, lightning stuck the vehicle shortly after liftoff. Many of the spacecraft systems were initially halted and the booster inertial guidance system had a small glitch but kept on working. The remainder of the launch went without a hitch. Not exactly sure of the orbital conditions or the integrity of the systems, the MOCR was holding its breath until data would be received from the ground station at Carnarvon, Australia. Much to the delight of the systems controllers, telemetry came in early. They were only too happy to get the early downlinked data and analyze the onboard equipment. However, Jay and I looked at each other with concern. Early acquisition of data could mean a shorter period and lower orbital altitude. But this was not the case, merely atmospheric multipath of the radio signals.

Of course Dave Reed and I had some interesting situations on Apollo XIII and Apollo XIV (discussed later). There are many stories about Apollo XIII. On several occasions, Dave and I have discussed our role in Apollo XIII. Never once did we, even remotely, consider that we might fail and lose the crew. Below I will describe an Apollo XIII issue that is known to only a few. A REFSMMAT is a mathematical expression that is used in the description of what direction the spacecraft is pointing. This description is in the terms of the values of three angles. By orienting to these angles the crew can point the vehicle in a desired attitude for a thrusting maneuver or entry into the atmosphere. REFSMMAT's were given names (for example, CUR001, OST005 or CUR003) and separate REFSMMAT's were assigned to both the CSM and LM. The associated numbers incremented every time a new REFSMMAT of a type was generated. Dave and I were the lead FIDO and RETRO on Apollo XIII and were on the entry team. The day before entry, Dave said, "let's go down to the RTCC room and practice the computations on one of the off-line computers." I responded, "good plan." Once there, I computed the final midcourse correction and entry solutions, Dave transferred them to his processors and then onto my entry displays. Lo and behold, the angles for the CM entry attitude were something I had never seen before and were completely wrong. It turns out the RTCC uses the last maneuver REFSMMAT for the CM entry attitude calculation. Since the last maneuver was done by the LM, using its unique REFSMMAT, the entry angles did not match those generated with a correct CM entry REFSMMAT. Dave and I came up with a work around for the next day, but in the future, RTCC LM REFSMMAT's started out with the number 500 to be completely distinguishable, e.g. CUR501 vs CUR001.

Although, the lead-time for upgrades or changes to the ground computer system was long, new capabilities that eliminated manual work-arounds or reflected vehicle changes were always being incorporated or improved. As the missions rolled along, we would add operational capabilities; some would be in the computer programs, others in our procedures supporting new crew activities, and some to expand our ability to handle lesser probable mishaps. Vehicle mass properties programs (weights and locations) became part of the real time computer, eliminating off line card deck processors. Originally, for a lunar module burn docked to the CSM, the thrust profile for the descent engine could only be approximated in the MCC computers. The proper profile was not modeled correctly until Apollo XIII. Also on Apollo XIII, we developed an accurate aerodynamic model for the reentry of the radioactive thermal generator fuel cask attached to the LM, which did reenter on Apollo XIII and was tracked by the AEC.

An Apollo XIII anecdote follows: shortly after retiring in 1994 and having moved to the Texas hill country, I found out that Jim Lovell would be signing his new book, "Lost Moon", at a local gift shop. With book in hand, I stood in the signing line. When Jim saw me, he invited me (almost insisted) to join him and sign books as well.

After TLI on Apollo XIV, the docking mechanism between the CSM and LM refused to connect the two vehicles. After about 1.5 hours and several attempts, some with hard contacts, docking was finally accomplished. Management decided to bring the probe back for inspection. Returning with the extra weight and finding a place to stow it in the CM were all handled in stride.

By the time Skylab came about, Mike Collins and Ron Epps were part of the Trench. These two, Bill Stoval and I along with GUIDO's George Guthrie, Ken Russell and Randy Stone provided the Trench support to the CSM and Skylab Workshop. Somewhere along the way, Phil Shaffer became a flight director. Being an old FIDO, Phil had a hard time giving up his background knowledge. If several options were in the offering, often Phil wouldn't pick the option the Trench recommended if he had any doubts. Quick learners and not to be outplayed, we would present the options but never recommended the one we preferred and of course Phil would select that option.

Stoval seemed to have an unwritten rule that one had to prove himself before he could be recognized with his middle initial. For example, Bill would be WMS and I would be CFD. After some maturing as Trench members (even though they had been top notch in the old Recovery Division), Collins and Epps received their middle initial, MFC and RCE, respectively. (Another time during launch simulations and when Bill Stoval had lost one of his contact lens, I had to help him read the launch plots to make abort calls).

For Skylab, the Trench continuously supported the active CSM phases, e.g. launch, rendezvous, maneuvers for repeating ground track, undocking, deorbit, and reentry. When the CSM was dormant, the FIDO's would come in daily for a few hours to update the trajectory for the other controllers and compute sets of emergency deorbit data. Of course, a Trench team member would always be on call with a pager in hand. During Apollo, the projection plotboards in the front of the MOCR were controlled by the Trench but with some agreements with the other controllers. Well, since we were only present for about 4 hours a day, the flight directors made their move. We would walk in and see either polka dots or butterflies on the 10 by 20 plotboard, sort of unsettling. Also during Apollo, we kept the lights in the front of the MOCR fairly dim to assure good plotboard contrast. On our every Skylab shift, Stoval had to dim the lights. Even Pat Patneski, the official JSC photographer, got used to the dim lighting.

Steve Bales headed the group that managed the Skylab Workshop on-board computers. These controllers sat at the Guidance console just to the right of the FIDO console. Routinely, the MOCR systems were checked from computer operations and telemetry parameters to the annunciation lights on the consoles. On one of my shifts, they were testing the consoles and all of the lights on the Guidance console were lit. Rudy Tunello happened to be supporting at the time. Steve walked in and in a panic screamed "Rudy what have you done." Rudy calmly turned around saying, "It is just a console function test."

After Skylab, the Apollo Soyuz Test Project (ASTP) came along. By this time the FIDO ranks consisted of Bill Stoval, Mike Collins, Ron Epps, and myself. I don't remember who the ASTP Guidos were. Many folks from JSC made trips to Russia to coordinate and plan the mission. I made one trip in September of 1974. Glynn Lunney was the NASA program manager for ASTP and met with the group before our trip. Some were concerned about the conditions in Russia especially dealing with their laws. His comment was "Just act like ladies and gentlemen and you will be fine." As usual, his advice was right on. The first day when I entered the Russian space office building, I started to take off my coat. One of the Russians said I should keep it, as the heat in the building will not be turned on until October, good suggestion. Our Russian hosts were all friendly and took us to several local points of interest including Star City and the monastery town of Zagorsk (now Sergiev Posad).

After two weeks in Russia, we headed home, but via Denmark and Germany. The hotel bed in Moscow seemed short, but not so in Denmark, those guys are tall. Touring about Copenhagen brought us to see the Little Mermaid in the harbor and the famous walking street. And then on to Germany.

The Munich Oktober Fest starts in September and ends the first week of October, thus we managed to get there in time to enjoy the festivities. The beer and food were good and I enjoyed the om-pah music. While in Munich, I rented a Volkswagen so several of us could take a ride to Garmisch in the Bavarian Alps. Our group consisted of Chuck Lewis, Chuck Horstman, Maurice Kennedy and me. Driving around in downtown Munich, I kept running into the same street. It took a bit for me to figure out that Einbahnstrasse meant One-Way-Street. (Note: At that time, JSC employees were allowed to take annual leave while on travel.)

When Ed Pavelka's son, Bruce was about 14, Ed bought him a Honda Mini Trail CT 70 motorcycle, a pretty small bike with only 10 inch wheel rims. Ed and I decided to get our motorcycle license on the CT 70 as it was street legal, although, we did look a bit awkward on it. Loading it in the back of my Ford station wagon (don't see these much any more, now they call them SUV's) we were off to the Dover Street Texas Drivers License office. After taking the written test, Ed was the first for the driving part. A DPS officer and I followed him in the station wagon. Using various horn blasts, the officer could direct Ed as he rode the test course. Ed passed with flying colors and I was next. I had barely gone a block when I was signaled to return to the starting point. The officer informed me that I had failed because the chase pilot, Ed, had sped in a school zone. It was really not Ed's fault as the route turned into the middle of a school zone where there were no signs. Back the next day, I passed too. On the subject of motorcycles, I told Bill I would never buy him one, which I did not. However, going into the Honda shop with Ed, I put Bill's name in a drawing for a prize. Several weeks later, Bill and Bruce attended the drawing at a local movie theater and as luck would have it, Bill's named was pulled out winning a Honda MT 125. Of course, I also ended up with a used Yamaha CT 175.

Again, my Dad, always the one to be thinking outside the box, had 5 quail eggs sent to our kids. After setting up the incubator, the eggs had to be turned over a couple of times daily for 24 days. My good buddy

Ed agreed to turn them while we were out of town for a few days, thus becoming a God Father. Finally, one egg, thank goodness only one, hatched out. It was a little rooster who made many trips to the lake in a canary cage during the five years he lived.

Then there were the carpools. When Jay Greene first arrived, he lived in apartments on Red Bluff Road in Pasadena. Since I drove Red Bluff to JSC (then MSC), we carpooled for a bit, his Corvair and my Renault Caravelle (with its weak front springs and seeming to be always going down hill). Car pooling from Friendswood mainly consisted of Ed Pavelka, Denny Holt, and me. Now while I drove an old 1960 Chevrolet red primered pickup truck (with vice-grip pliers for an inside door handle) and Denny had either Ruth Stoval's old Mustang or Ken Russell's old Pontiac, Ed had a nice shiny Mercedes as his carpool vehicle. So much for my being classy.

Speaking of Red Bluff Road, I will never forget the time Jim I'Anson showed up late for work. It had been raining and Jim, also driving on Red Bluff, got into a skid and ended up in the ditch between the divided lanes. Seeing what was about to happen, he dove for the floorboard, wrapped his hands about his head and managed to get out unscathed.

Some folks are just jumpy. I usually brown bagged for lunch. After eating, I would blow up the bag and pop it with a loud bang. Every time, and with his back to me, Jerry Elliot would come unglued at the bang. It got so that when I would start crinkling the bag, you could just see Jerry cringe, but that did not stop me.

However, the most fun project was the Orbiter Approach and Landing Tests (ALT). These flights were at Edwards AFB. Don Puddy led the MCC activity. While most of JSC was working the Shuttle program for orbital flight, a few of us, without a lot of interference, were gearing up for ALT. Being a short/small program with limited resources, I got to design the flights, check them out in the simulator, coordinate with the FAA Los Angeles Center, China Lake NAS, DFRC, Edwards AFB and of course the flight crews. A Boeing 747 was used to piggy back the orbiter and serve as an airborne launch platform. Using plotboards, like in the early days, I directed the trajectory from 747 takeoff through Orbiter separation, flight, and landing. I even got to ride the Shuttle Training Aircraft (STA) with Joe Engle and Dick Truly. Prior to my ride, the STA simulated a tail cone-on configuration. The tail cone-on flight path was shallow and relatively mild. The sim-engineer sat between the instructor pilot and the astronaut. On my flight, the simulation was configured for tail cone-off. Standing behind the astronaut and leaning on the bulkhead behind him, I held on to the shoulder harness of the sim-engineer, as he was not wearing it (it was his first tail cone-off approach). At 24 degrees down, all you can see is the ground; the horizon is above the top of the windscreen. We made 20 approaches. On the second approach, the sim-engineer had his shoulder harness secured! One time on travel to Downey and Edwards, I was with Don Puddy, Gene Kranz, and Harold Draughon. Driving back to Downey from Edwards, Gene asked to stop in Lancaster so he could get some beer. Although I decided to abstain, the rest enjoyed the ride. Little did we know that California had an open container law. Fortunately we were not stopped.

Way back in 1964 and while moonlighting on airplane simulators at Houston Northwest Airport (now D. W. Hooks Airport), I started flying lessons. Trading my labor for flight time, I was much better at fixing simulators than learning to fly. Tom McElmurry, working ALT for Deke Slayton, was a flight instructor. Under his tutelage I passed my FAA checkride in 1976. However, Tom's confidence in me always seemed to be much greater than my own. After several hours of instruction, it became time to "solo." As soon as the wheels left the ground I said to myself, "what have I gotten myself into....I have got to land this thing." On my first flight as a licensed pilot, and as to be expected, Ed Pavelka was my first passenger.

Living a few doors away from Ed and Joyce Pavelka, many games of dominos, chips and dips, and rum and cokes were experienced. Then on July 24-25 1979, came Tropical Storm Claudette with 43" of rain in Alvin in 24 hours. Most all of Friendswood flooded. While watching the water rise in the street, and as best we could, we raised our furniture and thank God we saved most of it. It was night and as the water came into the house, we turned off the power and met the Pavelkas as we headed up the street to our car pool buddy's home, Denny and Kathleen Holt's. Being about a foot higher than ours, Holt's home barely escaped being flooded too. As I remember, there were about 22 folks, including Denny's expectant cousin, there that night. The folks in our neighborhood banded together and recovered nicely from this ordeal.

After the kids were out of the nest, Betty and I drove to New Orleans to visit my sister, Molly. Molly, a.k.a. Sister Marie Celine, had been a Nun since 1954. Her convent, which had a guest apartment, was an old mansion near Tulane University off St. Charles Street. And of course, we made the trip during Mardi Gras. One day, all three of us were walking through the French Quarter and were "mooned" from a balcony above the street. Betty and I turned red, but Molly just smiled.

As I felt I had the best job at JSC, I really never had the desire to enter management until after ALT. As head of the Ascent and Entry Procedures section, I was responsible for the onboard checklists and cue cards for shuttle launch and landing procedures. We developed the first laptop computer system to be carried into orbit as well as the shuttle night landing lighting system (both are still in use).

Early in the Shuttle program, my Ascent and Entry Procedures section was moved to the Mission Operations Branch (current home of the Trenchmen) under Jay Greene. I was back home, and not much later, Jay joined the Flight Directors Office, leaving me as branch chief of MOB and responsible for the Trench. Finding a more regular daily schedule I was able to enroll at the U. of Houston Clear Lake and earn an MS in physical science.

Some of the JSC reorganizations are a bit hazy with the merging of the operations functions and later the mission planning activities. Along they way, I was Jon Harpold's deputy in the Flight Design and Dynamics Division. This division combined the areas of flight dynamics, ascent and entry crew procedures, and flight design (the old Mission Planning and Analysis Division). While there, I worked the JSC range safety coordination with the DoD. After the Challenger accident, I led the team that reviewed the entire flight design process as well as a review of the range safety methodology. With this background, but very little computing platform design experience, I was tasked to lead the effort to develop an integrated flight analysis and design system (FADS). The players in this effort were contractor ground systems developers (Loral) and flight design users (RSOC). I had quite a juggling act but with Leroy Hall at Loral and Glynn Lunney at RSOC, I had strong support for all of my decisions. With lots of good people, contractors and civil servants, the FADS project turned out to be very successful.

As the FADS was significantly more powerful than the systems it replaced, it morphed into the Integrated Planning System which would take in the crew activities planning in addition to its original task of trajectory analysis, design, and planning. Alas, my last assignment at JSC was Chief of the Integrated Planning System Office.

The many learning experience opportunities at JSC and the guidance of my leaders have given me a greater education than can be found at any institution throughout the world. The privilege of participating in one of man's greatest adventures is an absolute highlight of my life. The Presidential Medal of Freedom (for Apollo 13) and the NASA Outstanding

Leadership Award (for the Flight Analysis and Design System) are my tangible components that represent this honor.

Retiring to 26 acres in the hill country near Austin, Texas, we have raised goats, and built a house, a hanger, an airplane, and a landing strip. I have had several aerospace consulting projects, primarily in Seattle, and have published several aircraft oriented articles. For recreation, we have traveled to all 50 states and also have visited Canada, Australia, New Zealand, Central America and South America. I even managed to get a ride on a Navy Greyhound aircraft when it landed on the aircraft carrier Eisenhower. After spending the night onboard, I was subsequently catapulted off the carrier the next day. What a great experience.

Back in 2008, my good friend and colleague, Mike Collins, retired from JSC after more than 40 years of service. At his retirement party and during his farewell speech, he made a most surprising statement, certainly unexpected by me, when he said, "the most influential person in my career is Chuck Deiterich." What an honor.

Life's adventures continue.

V - Stephen G. Bales

FROM IOWA TO THE TRENCH - A GUIDO'S TALE

Copyright © 2012

By Stephen G. Bales
17 Hart Lane
Sewell, NJ 08080

On October 7, 1942 the Germans and Russians were desperately fighting for control of Stalingrad, the Japanese were trying to reinforce their positions on Guadalcanal, President Franklin Roosevelt was deciding on how to allocate American resources among numerous choices (Britain, Russia, our own military), and ….. Stephen G. Bales was born to Katherine Alice and Lyle M. Bales[1] in the Ottumwa Hospital. The attending was a Dr. Whitehouse who would be delivering his last baby before leaving for duty as a Navy officer. Mom would later tell me that when Dr. Whitehouse made a follow up house call (they did that in 1942) to 169 North Davis, Ottumwa, IA where she was living with her parents – John Ray and Eunice "Bessie" Glaze—he was in his Naval uniform and would be leaving for duty in days.

Dr. Whitehouse was one of millions of Americans who would leave for the service in 1942. Another was my dad, Lyle M. Bales, who had been drafted for service in August but asked for a three month deferment to be at home until I was born. At 39 he was one of the older US draftees. Mom visited him during basic training in Texas. She vowed never to go to Texas again as it was so hot and the residents took advantage of the visiting relatives by charging them large prices to stay in chicken coop type places. Decades later I had to convince her Houston wasn't really like west Texas and anyway we all had air conditioning now. Following basic training T/5 Lyle Bales was sent to France, arriving in September 1944 as part of the 102nd infantry division.

For the next 10 months the division fought from the German-Netherlands border to the Elbe River where they met Russian soldiers on May 3, 1945 only four days before the war in Europe was over. Dad never talked much about the war to anyone including mom. Once he did talk about seeing a barn where the Germans had burned and then shot many people. Researching this decades later I found the 102nd uncovered the massacre of a thousand concentration camp inmates at Gardelegen – this became a documented war crime site and today is a German national memorial.

So for the first three years of my life I grew up in mom's parents Ot-

---

1   *Dad had been married twice before marrying mom in 1941; both wives had died. He had two sons (William and Melvin) from his first marriage who were in High School at the time and living in Eldon IA with their grandparents. Mom offered to take both into their home as soon as Dad came back from the War but both boys had lived many years in that environment and wanted to stay. Mom did become close to both and when she made special comforters for all her sons in 1990 she made one for William (Melvin was killed in a car wreck in 1970) which William told her he treasured.*

tumwa home, watched by my grandmother while mom worked as a beauty operator and my grandfather worked at the Ottumwa John Deere plant (a.k.a. "the Dane") in the paint department. At that time the paint contained lead. Today we know that lead is extremely dangerous and remove any leaded paint from our homes. But nack then the workers dipped the equipment in the paint and got it on themselves. John Ray Glaze died in April, 1956 from a disease that was never clearly diagnosed, but in retrospect I believe the lead poisoning was a major contributor to his death. Grandfather was small (5'2") and strong. When mom was young they lived on a farm and later they owned a service station in Humphreys, MO. She said that many times grandpa was easily able to best the high school boys that tried to best him in a strength contest –probably she meant arm wrestling.

Mom told me that every day my dad was in Europe she read the battlefield situation map in the Ottumwa Courier. She would also point out each of the countries to me such as France, Belgium, and England and Germany. Turns out that without knowing it she was using a technique similar to the one we used to teach our boys which followed the Glen Domman "Better Baby Series." To her surprise, and the surprise of many others, at age two I was pointing to many of the European countries, saying their names, and when I came to France I said "my daddy's in France".[2]

Age 3

Dad came home in August 1945 when I was almost three. Apparently I was in the habit of going up to people and biting them. Since my grandparents and mother were overprotective, they hadn't done much about it. Although I don't recall doing it , mom told me that one day I decided to crawl up to my dad and bit him on the leg. That was the end of my biting anyone!! Dad reflexively backhanded me so hard that I rolled over twice.

Another trait I'd developed was taking off my jumper and running naked on the sidewalk in front of 169 Davis. I do remember how my streaking career

---

2 *It wasn't always a treat for either my relatives or me. My Aunt Elaine saw me do this and later decided to "show me off". Well as you might guess I apparently was totally silent during this session, as mom later told me.*

was terminated. I recall removing my blue jumper and feeling nice and cool, but as I passed the edge of the house I heard a WHAT! from the back yard. It was my dad spotting me running around without any clothes. Well that was all of the streaking I ever wanted to do.

Move to Agency Iowa

Sometime in 1946 we moved to a little house across the street from the school building in Agency, Iowa. I remember my twin brothers, Max & Jack coming home in big baskets having been delivered by the same Dr. Whitehouse who had survived the war and would later deliver my youngest brother Richard. Since they were born in August, we must have moved there earlier in the summer.

At the time I didn't realize it, but with the medical technology of the mid 40's my brothers were lucky to be alive. They were just over two lbs. each – not a huge problem today but a very serious one in 1946. Both were in an incubator for many days (probably 100% oxygen so they were fortunate to keep their eyesight—others in that environment did not); and they had other problems as well. And when they finally got home mom told me that she often had to keep them in the oven since there were no home incubators available to us (nor probably to most in 1946). And since there were no oxygen masks either, they simply were kept warm with normal air, which may have kept them from going blind later in life.

On top of everything else, both twins caught whooping cough before they were a year old and my parents had to constantly watch over them for weeks. Fortunately God blessed our family and both became healthy but not without a lot of concern from my parents (with little being communicated to me at the time).

I remember watching all the kids go to school starting that fall and asking my mother why I couldn't go there. With an October birthday, by the rules I wouldn't have started the 1st grade (there was no kindergarden) until I was six. Apparently my parents asked the principal, who was a Mr. Schriber, to let me go early. So one early Sept in 1947 I started 1st grade. The biggest thing I remember was that mom had to be gone that morning. It was one of the few times I recall she was gone, as she had stopped working in 1946 to be at home with us. So I had to start school alone. I remember every other kid coming with their mother who talked several minutes with the teacher. This doesn't seem like anything today, but it must have had a big impact on me as it's the main thing I remember from the first year in school.

In the third grade I learned about death as my Grandmother Bales passed away at the age of 90. I recall sitting in the family room at the funeral home between my father and my Uncle Paul. My uncle cried several times during the service but dad was dry eyed. At that time I suppose I thought that men didn't cry, so I was shocked at my Uncle's behavior. Later I asked mom why Uncle Paul cried and dad didn't; she said that was the way dad had been since coming back. The day he came home from Europe he said: "I have a lot to tell you some day". But she said that day hadn't come yet and I wonder if it ever did.

I was good at one sport –the American pastime in the 50's—baseball. My mother loved baseball and I would usually come home after school finding her listening to the Chicago Cubs playing someone. I learned the names of most of the players on the Cubs and their National League opponents. Two decades later, one of my NASA co-workers and Apollo XI teammate Jay Greene from Brooklyn, was quite surprised as I named the entire starting lineup of the 1951 Brooklyn Dodgers.

I started playing Little League baseball on the Agency Cardinals at nine. We didn't have any uniforms, didn't play in a league, and lost the 5 or 6 games we played which were essentially tune up games for some of the Little League teams in the "big city" of Ottumwa (pop 30,000). The next year the town bought us uniforms, built a nice field, and along with six other small towns formed a league. We had a 3 -13 record. However there were several of us the same age and we matured as a team, winning all of our games in 1953. The next year, and my last year in Little League baseball, the Agency Cardinals were invited to participate in a July 4th tournament in Ottumwa. In the first round we were matched against the best team in the 24 team Ottumwa league. I believe the tournament organizers thought a small town team would be a good first round tune up for their powerful league leader. You can imagine their surprise and dismay when we beat them soundly. I still remember the great game our excellent pitcher, Mike Whitman, pitched and the two times our center fielder, Clark Yeager, hit the fence with long drives. As shortstop I made two backhand catches that killed their attempt to rally. July 4th, 1954 was a very special day!!

Later that year my parents and my grandparents Glaze decided to buy a large home surrounded by ten acres on the outskirts of Agency. This place had a barn, two cows which I learned to milk, pigs, chickens, and a 2 acre orchard with cherry, plumb, and peach trees. The chickens roamed the orchard and part of their diet was the bugs in it.

In back of the house was a dilapidated old barn. My father, Uncle Paul (his brother), and a couple of other men laid out the foundations for a new one. After digging the trench that outlined the new building and pouring the concrete for it, the rest of the building was assembled little by little over the next year. Dad did most of the work; sometimes I could help –like nailing boards to a part of the framing he had constructed. When it was completed we painted the barn a clean white – it actually looked much better than the old gray stucco house. Later we painted the house white and rebuilt the front porch to make the house much better. In 2010 I returned to view the old house. It still looks good but the ten acres and the orchard have been replaced with new houses. Even in a small Iowa town urbanization goes forward (or backward depending on your point of view).

The old barn was about 40 feet behind the house and the new barn was built on the opposite side of it. One Sunday afternoon, before we tore the old one down, several of us heard a noise between the barns. There was a small pup that had been abandoned and somehow found her way across two fences and ended up between those barns. Although we had many animals, our family had never had a dog. So after some begging by me and my brothers, our parents agreed to adopt it. That dog stayed with the family for over 17 more years and finally died after I had long left the family home. That had to be one of the best days for our old family dog –Ginger; she had just fallen into a big tub of butter!

I remember one particular event that happened sometime in the summer of 1955. For some reason we decided to sleep out under the stars. It was a beautiful night and my dad pointed out the milky way and the big dipper. I was fascinated and awed by the heavens –maybe this was a precursor of how awed I would be when humans started to actually leave the earth and see the stars in a different way.

Move to Fremont, Iowa

When my dad was released from the army in 1945, he had gone back to work at the Morrell's Meat Packing plant in Ottumwa. During the next 4 years the union at the plant had called at least one long duration strike –during that time he worked for Grover Elsenson at Grover's hardware in Agency. Grover offered him a permanent job and he continued to work there until 1956. Dad then decided to try owning a hardware store and after several months of looking our family and another (the McDaniels—Opie & Charlotte) went together and bought one in Fremont.

At this time I thought I would grow up to be a small town businessman, probably in the hardware business like Mr. Elsenson. I had an interest in business even at an early age and had a million questions about one— how does someone get started? How do you get people to work for you? How much to pay them? Where do you get the hardware to sell? How do you know people will come into the store and spend money with you and if they do how much do you need to make on each item? This interest would be with me forever, but my life was going to go in a different direction for several decades due to events that would shake up in the US and the world in the late 50's.

We moved to Fremont in Sept 1956. I wasn't particularly happy about doing it since I had made good friends in Agency – Mike, Clark, and others like Denny Nelson, John Moyer, and Alan Tarbell. But life went on and soon of course I had new friends like Larry Deutchle (lived on a farm), Ron Clark, Doyle Fielder, John Garbison (a preachers son who also lived on a farm), Keith Dinsmore and others. When I transferred I was in 8th grade and the teacher was Mr. Earnest McBeth [in 2010 I attended a class reunion – Mr. McBeth looked almost identically like he looked in 1956—it was amazing].

Two things happened in the 15 months that directed my future into something other than business – both had to do with space. In October, 1956 the Disney network has a multi hour special describing how the experts at that time though humans would first go to the moon. The animated film turned out to be surprisingly accurate – at least on how we would first go around the moon. Fourteen years later I would be discussing this film at a dinner with many other space dignitaries. One of the men at the table started to smile, and said he had been the technical director on the project. He then introduced me to the producer; both said they had been surprised at the level of positive reaction the film had on many young people who had later become space scientists and engineers.

On October 4, 1957, three days before my 15th birthday, the Soviet Union launched Sputnik and the world changed for me and millions of Americans. It is hard to describe how worried and angry most people I talked to during the next few months were. Sputnik launched many things – including an immense amount of American government money into research and education. Two organizations started would really influence our lives –NASA and the Defense Advanced Research Projects Agency (DARPA) –NASA would put a man on the moon in 1969 and DARPA would make many technological advances, not the least of which was the initial development of a network that would become today's internet.

All this affected me both immediately and in the long term. Immediately I was angry and humiliated that our country, either did not –or could not—be first into space. Later we learned that in fact the US could have easily been first with a satellite but no one in Washington really understood the political significance of launching first (what an irony –politics is what our politicians are supposed to know). Later it would really encourage me to be part of this new space race. The fact that the government was encouraging science and technology made it possible for me to get scholarships and low interest loans to attend Iowa State University as an aerospace engineering student; things that would not have been available a few years earlier.

I was not a great athlete in high school, but I could run fast for the short distance races. I ran the 100 and 220 yd dash and came in fourth at two regional track meets held at Oskaloosa and Ottumwa. I really did like school – all subjects. Although our school was very small (Fremont had 600 people, my class had 22 students) we had very good teachers who prepared me well for both college and later life. My Freshman English teacher was a Ms. Beaver – she attended the 2010 reunion at the age of 91. Ms. Beaver gave us a good basic foundation in English grammar. Our math and science teacher was Mr. Donald Allen – he had attended Iowa State University as a chemistry student and was an excellent teacher for the basic sciences.

As a high school freshman I knew that I wanted to go to college but didn't know how our family could afford it. Starting in 1955 I worked every summer to make money. For the first 3 years I mowed yards –at one time I had over 40 yards to keep up. This not only made money but gave me a chance to talk with some of the interesting adults in the town that I otherwise would not have known. One was Mr. Bob Fell, who was a graduate of Grinnell College and an excellent writer. At the 2010 reunion I read from a very funny article about a dog that had been a town favorite in the 30's. Another was a Mr. Lincoln Ackerman, the local real estate agent and a man very involved in Democratic Party politics (he was a delegate to the 1956 Democratic national convention). Also a Grinnell College graduate, Mr. Ackerman wrote an important recommendation for me to get a scholarship at Iowa State. And he, Bob Fell, and others I got to know by talking with them a few minutes after completing their yards, gave me insight into business and how government impacted it (i.e., how much a typical farm was selling for, what impact the federal farm subsidy laws had to sales price, etc).

Other clients were older citizens who no longer had the strength to mow their own yards. Many were elderly ladies, such as Ms. Blanch Fell

(Bob's mother), who from time to time spent a few minutes discussing life as it existed in the late 1800's and early 1900's.

Then for five summers I worked summers as a farm hired hand. Sometimes it was just miserable –especially cleaning out the hog pens in mid July. Often it was lonely, like those many days when I walked fence lines or open fields cutting out thistles and sour dock. Then it could be fun, especially on those days when I worked the fields in a tractor mowing hay. For sure it made me realize how hard farmers labored.

Going to Iowa State University

In 1960 I was accepted as a student in Aerospace Engineering at Iowa State University (ISU); the first person in our family to go to college. I had a scholarship covering most of the first year costs and planned to work and borrow enough to get through the other three years. Although there were no aerospace firms in Iowa the department was highly rated – in part because ISU was very strong in engineering and the Dean at that time (Dean Towne –who had been one of the designers of the original color TV system) had demanded all his departments be strong. The department had started in1929 and in 1941 a Professor Bevan constructed one of the first large wind tunnels which was used in support of our World War II effort. It was still operating when I was a student. Two early graduates were T.A. Wilson (1943) who was the project manager for the B-52 and later President of the Boeing Company and John Yardley (1944).

This was my first time to be away from home for more than a few days and the experience was overwhelming for several months. On the first week of engineering orientation the lecturer said "look to your right and look to your left – two of you will be gone before next year". He was correct but it sure didn't do much for my confidence.

The dorm I lived in was called Friley Hall, a men only dorm with about 5,000 people[3]. Friley is broken up into 40 person "Houses" each of which had a Head Resident (HR) who represented the dorm system and enforced rules as well as a governing unit with a President, Treasurer and Secretary -- this governing body primarily arranged social events and tried to form a cohesive 40 man group. A House was a corridor about 100 yards long and each one had a den composed of 15 chairs and a TV. I lived in Lange House for all 4 years and it really was a cohesive group; probably because, unlike most Houses, in the Fall of 1960 35

---

[3] *All dorms at ISU in 1960 were either men only or women only and the women had to be inside the dorm by 10pm on weekdays and midnight on Saturdays.*

new Freshmen came to Lange House. Most of us stayed for the full 4 years and I formed several very strong friendships with these men.

ISU was on the quarter system, with Fall Quarter starting in early September and finishing just prior to Thanksgiving. I managed to get B's in all courses except engineering drawing (today everyone uses CAD, but then it was pencil, drafting table, T-Square, etc) where I got my first and only D.

In the Fall quarter I was in a three man room; at the end of the quarter one of my roommates flunked out and the other moved to another House where he had friends from his high school. The Head Resident (HR) assigned me another roommate – Craig McLaughlin and I stayed roommates and close friends for the next two years.

Craig had been in the Navy for four years where he had been an electronic technician stationed at the ground base in Naples. He was returning to school to become an electrical engineer. Craig was easy to get along with and gave me a little insight into what might await after college.

Most of the time during my college years I was so busy that the outside world didn't penetrate. But there were times it did –JFK's inaugural address in 1961 (Ask not...), President Kennedy's goal to reach the moon in a decade, the first US man in orbit, the Cuban Missile Crisis, and the President's assassination.

It is hard to describe in 2012 how the Glenn flight caught the attention of the nation and this aerospace student. I caught a glimpse of the original Mission Control Center on TV and wondered what it would be like to work there, never imagining that someday I would do so, but in the new one at Houston.

Since Craig was a former serviceman, he was more aware of the dangers we faced during that almost fatal October in 1962. I remember one night when he said "the Navy told everyone to get out of those waters close to Cuba now!" and then saying that means there could be real trouble by tomorrow. I fell asleep that night for the first time thinking that we all might not be there the next day. After reading two days later in the Des Moines Register that the crisis seemed to have been defused, I thought we probably all overreacted. Reading accounts written 30 years later, it appears that if anything I under reacted to what possibly was mankind's most serious crisis.

My grades steadily improved after the first quarter and by my sophomore year they really improved. At the end of that year I started making the Dean's List and stayed there throughout my college career. This was no small feat given the talent that was in the ISU aerospace classes of 1964, '65, &' 67. One I knew well, Ron Bailey ('64), went on to get his PhD then go to NASA Ames where he became the founder of NASA's Numerical Aerodynamics Simulation and High Performance and Communication Programs. Jim Johnson ('64) was Boeing's VP for Engineering and then President of Gulfstream Aerospace. John Tannehill ('65) also was a leader in computational fluid dynamics (CFD). Vance Coffman ('67) became the CEO of Lockheed Martin.

In November 1963, just minutes before leaving my room to take a final Fall Quarter exam in aeronautics, I heard a confused radio announcement that there was a report the President had been shot in Dallas. I waited to hear something else for as long as I could, then frustrated at learning nothing else walked to the test listening to the buzz from others also going to and from final exams. About halfway through the test our instructor, Dale Anderson (who developed a major computational fluid dynamics capability at ISU and became Dean of Graduate Studies at Univ. of Texas) announced: "the President died at 1:30 pm this afternoon". My fall vacation turned out much differently than planned. The continuous TV coverage of President Kennedy's burial was a sobering experience that nothing or no one was invulnerable and that anything could unexpectedly end up badly.

Summer of '64 at NASA Houston

Because I started to work 20+ hrs/week in my Junior year, I had not taken three electives required to graduate in May 1964 and would not graduate until November 1964. That spring, as I heard my classmates talk about the jobs they had secured at different aerospace firms, I decided this had been a big mistake. I should have taken the extra load and accepted whatever it did to my grades. But as often happens events worked out differently. Fortunately delaying graduation made things turn out better than I ever could have imagined.

None of my classmates knew much about, or talked about NASA as a career. But motivated by my interest in the Glenn flight, I had gone to the library and read about this relatively new government agency and its work. It seemed that the Kennedy Center in Florida or the new Manned Spacecraft Center in Houston were the places to go if you wanted to be involved in the manned spaceflight business. I found the government job application form and sent one to Houston (and maybe to Florida also, but I can't remember).

When I came home that May mom said "there is a big manila envelope that just arrived for you and it looks like it's from the government". Two weeks later I was driving a newly purchased, rough '57 Ford the 1,200 miles from Iowa to Houston not having a clue what to expect.

I was assigned to help Dick Holt who was chief of the Operations Branch, Flight Support Division, Flight Operations Directorate. Dick had requested an intern because his time was constantly being drained by requests to give tours of the new Houston Mission Control Center (MCC). What an opportunity!! My job was to learn as much about the control center -- I was going to get paid to learn about the exact place I wanted to work.

Weeks later I started giving tours. The first few were somewhat rough I suspect, but no one complained to Dick. Getting inside the new MCC was enough for most of the people. After awhile, as I learned more about the building and the control positions and was giving a tour each day. Dick only had to give one on special occasions where the visitor had enough gravitas to warrant his personal attention.

What a great place to be for someone who was interested in someday working in the MCC. When I arrived in June NASA had completed Project Mercury and Gemini had not yet started. It was clear that the old Kennedy MCC was not capable of performing the more complex Gemini Rendezvous missions (not to mention the lunar missions) and work on the Houston MCC had just started. The building structure was finished, carpet was on the third and second floors, computers installed in the first floor, and that was about it. During the first week Dick's assistant Joel Moore briefed me on the basics of the building where I struggled to learn the names of the rooms and their functions. There was a Mission Operations Control Room –MOCR pronounced MOK-ER) – where it looked like all the final decisions were made, the Staff Support Rooms (SSR's) somehow were to help each of the operators in the FCR, the Main Computer Room with four IBM 7094's, and other support computer and electronic areas such as the Master Digital Command System (MCDS) and the Communications Computer Processor.

Joel gave me a layout of the FCR consoles, the computer room floor plans, a phone book, and encouraged me to talk to as many people in each of the different areas as possible in order to give a better tour. Dick Holt also assigned me the task of developing a first cut of an MCC brochure that could be used to help future tour guides. As a shy young intern the last thing I would have ever done was to call up someone and ask them about their job – especially since I assumed that if every man (there didn't seem to be any women engineers) in the building wasn't studying something every minute of the day that the Gemini Program would fail.

But I wanted to do a good job and Joel helped. Many of the computer operators and engineers worked as contractor support for the Mission Support Division and were willing to spend some time explaining what each of their computers were and what they were going to do in the mission. Some of them gave me books to read while others, like John Hatcher and Jim Fucci liked to tell stories about Mercury and something called the "remote sites". I learned these were small control centers placed around the globe that monitored the spacecraft when it was not over the US. For Apollo these would all become remote sites and route their data on "high speed" lines to the MCC, but for Gemini there were small teams of flight controllers who would deploy to these sites to support the program.

A few weeks after I arrived, the Division Chief, Pete Clements, invited several of the interns to his office for a visit. I was surprised to find out he knew who I was and the job I had been assigned. Later I discovered that Mr. Clements was the first Network Controller in the Mercury MCC responsible for the status of all the remote sites supporting the Mercury missions. Pete said he would call John Hodge, the chief of the Flight Control Division, where all the flight controllers worked and ask that his Branch Chiefs give me a short interview on what they did. What an opening.

For the next month I visited every branch in the Flight Control Division. All these branches were headed by veterans of Mercury control who were going to become leaders in Gemini and beyond. I met Gene Kranz who had his assistant Joe Roach give me a briefing on the role of the Procedures Officer. Mel Brooks took time to explain Agena (the unmanned vehicle that the Gemini spacecraft would rendezvous with) systems and someone (forget who) gave the rundown on Gemini systems.

Next I had the chance to meet with Glynn Lunney who spent almost an hour of his time explaining the Flight Dynamics Branch responsibilities. There was the Flight Dynamics Officer (call sign FIDO), Retrofire Officer (RETRO) and Guidance Officer (GUIDO) positions. After leaving his office I was sure that I wanted to work in this Branch and send Glynn a note to this effect before I returned to school.

Flight Dynamics Branch (FDB) Dec 1964

Four months later I arrived in Houston assigned to the Flight Dynamics Branch thanks to Glynn. A good recommendation from Pete Clements may also have helped as he had been pleased how I had offloaded from Dick Holt and completed the final tour guide package.

My wife, Sandra, says "you must have driven the real engineers crazy". She has long recognized that my thought patterns and behavior are not as organized and methodical as those usually associated with excellent engineers. If it had not been for Sputnik and the early manned spaceflight programs, I probably would have gone into accounting or business.

There were some really great logical, organized thinkers in the Flight Dynamics Branch –Phil Shaffer and Charlie Parker come to mind immediately. But at first I didn't drive them crazy because I was too intimidated to say much. Glynn assigned me to the Gemini Section which was getting close to flying their first manned mission –Gemini 3. The leading Gemini operators, including the Section Chief Cliff Charlesworth, were coming back from Florida after the unmanned Gemini 2 booster that had shutdown on the pad (the old Mercury Control Center would be used until Gemini 4).

When he came back to Houston, Cliff assigned me to the FIDO group and I took an open desk in an office with Ed Pavelka, Charlie Parker (senior GUIDO), and Ken Russell (backup GUIDO). Once again I enjoyed good fortune. By sitting in the same room as Charlie I was able to learn more about guidance systems and spaceflight in six months than I could have learned from others in years. Charlie had worked on guidance systems for Western Electric, really knew those systems, and could explain complex concepts clearly and simply. I don't think he ever taught school either before or after his NASA career; he would have been a great instructor. I also lucked out because both Ken and Ed, who had some experience but were also still learning their jobs, were both helpful and courteous to this "newbie".

The first manned Gemini mission was just months away, and I was able to watch the back team Ed (FDO), Ken (GUIDO), and Dave Massaro (RETRO) perform in launch and entry simulations. At first I didn't have a clue as to what they were doing, or understand half of what they said, because the acronyms were coming so fast and often. Fortunately Glynn had directed that the section write a procedures handbook which gave a detailed description of each position's responsibilities. Between reading the book, asking questions, and listening to Charlie describe the guidance system and various aspects of trajectory design and rendezvous I started to catch onto what the section really did.

In mid 1965 one of the new Guidance Officer candidates decided to leave and Cliff assigned me to the Guidance group. This fit in perfectly as I now had reason to ask both Charlie and Ken more and more about guidance systems and watch them during simulation training.

In addition to the fun (yes fun) of working in the Flight Dynamics Branch, I soon discovered that being in the branch was like becoming a member of a large extended family. The people really cared about each other. Several of us were single and the Lunneys and the Charlesworths routinely invited us to their homes for holiday meals. I vividly remember those special afternoons where we watched football games, played with the kids at halftime, ate a wonderful meal, and then talked about everything under the sun until late in the evening. We were building relationships that would carry us through many long and sometimes tense days.

The Guidance Officer Role

Unlike the FIDO and RETRO positions, the Guidance Officer did not exist in Mercury. Gemini was the first manned spacecraft to have an onboard computer system that could control the spacecraft in orbit and the entire launch vehicle during powered flight. I believe there was considerable discussion about whether or not a third position was even needed. Finally the decision was made to add the Guidance slot; one that turned out well.

The basic job of the Guidance Officer in mission control was defined by Charlie, along with help from Ken Russell and Will Fenner (who like Charlie had also worked with Western Electric). Reading the procedures and listening to Charlie, Ken and Will I found out that GUIDO had to understand how things worked in three separate technical worlds:

The MCC

GUIDO was an MCC position so he had to understand how to work there –when and how to talk and monitor, when to speak and when to be quiet, how to help the FIDO and RETRO, how to write mission rules concerning the guidance system, when to be quick with an answer and when to think about the problem, and how to work with your back room support.

GUIDO had to understand how all parts of the guidance system worked and really understand where it was strong and where it was vulnerable. All manned guidance systems consisted of a computer that took inputs from both external sensors and the MCC via electronic commands uplinked to the spacecraft. The computer used this information to determine the vehicle's position, velocity, and attitude. Knowing this information the machine would either automatically issue commands to control the vehicle's acceleration and direction or it would display information to the crew to allow them to do this task. This is how the system "guides" the spacecraft.

A major external sensor is called the inertial platform consisting of three gyroscopes to hold the device fixed in space and three accelerometers to measure forces when the vehicle is in powered flight. Usually the gyros and accelerometers work well and the computer has an accurate knowledge of its environment and can issue the correct commands. But these sensors can fail –sometimes totally which is fairly easy to detect but sometimes subtly which is not. That is why GUDIO had to know all about the "world" of radars and how they measured trajectories.

Trajectory Measurement

The Gemini launch vehicle (GLV) had a primary guidance system called GE/Burroughs. This system used ground based radar to feed a ground computing system that in turn sent radio signals to guide the launch vehicle.

The Gemini computer also had the ability to guide the GLV, but only if the crew threw a switch to put it in control. GUIDO's job during launch was to determine if this switch needed to be thrown. He would monitor the difference between where the two systems wanted to drive the vehicle. If they agreed all was fine, but once a divergence started one of the systems was wrong and a choice had to be made.

Unless there is a vehicle control problem, for example if one of the engines failed or went to half thrust and the vehicle simply could not respond to the primary system, the guidance system in control believes everything is going perfectly (somewhat like most of us do when we think we are in control). And the backup system trying to drive the vehicle elsewhere also thinks it is perfect. So GUIDO had to come up with a way to break the tie. Fortunately other radars also tracked the GLV and by paying attention to whether or not FIDO had confidence in them GUIDO could use one to break the tie.

That was the theory; in practice things were harder. Usually the radar data was quite noisy, there could be confusing signals from one or both systems, the GUIDO had to monitor deviations in three axis (roll, pitch, and yaw), there were times to normally expect some deviations between the two systems such as immediately following staging when the two guidance equations could slightly diverge, and so on. To help, a second position called YAW was added to the Guidance Console as a switchover capability was now possible. Because the GLV was built by the Martin Co., Clay Long from the Martin company, would man the YAW position for all Gemini flights.

Doing the Guidance Officer Job

One of the signs you are mastering a rapidly moving task is when you can get things to seem to "slow down" when the action gets the fastest. Sometimes a football quarterback will say he had to get used to the speed of the college, or pro, game – he had to get the game to "slow down" The Gemini and Apollo launch phases and the Apollo landing and ascent phases were like this – you either were able to get them to "slow down" or you were not ready.

I never was ready for the Gemini launch phase. I hoped it was because I was still green and there wasn't much time to learn. Or maybe I was never going to be able to make it happen. I would find out in Apollo.

However I was slowly learning the subtle behavior of the guidance systems that could indicate upcoming problems. Also it became clear that keeping the other Trench members informed was critical. I listened as Charlie and later Will did this in simulations and actual flights. I tried to learn as much as I could about how they were able to read the guidance systems. Although I never totally mastered it I did learn a lot that would be invaluable in Apollo. And I learned how much a "heads up" can be valuable in any profession – as long as it is accurate!

Another lesson I learned the hard way – when someone sits beside a flight control operator and watches them work it becomes easy to believe you could do as well or better. After being in the section for several months I decided that I was ready to start simulating as a GUIDO. So the next week I scheduled my first private session with Cliff to announce that I wanted some time on the console. He got that strange sort of smile on his face and then proceeded to ask several questions to which I had could answer some answers, but fell short on others. Cliff then thanked me for coming in but reminded me that he was the one to decide when and how operators would get a chance in the MCC. I left the office thinking that I had made the worst blunder of my life, but it turned out that Cliff was actually pleased to see his engineers ready to try their best. And it wasn't too many weeks after the meeting that I was given the chance to try my hand at a simulation.

Although I was not ready to be a launch phase GUIDO I was able to work orbit phases. My first real chance to help was not as a full fledged operator, but rather as an assistant to Charlie during the first rendezvous mission. Once FIDO computed the actual maneuver plan, GUIDO was responsible for filling out the detailed messages that were read to the crew. But as usual there was more to it that simply filling out forms. GUIDO was constantly checking the total plan and giving Cliff, who was the prime FIDO for this first of a kind flight, a lot of good inputs. My role was to check the checker –before the final message was sent to the crew Charlie would hand it to me and I would compare it with the information on the MCC displays. What an exciting time when the MCC and Gemini 6 and 7 pulled it off! I wish I had kept one of the flags Jerry Bostick brought in to celebrate the event.

I worked with Ed Pavelka as we planned and executed a first orbit rendezvous (called M = 1) on Gemini 11. This was the highlight of my Gemini experience and when the program finished with a successful Gemini 12 flight in November 1966 I'd come a long way from the kid who knew absolute nothing about NASA or the manned space program in June 1964. The Branch had been reorganized in late '66 with Cliff and Glynn leaving to become full time Flight Directors and Jerry becoming our new Chief. There were three sections—FIDO (led by Phil Shaffer who had been a leader in the Apollo FDO area), GDO (Charlie Parker), and RETRO (John Llewellyn). We were getting ready, or so I thought, to be flying Apollo missions the next year.

Apollo – 1967

The first few weeks of 1967 went well as I began to learn about the Command Module and Landing Module spacecrafts and their respective guidance systems. Will Presley and Gary Renick had been following the Command Module (CM) and Landing Module (LM) guidance systems while Gran Paules would be the lead launch GUIDO having extensively studied the Saturn guidance system. I was particularly intrigued by Gary's description of the LM which had a primary navigation and guidance system (PNGS but pronounced PINGS) and an abort guidance system (AGS pronounced AGGS which sounded like eggs but starting with an "a"). They were dramatically different animals.

The PNGS was capable of performing lunar powered descent, abort to orbit from descent, lunar ascent, and rendezvous. Its computer was called the LM Guidance Computer (LGC) and was the same hardware as that used in the Command Module. Programmed by MIT by today's standards they were less capable than a cell phone; compared to the Gemini computer they were powerful indeed. In order to perform the lunar landing the PNGS had to connect with many different systems including a landing radar, a rendezvous radar, and an inertial measurement unit (IMU). This IMU, unlike that in Gemini, would have to be aligned in lunar orbit by the crew and not by a ground team at KSC. And it also took inputs from the crew via a device called an Apollo Optical Telescope (AOT) for alignment purposes.

The AGS was about 20% the size of the PNGS and could only perform abort and rendezvous. It navigated during powered flight by body mounted gyros and accelerometers. Although it didn't have the equations needed to steer the LM during powered descent, the AGS could navigate during all portions of the landing as it had to be prepared to perform an abort in the case of a PNGS failure. Finally, if the PNGS failed on the surface we had to have yet another method of aligning this system –just one more puzzle in a whole boxful.

Then on January 27th the world changed for Apollo, NASA, and the country. I was at home when a TV report said that all three Apollo I astronauts have been killed by a fire in the capsule. This was a major shock. Although I didn't personally know these crewmen I was deeply saddened. And for the first time in two years I did not look forward to going to work the next day.

[A personal note—since 1997 I have been involved with chemicals that retard fires. From time to time people have challenged the concept of putting chemicals in plastic and rubber products saying they only keep the problem away for a couple of minutes or less. I think they are surprised at how strongly I've responded that at least people will have a fighting chance to escape.]

After a short time it was clear that the best thing I could do was to keep studying and thinking about Apollo systems as the NASA and contractor leaders struggled with the technical and political issues that immediately consumed the agency. I believe their determination to continue combined with a general public awareness that this program was of vital interest to a nation in a struggle with another superpower allowed the return to flight in less than two years. And frankly I am glad that the only insight I had into most of these power struggles was a brief glimpse on the nightly news. If I had been bombarded by the non-stop reports we get today I could have wasted a lot of time.

Early in 1968 I was assigned two tasks – (1) be part of the Apollo VII GUIDO team that would be lead by Will Presley and (2) start following lunar ascent & descent very closely. I had been studying Command Module systems and looked forward to the Apollo VII assignment. The ascent/descent task was a different matter. The more I learned about LM guidance itself, let alone how to use it during landing, surface operations, ascent and rendezvous, the more overwhelmed I became. I had watched Dave Reed and Gary Renick, assisted by Ken Russell, really have to fight hard to complete the unmanned LM mission (Apollo V). And the lunar landing would require many new tools and procedures that this flight didn't have to cope with.

At first I thought this assignment was a preliminary data collection one and that in a month or two another person would also be assigned. It soon became clear the projected mission schedule wouldn't allow more people to be assigned to ascent/descent right away. So I concentrated on the first thing that had to be done for any new mission –writing the requirements the computing complex would have to implement.

In 1968 flight controllers didn't design or code software—either for the onboard or ground system. What we did was write requirements for the ground computing complex that the Flight Support Division (FSD) and IBM would implement. FSD was often assisted by the Mission Planning and Analysis Division (MPAD) who for many of our requirements developed the theory, equations, and sometimes the prototype software.

Although many questions were open concerning the practical operations procedures that would be used to actually get the guidance systems ready to do descent and ascent, an immense amount of work had been accomplished. MPAD had been working on trajectory analysis for several years and along with JPL and others had been focusing on lunar trajectory design and tracking analysis since at least 1966. MIT who was developing the LM software, MPAD, and TRW (the MPAD support contractor) had written technical papers that gave me an idea of the best thinking to date on what had to be done if the PNGS and AGS were going to successfully perform ascent and descent. But the picture was a long way from being complete.

The Gemini and Command Module guidance systems were successfully powered up, initialized, and aligned by a large ground crew or the launch did not happen. But the LM was launched in a powered down condition. The PNGS and AGS had to be powered up and initialized by two people in the LM assisted by an MCC that was 250,000 miles away. And this had to be done twice –once in lunar orbit prior to descent and again on the surface before ascent. The more I thought about this the more overwhelmed I became – could it really be done?

Turning on the computers would be the easiest part. But how were we going to get the IMU aligned? I discovered that when the vehicles were docked the AOT view was blocked. The only way to start was to use the CSM IMU, assume the vehicles were docked together just like the theory said they would be, and give the LM crew instructions on how to initially fix their IMU in space. But was only a start – could it guarantee enough accuracy? What was enough accuracy? And when the LM finally undocked and did get an accurate alignment and then we saw a big change how would we ever know if it was due to the initial inaccuracy ('GO' for lunar descent) or a big drift in the platform ('NO-GO')?

While I wasn't worrying about the pre-descent setup and thought about monitoring the powered descent things seemed even worse. What was the GUIDO (I didn't know it was going to actually be me until some months later) going to do if the PNGS and AGS started to disagree. The only third source was the MSFN (Manned Spaceflight Network) doppler which measured instantaneous range rate to the LM –unless the error was primarily along that axis it wouldn't help. One paper said that in that case just pick the PMGS –what a deal! GUIDO would just guess and hope? And by the way what were the criteria for calling an abort during the descent even if both systems were working perfectly?

Fortunately there were a lot of talented people who were completing their work on trans lunar and circumlunar techniques that started working the lunar landing problem. Phil & Dave were a help because they knew a lot about the LM and could offer advice about what had been considered in the past and discarded. Then things really picked up when Bill Tindall finally had time to emphasize his Lunar Landing Flight Techniques Panel. Reading Bill's old techniques schedules one can see that in the late summer & fall of '68 the first drafts of the following were due: power on to touchdown (Aug), powered descent (Sept), lunar surface (Sept), ascent (Oct) and descent aborts (Dec).

It is no exaggeration to say that without William Howard (Bill) Tindall we would not have been ready to get the LM guidance systems prepared for lunar landing. Bill had successfully conducted Flight Techniques panels for other phases of the lunar mission, had a great knowledge of trajectories and guidance systems, knew people at most NASA centers and contractor facilities, and had boundless energy. He brought together people from all these places in meetings of 60-70 people to go through what we were going to do every minute from LM power up until touchdown plus two hours. The first meeting was going to be a two day marathon.

Meeting 1, day 1: For the initial meeting Bill got most of the players into one room so we would all know each other: MIT, Grumman, AC/ Delco, MPAD, TRW, astronauts, flight controllers, engineering specialists and flight planners. He said this meeting would be about power up and initialization procedures – i.e., what had to be done from LM power up through powered descent ignition. He started by asking what needed to be done the first hour after the crew entered the LM.

There was a total cacophony of opinions; sometimes complementary, sometimes not. There were people talking at once, sometimes shouting. Once in awhile someone would get so mad they would have to leave the room. But by noon there was some agreement on the major tasks that had to be done that first hour. Then we came back from lunch and started on the second and third hours.

Day 2: We started on hour four and went through descent ignition. And the second part of the day the group addressed the basic lunar surface operations. Bill kept the actual powered descent procedures separate since they would involve a smaller number of people and there were many open questions that were related to, but somewhat different from, those we were discussing in this marathon. By the end of day two we had baselined a big picture of what needed to be done.

There were over fifty action items to be completed by the next month's meeting, but now each major organization knew what they really had to work on if we were going to pull this thing off. Meeting at least monthly from then on, the power up and initialization procedures came together in time for the start of Apollo XI simulations.

None of this would have worked without Bill Tindall's management style. He always allowed anyone to say anything without being judgmental. No one, no matter how bad their ideas, was belittled – at least the first time. After awhile, when time ran tight, some off the wall ideas were fairly quickly cut short, but even then not in an abrupt manner. At least by him; others in the group, including myself, were not always so patient with what we considered a time waster.

Bill published the descent aborts document last because no one had a good idea why and when to stop for PNGS navigation errors. Clearly we didn't want to fly below the "dead mans curve" that region where the descent engine at full throttle could not have prevented a crash. But that curve didn't come into play until late in the descent phase which lasted over twelve minutes. And an abort and subsequent rendezvous would be one of the most tricky procedures accomplished in manned spaceflight history.

A major breakthrough in ascent and descent monitoring occurred when Dr. William Murphy (Bill) Lear began to demonstrate a twenty-one state Kalman filter that would be able to take the MSFN doppler and generate a three axis velocity vector. We called these MSFN velocities. Now there was a chance we would be able to break a tie between the PNGS and AGS if needed. Charlie Parker immediately wrote a requirement for displaying the velocity differences between these three sources. This display would be invaluable on every lunar descent and ascent.

The next breakthrough in descent monitoring occurred when the concept of protecting abortability took hold. I think Dave Reed first mentioned it. The idea was that if a landing was still possible, but the PNGS errors had grown to a point where it could not safely perform an abort, then you should stop the landing –ie abort -- because if you don't the next problem, like a descent engine failure, would be catastrophic. The entire descent abort group discussed this for weeks and finally most backed the concept.

Looking back forty years I still believe it was a good technical decision. But like many of the decisions we had to make in Apollo, if something went wrong it would have been very difficult to explain to a review board, let alone others not as familiar with spaceflight. For example, it we had aborted under this scenario and then failed to complete the rendezvous, the immediate question would have been "could you have completed the landing"? And the answer would have been maybe or even yes. The next inquiry would be—"so you caused a disaster because you were afraid there might be a disaster". And so it would have gone. I am very grateful for two things –in 1969 I didn't spend much time thinking about what would happen if we failed and although it was close I didn't have to call an abort on Apollo XI.

Once the concept was decided upon, MPAD & TRW had direction to figure out how we could use the MCC descent displays to implement it. A few weeks later they presented the data and I really didn't like their answer. Their conclusion was that small (35 ft/sec) errors caused by alignment or accelerometer errors were enough to keep the PNGS from being able to pull off an abort. The FIDO displays were not granular enough to detect them but the conclusion was the Guidance Officer displays designed by Charlie Parker would be perfect for the task.

I was shocked. GUIDO didn't call aborts. In fact one of the first Guidance Officer mission rules was –The Guidance Officer does not request or initiate aborts. I said this was a bad idea; that the analysts hadn't done enough homework. They needed to look at our operation and figure out a way where we could work as we did in launch phase – GUIDO monitoring the systems and warning FIDO about possible deviations and FIDO calling for an abort when a trajectory limit has been violated. I really stirred things up, but the MPAD/TRW people stuck to their guns –this was the only tool that would work.   Bill appeared to be leaning in their direction but closed the meeting by asking me to thoroughly discuss this approach with the rest of the Flight Dynamics Branch.

I recall that the reaction by other branch members was similar to mine. But after talking and talking no one could come up with either an alternate concept or a better way to implement the abortability concept. So, with great apprehension, the general rule about GUIDO not recommending aborts was replaced with several detailed rules describing how the Guidance Officer would call descent aborts based on PNGS navigation errors.

Apollo X often gets lost between discussion of Apollo VIII and XI, but for those of us trying to make sure XI happened it was absolutely essential. The mission exercised the entire LM preparation timeline from power up through preparation for engine ignition. The flight proved many things that might not be exciting to an average observer but were totally fascinating and encouraging to this Guidance Officer. Recall the problem about getting an accurate IMU alignment while docked. Well one month prior to the flight an MIT engineer named Bob White presented an approach to assure we could get exactly that. Bob explained that if we performed two docked attitude maneuvers in a certain manner, recording the CSM and LM attitude readouts before and after each rotation we could compute a very accurate IMU orientation. I immediately wrote a requirement for this computation to be put in the ground system. MPAD supplied the equations in a couple of days, FSD/IBM had it in the system in a week (a record I think), and working with the Apollo X crew we demonstrated it could be done!!!

Apollo XI simulations could not start until three months prior to the mission because the simulator and flight software was not ready until then. I would be GUIDO on ascent and descent while Jay Greene would be the descent FIDO with Phil Shaffer on for ascent. Both were solid rocks of support. Phil and I had worked together on Apollo X while Jay and I spent hundreds of hours in flight techniques and mission rules meetings trying to get a total handle on the landing and lunar surface phase. This was an intense time for everyone, but I can not recall having an angry word with either man during those difficult months.

Three months before the first Apollo XI simulations, two MPAD engineers, Stan Mann and Claude Graves, scheduled several Guidance Officers for a training session using a guidance only simulation system their division had developed. There in a small room was a TV tube and two strip chart recorders imitating the GUIDO descent and ascent displays. Better yet they and TRW had programmed each type of guidance failure we might see in both phases –accelerometer biases, g sensitive biases, IMU misalignment, IMU drift, and landing radar errors. Dave called it the Guidance Officer's training school and indeed it was. For the next two months I spent many hours each week up in that room, probably driving the computer operator to want to get another job. But this was incredible—I got ascent and descent monitoring to "slow down". No longer did I have to think about what was causing a deviation –I could diagnose the cause of systems failures also paying attention to other events, such as computer modes and alerts. Thanks Stan and Claude; your system really helped.

Apollo XI simulations started one month before Apollo X flew. While I recall pieces of many of them, two remain totally clear. As we were starting the first powered descent simulation, I heard a headset plug into the spare port in my console. Thinking it might be Jerry or Charlie, I looked up and saw Chris Kraft. This was the only time I have ever heard that Dr. Kraft plugged into an operator's console during a simulation –he either listened from his office or was stationed on the "back row" in the MOCR. Since I really didn't know him very well, I just said hello and the sim proceeded. Half way down my velocity errors grew to the point where I had to call an abort.

As the vehicle climbed back toward orbit, Jay called out that the errors seemed to be going away -- I told him that is exactly what would happen for a platform misalignment and told Gene Kranz the platform had a pitch misalignment of about 0.5 deg/ I also recommended the crew perform an emergency alignment post insertion to verify it. Sure enough Neil reported a misalignment angle of 0.5 in pitch –turned out that the simulation people wanted to have a nominal case to start training but this error had somehow gotten into their system. After hearing the crew readout Dr. Kraft slapped me on the shoulder, said well done, and left.

I suspect that either Bill Tindall or Gene had told him that given the new abortability rules the GUIDO might be carrying a decisive load in descent and he wanted to see if I was up to the task. If not this would have been the time to make a change.

The second sim I recall was the last one before the flight and it didn't go as well –or maybe it went even better than expected. About five minutes into the descent the computer gave a 1210 alarm, which I recall meant the computer was trying to access two separate hardware devices at once. My software support was Jack Garman who provided excellent real time software advice to every GUIDO in every Apollo mission. Jack could only verify what the alarm was telling us and of course couldn't know what caused it. Based on the fact it should never have occurred and that meant something was seriously wrong I called for an abort.

During the debriefing I stated that we really didn't have a rule on alarms that had been programmed to be useful in testing and were never designed to occur in flight. I explained my rationale, and listened to others comment. The Simulation Supervisor didn't believe we had done the right thing, but was also not as confident as he normally was when he disagreed about our calls. For this reason I have always suspected this was not a scripted failure. The simulation system used a real LGC but modeled the other guidance hardware and there easily could have been was a LCG-model interaction that created this alarm. But the simulation folks were like the CIA – never admit anything and always keep them guessing; Bob Carlton the team's Control Officer simply called them devious. In any event they did their job by challenging our decision. Thanks Dick Koos, Carl Shelley, John Cox, Bob Holkan, and everyone else who ran the Apollo simulations.

Obviously we needed to do more work on these type of alarms, even if the experts said they wouldn't happen in flight. Gene gave orders to get it resolved before launch. Since I was still working a dozen open items, I asked Jack to assemble the software people from MIT and the hardware designers from AC/DELCO to develop a set of guidelines we could turn into rules. A few days later Jack reported that after being told many times that alarms like the 1210 would never come up, he had been able to get the group to categorize them into actionable types. There were several where a decision would have to be made –if the alarm wasn't coming too fast and we still thought the PNGS was guiding properly we should continue. Gran Paules, who not only was GUIDO for the launch but also worked as YAW support during descent, turned these conclusions into mission rules which I thought we would never use.

Although we had worked on hundreds of contingency landing and entry issues, it seemed like another hundred popped up between the last simulation and LM activation. I guess it was to be expected given all the smart engineers trying to make sure that their system or issues would not be the one that would stop the first landing. But once the crew was no longer available the flight control team became their last chance to get a new procedure or plan considered. As an example, the day before landing we were working on the case of the stuck landing radar.

The landing radar had two positions –No 1 was positioned such that the radar could lock on at altitudes of 40,000 ft. When the vehicle pitched up at 7000 ft to give the crew a visual display of the landing site, the radar was moved to position 2 to adjust to the more upright vehicle attitude in order to stay locked on the surface. Because operation in position 2 was critical the checklist had the crew moving the radar to position 2 and then back to 1. But now there was a worry that the radar would never go back to the 1 position or the position indicator would have a problem and the LGC would think the radar was in position 2 when it was really in 1 (and compute altitude incorrectly). This meeting went on for at least two hours and I can't remember what we finally decided -- but this is typical of the issues that went on and on and on until we finally started the preparation for landing.

After working the radar problem I do remember the best thing that happened the evening of July 19th. I saw Jay and Ken who suggested we go out to dinner at a good steakhouse. After a great meal I went back and slept in the flight controller bunkroom, which had been outfitted in Gemini to hold 20 or more controllers. That night I don't recall more than two others in the place. Surprisingly I slept like a rock and woke feeling absolutely wonderful. I went to eat at the temp cafeteria set up next to the bunkroom and arrived in the MOCR around 7:30 AM CDT feeling great and relaxed.

The feeling didn't last. Members of the descent team were coming on shift and no one, I mean no one, was smiling. For the first and only time that day I glanced up into the VIP viewing area and already it was starting to fill up – eight hours before landing.

The crew was preparing to enter the LM. Gene polled all flight controllers and the rhythm of the pre-landing preparation started. The docked CSM/LM were in a 60 nautical mile orbit with a period of about two hrs; for about an hour and 20 minutes MSFN had contact; then they were gone for about 40 minutes. After starting the shift, the LM/CSM would make three more "front side" passes.

At loss of signal (LOS) we would take a quick break, Jay would work with the trajectory specialists to determine the new orbit based on the latest doppler tracking. Until he had the orbit nailed down I would work on anything non orbit dependent, like selecting stars to use as alignment checks. Then I would use his new orbit predictions to generate information that would be electronically transmitted to the PNGS on the upcoming pass. Working as hard as possible, yet checking each number and command at least twice, would get everything ready for the next pass with about three minutes to spare before the vehicles appeared again.

This rhythm lasted for seven more hours and everything was going well as the LM undocked and the two vehicles disappeared behind the moon for the last time before powered descent. Jay had computed a maneuver the LM would perform behind the moon to lower its orbit to 50,000 ft at a point just prior to starting the final descent maneuver.

For the first time in seven hours I had a thirty minute breather. After five minutes I realized this might not be a good thing. In a few minutes the vehicles would appear and 13 minutes after that the crew would start the descent engine. The air seemed heavy; that is hard to describe but the air just seemed to be heavy. Then Gene announced "all flight controllers go to AFD Conference". The Flight Director loop went all over NASA and the contractor plants --and maybe even into the White House. But AFD Conference could only be heard inside the building. Something special was coming.

"We are about to make history. We have trained and prepared for this moment and we are ready. But I want you to know this—whatever happens when we walk out of this room we walk out together as a team." I can still recall that moment forty years later. It was exactly the right thing at the right time.

Gene then proceeded to have the doors of the control room locked and they would not be opened until this first attempt to land on the moon was over however it turned out. The only people at the Guidance console were me, Gran as YAW, and Charlie who was acting as the official observer. The air got heavy again.

The vehicles came into view. Less than twelve minutes remained to assess the LM before making a Go/No-Go for descent engine ignition. In simulations this seemed short; now with data dropping out about half the time it seemed like seconds. Fortunately everything we could see indicated the guidance systems were still in great shape.

Just as a 'GO' for Powered Descent was voiced to the crew all data was lost again. Don Puddy[4] was responsible for communications and was coping with a situation where the high gain antenna was bouncing a signal off the LM vehicle instead of pointing directly at the earth. He recommended a slight yaw maneuver that recovered data a minute into the descent.

At first things looked good –the PNGS and AGS velocities agreed. And I could hear Jay and his support restarting the Lear Filter. Soon the MSFN velocities would confirm all was well. But they didn't – MSFN said there was a 20 foot per second (fps) vertical velocity error in both systems. The LM was going toward the moon faster than it should have been. And if this error grew to 35 fps I would have to cause an abort.

There could only be two reasons for this error. The worst was the IMU had been misaligned or it was drifting badly. If so we would hit the abort limit in another minute[5]. The second possibility was that the vehicle was several miles further downrange than we had predicted. In this case the velocity error would hold at 20 ft/sec and be corrected later by the landing radar. But the landing would be several miles downrange from the relatively smooth planned location.

Thirty seconds later I'd seen enough to believe it was a downrange error and reported that to flight—20 ft per second probably due to a down track error. The LM was still over 40,000 ft in altitude and the crew had just started a yaw[6] maneuver to put the LM in a position where the radar could track the surface. Immediately the radar locked on and confirmed the 20 fps and an altitude error of 2900 ft. This was what I expected and advised flight to have the crew let the PNGS use this data to correct its altitude and velocity. Buzz Aldrin made the keystrokes to do this and the radar gradually started to correct the PNGS velocity error. I thought

---

4   *Don and Phil would become Flight Directors on later Apollo missions. Several years later Don became the Division Chief of the systems flight controllers and I served as his deputy.*

5   *Unfortunately we didn't have the luxury of two independent attitude references—the AGS rate gyros were projected to drift at such a rate that unlike the IMU we could not independently align that system an hour before landing. So if the IMU was misaligned so was the AGS.*

6   *Unlike other spacecraft where the pilots were seated and the engine thrust was through their back, the LM crew was standing and the thrust ran vertically through their body. So while most engineers call a maneuver around the thrust vector a roll, in the LM it was a yaw.*

my big problem was over.

Per the checklist, Buzz Aldrin keyed in V16 N68[7] to start up a special PNGS display that allowed him to watch the landing radar data gradually corrected the PNGS velocity and altitude. Immediately there was a report: Program Alarm 1202; seconds later we saw it in the MCC. I heard Gran say that's like the one we had in the sim. A few seconds later Neil said " give us a reading on that alarm." Buzz normally did the talking during descent; it was clear the 1202 was causing the crew serious concern (as well it should have been). Simultaneously Jack was reporting on the guidance support loop that this was one where we are GO if it doesn't happen too often[8].

This triggered my memory; I would have to make the call based on how well the PNGS was performing and a huge factor was whether or not this alarm wasn't coming up "too often". Now I was doubly glad for all the pre flight training and simulations because it only took a quick glance to verify that all was still OK with the PNGS. We had never defined exactly what "too often" meant, but since it hadn't repeated for several seconds and everything else was good I gave a loud GO. Gene and Capcom Charlie Duke heard it simultaneously. Usually the Capcom waits for Flight to confirm it's OK to pass anything to the crew. In this case I believe Charlie sensed it was critical the crew be assured that MCC was Go on the alarm. In any event he didn't wait and voiced to Neil "you are Go on that alarm."

The computer alarm killed the N68 display, so Buzz keyed V16N68 again and immediately got another 1202 alarm. It had taken 20 seconds to decide on the first alarm; this time Jack and I were able to confer quickly and I gave a GO within 10 sec. The 1202 was telling us the computer was performing a restart which could be caused by hardware or software problems. The computer had to complete all guidance computations every two seconds. Now twice it hadn't been able to get everything done and had to restart the process on the fly. So far the computer had successfully done enough to preserve critical functions, but would this continue? The best thing we could do was to tell the crew to quit trying N68 and keep monitoring. Charlie Duke relayed this advice telling Buzz we would monitor the radar data for him.

---

7   *The Apollo computers used Verbs & Nouns for crew input. Verb meant do some task and Noun described the task. V16N68 meant display landing radar data on the three computer readouts.*

8   *Russ Larson from MIT was next to Jack at the software support console in the Flight Dynamics support room. Russ later said he couldn't even speak – so he gave a thumbs up just before Jack made his report..*

There were no more alarms for two more minutes, Maybe this display had caused the restart. All the PNGS data said it was fine. Even so it was a confidence builder to hear "throttle down on time". It must have been even more reassuring to the crew as Buzz reported "Ah! Throttle down .. better than the simulator." Since the descent engine couldn't operate between full throttle and 65% thrust without damage, the guidance equations were programmed to only allow throttle down when thrust would never be required to go above 65%. That this had occurred on time was a good indication that the system was still performing well.

Eight and a half minutes into the descent the computer switched programs indicating the "high gate" had been achieved. The first period of landing was devoted to eliminating most of the LM's forward velocity, setting up "high gate" conditions at 7400 feet. The vehicle now could be pitched up to give the crew visual contact with the landing site.

This was the time where the plan was for Neil to determine where the PNGS was trying to land, and use his controller if necessary to instruct the PNGS to select another spot. However forty seconds later a 1201 program alarm flashed on the crew display to which I responded "same type, we're GO" – the only difference between 1202 and 1201 was the programs that the restart had to discard. Seconds later there was a 1202 followed shortly by another.

This last 1202 happened at an altitude of less than 1000 feet. Most thought that below 2000 feet the crew would be able to manually land the vehicle, even if the PNGS totally failed. But this was far from a normal landing.

From high gate on, the plan was for the crew to concentrate on selecting a good landing site and directing the PNGS to head there. But now, at this most critical period, they had to continually clear program alarms and listen for the MCC recommendations. Somehow Neil was able to do all this, determine the computer was going to take them to the edge of a rocky crater, understand that the vehicle momentum was too great to stop short, and decide to manually fly over this obstacle.

On the ground we didn't know about the crater. All I could see was that unlike the simulations, the crew was flying very fast over the surface and taking much longer to descend the final 500 feet. Soon Bob Carlton at the Control console called low level, which was the last fuel indication the vehicle provided. At that point he started a stopwatch reading 120 seconds. When Bob said zero the MCC would call an abort. Bob called sixty seconds, then thirty seconds as the crew reported picking up some dust; Charlie Duke repeating these calls to the crew.

Any landing abort was difficult; aborts just off the surface were the worst. I was getting ready to start my abort procedures when Buzz reported contact light and engine stop. This was followed by Neil's: "Houston, Tranquility Base here, the Eagle has landed." Believe it or not I had a second to think -- what a super name. It was unexpected – in the simulations the crew had always used Eagle even after touchdown.

Charlie Duke's console offered a good view of the Guidance position so I've always thought his "We copy you down Eagle, you've got a bunch of guys about to turn blue" was directed at me.

I quietly celebrated for 10 seconds and then had to start our Stay/No-Stay procedures. The first few minutes went well enough, but then there was a problem with the descent engine helium tank overpressure. I thought we might be taking off two hours after landing. Flight came to me and said he was going to be busy with a propulsion problem and to let him know when the PNGS and AGS were fully prepared for an emergency ascent. Fortunately the problem was resolved without damage to the vehicle and a few minutes later our shift was finally over.

I was one of several flight controllers that went to the post shift press meeting. I don't remember much about it. I may have been one of the few people to almost fall asleep at a NASA press conference. As soon as possible I went up to the flight controller lounge and just sat in a chair for 30 minutes. Soon the room filled up with other descent team members and like millions around the world we watched on TV as Neil descended the ladder and stepped on the moon. I watched until Buzz was on the surface and the flag has been planted, then went across the hall to the bunk room.

Eating in the cafeteria the next morning I went over what was likely to be in store during the Ascent shift which would start in about an hour. Just after the press conference I had checked in with the GUIDO and FIDO on duty. There were two major open items: we weren't sure exactly where the vehicle had landed and no one could explain the cause of the alarms. The first problem had been worked hard by every position in our branch in the office, in flight techniques, and during simulations. The important thing was to get the LM back to the Command Module and doing this rendezvous was a relative, not absolute, problem. I felt our joint procedures would work even if the exact landing position was never known.

The issue with the alarms was that we didn't know what had caused them, so the problem could reoccur at any point from LM liftoff through docking. We'd developed backup procedures covering numerous PNGS failure scenarios but I hoped they wouldn't be necessary.

Glynn was the Ascent Flight Director. The first four hours of our shift would be the preparation of the LM for takeoff, followed by the powered ascent, and finally the rendezvous of the LM and Command Module. At the handover briefing I told Glynn we still didn't know what had caused the alarms. He didn't seem surprised. He knew that if the PNGS did fail we had backup procedures using the AGS.

The surface preparation went smoothly. The LM radar was able to track the Command Module giving us confidence in the relative position of the vehicles. Then about thirty minutes before igniting the ascent engine, Jack came on our loop and announced that the large team working on the alarm problem thought they had the answer. And they wanted us to move the Rendezvous Mode switch to a new position now.

No flight controller likes last minute procedure changes and I was no exception – in fact I may have been worse than most. Too many times I had seen last minute improvements be just the wrong thing to do. I asked Jack if this had been absolutely agreed on by the team and to ask one more time was there any possibility the change could make matters worse. Soon he was back with yes to the first and no to the second. We didn't have time to discuss the details of the cause with the MIT team in Boston; it was either believe them or not. After getting assurance this couldn't make things worse, and knowing enough about the system to have some confidence it wouldn't, I was ready to make the change.

I had to ask Glynn to call for this switch change less than twenty minutes prior to liftoff. I recall he was not too pleased at getting this late input but understood what was at stake and told the Capcom to relay the message. Telemetry confirmed the switch change and shortly thereafter the crew lit the ascent stage and we were off.

Everything from liftoff until docking went as planned (athough there was a control issue post docking). Both guidance systems agreed perfectly and the PNGS put the LM into the preplanned orbit. From there on the rendezvous was essentially a repeat of the Apollo X sequence that Phil and I had worked together and it too went perfectly. Shortly before docking our shift was through and my direct console work on Apollo XI was over. From there on I was an observer watching the other controllers work with the crew to leave lunar orbit and finally re-enter the earth's atmosphere.

Post Flight Analysis

The Downrange Error

The NASA post flight analysis team was excellent at digging into problems and using the lessons learned in future missions. Needless to say there was a lot of digging into the two descent issues.

The reason for the downrange error was unanticipated forces from venting and uncoupled attitude thruster firings that occurred when the LM was behind the moon prior to landing. The MCC trajectory processor had very accurately predicted the orbit from LOS taking into account the maneuver that lowered the LM orbit to 50,000 feet. But it could not have known about these unexpected forces and as a result the closest point of the orbit was actually lowered to less than 50,000 feet. Thus at descent engine ignition the LM was 3.5 miles further downrange and traveling 20 fps toward the moon more than predicted.

For future missions the first step was to review those things that caused the venting and absolutely minimize them. Then recognizing venting still might exist in small measure the NASA team used the GUIDO displays and a new software change developed by MIT to perform a precise landing. For every 1 fps of radial velocity error the LM was going 1,000 ft off the nominal. So for Apollo XII GUIDO would note the velocity error and read up a number that the crew input to inform the PNGS how far downrange (or uprange) it was in error. Since this was done early in descent the guidance equations could easily accommodate this change.

On Apollo XII Dave Reed and I used this technique to help Pete Conrad land the LM within a few hundred feet of the Surveyor vehicle.

The Program Alarms

The alarms were caused by a problem only an electrical engineer could love[9]. In short the PNGS was constantly overloaded by an average of 13% during the entire landing phase. This overload was caused by an

---

9   *The ultimate description was a 1969 memo by George Silver, the MIT engineer who solved the problem during those hours between landing and ascent. Since that memo does not appear to be available, Don Eyles "Tales from the Lunar Module Computer" is a good alternative.*

electrical mismatch between the rendezvous radar Coupling Data Unit (CDU) that provided rendezvous radar angles to the PNGS and the Attitude and Translation Control Assembly (ATCA) which provided radar display reading to the crew. These two electronics boxes were frequency but not phase synchronized due to an incomplete requirements statement.

The ATCA was turned on first. When the PNGS was turned on the phase relationship between these two boxes was fixed until one was turned off (which didn't happen until after landing). Even then this was not a problem if the RR mode switch was in the computer (LGC) position. Unfortunately the PNGS happened to be turned on at exactly the wrong millisecond and the result was the worst possible phase difference of 90 (or 270) deg. And the checklist called for the switch to be in the SLEW position to make sure it didn't move during powered descent. As a result this phase difference caused the CDU to continually decrement angle commands to the PNGS which constantly robbed the computer an average of 13% of its time.

The PNGS margin from engine ignition until high gate was about 15%; for the first four minutes of descent the computer was scraping through. Processing landing radar added 2% duty cycle, so when we acquired radar data it was probably just luck that an alarm didn't immediately come up. But the radar display Buzz called up added another 3% and immediately triggered the 1202. By telling him to stop pulling up this display we did stop more alarms – for awhile.

When the vehicle reached high gate a new program started called P64 which only had about 10% margin and the alarms started coming in earnest. In fact I am not sure to this day why we didn't get even more than three in forty seconds. The good news was that when Neil switched to manual mode to fly over the crater the duty cycle dropped and the alarms stopped.

MIT made a software change to not read the radar angles during descent if the switch was not in the LGC position and the problem never occurred again.

EPILOGUE

NASA

After Apollo XI I would stay at NASA over two more decades and work for many excellent bosses including Gene Kranz, Neil Hutchinson, Pete Frank, Don Puddy, and John O'Neil. In 1990 Gene would put me in charge of developing the new Mission Control Center and together with help of many fine young engineers we built one that contitnues to serve the Agency (albeit I'm sure with several upgrades during these last 15 years).

The years from 1964 – 1969 were so packed with so much challenge and excitement that I never had time to really think about how fortunate I had been to be part of the Flight Dynamics family, aka The Trench. Glynn, Cliff, Jerry, and Charlie had been great bosses, mentors, and technical leaders. Each in a different way had helped me get ready for Apollo and whatever would come next. And FDB was filled with outstanding people to work with.

I was also lucky to be part of the Flight Operations Directorate, led by Dr. Kraft, one of the giants of the space business. Although I didn't ever know him as well as others did, in two different mission rule meetings I saw part of what Jerry writes about in his chapter. These meetings were packed with astronauts, flight controllers, and engineering managers, and many others. The issues were hot and the decisions could well make the difference in how the missions would turn out. That type of meeting can get very personal, especially if you're going to fly the spacecraft or have to make the call from the MCC. And in both meetings, after listening to everyone, he would say: "This is what we are going to do—unless someone wants to argue." No one did. It wasn't because of his title; there were people at NASA with bigger titles. It was what he had accomplished and the confidence he inspired.

Finally I am grateful to God that every Apollo mission ended with the successful recovery of the crew; not only because they were friends and coworkers but because Apollo accomplished so much for our country. During the cold war it was especially critical that America be associated with success and confidence. Even forty two years later the words "lunar landing" is universally associated with United States and Success. The alternative would have been: "United States, Failure, Can't Do," and "Tragedy" every time the words were uttered or someone looked at a beautiful full moon.

Family

In 1985 I was lucky enough to have Sandra J. Belinsky accept my proposal of marriage. Both our parents and many NASA friends attended the wedding. Dad was 85 and was heard to say "I never thought this boy would ever get married." When he and mom met Sandra they were more than pleased that I had finally decided on family life.

Our first son Jonathan was born a year later and the second, David, came along in 1990.

Shortly after David was born Sandra retired as a practicing Pediatrician to home school the boys. Then in 1997 we moved to Sewell, New Jersey, about 20 miles from Philadelphia, where I managed a chemical company for three years. In 2000, Sandra and I started a chemical additives company which we named Lord's Additives LLC as we try to run it using biblical principles. The last ten years have seen us in meetings with the EPA, chemical companies from China, India, and Europe, and customers in several states.

Jonathan has just begun the practice of law with a Leesburg, VA firm. He and Carolyn Kyte were married in 2007 and have a two year old daughter, Margaret. David is a junior studying neuroscience at the College of William & Mary in Williamsburg VA.

David, Steve and Jonathan

VI - William Gravett

THE SKY'S THE LIMIT

Copyright © 2012
By William Gravett
807 Voyager Drive
Houston, TX 77062

BEGINNINGS

I was born in Cincinnati, Ohio, on March 9, 1940. One grandfather (Mom's dad) was Pierce Schaeffer, a successful Dayton, Ohio, business man. The other grandfather was Dr. William Allen Gravett, another Daytonian. He was a highly respected osteopathic physician (and had a hospital there dedicated to him in honor of his work. The hospital still stands today.) I was named after both grandfathers, hence William Pierce Gravett.

In Dayton "Doc" Gravett's family (three boys and one girl) lived in the middle of a block remarkable for its inhabitants. Charles Kettering, who invented the electric starter for automobiles, lived on one end of the block and the Wright brothers, flyers of the first powered aircraft, lived on the other end. Doc Gravett knew them all and told me that the Wrights were pretty reserved and mostly stayed to themselves. At the time of their work on the Wright flyer, they owned a bicycle shop there in Dayton.

The year 1940 was very interesting. The nation was still recovering from the Great Depression; and while there was a lot of optimism, war clouds were gathering over Europe. Many felt that we should absolutely stay out of European affairs while others believed the longer we waited the worse the inevitable struggle would become. When the Japanese attacked Pearl Harbor on December 7th, 1941, Dad became the air raid warden on our block there in Columbus.

Soon after I was born, Mom and Dad (Betty Frances Gravett and Charles Hugh Gravett) and I moved to an apartment in Columbus, Ohio, where Dad took a job with the Scioto Paper Company. Dad was the dreamer in the family and was quite personable and a very good actor. He attended Ohio State University for two years and had an opportunity to attend the Juilliard Academy in New York to hone his acting skills. He had extensive radio broadcasting experience and was a character on the first soap opera ever broadcast, "Ma Perkins." But there was a restless side to my Dad that plagued him and he never seemed to find his professional niche in life.

Mom, on the other hand, was the anchor. As I look back now, I realize I appreciated my Dad's flamboyance, but I really grew to respect my Mom's consistency. I always knew that each in their own way really loved me.

Soon after I was born I suffered an asthma attack. In those days asthmatic infants really had a tough time and there were few options available, (short of being hospitalized, which my parents could not afford). Many times Grandpa Gravett would drive all the way from Dayton to Columbus to help. The nerve center for breathing is in the lumbar region of the spine, and Grandpa would hold me cradled in his left arm and manipulate my lumbar vertebrae with his right hand. He and my parents would stay up all night with me during severe attacks. My parents told me that I almost suffocated on three different occasions. Pediatricians later determined that the triggers were allergies (especially animal dander) and cold air.

As I grew older the attacks seemed to become more severe and were a constant worry to my family. My parents began taking me to church and Sunday School when I was very young. I still remember the teacher in my class was a little old lady known as "Auntie Gruebler." She taught us that God is love and that we could call on Him to help us. One night I had an especially bad asthma attack and tried to call Mom and Dad for help, but I could not make a sound. So I took my Sunday School teacher's advice and prayed to God for that next breath. The next morning my parents found me propped up in my bed wheezing severely but able to breathe. It was then I knew that Auntie Gruebler knew what she was talking about, and I called on Him many times during subsequent attacks.

For Christmas 1943, Santa Claus brought me a little pedal-driven fighter aircraft that I could sit in and drive around the house. It was beautiful: red, white, and blue with a propeller that turned as I pedaled. I was told that I became a highly skilled "pilot;" and to Mom's relief, never banged up the furniture – much. Here's a picture of me in Columbus with my Army Air Force cap and my cocker spaniel, Jeff.

In 1944, the war was raging in Europe and

in the Pacific and Dad was drafted in to the Army Air Force. He was stationed at Duckworth Air Force Base near College Station, Texas, where the primary function was to teach pilots blind (or instrument) flying. The Air Force discovered Dad's acting capabilities, and he became an entertainment specialist. After basic training was completed, Dad scheduled big-name entertainers, put on plays, and provided many different types of entertainment to boost morale for airmen and their families.

HEADING FOR TEXAS

Mom decided she wanted to be close to Dad. So she put our furniture in storage, packed our clothes, bought train tickets; and we headed for Texas. Enlisted airmen were not allowed to have their families on the base, so Dad found a family living close by the field who had available rooms to rent. These folks were salt-of-the-earth people, and they really grew to love Mom and me. In fact, they let me do more things than Mom would normally, including make a horrendous racket with their son's trumpet. They would tell my Mom, "He's just being a boy…we don't mind, Betty,…let him be!" The home sat on a couple acres, and in the Spring the lot would be covered with Indian paint brushes – all red and yellow. (I still had asthma attacks during this time, but in the warmer Texas weather, I seemed to do better, especially in winter.) One day I found a possum's nest. The mother had been killed, and there were four babies so I ran to Mom with the news. She put newspaper in a shoe box and they moved in with us. We fed them with an eye dropper, holding them up as they curled their tails around our fingers, eyes closed, hanging upside down.

Mom and I attended plays that Dad produced or acted in. In one mystery play, Dad was "stabbed" during a scene. Even though Mom had briefed me several times that it was only a play and not really happening… Dad was not really hurt…no matter…the actors did a great job. It scared me, and I stood on my chair yelling at the top of my lungs, "Don't you hurt my Daddy!"

BACK TO OHIO

Immediately after VE day, Mom and I headed back to Columbus. I snuck a horned toad on the train; and all went well until a conductor noticed me peeking into a shoe box. Of course this was "Jerry"-the-horned toad's home. When the conductor saw the strange creature he let out a yell, Jerry jumped out of the box, and for all I know he's still riding somewhere on the Atchison, Topeka, and Santa Fe line. I did catch some grief from my mother over the whole episode.

Back in Columbus after Japan surrendered, the kids on the block  got together for a VJ parade. That's me with a red, white, and blue fan on the front of my hat.

Dad was honorably discharged a few months later. When he got back to Columbus, he returned to the Scioto Paper Company. Unfortunately I had returned to my battles with asthma. The attacks worsened, I missed a lot of school, and at this point the doctors told my parents that my best chance was to live in a warm, moist climate. Grandma and Grandpa Gravett had just retired to Fort Lauderdale, Florida; and a home became available nearby. Dad reasoned that the move to Florida would help my asthma attacks subside; and as the oldest son he could look after his aging parents. So in late 1946 Dad quit his job and we headed for the sunshine state.

IN FLORIDA

I started the third grade at East Side Elementary which was within walking distance from our home on North East First Street. Unfortunately, because of the varied tropical flora, the asthma returned with a vengeance. I missed many days of school and was in a constant catch-up mode, always behind the other students. However, I somehow was able to achieve fairly good grades.

To relieve the suffocating effects of asthma, the doctors "shot" me up with large doses of adrenaline. The adrenaline made my already overworked heart work even harder. To this day I believe that because of that adrenaline therapy, my system prematurely goes into the fight or flight mode which sometimes results in a real struggle to control that situation.

On the days I was able to go to school I had a lot of friends and was a pretty good student. I did worry, though, over my grades since I was always playing catch-up as a result of the excessive absences. I couldn't excel in sports, but I was a good musician and had a good singing voice (inherited from Grandpa Gravett, who was a professional vocalist).

One day I was riding in the car with Dad and heard for the first time Earl Scruggs play the five-string banjo. I had no idea what kind of instrument it was, but I was so impressed with its hard-driving syncopated sound that I told my parents that I was going to find out what it was and learn to play it. There began my life-long love affair with the five-string banjo.

Mom and Dad soon joined the First Presbyterian Church in Fort Lauderdale. Many of my school buddies went there, and we had a lot of fun in the active youth program. The music department was also very good and I joined the youth choir. A choir director of some renown came to direct one Sunday. He was a great guy, but he wore a "rug" (ill fitting, I might add). The composition we were singing got quite frantic in some places, and so did his directing. The problem was he'd get to thrashing about on the podium, and the leading edge of the rug would fly up, then flop back down on his head. The congregation couldn't see this action, but a bunch of singing youngsters could; and we were trying so hard to stifle the laughter that several of us almost wet our pants.

Dad took a job as a radio announcer on radio station WBRD in Fort Lauderdale. He really enjoyed his work but it didn't pay very well. However, his early morning show called, "Morning Merry-Go-Round," became quite popular around the town.

The Gravett family had some good times in Fort Lauderdale. On weekends, when possible, the family headed for the beach where there was surf fishing, swimming and beach picnics galore. In the evenings the family would sit outside under a huge tree at Grandpa and Grandma's, and when I finished my homework I could walk over and join the family circle that talked and laughed and sang until bedtime. The circle expanded as my Aunt Pat, newly divorced, moved to our town with her two daughters, Patty Joan and Kathleen. Those two cousins became like sisters to me, and to this day we remain close.

In school my favorite subjects were science and English. At that time I didn't like math or history. In fact I really struggled with math. Aunt Pat was very good with math and helped me a lot, but I just didn't get it.

In 1953 I started middle school. I enjoyed taking trumpet lessons and joined the band. I became a pretty good trumpet player and went to the State Band Contest where I won first chair, second trumpet. Mr. Kephart, the junior high band director really needed heavy brass players so I volunteered and became a bass (sousaphone) player. I loved music. Dad played the ukulele and taught me how to play it as well. The family really enjoyed singing, and we would get many three-part harmonies going.

About this time in my life, the asthma attacks were beginning to slack off. I guess I was slowly outgrowing the asthma which was certainly a blessing. Asthma had truly made my early life miserable and even frightening. Dad later in my life told me that Grandpa Gravett had said that many asthmatic children grew to be anxious adults. In school I still was a "worry-wart" although my grades were not bad. I worked very diligently at my studies and was known as a good student and in general a good kid.

It was at a Junior High science fair that a friend of mine, Randy Williams, brought his ham radio station and set it up. He was a novice class operator and was allowed only to transmit Morse code on the amateur bands. He showed me his Heathkit AT-1 transmitter which he had built and allowed me to send out one "CQ"…a signal inviting any other amateur receiving the signal to answer. I was hooked! I learned the Morse code and some radio theory as well as operating rules, and my parents gave me a short wave receiver for my 14th birthday. I passed the FCC examination, built an AT-1 like Randy's, and was on the air. It was really fun and I enjoyed hours of world-wide communications. The novice license was only good for one year; and to progress to the next level, I had to improve my code speed from five words per minute to thirteen and pass a more difficult radio theory and regulations test.

I started as a freshman at Fort Lauderdale High School in 1955. I was fifteen years old. I still enjoyed science and English but struggled with math and history. Band was fun and things were going well. I passed my general class amateur radio test, received my license and was really into ham radio. I had many friends and was active at church.

After school and on weekends I got a job selling newspapers next to a grocery store. I soon decided I wanted to make more money, so I interviewed for a stock boy position at the grocery store and got the job. One weekend I was unloading a trailer at the grocery store when one of the guys threw a huge carton with 500 rolls of toilet paper in it. I caught the carton but something snapped in my back and I went down. It also knocked the wind out of me. I limped up to see the manager and he released me to go home. My back stayed sore, so Mom took me to the doctor who noticed during the examination that my hips were not level. Further examination revealed that my left leg was about an inch shorter than my right leg. These were the days before Dr. Jonas Salk developed his polio vaccine and polio was a real threat to the general population…especially children. The doctor surmised I had contracted a mild case of polio which had affected my left side causing the left leg to stop growing. At a subsequent visit it was noted that the left leg had started growing again but it never caught up to the right leg. So I was fitted with special lifts in my left shoe and they did the trick. I soon returned to work. All went well and my freshman and sophomore years passed quickly. In my junior year, the Russians launched Sputnik and the nation was incensed. How dare they fly anything over our air space! I still remember that cool October evening when I walked out on Northeast First Street, looked up into the clear, starry sky and saw that small faint point of light racing across the heavens. The space race with Russia was on!

My senior year I took Algebra II from a teacher who turned my (and many others) math study habits around. This teacher was really tough. Others said receiving a C grade from him was equivalent to an A from anyone else. He was an absolute stickler for detail and accuracy, and you had better have your homework assignment done or else. He would make you come to the blackboard and work problems before the whole class and if you weren't prepared there was pure hell to pay. Well, I struggled through and was thankful for the C that I got; but more importantly, I had learned how to study math. This newly-learned skill served me well in college and I will always be indebted to that Algebra II teacher, George P. Spaulding, or "Uncle George" as we called him (NEVER to his face!)

The nation now had a shortage of technical people. There were plenty of business and liberal arts folks, but not enough engineers, scientists and chemists. Meanwhile, it struggled with the new technology and concepts required to orbit a satellite. Failure after failure occurred but finally the U.S. succeeded in orbiting a satellite; the Russians, however, trumped us by orbiting a living creature... a little dog named Laika

I became intrigued by this competition to establish a presence in space, and Dad suggested that I consider engineering as a career. I was still enjoying my amateur radio hobby (call sign K4EHL) and electronics was really interesting, so I thought I would become an electrical engineer with an electronics option. I wrote the poem, "The Sky's the Limit" in my senior year as a project for an English class.

THE SKY'S THE LIMIT

The sky's the limit, they've always claimed;

But in man's soul a consuming flame

Has turned his eyes to the Heavens above;

His searching mind has found a new love.

With monstrous spikes of steel and fire

He feeds and quenches this new desire,

To conquer the infinitum of space

To seek new knowledge, to touch God's face.

His efforts to push back this new frontier,

New alloys of hope...of courage...and fear.

Ever higher he pierces the haze

With a roaring spear...a crimson blaze.

Astride this heaven-bound holocaust

He'll limit the limitless sky at last!

I had learned ballroom dancing at some YMCA dance classes. My Senior Prom was a lot of fun, and my date, Patricia, and I danced the night away. Life was good!

Dad and I joined the Civilian Aircraft Observer Corps. The cold war with Russia was in full swing and there was a genuine fear that the Russians could launch an undetected aircraft attack by flying under the protective cover of our radar. To preclude this, volunteers were enlisted to man observation posts all over the U.S. to track the paths of all air traffic. An observation post was established on top of the Sweet building in downtown Fort Lauderdale. On our duty days Dad and I would go to the top of the building (below) at about 5:30 am, spot aircraft and phone in observations to the Miami plotting and civil defense center. There, volunteers would check the progress of aircraft flights, watching for evidence of Russian intruders. It could be really miserable at the Broward County observation station whose call sign was "kilo metro five zero black." The roof leaked during heavy rain, and in winter it got plenty cold for us Florida folks several stories up

in the air. The small white structure atop the Sweet building in the picture is the station.

I graduated from Fort Lauderdale High School in June 1958 in the upper half of my class. I was a hard worker and was now working for Sears-Roebuck as a salesman in the paint and hardware department after school and on weekends. I applied to Georgia Tech and the University of Florida and was accepted at both schools. Because of financial considerations, I chose the University of Florida in Gainesville. My best friend, Paul Miller, was enrolled there also and we became roommates.

COLLEGE DAYS

I really felt sort of burned out from high school and when college classes began I didn't get behind, but I didn't really apply myself in earnest either. I was also a bit homesick since I hadn't been away from the family for any extended period of time. The first round of "progress" tests (as they were called) came and went, and the grades indicated that I hadn't made much "progress" in my higher education. That concerned me so I kicked it up to high gear. It became abundantly clear that I was literally fighting for a good future. I put everything I had into my studies. While I didn't have much fun, it was satisfying to see those grades turn around. I earned a B average my first semester and was headed for the Dean's list. I never quite made the "good" Dean's list; but going into my junior year, I had a solid B average.

The summer before my junior year was filled with work at Sears-Roebuck in Fort Lauderdale. A high school classmate of mine, Millie Moore, came to work in the hardware department. She was a very quiet girl and came to me often with questions from customers about the features of the various tools available in the department . I enjoyed helping her out as she was a very sweet person. One day I was working with a customer of my own when Millie asked me if I would help her customer. "What does he want, Millie?" I asked. She was obviously embarrassed because she looked at her feet and shifted from one foot to the other. She mumbled something, but I couldn't make it out. I said something like, "Come on Millie, my customer is waiting; what does he want?" Millie looked at me with the crimson glow of embarrassment spreading across her face and said in a louder voice, "He wants a rat-tailed bastard!" I looked over at her customer, and there he was, a grizzled old plumber who often came into the store, smiling a toothless grin at Millie and me. A bastard file is the second coarsest flat file, and a rat-tail file looks just like a rat's tail. Technically speaking, there is no such thing as a "rat-tail bastard," but the plumber decided that he was going to have some fun with young and innocent Millie.

About a month before school started our youth group at First Presbyterian decided to have a mid-summer's dance as a fund raiser. The theme was Hawaiian, and the activities auditorium had been transformed into an island setting. I did carpentry work and some other chores to help out. I was 20 years old and at the time not dating anyone in particular. Then <u>she</u> walked into my life. She was new in town, had joined First Presbyterian, and became involved in the youth activities. She was sweet, petite, blond, and beautiful; and I flipped out! She had graduated from high school and was going to be in the freshman class at Texas Christian University in Fort Worth. She had just turned 18. We went out every one of those thirty days before she had to leave for Texas. We really had fun together and that last week confessed our love for each other. I went with her and her parents to the airport, and we both shed tears at the parting. Lovesick, I started back for my junior year. I moved into a dorm room with a roommate who was going through the same thing. What a couple of "sad sacks" we were. Telephone romances usually don't work out, and ours surely didn't. Try as I might, I could not keep my mind off her, and my grades started slipping. I started heading for the "bad" dean's list. At the end of that semester, I ended up on "scholastic probation."

The second semester started, and I was taking heavy duty courses including a graduate level course in partial differential equations. I was still pretty heartsick, felt emotionally worn out, and was tempted to throw in the towel and join the Navy. My Aunt Pat talked me out of that and convinced me to finish school. My senior year was better, and I managed to graduate in June 1962 in the upper half of my class. I still remember walking across the campus with a new girl friend and sticking that last lab report under the professor's door. Thank goodness college was over.

TO THE CAPE

By now Project Mercury was in full swing, and I was interviewed by the RCA Service Company located in the Tech Lab just south of the

Cape. I was hired as a Range Safety Analyst. Basically I worked for the Range Safety Officers, (Air Force Officers) whose responsibility was to protect the eastern seaboard of the U.S. and the down range islands from a rocket gone wrong.

To do my work I dealt with missile performance data classified "Secret," and the data I generated from that was in turn classified "Secret." Multiple copies of the data were required; sometimes four or five-ply paper had to be used to satisfy the requirements. In that case, the carbon sheets between the sheets of paper were also classified.

On one data run I goofed and forgot to specify to the computer center that my job was to be printed on five-ply paper labeled "SECRET." When I got the job back and realized my mistake, correcting the problem on the printed sheets was quite easy. We had a rubber "SECRET" stamp and all I had to do was stamp each page. A big problem remained though. Since there was no requirement for secret-stamped paper, the computer operators thought the data was unclassified and when they stripped out the carbon sheets, they threw them in the unclassified trash which was carried outside to two dempster dumpsters. That would have been a big-time security violation.

I notified RCA security and my boss immediately. As expected, the word came back, "You had BETTER find those carbons!" I ran to the dumpsters and luckily found they had not been emptied yet. They were full of old carbon sheets. My boss helped me into the dumpsters, and I started digging through carbons, all the while getting dirtier and blacker. Finally I found the correct carbons and was able to retrieve all of them. Believe me, I never again had a close security call after that one.

I worked the night shift in the Tech Lab since I was single and enjoyed the increased pay differential. Consequently, I saw some spectacular night launches, which included a Minute Man Missile test. Since these missiles were solid fuel and launched from silos, a silo had been constructed on the Cape. This particular test failed spectacularly. The missile just cleared the silo and for whatever reason blew to smithereens dispensing chunks of burning solid fuel all over the Cape. It looked surreal, like a scene out of hell with fires everywhere.

During the early days, the most dramatic launches were the Atlas missiles. There was no mistaking the roar and thunder of the Atlas. My beach apartment out on Washington Avenue shook, and pictures came crashing down from the walls. These were amazing vehicles. Their "skin" and frame was so light that they couldn't stand unsupported and had to be pressurized with a gas charge to stand unfueled. The Cuban missile crisis occurred in October of 1962, only three months after I hired on with RCA. A squadron of U2's that took the photos of the Russian missiles in Cuba was stationed at Patrick Air Force Base just behind the Tech Lab. Before the first shift would arrive, I could hear the weird whistling sound of those U2 engines as they prepared for another reconnaissance mission. At night troop convoys moved down highway A1A; and near our Tech Lab in a clump of trees, a portable NIKE anti aircraft battery was stationed. I could see the noses of those missiles above the tree tops. Every gun shop in the Cape area was sold out. Rumors abounded that nuclear warheads had been moved out to the Cape, and 50-gallon drums of gasoline had been placed by the elevator doors of the Tech Lab. In the event of an attack, we were to send the elevators to the bottom of their shaft, dump all our classified documents, computer punch card decks, computer tapes, etc., down the elevator shaft, use a fire ax on the 50-gallon gasoline drums spilling their contents into the shaft, light torches, throw them down the shaft, then evacuate via the stairwells. No kidding! It was a very scary thirteen days.

Since I was earning about $7000 per year with night differential (a really great salary in the early 60's), I decided to trade in the Ford sedan I had bought from Grandma Gravett on a beautiful blue, brand new MG-B. It was a British two-seater convertible, and I really loved that little car. I quickly found out that I was going to have to become a shade-tree mechanic to afford repairs and tune-ups. The fuel pump was behind the passenger seat in the battery compartment, and when you turned on the ignition you could hear it chatter as it primed the engine. After many miles, it would get cranky and sputter and die in the middle of the road. Then I would have to coast over to the side of the road, open the battery compartment, push in the mechanical assembly of the pump until it produced the familiar chatter priming the engine, replace the battery cover, and go on. It grew to be a hassle. One day I was driving down the freeway, and the engine went into the sputter mode...the fuel pump again! I got very angry and called the fuel pump some unprintable names as I banged the battery compartment with my fist. The pump suddenly chattered and the engine fired up again. About ten more miles down the road, the sputter began again…banged on the battery compartment…the whole sequence was repeated. I bought a new fuel pump; but until I had time to install it, I acquired a rubber mallet and stashed it to wallop the battery cover. During this time I was getting about twenty miles to the "bang" on the average.

The twin carburetors had to be "balanced" by inserting a pitot tube type assembly (that used pith balls in a glass tube) into each carburetor intake, idling the engine and adjusting for equal heights of the pith ball displacements. I faithfully adhered to the service manual procedure until one day I just completely cut out one carburetor, just to see what would happen. All that happened was a slight drop in engine RPMs. I tried the experiment with the other carburetor… same result! So I quit balancing the intakes – didn't seem to make any difference.

Although the girls liked my MG-B, I used to tell them that it was air-conditioned in the winter and heated in the summer. The only "air conditioning" was to put the top down. Some of my dates would say, "Why don't we just take MY car next time?" I never complained.

The assassination of President Kennedy was a horrendous event. Some historians have called it the, "loss of our innocence as a nation." I had been asleep at home since I was still on the night shift and I woke up to get a snack and some milk when I found out about it. I was glued to the television for the rest of the day watching the events unfold. At work that night everyone had gone without sleep and was emotionally worn out. Some days later, a rumor floated around that the Cape was to undergo a name change in honor of our fallen President. Sure enough, a few days later Cape Canaveral became Cape Kennedy. Some were incensed at the change. I was not.

About this time, NASA and NASA contractors involved in designing and building the Mission Control Center in Houston (MCC-H) began to advertise in local newspapers for engineers. Everybody on our shift sent in resumes. I also flew up to Binghamton, New York, to interview with Singer Link who was building the Gemini and Apollo simulators. I was not impressed with Binghamton, so I declined that offer. Johns Hopkins advertised for engineers to go out on nuclear subs staging from Holy Loch, Scotland and evaluate

Polaris Missile launch tests.

I applied for that, but nothing came of it. Soon afterwards I got a phone call from a Philco Ford manager in Houston. He was looking for engineers to work with NASA flight controllers in designing displays they would use to conduct missions. That sounded interesting to me so I agreed to an interview. All went well and there was a nice pay increase offered. They flew me out to Houston, and I got a chance to see the city. I was really impressed so I accepted the position.

TO HOUSTON

In April of 1964 I packed the little blue MG-B with some personal belongings including a brand new Gibson RB-175 long neck banjo – my first really good banjo (I still have it!), and headed for Houston. I found a suitable apartment near the HPC (Houston Petroleum Center) which was the interim Manned Spacecraft Center while the real facility was finished.

The first person I met at HPC was Linda Bostick. She was absolutely beautiful and struck me as a very nice person. My Philco boss whispered in my ear that she was married and unavailable. My heart sank – oh, well. Then Jerry Bostick walked in and I was introduced to him. I was told that he was a flight controller and had worked on Project Mercury.

I was assigned the task of developing real time data displays for the Flight Dynamics controllers. I worked with Ed Pavelka, Ken Russell and Dave Massaro who were in the Gemini Flight Dynamics Branch. Glynn Lunney was the Branch Chief. As time went on I began to develop a relationship with these guys and really enjoyed working with them.

In September of 1964 I decided I would like to try my hand at being a flight controller, so I caught Glynn in his office one day and told him of my dream and that I wanted to work for him. He told me to fill out a form 52 and then made some suggestions on how I should word my qualifications. After a month or so I received a job offer from NASA. The salary offered was quite a bit less than my current one which didn't matter to me, so I joined the Gemini Flight Dynamics team. I was thrilled! So was my whole family. Soon after I was hired, Glynn and Marilyn invited the new guys to dinner at their home. The Lunneys were very gracious and kind and made us feel right at home and part of the Flight Dynamics Branch family.

WORKING FOR NASA

My official start date with NASA was January 11, 1965. By this time the Manned Spacecraft Center was open, and I reported for duty there. After the second unmanned test of the Gemini Launch Vehicle (GLV), GT-2 which launched January 19 with a Gemini spacecraft (s/c), I was told I would be working with John Llewellyn and the Gemini Retrofire Officers (MCC call sign: RETRO). The RETRO was the abort specialist of the Flight Dynamics team, responsible for getting the crew safely back to earth during the launch or orbit phase of the mission, and for the conduct of the nominal (or normal) end-of-mission reentry. That sounded great to me. The Flight Dynamics officer (MCC call sign: FIDO) was the team lead and evaluated trajectory data to be used for computing all s/c maneuvers, as well as generating s/c maneuvers to accomplish rendezvous with target vehicles. The Guidance officer (MCC call sign: GUIDANCE) monitored all of the guidance systems involved in the mission with a particular eye on how those systems and their failures affected the s/c trajectory.

During mission simulations John had noticed that the inertial velocity indicators (IVI's) in the simulators did not show the proper values when the retrorocket models fired. He was suspect of the rocket cant angles modeled in the simulator and wanted me to fix that. He asked me to be liaison between the Landing and Recovery Division (LRD) and Flight Control Division (FCD) on s/c landing point selection. Finally, he wanted me to become proficient in supporting Launch Complex 19 (the Gemini launch pad) on pad tests with the s/c and booster. This would be in addition to becoming qualified as a RETRO. It surely sounded like a "full plate" to me, and indeed it was.

During this time there were only three qualified RETRO's: John Llewellyn, Jerry Bostick and Carl Huss. Carl had a heart attack and that left John and Jerry. Tom Carter, a friend of Jerry's from the Mission Planning and Analysis Division (MPAD), was selected to be on the Gemini RETRO team. It was around this time that Dave Massaro, then Bob White, and I joined the Gemini Flight Dynamics group, RETRO section. Jerry was moved to the FIDO section. Bob White later decided to go to the Engineering Directorate (I believe), so that left John, Tom, Dave, and me to handle the RETRO function for all the upcoming Gemini flights. There wasn't much time to get ready as NASA management had decided the Gemini program would be concluded by 1967. I found myself in a "hurry-up, catch-up" mode as the newest Gemini RETRO candidate. Many times throughout my NASA career I found myself in that same predicament, "hurry-up, catch-up;" it's a tough place to be and required much hard work. The Gemini assignment was particularly difficult because it dealt with orbit and reentry trajectory management. In college, I had not taken any courses dealing directly with these subjects.

The simulator retrorocket cant angle situation had a pretty simple fix. I was able to get the cant angles used in the simulator and compare them to the McDonnell (the folks that built the Gemini s/c) data showing the spacecraft actuals. Sure enough, there was a problem, and with that information the IVI readout trouble went away once the actuals were inserted in the models.

The LRD liaison was quite another story and was ongoing for the entire Gemini project. Gemini and Apollo s/c's had to land in the ocean. To sum it up, LRD was interested in the most efficient use of their recovery ships (U.S. Navy vessels), but the RETRO's were most interested in getting adequate radar, telemetry, and voice coverage for critical portions of the reentry trajectory. As an example, we always wanted to have voice, tracking, and telemetry data available at the retrofire point in the orbit, as well as a spacecraft-visible horizon. Just prior to s/c blackout, backup guidance quantities to be used in the event of an onboard computer failure would be radioed to the astronauts. These quantities were a roll-left bank angle, a roll-right bank angle, and a time to reverse from the roll-left to the roll-right attitude. Tracking data and voice coverage post blackout was good to have since drogue and main parachute deploy times based on the latest tracking data could be updated to the crew. Also this data would result in a more confident prediction of the actual s/c landing point.

For hours and hours we would examine landing points and the coverage available and make tradeoffs. In case of a standoff, I would get John Llewellyn in on the situation with LRD management, and it would be resolved.

PAD CHECKS

The pad check job was very important but highly time consuming. Basically test data would be transmitted from the RETRO console to the Gemini onboard computer to help the Cape guys and our Guidance and Navigation (GNC) controllers check out the Gemini computer. As an example, the primary mode of guidance during launch for the GLV was a radio guidance system (RGS) backed up by the spacecraft inertial guidance system (IGS). In the former, radio signals with steering commands were sent from the General Electric/ Burroughs mod III guidance complex (GE/B) on the Cape. In the latter, a guidance scheme (simple but effective) using the Gemini inertial platform (gyroscopes and accelerometers) and the onboard Gemini computer could be astronaut-selected in case of loss of the RGS. To minimize any differences between the two systems, GE/B would transmit position and velocity updates at two specific times during the launch to the Gemini computer. The GLV/Gemini/GE/B interfaces were checked in separate pad tests, so there was no point in tying up GE/B to transmit two updates during the spacecraft pad test. RETRO simulated GE/B and would transmit these updates at the specified time during the simulated launch. The Cape guys could actually fool the onboard computer into thinking it was steering the GLV, and it would send out steering commands to the engine package and actually gimbal the engines as if the vehicle were flying.

The specific data tables and values the Cape wanted us to send during the pad checks were found in a typically huge document called a Systems Engineering Design Report (SEDR, pronounced "cedar") Several SEDR's were run to support every mission and RETRO had to send the data.

The Cape might start a Pad check specifying a particular SEDR at two a.m. I would get to MCC-H typically two hours before the Cape started the test. I would supervise the MCC-H Master Digital Command system (MDCS) controllers as they loaded the data tables into the various sectors of the MDCS and make a list of the tables loaded in each sector. By the way, the MDCS was the computer system that handled all data transfers during pad tests and the real mission from MCC-H to the Gemini's onboard computer.

On the RETRO console, there was a matrix of buttons, each having a spring-loaded closed clear plastic cover over it to preclude inadvertent closure. When the SEDR commenced, all the required steps were sequentially listed in the document, and you did your best to keep up with where the engineers in the blockhouse were by listening to the blockhouse communication loops. When required, the Cape spacecraft test conductor (STC) or test conductor (TC) would say over his loop something like, "Houston RETRO, STC transmit table so and so, verify MAP." A MAP is an acronym for a message acceptance pulse. RETRO would respond, "STC, RETRO transmitting table so and so on my mark, 3-2-1 mark." RETRO would lift the clear plastic cover and push the appropriate button. The top half of the rectangular button would light up indicating that the MDCS was transmitting the data table. If all went well, the bottom part of the button would light up indicating receipt of a MAP (now the whole button was lit). RETRO would tell STC, "MAP received," and all would be well. But if the top of the button extinguished, and only the bottom half was lit, that was bad news. That meant the Gemini computer had not issued a MAP and had not received the data table. The s/c computer engineer would tell STC that the data was not in the computer, and STC would request a retransmit. If a MAP was received, all was well. If not, it could become a real mess. STC would either hold the progress of the SEDR until the problem was fixed or multitask, that is, skip the problematical part and jump to another part in the SEDR. It was a complex operation, to say the least, and one switch out of configuration either at MCC-H or at the Cape could temporarily derail the whole procedure. The Cape was almost always under severe time constraints and would juggle the steps in the SEDR to keep things going. RETRO would have to stay right in step with all this, always keeping the correct data tables loaded in the MDCS sectors to support. Many times I arrived at MCC-H in the pitch blackness of near midnight and left MCC-H in the blackness of the next night, approaching 18-20 hours on the console.

Having been trained by John, Tom, and Dave, I was turned loose to handle most of the pad checks after GT-5. I actually enjoyed these checks, and the Cape STC's began to recognize my voice and knew that I could be trusted to send the right data at the right time. While I never saw their faces, I would recognize the STC's and TC's voices; and I began to anticipate how each individual would conduct the pad test and be ready on time to support whatever they would throw at me. It was fun!

Learning to be a manned-mission qualified RETRO in those days was another ballgame completely. The only active experienced RETRO was John Llewellyn, our section head. John was incredible: highly dedicated and one of the hardest workers I have ever known. He not only had to pull things together to prepare himself for an upcoming mission, but he also had to shepherd Dave, Tom and me. A lot of times he was so busy that the only time I could get answers to my questions was after normal week-day work hours and on weekends.

STAFF SUPPORT ROOMS (SSR's)

The front room positions of the Flight Dynamics team were the FIDO, RETRO and GUIDANCE Officer. Together, they handled all aspects of spacecraft trajectory control. Off to one side of the Mission Operations Control Room (MOCR) (or front room) were Staff Support rooms (SSR's). In the Flight Dynamics SSR there were three consoles, each one dedicated to supporting its front room counterpart.; i.e., RETRO support, FIDO support and GUIDANCE support. During mission simulations or during real-time conduct of a mission, these positions were manned by trainees who ostensibly would move into the MOCR position. Some candidates working in the SSR's would decide that the life of a flight controller was not for them and move elsewhere.

I started out as RETRO support. I would basically help the MOCR RETRO in any way I could. As an example, loss of the s/c on-board computer or inertial platform had a significant effect on re-entry preparations. At that time we did not have continual communication satellite coverage around the orbit. Remote sites scattered around the world gave us maybe 10 or 12 minutes of coverage per site followed by long periods with no coverage. The remote sites mimicked MCC-H in the hierarchy of responsibilities. There was the capsule communicator (CAPCOM), the boss who talked directly to the astronauts as they passed over the site. Spacecraft systems flight controllers were there to observe telemetered systems data. After a pass, systems status summaries were sent via teletype to the MCC-H systems controllers' SSR's. RETRO support's console was located by the teletype machines in the Flight Dynamics SSR (continuous clatter of those machines was sometimes hard to deal with). I scoured those incoming systems summaries for any hint of a spacecraft s/c computer or inertial platform problem. If I found something that hinted of a problem, I would notify the RETRO to check with the MOCR computer hardware engineers (GNC) to see if indeed a problem had been discovered which would require immediate planning for manual reentries. In the picture, the RETRO support console is at the far left. In front of it is plot board 4.

The RETRO position generated what was called BLOCK data. These were "blocks" of retrofire times to hit planned or contingency landing areas in the event the astronauts lost communications with the ground and subsequently developed some serious problem requiring a reentry. Before these times were read up to the astronauts, I would check to insure that the times were correctly entered on the forms used by the astronauts. There were other messages called pre-burn advisories (PADS) that were sent out and also had to be checked. Prior to a reentry, at the retrofire point, I had to determine if the s/c horizon was visible or not. The astronauts could use the horizon as an attitude check for the retrofire maneuver.

During the launch phase, I would closely observe plot board 4 which showed latitude and longitude of the s/c landing point assuming a premature booster cutoff. A deviation north or south of the nominal (expected) trace could confirm a potential booster guidance problem. When retrofire occurred, the s/c IVI's could be plotted to verify that the braking velocity imparted by the retrorockets and the retrofire attitude (normally 30 degrees below the local horizon) were correct.

RETRO support was an important job, but it was nothing like being in the front room position as RETRO and being totally responsible for conducting a reentry during launch or orbit. Math model simulations without crew simulators or astronauts were used by Flight Control Division (FCD) to "get its house in order" before integrated training with the astronauts. Another trying situation existed because the flight crew simulators then were very troublesome; I remember that many training hours were lost. Coupled with all this were the problems involved in getting the new control center bugs ironed out.

I might mention at this point that the control center subcontractor responsible for the large display on the front center wall of the MOCR that shows the sub-satellite point (ground tracks) was having a terrible time getting the system to function properly. This system, I think, was possessed! The basic scheme was a scribe pen driven by a display computer that received position data from the mission operations computer (MOC) and would etch the tracks on a small slide that was then magnified and optically mixed with a background slide showing an image of the world.

In the middle of a simulation, the scribe pen would go crazy, racing madly around, drawing lines all over and mixing every color it had. It was pretty laughable to see this thing take off on its own. Confidence in the reliability of that system was low enough, however, that up to the Gemini 5 mission, I believe, the X-Y plot boards, the types used in Mercury Control and in the MCC-H Flight Dynamics SSR were rolled into the MOCR right in front of the trench consoles.
The training simulations were for the most part very good and presented many taxing problems for the flight control team to solve. Frankly, my heart would pound and my palms would sweat, even though it was just a training session.

LAUNCH ABORT TRAINING

The most difficult simulations for me and most of the controllers were the launch aborts. Spacecraft launches have been, are now, and arguably will continue to be the most dangerous phase of any manned mission, no matter how routine they appear to become. Launch aborts (or early termination of the flight) fall basically into three broad categories: booster, spacecraft, and astronaut problems (or combinations of these). Trajectory-wise, depending on when the abort occurred, there were five Gemini abort modes; although the fourth mode was actually a maneuver using the s/c propulsion system to get into orbit. The flight control team could aid the flight crew in detecting, and in many cases, remedying insidious s/c failures; but for rapid, violent failures (as seen during the fatal launch phase of the Challenger) there is little anyone can do.

Portions of the normal launch trajectory are extremely hard on the spacecraft, booster and crew. The region the vehicle passes through at roughly one minute into the launch called MAX Q (or maximum dynamic pressure) is due to atmospheric density and vehicle acceleration. Extreme vibration and bouncing around is occurring. Imagine the potential effect on sensitive equipment in the booster and s/c or a crew member trying to push a button or throw the correct switch at this time. Very difficult indeed!

For Gemini the pad or low altitude aborts (prelaunch to about 50 seconds or 15,000 feet altitude) were called mode I aborts. The s/c had jet-fighter type ejection seats and either of the two astronauts could initiate the abort sequence. When a D-ring was pulled, the two hatches were blown open followed by ignition of the seat-escape rockets. When the seat rockets burned out, the astronauts were separated from the seats, their parachutes opened, and they floated to the ground to be picked up by rescue personnel. Sounds fairly ho-hum, doesn't it? Everybody has heard of or seen video sequences of fighter pilots ejecting from their damaged aircrafts. How was adequate sizing of those seat-escape rockets for Gemini accomplished? The answer is that engineers were able to model a catastrophic explosion of the GLV on the launch pad and the resulting expanding fireball. The Gemini seat rockets had to be able to clear the astronauts away from that fireball; and to do that, the rockets subjected the pilots to forces of about 60 G's along the spine, sufficient to severely injure or cripple. The astronauts knew this; and although on the first launch of Gemini 6, the crew had indications to execute the mode I abort, they chose not to. We found out later that the astronauts had agreed not to eject until they heard the sound of "tinkling glass falling around them." (Talk about some cool heads!)

The mode I–II abort region occurred between about 50 to 100 seconds. Here the flight crew activated the abort control handle in the s/c to the shutdown position, waited around 5 seconds for booster thrust to tail off, then moved the handle to the abort position. The s/c separated from the booster, leaving the adapter section behind, and the retrorockets were salvo-fired. This mode sometimes called the "ride-it-out" mode allowed the crew the options of staying with the s/c or ejecting. In the event that they elected to stay with the s/c, RETRO would pass to them drogue and main parachute deployment times and aid the recovery forces with predicted landing point coordinates.

Abort mode II started at 100 seconds after liftoff (or about 75,000 feet altitude) to a s/c velocity of roughly 21,000 feet per second (14,318 miles per hour). For this mode RETRO would announce to the MOCR operators, "mode II, full lift." This information was relayed to the flight crew. The booster was shut down, and the s/c separated. The adapter section and retropack were jettisoned and the crew oriented to the full lift attitude. The astronauts' heads were pointed toward the earth, and they were "seeing where they had been rather than where they were going." The s/c developed a small amount of lift during the reentry because there was a displacement of the center of pressure from the center of gravity. The "heads-down" attitude caused the lift vector to be pointed up, and full lift helped minimize the G-forces on the astronauts. RETRO would, via the CAPCOM, pass drogue and main chute deploy times; and as in mode I-II, aid landing and recovery forces to recover the s/c by providing landing coordinates generated from radar tracking data..

There were three preferred (because emergency recovery vessels were present there) fixed time aborts for s/c systems problems (but depending on the severity of the problem, an abort could be called anytime, of course). These were at ground elapsed times of 1:40, 2:40 and 4:40. They were all mode II, full lift aborts. When the landing point on plot board four would touch the fixed time abort hacks on the nominal trace, RETRO would give a "mark" call over the loops, CAPCOM would mark it to the crew and the astronauts would go through their booster shutdown, separation, and mode II abort procedures.

The mode III aborts were the really tough ones to handle because RETRO had a lot to do and very little time to do it. The s/c was still sub-orbital if a booster cutoff occurred in the mode III region. The basic flow of the abort went something like this. When cutoff occurred, RETRO announced mode III to the MOCR operators over the MOCR communication loops. The RETRO abort digitals would show an elapsed time from liftoff (ground elapsed time or GET) to fire the retrorockets to hit a target point in the Atlantic selected by the abort processors in the Real Time Computer Complex (RTCC) and based on the radar tracking data selected by the FIDO. The alphabetic code (A-B-C-D-E or F) of that area was also displayed. RETRO had to check the reasonableness of the abort processor's solution. A "noisy" radar vector may have been used by the abort processors, and the displayed solution could be erroneous. If the solution looked good, RETRO announced the abort area and the retrofire time which was typically 1 minute:30 seconds to 2 minutes after the booster cutoff time. He went to a command panel on the RETRO console with the code of the selected landing area on it and depressed the appropriate button. The top half of the button lit, indicating the MDCS was transmitting the target latitude and longitude to the Gemini computer. If the s/c got those targets, it sent back a MAP (message acceptance pulse), and the whole button lit up. RETRO waited until 10 seconds prior to the predicted retrofire time and initiated a countdown over the MOCR communication loops. The CAPCOM echoed that countdown to the crew. When the crew heard the count reach zero, they pushed the manual retrofire button. They, in the meantime, had been busy separating from the booster, jettisoning the adapter section, turning the s/c around 180 degrees, and pitching down 30 degrees below the local horizontal (the normal retrofire attitude). After the retrorockets fired, slowing the s/c down 320 ft/sec (218 miles per hour), the crew jettisoned the retrorocket pack and read out the IVI's to the ground. RETRO read these values into the MOC, and the RETRO abort digitals display updated using the components of the retrofire burn as displayed on the Gemini IVI's. RETRO passed blackout begin and end times, backup guidance quantities roll left angle, roll right angle, and a time to reverse the bank angle, drogue and main chute display times. All these times were now referenced to the time of retrofire.

RETRO gave the recovery personnel the predicted landing coordinates and landing times. The recovery ships moved in to pick up the s/c. When the s/c came out of blackout, assuming there was tracking data available, RETRO updated the bank, reverse bank, and time to reverse bank, etc., based on the latest tracking data.

In the case in which the abort digitals showed an erroneous solution based on a bad radar vector, RETRO would give up trying to get them to a specific target point, and do a minimum time to fire (firing the retrorockets one minute and twenty seconds after booster cutoff time). After retrofire the crew would roll the s/c around its center line to 90 degrees (roll left 90), and hold that bank angle for the remainder of the reentry. If all else failed, RETRO had prelaunch generated plots with which he could estimate blackout, chute deploy, and landing times. It was tough to pull off a clean mode III abort; but after many training sessions and John Llewellyn's help, I got pretty good at it.

Shown below is the primary Flight Dynamics plot used by the "Trench" operators during a Gemini launch. The cusp point represents launch vehicle staging (stage one burns out, stage two lights up). The feathered lines are abort limits. The upper feathered line is a 16.5 g full lift limit. If the launch data showed that this limit was violated, the GLV would be shut down and the crew would perform a mode II abort and full lift reentry. If the lower feathered line was crossed, this meant that the Reaction Control System (RCS) thrusters in the nose of the Gemini did not have sufficient thrust to swing the s/c around to reentry attitude; i.e., heat shield into the

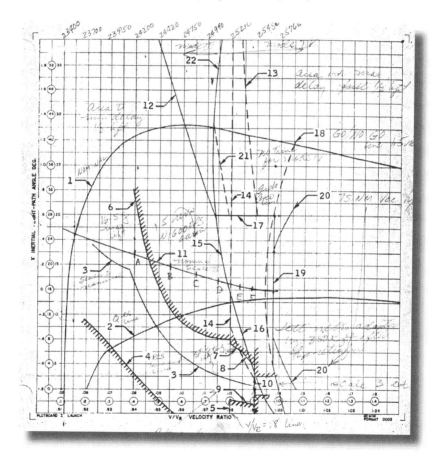

atmosphere. The dark line in the area between the two feathered lines is the normal expected trace or the nominal. All of the other lines, of course, had specific meaning but they are too numerous to mention here.

The good news is that we never had to use any of those abort procedures. We did come close. On the first launch attempt of Gemini 6 in December of 1965 (previously mentioned) we experienced a pad shutdown because a plug vibrated loose prematurely after booster ignition and caused the ground launch sequence computer in the blockhouse to shut down the GLV. To this day I remember Charley Harlan, the Booster Systems Engineer (BSE) calling out, "Pad shutdown, Flight!" We later found that the thrust in one of the two GLV engines was decreasing because of a dust cap that should have been removed at the Martin Plant in Baltimore, Maryland. If that tail plug had not vibrated loose and hold-down release issued by the ground launch sequencer we would have had a terrible situation. We had closed circuit TV down to the Cape and a couple of those cameras were focused in on the GLV engine package. There was fluid dripping all over the engine components and suddenly two figures completely clothed and hooded in white chemical/fire retardant suits moved into view. I was thinking at that time that I would not have their jobs for anything in the world!

NOMINAL PROCEDURES

For a nominal launch, things were fairly simple at the RETRO console. At liftoff RETRO verified that the Gemini computer's clock had started and announced to the MOCR operators, "clock start!" over the MOCR communication loops. The GE/B test conductor would give ten-second verbal "marks" and RETRO would compare the time in the Gemini onboard computer with GE/B time. He would announce any timing differences over the communication loops (usually the clocks were "in sync"). If they were not within about two seconds (I believe that was the number), RETRO would say something like, "Spacecraft clock leads or lags the ground by the number of seconds." This was the cue to the GUIDANCE officer to inhibit the GE/B update transmissions to the Gemini computer (previously discussed) at one minute forty seconds and two minutes and forty seconds. The updates to the IGS from GE/B were inhibited because with an excessive time difference, it was better to let the IGS knowledge of the vehicle's time position and velocity stand if a switchover to it was required. The official GMT of liftoff from the GE/B complex (or sometimes Cape Superintendant of Range Operations (SRO) was obtained by RETRO, input to the mission operations computer, and announced over the MCC-H loops.

RETRO would then monitor all prime flight dynamics displays: V/ VR (a ratio of actual vehicle velocity to required velocity to reach orbit), versus inertial flight path angle (angle between vehicles velocity vector and the local horizontal), h v d (altitude versus downrange distance from the pad), latitude and longitude of instantaneous s/c impact point (where the Gemini would land assuming booster cutoff). When V/VR reached 0.8, FIDO would announce, "Mark .8" over the loops, and the CAPCOM would notify the crew. V/VR reaching .8 meant we were not only 80 percent of the way velocity-wise to orbit but also at the beginning of the mode III abort region if anything bad happened (like a premature booster sustainer stage cutoff).

At normal cutoff GE/B would announce, "Burroughs GO;" FIDO likewise would announce, "GO" to the MOCR team. Next FIDO would gather as much good tracking data as possible, and RETRO would check the RETRO fire time to hit area 1-A (off the east African coast) which the crew had been given pre-launch with the time computed based on real-world, "what-actually-happened" data. If they were reasonably close, the crew would be told that no 1-A updates were required; and the whole operation would proceed to the orbital phase.

The orbital phase was very busy. RETRO generated BLOCK data to be uplinked by voice to the crew. These were retrofire times to target preferred landing areas (PLA's); or if no PLA's were available, contingency landing areas (CLA's). (Gemini 8, Neil Armstrong's aborted first flight, landed at a CLA in the Pacific.) Once a day, on the average, RETRO would send a pre-retro "load" up to the s/c computer providing state vector information to navigate to the selected PLA for the day, if a retrofire and subsequent reentry was required.

Two or three days prior to the planned reentry day, RETRO and the McDonnell weight and balance people began work calculating the latest vehicle center of gravity (CG) location at end-of-mission (EOM) retrofire time. Based on where the crew would store items used during the mission, the CG would shift.

CG location was important in determining the aerodynamic behavior of the Gemini in the atmosphere. The vehicle had a small lifting capability which could be used to "fly" to the target. Aerodynamic data (lift versus mach number) would be updated to the ground computers so that this lifting capability would be accurately modeled for retrofire times and backup guidance quantities calculations.

On the "big day" for end-of-mission (EOM), RETRO would update the latest and best pre-retro load to the onboard computer and retrofire time to the spacecraft TR clock. This was a decrementing clock. When it went to zero the retrorockets would automatically fire (backed up one second later by the crew depressing the manual retrofire button). The reentry sequence had begun! Updates would be passed to the crew based on the actual data provided by tracking radars. The world would see on TV the s/c coming down on the chutes, usually very close to the recovery aircraft carrier. We would cheer and clap in the MOCR, sit back at our consoles, and heave a sigh of great relief...And <u>that</u>, folks, in a nut shell, is what the Gemini RETRO's did! (Apologies to super RETRO John S. Llewellyn for any glaring errors or omissions.)

ON TO APOLLO

After Gemini, Dave and Tom left. I went to the Apollo RETRO section. I was given Dave's tasks (I don't remember what they were). I was also tasked with defining the RETRO operational computing requirements for managing aborts out of cislunar space (between the earth and the moon), and lunar orbit. The processor that was born out of all this work was the return to earth abort processor (RTEAP).

I was on the RETRO console for the shift just before the loss of the Apollo 1 s/c and crew in 1967. At the end of my shift I handed over to Chuck Deiterich and headed out for a date on the other side of town. I was in the MG-B listening to music on the radio when the awful news of the pad fire was announced.

Dad came to Houston for a Kiwanis International meeting. He joined me for this picture in the MOCR.

I pulled off I-45 and headed for a phone booth (no cell phones back then). I called Chuck on the console and was absolutely shocked when he verified the radio broadcast. He told me that I didn't need to come in because there was little that could be done. I met my date; she had heard the news. I remember that we had a pretty quiet and subdued dinner. I begged off and went home. She understood.

Jim Payne was the prime RETRO on the first unmanned test of the Saturn V and I was his understudy. The flight was amazing. That monster vehicle lifted off and flew like a veteran although the launch trajectory was slightly dispersed. We watched in awe as all that hardware performed flawlessly through its paces. We were also treated to a great reentry sequence with the s/c guiding itself to within a few miles of the target that Jim had specified. The Cape RSO for that mission later came to work for our directorate. He told us that the roar heard in his control room in Central Control was incredible; his X-Y plot boards were shaking and vibrating, and one of the plot board arms vibrated loose and fell on the floor. Plaster was falling from the ceiling. It must have been a real spectacle to behold that close up.

APOLLO 502

I was made prime RETRO on AS-502, the second unmanned test of the Saturn V. The Saturn BSE's console was located next to the RETRO console. The training sessions went pretty well, and I felt that I was ready. Then it happened. About one day prior to liftoff, the reentry software experts told me they had found a bug that only occurred in alternate mission sequences. Basically, during the early phase of the entry, the software "thought" it had more lift available than was actually available. When it got into the final phase of the reentry, it discovered the problem too late and was not able guide the s/c to the target.

One of the prime objectives of this mission was to subject the Apollo heat shield to conditions approximating those of a reentry from a manned mission to the moon. The normal sequence involved a translunar injection (TLI) burn out of low earth orbit (nominally, a 100 mile circular orbit) performed by a relight of the SIVB, the third stage of the Saturn V rocket. Then the Apollo s/c would execute a high-energy reentry.

An alternate sequence involved a situation where, for whatever reason, the SIVB failed to relight, and the Apollo s/c's propulsion system lit off to simulate an SIVB full-blown TLI. The alternate mission resulted in a less severe test of the heat shield, but it was the best that could be accomplished under the circumstances. Because of the timing of when this problem was discovered the Flight Control team had not been trained for the flawed reentry software situation. The simulations were over!

Launch day came. Pre-launch was smooth, and liftoff occurred on time, as I recall. I verified spacecraft clock start and announced the same over the MOCR communication loops. I called the SRO, got the GMT of liftoff and had it entered into the MOC, then started monitoring the prime launch display. We saw S1C staging on the plot boards. From where we sat, the S1C (booster first stage) worked normally. Little did we know that rough combustion had occurred, and the Saturn V had experienced severe vibration. A short time later over the "air waves" I heard BSE begin to talk to his back room and I picked up some alarming words, "Which one did you lose?" As I recall, I told FIDO and GUIDANCE over the air waves that we had lost an engine on the SII. The Saturn V instrument unit (IU), the guidance system, knew how to handle that failure, but tension was beginning to build. Then, again over the air waves I heard BSE say to his support engineers something like, "What? You say you've lost another one?" He now reported to the Flight Director (FD or FLIGHT) that a second engine on the SII was out. I couldn't believe this was happening. The FD said very quietly, "OK, Booster – your call!" Right after that the Cape RSO came up and said, "Houston FLIGHT, RSO, we have indication of two engines out." The FD said, "It's OK, RSO, we see that and we're watching it." The condition clearly called for a BSE initiated abort sequence; but BSE, after quickly talking to the Marshall Space Flight Center (the NASA center that designed and built the Saturn V) powers- that- be, told the FD that they would just like to let it fly. So we just let this wounded bird fly, and she was flying low and slow, confirmed by the flight dynamics displays. It seemed to me that we were on that crippled stage for eons when finally staging occurred, and the SIVB lit up. We saw traces on the V-gamma plot like I had never seen before. The SIVB was "pedal-to-the-metal" trying to make up for the low slow trajectory. When we finally got cutoff, we were in an overspeed condition. Instead of a nice 100-mile circular orbit we were in a large elliptical orbit with an apogee (high point) at about 400 miles. Needless to say, tension was pretty high in the trench and in the rest of the MOCR. The question now became: could the IU computer converge on a TLI solution out of this "big egg" orbit we were in. We knew it could out of a 100-mile circular. In the meantime, I configured my console clocks to automatically start a countdown to the TLI burn. When the SIVB telemetered down a discrete at ignition minus 10 seconds, my 10-second clock would start decrementing, and I would count down to the TLI over the MOCR communication loops. We breathed relief when we got the report that the IU converged on a TLI solution.

We came up on TLI minus 10 seconds. I heard the clock relays set from the discrete, but the clock didn't decrement and I missed the call. No matter! The SIVB did not relight. Backup ignition commands were sent by BSE – no joy. So the backup mission sequence was initiated; and there I was, right in the middle of the reentry mess. I had about two or three hours before the spacecraft reached the entry interface (EI) altitude of 400,000 feet. The velocity and flight path angle were nominal there, indicating that the s/c itself should be OK. My problem was telling everybody where it would land. Several discussions among the team occurred – like loading a new landing target closer to the EI latitude and longitude into the launch abort target locations and then "fooling" the s/c to think it was in a launch abort so that it would use these new target locations. But when the smoke cleared, logic had prevailed; and in this case, "When you don't know what to do, don't do anything." So we did nothing! We had never been trained during simulations to attempt this scheme.

As tracking data came in, my displays showed landing points pretty much all over the place, but in general they grouped short of reaching the target where the recovery aircraft carrier was located. I hesitated until the last possible minute to predict a landing point, since I wanted as much data as possible to use to make my best educated guess. I came up with my best estimate and gave it to the MOCR team. As I recall, it was about 100 miles short of the target loaded in the s/c. The aircraft carrier lit up all boilers and started steaming toward the new target point. The s/c reached EI and was in the proper attitude when the entry sequence started. I was holding my breath; it had been a bad day so far. Suddenly I heard the report that the aircraft carrier's radar had acquired the s/c. The carrier's radar operator began to give altitude and range hacks on the s/c. It was getting closer to the carrier. Then I heard the call I hoped I wouldn't hear, "The s/c is directly overhead." The carrier had to wheel around and chase the s/c. I am sure that carrier skipper had a few choice words for me.

On this mission Advanced Range Instrumentation Aircraft (ARIA) were being checked out, and since I couldn't tell where the s/c was, the ARIA began a search. When they thought they had found it, they would dive down to check it out. As I recall, one ARIA spotted what they thought was the s/c, though it turned out to be a whale. Finally they found it bobbing up and down in flotation two attitude. Instead of the heat shield being in the water, the nose was in the water. I stayed in the MOCR to listen to the ARIA for a while. They had radioed the landing coordinates to the aircraft carrier, and the carrier recovered the s/c. The s/c actually went long (or beyond the original target). I was mentally beat and disappointed to say the least. When I drove home I learned of the assassination of Martin Luther King. It was a bad, bad day.

FAREWELL

After this mission I began to ask myself some hard questions. I had been assigned Dave Massaro's tasks as well as the responsibility for the RTEAP display development. I also had to prepare myself for upcoming Apollo missions. After the failures I had seen, could I feel confident sitting at the RETRO console on a manned mission? Sadly for me, the answer was no. I felt that I had given it my best; but I needed to move on. In 1968 I said farewell to the Flight Dynamics team and hello to the Mission Simulation and Training team. I began working on training simulations for the astronauts and flight controller personnel. I did that through Apollo 16.

During the Apollo 11 mission Lunar descent, I stood in the simulation control area whose front window looked out into the MOCR. I had helped train the Apollo 11 flight control and flight crew teams for that mission. I will never forget the look on super RETRO John Llewellyn's face when we all heard Neil call out, "Houston, Tranquility Base; the Eagle has landed!" It was a look of relief and a look that said, "I've been waiting to hear that call for a long time!"

EPILOGUE

I am so pleased that I was asked by Glynn Lunney to write my story and to contribute to this book. Currently I am a substitute teacher here in the Clear Creek Independent School District. Whenever I have a chance, I like to tell students a little bit about being a NASA flight controller, especially on the Flight Dynamics team. Several students have asked me to describe exactly what tasks were required on the console. So I thought that along with my life story, I would devote some pages to the real "nuts and bolts" of what I and other RETRO Trenchmen really did at that front row console.

I participated as a flight controller on Gemini, Apollo, Skylab, Skylab Rescue, and Shuttle during my career. I finished my thirty-plus years with NASA in 1995. I lost my Dad that year and in September married my best friend, Faye Chaviers. We have been happily married for nearly 17 years now.

WHITE DOVE

Bill Gravett, Angela and Glenn Beauboeuf, and Ron Appleton

I have also continued my love affair with the 5-string banjo. In 1999 I joined a bluegrass gospel band called WHITE DOVE and have been with them ever since. In 2001 we turned out a cd called, "The Gathering," that was submitted for a Grammy. We have made TV and radio appearances. In 2005, I went to New York City and there appeared with the great Les Paul and his band. Les began his career as a bluegrass guitar picker. While on the stage, I presented him with a T-shirt that had silk-screened on it an Apollo astronaut standing on the moon picking a 5-string banjo. I kidded Les that guitar players aren't the only ones with "firsts!" – He got a real kick out of that.

In closing I wish to first of all thank my Lord and Savior, Jesus Christ, whose Spirit has been threaded through the fabric of my life since I first knew of Him as a young boy. He has remained faithful to me even when I was unfaithful to Him. I know that without Him, I could do nothing. I want to thank my wife, Faye, for all the good years. For a long time, we passed each other in life like ships in the night; but when we got married I knew that at long last my ship had come in.

And finally, to Glynn Lunney, Gene Kranz, Christopher Kraft, and John Llewellyn, I thank you. You were my leaders, champions, and inspiration during all those exciting 30 years.

VII- Maurice Kennedy

MAURICE KENNEDY'S STORY

Copyright © 2010

By Maurice Kennedy
15423 Torry Pines
Houston, Texas 77062

The Beginning

I was born December 1, 1940, in Cameron, Texas. Cameron is a small rural community in central Texas. The most interesting thing about my first few years is where I lived the first few months. My parents (Bert and Pauline Kennedy) and I lived in the Milam County jail, which was located in Cameron. You see, my grandfather was the county sheriff and the immediate family of the sheriff lived in the first floor of the county jail, which was configured similar to a two bedroom home. Although I obviously don't remember anything about this time frame, I was teased about serving time and being a county jail inmate as I grew older.

Before my first birthday, we moved to a small home on the out skirts of Cameron, where we lived for about one year. We then moved to Freeport, Texas, a small blue collar community about 50 miles South of Houston on the Texas coast. We moved to Freeport so my dad could work at Dow Chemical Company. They were hiring and he could make more money working for Dow Chemical Company than he could make in Cameron. This is where both of my sisters (Brenda Joyce and Sherry Lee) were born and where I lived until leaving for college in September 1959.

A few years after moving to Freeport, I developed an interest in rockets and space. I am not sure how I developed this interest. There were no air or space related government agencies or private companies in or near Freeport. In fact the only non-fishing and non-agricultural business in or near Freeport was Dow Chemical Company. Maybe my interest grew out of post World War II news and/or movies, particularly the Flash Gordon serials.

Almost every Saturday, all of the kids in our neighborhood would go to the Ora Theater. It had a double feature and a serial and it only cost nine cents. Our parents knew what they were doing because it gave them three to four hours of free time, to get things done without the kids. The most memorable Saturday mornings were the ones with the Flash Gordon serials.

Building Rockets

Both of my parents worked the entire time I was growing up, which gave me the freedom to do things I might not have been able to do otherwise (like building model rockets). My dad started out as a journeyman painter in the Dow Chemical Company paint department and retired as a foreman, in the late 1970s. My mom was a shoe sales person in the

Weiner's Department Store and later was a receptionist at the Dow Hotel, which was the only hotel in the Freeport area.

At the age of nine or ten, I decided to start building and flying model rockets. I would form a small tube from cardboard and tape or use a portion of a spent roman candle tube. I would close one end and put three or four cardboard fins near the open end of the tube. The propellant was gun powder, which I initially obtained by cutting open several firecrackers and later made myself. The fuse was formed by connecting firecracker fuses together. These model rockets did pretty good but, there were many changes over the next several years.

At the age of 12 or 13, I was ordering chemicals from W. H. Curtin, a chemical supply company in Houston. The first chemicals were sulfur and powdered zinc, which were relatively inexpensive and easy to mix. By this time, I had been working part time jobs (delivering circulars and mowing grass) and had a small bank account and could pay for the chemicals. Also, my dad began to "help" me build the model rockets. I would draw simple plans for the rockets and he would take them to the plant and have friends (pipe fitters, machinist, and welders) construct the rockets, during their off time. The model rockets were initially a single stage constructed from left over thin wall conduit and aluminum. The nose was formed by cutting triangle slots, pressing the remaining pieces together, and then welding them. Four aluminum triangular fins were welded to the bottom of the tube. The fuse was a squib which was connected to a battery and switch. This type of fuse allowed me to be further away from the rocket during the ignition phase and provided better control over the ignition timing. If one of my earlier rockets tipped over or someone came into the launch area while the fuse was lit it could have resulted in a serious accident. The new ignition system eliminated this potential problem. These model rockets were larger (typically 18-24 inches tall) and performed much better than the smaller gun powder rockets.

By the time I was 14, I made two significant changes. The first was to use the same propellant the Army was using in their rockets, which was potassium chlorate and asphalt. The second was to migrate to somewhat larger rockets, some of which had a second stage. The second stage could carry a small payload and/or a recovery parachute. I learned a lot about building these model rockets and mixing the propellant from the book Rocket Propulsion Elements. The fuse for these model rockets was also a squib connected to a battery and switch. The trajectory was controlled by using two small rings on the body and a steel rod with a base which kept it fixed to the ground. The two rings slid on the steel rod and controlled the initial trajectory, which was defined by the angle of the steel rod. These model rockets were the most fun to build and fly. However, I only flew a few of these and most of them flew out of sight. Unfortunately, this phase of my model rocket building and flying days did not last long.

One day, I was in the back bathroom of our home heating the asphalt in an old metal coffee pot, which had an open top so that I could easily mix in the appropriate amount of potassium chlorate and then pour the mixture into cylindrical forms. Unfortunately, I left the coffee pot over the Bunsen burner too long and the mixture exploded shooting flames to the ceiling and blowing the bottom out of the coffee pot. It singed the ceiling and the hair on my head. I was lucky to not have any serious injuries. However, my model rocket building and flying days were over.

High School and College

I went to Brazosport High School and took all of the math and science classes available, in preparation for college and a future in aerospace. I was also involved in the science club and one of six students invited to special computer classes at Dow Chemical Company. Dow had just bought a new IBM mainframe (I believe it was an IBM 360), which was the largest computer available on the market at that time and they wanted to use it to help educate the greater Brazosport community via special night classes for six selected seniors from Brazosport High School. Although I participated in the above activities, I was still considered a jock and played football all three years.

Upon graduation, I wanted to go to Cal Tech. However, I could not afford the out of state tuition and living expenses and I did not have the grades for a significant scholarship. I made As in most of my math and science classes but, I made Bs and Cs in most of my other classes and a D in French one semester. I did not like French but, needed two years of a foreign language for college.

Fortunately, one state school offered an aerospace engineering degree, the University of Texas in Austin. After making a good grade on the SAT, I was accepted for entrance into the university's engineering school. In September 1959, I began my college career. It was an exciting time and a lot of high school graduates were going into engineering. The Russians had launched Sputnik in 1957 and the U.S. was in a space race. Several schools across the country (including the University of Texas) were expanding their engineering, math, and science programs - it was called "operation bootstrap."

The first few days at the university were spent in orientation. During this orientation, we were told 1959 was a record year for enrollment in the engineering school. I also learned that the relatively new aerospace engineering department was the second largest engineering department (second only to the electrical engineering department). We had about 450 freshman students enrolled in the aerospace engineering department.

It was a five year program and I married my wife, the former Trudy Lynn Rabourn, during my third school year. I met her my senior year in high school and thought she was an interesting and beautiful young woman. She was a sophomore and dating one of my friends. However, a couple of years later she was no longer dating my friend and we went out on our first date. The day before going back to school for my sophomore year, she called and ask what I was doing. I told her I was packing to go back to college and she said she would like to help me pack. I really didn't need the help but, I wanted to see her before I left for college. To make a long story short, we completed packing in a few minutes and then went to a movie. The next day, I left for college and a few days later Trudy and I began writing each other. A few months later, I gave her a fraternity drop pin. The next school year, Trudy enrolled at the university and on January 28, 1962 (between the Fall and Spring semesters) we were married. Note: It must have been a good decision because we are still married after 48 years.

We both immediately went to work; Trudy full time and me part time so I could continue with school, at a reduced number of hours. Nine months later, my son (Ted Graves) was born and we were fortunate to have a neighbor take care of him when we were at work and I was at school. It was a tough couple of years but, I graduated in January 1965, along with 11 other aerospace engineering students.

Note: I think the above three sections are important because they show where I came from, how I developed an interest in aerospace, and my education and preparations for a career in aerospace.

Career Decision

During my last semester at the university, I interviewed a couple of companies and NASA. I received and accepted an offer from Pratt and Whitney, in West Palm Beach, Florida. I really wanted to work for NASA, at the Manned Spacecraft Center (later renamed the Johnson Space Center) near Houston. However, the Manned Spacecraft Center had a temporary hiring freeze and was not able to extend an offer prior to the Pratt and Whitney offer acceptance date.

The last day at school, we had packed our meager belongings and were about to leave our married student housing (old World War II barracks) and head to Freeport and Lake Jackson (Trudy's parents) before going to Florida when the telephone rang. I was tired and immediately angry at Trudy because she was supposed to go to the telephone company the previous day and have our telephone service disconnected.

I answered the telephone and it was Jack Lister from the personnel office at the Manned Spacecraft Center. He told me the temporary freeze had been lifted and NASA wanted to extend an offer to me. He then asked if I could come to the Manned Spacecraft Center for interviews. I told him I really wanted to work for NASA at the Manned Spacecraft Center but, couldn't wait any longer for an offer. A few days earlier, I had verbally accepted an offer from Pratt and Whitney. Mr. Lister then told me he understood and suggested I call Pratt and Whitney back and ask them to release me from my commitment. I had mixed emotions about doing this but, my strong desire to be part of America's next great adventure and to be located near our families lead me to my decision. I agreed and immediately called the Pratt and Whitney personnel office, explained the situation, and asked them to release me from my verbal commitment. To my surprise, the representative said that he understood and the company would release me from my commitment. He then suggested I call him back after one year at NASA and tell him whether or not I was happy with my decision. If not, Pratt and Whitney would still like to hire me. I thanked the representative and told him I would call him back in one year. I then hung up the telephone and immediately called the Manned Spacecraft Center personnel office and told them I could come down for interviews in two days.

One year later, I called the Pratt and Whitney representative back and told him I was still happy with my decision. I also thanked him for agreeing to release me from my commitment and giving me a second opportunity to work for Pratt and Whitney.

Going to NASA's Manned Spacecraft Center

After leaving Austin, Trudy, Ted, and I drove to Freeport and Lake Jackson to visit our parents and make this our home base while looking for a place to live near the Manned Spacecraft Center. Both families were happy to know we would be living less than 50 miles from them; particularly since Ted was their first grandchild.

The next day, I put on my only suit and headed to the Manned Spacecraft Center for four previously scheduled interviews. My first interview was with Mr. Glynn Lunney, a flight director and head of the Flight Dynamics Branch (FDB). As the interview progressed, I realized this was not only the right job but, even more importantly the right person. After the interview, I called the personnel office and asked if I could cancel the other interviews because I had decided I wanted to work for Mr. Lunney. They agreed and subsequently cancelled the other interviews.

The Flight Dynamics Branch

On February 9, 1965, I completed new employee processing and went to my first NASA job, in the FDB. NASA had completed the Mercury Program, was preparing to fly the first Gemini flight, and was staffing up to prepare for the Apollo Program.

The branch had three sections: a Flight Dynamics Officer (FDO) section, a Guidance Officer section, and a Retrofire Officer section. I was assigned to the FDO section, to work on the Apollo Program. I think this assignment was based on my Aerospace Engineering degree and my senior project. I had built a scale model of the Apollo Command Module (CM) and used it to test low speed re-entry aerodynamic conditions in the university wind tunnel.

As I stated earlier, Mr. Lunney was the branch chief. Other key members of the branch included Mr. Cliff Charlesworth (Deputy Branch Chief), Mr. Grady Meyer (FDO Section Head), Mr. Charlie Parker (Guidance Office Section Head), and Mr. John Llewellyn (Retrofire Office Section Head). However, about a year after I joined the branch Mr. Meyers left the branch and Mr. Jerry Bostick took his place. In addition to these branch managers, there were several other key personnel. Some of these personnel will be mentioned in the remainder of my story.

My desk was temporarily located near the primary entrance to the FDB office complex. This proved to be an unexpected advantage because most of the members of the branch walked through this doorway to go to and from their offices/desks, which allowed me to get to know branch and other key personnel during the first few weeks in the job.

It was immediately obvious that the FDB was a key element of the NASA human space operations team, with overall ground responsibility for the space vehicle trajectory. This included all related near-term planning, ground control procedures and flight rules, ground computation of in-flight maneuvers, ground monitoring of vehicle and crew performance, and ground execution of assigned maneuvers. These responsibilities were shared by the three sections and their corresponding Mission Control Center (MCC) console positions, which were located on the front row and referred to as "The Trench." The FDO was the team lead and had overall responsibility for ground trajectory planning and execution, the Guidance Officer was responsible for all related guidance and navigation, and the Retrofire Officer was responsible for ensuring the crew's safe return to Earth.

In summary, the FDB was composed of a diverse group of men who worked together as a cohesive team and performed extraordinary things in support of America's great adventure. It was led by an outstanding branch chief and deputy branch chief, with a lot of input from the other members of the branch, particularly the section heads and lead position operators.

Not all Work

Although branch personnel were clearly focused on assigned programs and specific mission objectives and worked long hours to implement those objectives, we found time to participate in joint family activities and to play a round of golf once or twice a month.

The FDB was a family of families and most of us were married and had children. As I indicated earlier, our son (Ted) was two years old when we moved to the Clear Lake area. Two years later, our daughter (Kristi Lynn) was born. The four of us were active members of the FDB family of families. We participated in virtually all of the FDB and NASA family related activities, which included branch get togethers, NASA picnics and children parties, holiday related activities, and other special events. Most of the other FDB families did the same and we enjoyed participating with them. This part of the FDB experience was very important to me because I wanted my family to be a part of the great adventure.

The golf outings usually involved six people (Cliff Charlesworth, Phil Shaffer, Charlie Parker, Bill Stoval, Bill Boone, and sometimes myself). I would play when I didn't have a work or family obligation and two of the other five could not play on that Saturday or Sunday. These outings were special for me because I loved the game and the interaction with the other players, which always ensured it was a fun day regardless of my score. One of the most memorable outings involved small bets (I think we were playing for a dime a hole) and the interaction between Cliff and big Phil. At the time, Phil weighed about 300 pounds and could hit the ball a country mile. Phil had out driven the rest of us on the first few par four and five holes. On the next par four hole, Phil teed off first and hit the ball over 250 yards. He then turned towards the rest of us with a big grin on his face. That was about all Cliff could take. He looked at Phil and said "You drive for show but putt for dough." That had the effect Cliff intended. From that point on, Phil lost his concentration and most of the remaining holes. I believe Cliff won 40 cents that day.

Trench Memories

First Flight Rules Review with Dr. Kraft

Initially, I was assigned to two of the unmanned test flights. During the planning and preparation phase for these flights, our team worked hard to develop Flight Rules, which would be used to help the flight control team and others make decisions during the planning and conduct of the flights.

The final flight rules reviews were conducted under the direction of Dr. Chris Kraft (Director of Flight Operations). Some of the most memorable reviews were conducted on Saturdays and included representatives from the ground support team, the planning team, the MCC prime console positions, and the crew office (the unmanned flights as well as the manned flights).

Prior to participating in my first formal flight rules review with Dr. Kraft, I got some unusual advice from another member of the FDB. Jerry Bostick (my section head and a respected member of the larger operations team) told me to watch Dr. Kraft during my presentation and move on to the next topic when Dr. Kraft reaches into his pocket, pulls out several coins, places them on the table, and begins to rotate them through his fingers. This proved to be an accurate and valuable observation. I got through the review with good marks.

Note: Early on, Jerry gave me one other memorable piece of advice "Don't do nothing because you can't do all you want to do in the time available." I tended to be a perfectionist and sometimes went too far or avoided a particular challenge/opportunity because I didn't believe I could do all I thought was required in the time available. Jerrys advice helped me be a more productive member of the FDB.

Apollo I

My first assignment to a manned mission was Apollo I, the first scheduled manned Apollo flight. I was scheduled to be a third shift FDO and our team was assigned to support some of the preflight tests, including a countdown demonstration test on January 27, 1967. It was to be one of the last demonstration tests prior to the flight and included the crew.

I was on console supporting the countdown demonstration test when a fire broke out inside the command module (CM) cabin. Based on systems console displays and the air-to-ground loop, our MCC support team knew immediately there was a serious incident. In a matter of seconds, the CM was destroyed and tragically the crew (Gus Grissom, Ed White, and Roger Chaffee) were lost.

Although we knew there was a cabin fire and we had lost the crew, we needed to evaluate the events leading up to the fire and the events during the fire. The Flight Director ordered the MCC doors closed and all voice loops not needed to conduct our near-term evaluation turned off. However, a few key flight controllers and managers were called in to support the near-term evaluation. A few other key people were notified and given the limited details we had at the time.

The recorded telemetry and voice data was replayed a couple of times to make sure we could focus on what had happened in each of our areas and to allow us to document everything we saw and heard. It was hard to listen to the air-to-ground loop and I had several difficult nights over the next couple of years.

The incident resulted in a two year stand down, which was used to make the space vehicle, processes, tests, and our procedures safer. Two of the most significant changes included changing the cabin atmosphere from pure oxygen to an air mixture and making the cabin door easier and quicker to open.

Out of the ashes, emerged a better space vehicle and overall program. Two and a half years later we successfully landed Americans on the moon and returned them safely back to Earth.

Apollo IX

My next Mission Operations Control Room (MOCR) manned mission assignment was Apollo IX. During the flight, I was responsible for finalizing the overall Lunar Module (LM)/Command Service Module (CSM) separation and rendezvous demonstration plan. Our team had simulated this phase a couple of times and we knew our responsibilities and how to execute them. As it turned out, the actual separation and set-up phase execution was a little different than the pre-flight plan. However, the new sequence was well within expected potential deviations. The next shift would simply start with a slightly different rendezvous plan.

Soon after the crew had executed the LM/CSM separation and initial phasing sequence, the lead FDO (Dave Reed) arrived in the MCC. He came in early because he had heard the rendezvous plan was different than the pre-flight nominal and he wanted to know the rational and details associated with the change. Dave was an outstanding FDO and always strived for perfection, particularly when he was the lead FDO.

I was surprised he knew the rendezvous plan had been changed and he had come to the MCC earlier than the rest of his team. However, I soon learned Dave had been listening to local in-depth coverage while taking a shower and getting ready for his shift. This demonstrated Dave's dedication to the job and emphasized the importance of this flight to the program. It was the first time we had put crew members in a vehicle that could not return to Earth; they had to rendezvous and dock with the CSM in order to come home.

Prior to completing my shift handover to Dave, Dr. Kraft came down to our console and said "I have been listening to your loop and want to commend you for a job well done." I think this helped mitigate any disappointment associated with the slightly different rendezvous plan. Dave's team and the crew subsequently successfully executed the updated rendezvous plan and the mission was a tremendous success.

Most Memorable Trench Handover

I don't remember the flight but I remember the following handover. During one of the shift handovers, the Retrofire Office (John Llewellyn) assigned to my team did not show up for his hand over and the previous shift Retrofire Officer (Chuck Deiterich) had to stay on console. We were not able to contact John and did not know his status.

About four hours into our shift, John walked into the Mission Operations Control Room (MOCR), up to the Retrofire Officer console, and said he was ready to handover. It turns out, he had driven his car (I think it was a Triumph TR-3) off the road and through a barb wire fence. His car was stuck in a muddy field and he had walked the remainder of the way to the MCC.

Although John was noted for a variety of unusual activities (riding his horse to work when he had lost his site car sticker, Singing Wheel exploits, etc.), this is one I want to document in my story because it shows John's determination and dedication to The Trench. He had walked several miles in darkness and rain to get to the MCC for this shift.

Esprit de Corps

Webster's II New College Dictionary defines esprit de corps as "A common spirit of enthusiasm and devotion to a cause among the members of a group." This was certainly true for the Apollo MCC flight control team. It was reflected in the attitude and actions of the entire flight control team and The Trench in particular.

Early on, this common spirit became known as Captain REFSMMAT, the ideal flight controller. I don't know who first came up with the idea but, Ed Pavelka brought Captain REFSMMAT to life with a flipchart size cartoon drawing. He had a captain's military jacket, khaki shorts, and tennis shoes. Once the initial drawing was completed and put on display in the FDB office complex, word got out and the captain was immediately adopted as the flight control team mascot. However, he

Captain 'Refsmmat'

"The Ideal Flight Controller"

(Note: Ed Pavelka sketched the very first version of the "Captain" and chose to spell it with one "M." In subsequent drawings he also used two "M's" to spell REFSMMAT .which was an acronym for the "reference stable member matrix." It was the platform reference for all space maneuvers on a given Apollo mission.

soon had an arch enemy know as Victor Vector, who basically stood for just about everything that opposed the captain. He tried to challenge the captain and always failed miserably.

Over the years, the captain was fitted with several tools of the trade which included special glasses, a radar antenna, and several REFSM-MATs[1]. He also collected a lot of graffiti, which documented the memories, sentiments, frustrations, and pride of the flight control team and The Trench in particular. This required Ed to make several additional drawings during the remainder of the Apollo Program.

Finally, I will close my story with a final comment about The Trench and a short story about something that happened during the early days of the ISS program.

My seven years in the FDB/Trench was the highlight of my space career, which included 37 years at the NASA Manned Spacecraft Center/ Johnson Space Center and seven years at the United Space Alliance Company, also in Houston. This is because of the exceptional leadership (particularly Glynn Lunney), the outstanding co-workers, and the unprecedented opportunity we had to help America send the first humans to the Moon and return them safely to the Earth.

During the early days of the ISS Program, I was the Deputy Manager of the Mission Integration and Operation Office and had the good fortune to be included in the initial meetings with our International Partners, particularly the Russians.

In late 1993, the first significant contingent of Russians came to Houston to meet with several representatives from NASA. After several days of intensive discussions and negotiations, a few representatives from each side met to finalize negotiations and sign an important agreement. At the end of this meeting, the Russian representative across from me smiled, wiped his forehead, and said "whew." The lead Russian representative quickly looked at him and told him he should not react so quickly. He then told the following story.

In the late 1800 hundreds, a Russian farmer lost his only horse. The next morning, he gave his oldest son enough money to buy a new horse and sent him on his way to the nearest town, which was several kilo-

---

1 *REFSMMAT (two "'M's") was an acronym for the "reference stable member matrix." It was the platform reference for all space maneuvers on Apollo missions.*

meters from the farm. The son reached the town several hours later and went directly to the livery stable. As he entered the livery stable, he met the owner and told him he needed a good plow horse. The owner took him to the back of the building where several horses were located and told him they were all for sale. The son looked them over and selected a large gray horse, which was within his budget. The owner told the young man he had made a good selection but he needed to tell him something about the horse. He then said "you have to tell the horse 'whew' to go forward and 'whoa' to stop." The son said he understood and proceeded to pay the owner for the horse. He thanked the owner and began his trek back to the farm. About half way back, he realized it would be dark before he got home and decided to take an unfamiliar shortcut. After going down the shortcut a few kilometers, he suddenly came upon a deep ravine and immediately yelled whoa. The horse stopped with his front hoofs just centimeters from the edge. The son reached into his pocket, took out his handkerchief, wiped his forehead, and said "whew."

This short story has a good message for all of us and reminds me to always be careful about making decisions and always think about the possible consequences before I speak.

Post Script

To the best of my memory, the above short story documents where I came from, how I became interested in space, my preparation for a career in space, my perspective on the Flight Dynamics Branch (FDB...the Trench) and some of the more interesting memories relating to this path and my days in the FDB/Trench.

I hope my children and their spouses (Ted and Anne Kennedy and Kristi and Jason Pasinski), grandchildren (Payton Lynn Pasinski, Liam Graves Kennedy, Paige Eva Pasinski, and Ashby Lee Kennedy), etc. will read this short story to learn more about their father/grandfather/etc. and some of the more interesting and unusual things that happened to me and some of the other people in the FDB/Trench, leading up to and during the Apollo Program.

VIII - "Dutch" von Ehrenfried

THE GOLDEN AGE OF SPACEFLIGHT

Manfred Hans von Ehrenfried, II
"Defending" America During WWII
age 8

Copyright © 2011

By"Dutch" von Ehrenfried
3102 Point Cove
Lago Vista, TX 78645

The "Dutch" von Ehrenfried Story

BEFORE NASA

The year is 2011 and I am 75 years old! I will crawl back in time and record my faint memories of the "Golden Age" of space flight. Fortunately, the guys in the Mission Control Center "Trench" before me have refreshed my memory.

I was born in Dayton, Ohio in 1936; a depression year. The world was full of wars as it still is today. My father was a heel-clicking, hand-kissing young German who swept my teen-age Kentucky born mother off her feet. I had two older sisters and I was the spoiled little boy.

By the time WWII started, my parents were getting a divorce and went to work in the war effort. My sisters went to a convent and I went to a Catholic military school from 1942 to the end of the war in 1945. I dressed in an Army uniform and drilled with a parade version of a 1903 Springfield rifle. It was taller than me. We thought that if the enemy came to America, we would be the home guard. As you can imagine, I got a great education from the nuns; and a few disciplinary smacks on the hands with the ruler. The priests gave the spankings. I became a disciplined well-educated young man. We were even taught respect, manners and made our beds in the morning. Take note American teachers and parents!

By the end of the war, my mother had remarried and we moved East briefly and then to Amish country in Lancaster County, Pennsylvania. In 1947, I went to a two-room school house in Paradise, PA. There was a pot belly stove in each room. Many of my classmates were from Mennonite families. By 1950, I was heavily into the Boy Scouts, going to international jamborees, and going to camp in the summers. I got my Eagle Scout award at age 16.

I graduated in 1954 from East Lampeter High School just outside Lancaster. It is now the Mennonite School for the Deaf. I then went to nearby Franklin & Marshall College. Then we moved to Petersburg, VA. I worked in the Virginia Department of Highways Bituminous Lab as a technician and went to RPI night school for a year. I then transferred to the University of Richmond Virginia. I majored in Physics and minored in Math. I well remember when Sputnik went up in 1957. It really did cast a chill on Americans as we were very suspicious of the Russians. I was taking Russian history at the time and often hid my history book under other books because it had a big RED STAR on the cover and spine. Sounds silly now; but not during the height of the "Cold War."

In 1959, I had an occasion to hear Dr. Wernher von Braun speak at a conference. Little did I know that 8 years later, I would give him the briefing in Houston on the Apollo VII mission test objectives! Afterwards, I reminded him of the speech he gave us when I was in college and how he inspired us with visions of spaceflight. Many years later, I helped NASA Headquarters compile a book of testimonial letters from friends and colleagues for his 60th birthday. I wish I had kept a copy of it! He died from kidney cancer in 1977 at age 65. Later I found out that Chris Kraft and he tangled a few times.

After graduation in 1960, I went to look for a job. I realized that this would take a while so I took a temporary teaching job while I looked. By this time I was married to my first wife Jane Edmonds and had my first son, Manfred III; aka "Little Dutch." I was the first physics teacher at the Colonial Heights High School teaching physics, solid geometry, trigonometry, science and general math. I also coached basketball. In the meantime, I wrote the various National Laboratories for a job. The message was: get your PhD and reapply.

I thought that if I couldn't get a job as a physicist then I might as well go and become a pilot after I completed my year of teaching. Since I took Air Force ROTC in college, all I had to do was go take the physical and start training. So, I went to the nearby Langley Air Force Base in Hampton, VA and took the physical. I flunked! What? Apparently I had checked one of the many boxes that admitted that I had asthma as a child. That did it! As I left the base feeling very dejected, I saw a sign that said NASA Langley Research Center. I thought, "Well, while I'm here, I might as well see what's going on there." One door closed but, by divine providence, another door was about to open.

I walked in and told them my story. A gentleman named Chris Critzos told me what was going on and that they were looking for flight controllers. I thought he meant people to work on flight control systems for aircraft. Well I knew about airplanes; after all, I built many model airplanes! No, he went on to say that they were about to launch the first American into space and that they were building a world-wide network of tracking stations to monitor future flights. That was May 4, 1961.

I told him that I would have to finish my teaching job but I could report for work the next month. He said "Yes, come back then." I asked him, "What does the job pay?" He pulled out a chart and said, "Well, you

have a BS degree and one year of experience, so you'll be a GS-7."
I said, "what's that?' He said, "That's $6,345/year." I said, "Oh my,
I don't need that kind of money; I'm only making $3,700/year now."
"Well, that's what a starting GS-7 makes" he added. (I've learned a
little since then.)

The next day, May 5th, I had a radio on in the classroom and my students
and I listen to the launch of Alan Shepard on Mercury Redstone 3 with
the call sign, "Freedom 7." I was hooked!

After the school year, I rushed to Langley with my wife, baby and a
trailer. I went into the NASA building and announced my arrival for
work. Someone looked for my name and said they didn't have any record of me being hired. I said that Chris Critzos hired me and they went
to get him. He straightened things out and gave me a tour.

I met Gene Kranz, Gerry Brewer, Arnie Aldrich, John Hodge, Jack Ko-
slosky and others. Jack and I were assigned to Gene Kranz and that
began my career with NASA. I was 25 years old. I had no idea what I
was going to do. I was just glad to be there.

During those first days, I met the group of 16 Philco technicians that
were assigned to the flight operations organization. They were kept in a
separate room because they were contractors. However, they were there
to help us new, young NASA flight controllers with communications,
electronics and data systems. They had experience from other defense
tracking stations that would be helpful in augmenting our training and
staffing at our tracking stations. Credit must be given to these men who
became part of the NASA teams that manned the remote sites. Among
them I recall: Al Barker, John Gorman, Marv Rosenbluth, Jim Tomber-
lin, Richard Cross, Harry Hopp, Sy Rumbaugh, Bill Wafford. Louis De-
louca, Wilber Hubert, Jim Strickland Lloyd White, Dan Hunter, Dick
Rembert, Harold Stenfords, and Ted White.

PROJECT MERCURY

Space Task Group-1961

Flight Control Operations Branch

NASA Langley Research Center

Former F-86 pilot, Gene Kranz took me under his wing and pointed me to operational areas related to the world-wide tracking network and the Mercury Control Center (MCC). Most of 1961 was going to various classes to learn the Mercury spacecraft, the Atlas launch vehicle and capabilities of the tracking stations around the world. There were no college courses like those to prepare you for spaceflight support. This also began many years working with Mission Rules; now called Flight Rules. My first support was helping Gene with the MR-4 Mission Rules for Gus Grissom's flight. Within one month of my arrival I was involved in historic spaceflight. I was teaching kids in a classroom just one month earlier. The Grissom water landing caused some consternation. I have a photo of the recovery helicopter's wheels in the water just before the pilot cut the capsule loose. The summer of 1961 also included the Russian launch of Vostok II with Gherman Titov, and the first orbital flight of Mercury on the Atlas launch vehicle; MA-4.

I spent MA-4 and MA-5 at Goddard Space Flight Center learning how the flight controllers communicated with the Mercury Control Center. I was trained by a man (I think his name was Robby Robertson) whose call sign was "Goddard Voice" and by Bob Plaumann. This involved the NASA Communications Network (NASCOM) consisting of voice and teletype (TTY). The command and telemetry was handled by the Satellite Tracking and Data Acquisition Network (STADAN). This was an age before voice was handled by satellite communications. The Goddard controlled voice circuits allowed the Mercury Control Center and the remote sites to coordinate all the mission planning and operations data. From that position at Goddard, I could hear all the simulations and mission communications. This gave me a good understanding of how flight control works. It was great training for a new person with no concept of spaceflight operations.

Communications then were primitive compared to today. Some tracking stations had underwater cable and land-line communications back to Goddard and then on to Cape Canaveral. NASA paid AT&T extra to continuously monitor and tweak these lines for a mission. Very remote stations like the tracking ships in the Indian, Atlantic or Pacific Oceans, or stations on islands took up to a half an hour to establish contact. This was done with Single Side Band HF radio much like Ham radio.

I needed to learn how to communicate with all of the tracking stations at different times during the missions to be sure they had the latest information to pass up to the crew or what they should be looking for on telemetry. The remote site flight controllers would also be sending TTY back to MCC. The first women to ever be in the control center were runners from the TTY area to the various flight controllers' consoles. I would also update the remote sites on any changes to the Mission Rules. This would take a lot of time; depending on the quality of the voice links.

(The NASA book, "Read You Loud and Clear" by Sunny Tsiao, chronicles the history of the NASA Spaceflight Tracking and Data Network.")

MERCURY ATLAS-6

After the flight of the chimpanzee Enos on MA-5, it was time to launch the first American into orbit. By this time the preparations for MA-6 was in full swing. I spent most of the next few months helping Gene with the MA-6 Mission Rules, the procedures and communications to the launch pad and range people and the internal procedures within the control center. This position in the control center was called the "Operations & Procedures Officer; better known by the call sign; "Cape Procedures" or just "Procedures."

When Gene or I talked to the Atlantic Missile Range (AMR) (later called the Eastern Test Range) tracking stations our call sign was; "Devil Fox Brass One." I got a lot of help from the MCC support people to learn the Ham radio lingo and the communications flow into and out of the control center. Prior to Gene or I getting ready to communicate with the sites, George Metcalf, "ComTech" would get the links established for us. Voice quality often suffered in the early days. Wearing heavy Western Electric headsets for hours struggling to hear was very uncomfortable. Later we got much lighter Plantronics headsets.

One of my favorite guys was John Hatcher. His handle was "Support." He sat just inside the control center to the left. He knew the Cape and the AMR well. If anybody in the MCC needed something you could go to John. Sometimes, he would give us lessons on how the data flow worked from the range to the control center.

The Mercury Control Center had a viewing room with a big glass wall so the VIPs could see what we were doing on the main floor. Underneath the floor of the VIP room there was another small area where we could go for discussions and post simulation reviews. Many of the Mission Rules were discussed here as well as any operational matters that needed to be changed for the subsequent simulation. These discussions were often quite frank and sometimes "testy." The outcomes all had to be documented, reviewed and approved. I took copious notes but nobody could take notes like Gene Kranz. Gene taught me everything I needed to learn. Keeping up with him was a challenge to say the least.

Most of the MCC contract support people were very experienced with radar, data, voice, teletype, and communications having supported both military and NASA launches. My favorite teletype guy was Andy Anderson. He worked in a small room just off the control center that just reeked of teletype oil and sounded like a bunch of loud sewing machines. TTY was the primary way to communicate to the remote tracking stations. There was a strict protocol and format of the messages. They had to be cryptic but precise because they were transmitted at low speed but often of critical importance. The language of flight operations is unique. Say what you need to say in as few words as possible. Be to the point. (Note to the wise; learning this type of communications does not transfer to your home life!) My training at Goddard helped me learn how to facilitate the communications between the remote sites and the control center flight controllers.

John Glenn's "Friendship Seven" slipped many times. We seemed to be down at the Cape for months. We had "Scrub" parties at the motel in Cocoa Beach. We played volleyball, had pool parties and relaxed a little from what was often 10-16 hours days. It seemed weird at first to be playing volleyball with Chris Kraft, an Air Force General, a Mc-Donnell VP, a couple of flight surgeons and a bunch of us young flight controllers. The games were very competitive. I'll never forget onetime I spiked the ball right into Chris's face and cut his cheek. That was embarrassing.

One time at a pool party everybody was throwing people into the pool. Not to be left out of the fun, I grabbed one of the secretaries and started to push her in but she slipped out of my grasp and fell into the edge around the pool and broke her arm. Fortunately, one of the flight surgeons was there to administer first aid. Upon our return to Langely, my wife met me at the airplane and as the secretary came off the plane in a cast, my wife said, "Oh, what happened to her?" My explanation didn't go over very well.

During John Glenn's flight, the famous "Segment 51" signal indicated the heat shield had deployed. Since this was not supposed to happen in orbit, it posed a potential grave danger. Others have described the technical details. I think the best description is in Gene Kranz's book, "Failure is Not an Option." I will just point out what I was involved with which was helping to prepare all the teletype messages that Andy Anderson and a guy named just Eshleman, would send out to the tracking stations to see if they also had that signal and any other information that might shed light on the situation. Some people in MCC feared the worse. Sometimes just 4 or 5 people would be in the teletype room trying to figure out just what to ask the remote site flight controllers. I remember the McDonnell engineers Ed Niemann and John Yardley with Gene and me in this little room drafting up the messages to give to Andy to send out to the sites. It was extremely tense and at times grave. Meanwhile, Kraft, Williams, Faget and the spacecraft systems experts strategized on the proper response and the reentry procedures in the remaining time before retrofire. Would the heat shield come off, would the attached retro pack affect the aerodynamics, would John Glenn survive? That was my second manned spaceflight experience and the first one in the Mercury Control Center! I'm still only 25 years old.

While months were spent on the Mission Rules; it suddenly and permanently instilled the mindset that not all events could be envisioned and thoroughly discussed before they occur. In the introduction to the Mission Rules, it states; "Having analyzed the conditions and malfunctions herein prior to their occurrence provides those personnel involved with pre-thought, pre-arranged and pre-planned actions which are known from experience to be the best solution to the malfunction."

But, by having analyzed and simulated many different spacecraft, launch vehicle and network failures and problems, the flight controllers and managers gain a depth of understanding that enables them to tackle the unknown or unfamiliar. I became totally involved in helping Gene with coordinating and documenting this process throughout Project Mercury and up to Gemini 7.

Sometime after Glenn's flight, President Kennedy came to the Mercury Control Center to congratulate everybody. We all dressed up in suits and ties. The "Cape Procedures" console is the first one as you come through the door to the main room. Kennedy's back always gave him some pain so in going up the two steps to our floor level, he put his hand on my shoulder to give himself some support. I just sat there at attention. He went past Gene Kranz and greeted Chris Kraft who started to give him a tour and introduce him around. Meanwhile, General Curtis LeMay came over to my console and used the top of it to check out the medal they are going to give to John Glenn. He said, "Do you want to see Glenn's medal?" as he showed it to me. I just smiled and continued to sit at attention. A photo of that visit and Certificate of Participation for the team that launched the first American into orbit is on my office wall.

After this flight I was assigned to go find us a place to live in Houston. I found a flat field with some concrete slabs and I think there were one or two houses. This development was called Sun Valley. It was south of Hobby airport and a few miles north of were the Manned Spacecraft Center was going to be built. I borrowed $250 for the down payment and bought a lot on the corner of Regal and Welk. I reported back to Gene that you could get a new three bedroom house there for $16,500. I thought I could afford it; after all, I was making almost $7,000/year! A lot of the flight controllers and flight support people moved there. It was later called "Flight Controller Alley."

MERCURY ATLAS-7

Scott Carpenter's "Aurora 7" flight was launched on May 5, 1962. Prior to launch, I continued supporting the remote site flight controllers and became more involved with the Test Conductor's countdown and how it can drive the MCC and the remote sites. It started to be clear that we needed to integrate the various countdowns. There were a lot of groups supporting a launch and they each had to take certain actions at certain times. Later I would work on an "Integrated Countdown."

The most vivid memory of the MA 7 flight was the long reentry due to Scott not being in the right attitude, late for retrofire and misuse of fuel. As John Llewellyn, the "Retro" realized how far down range he would be from the desired recovery ship, it became a problem of getting new recovery forces to him. While the Recovery Team worked that problem, I began calling down the Atlantic Missile Range stations to determine if anybody had contact with Aurora 7.

This is the time that Chris Kraft had to tell an Air Force General who was in charge. The Air Force was in charge of the AMR. Kraft, the NASA Flight Director, was in charge of the mission. Now there was a race between the Navy and the Air Force as to who was going to recover Scott Carpenter. The General learned that the quiet civilian Chris Kraft was in charge. I watched that encounter from about 10 feet away.

There were usually a couple of Generals and Admirals and a few Captains (my favorite was Captain Pete Clements who helped me a lot over the years) and Colonels in monitoring positions in the control center. To the casual observer, you would think the military was in charge. They were older and in uniform with their hats, rank and medals. Then there were a lot of us twenty year olds. Chris Kraft was 37 years old. It was clear that he was in charge! I was learning a lot about a lot of things in Mercury Control!

After this flight, we moved into our just completed new home in Sun Valley. Life is good!

MERCURY ATLAS-8

The next mission was that of Wally Schirra's "Sigma 7" launched on October 3, 1962 on MA-8. By this time, I had some more experience and was helping coordinate the Mission Rules with various flight controllers. As you would expect, the crew had a big input. One time Wally invited me to come to his beach hotel to coordinate his inputs to the latest draft. We sat on the beach and went over the rules. I would give him some insight why a particular rule was written and he would give me his input which I would later take back and go over with Kranz and the other flight controllers. Then we would get into his Maserati and drive down to Cocoa Beach and get some lunch. Over the years, we developed a good relationship and after the fire on Apollo 1, I worked with Wally, Walt Cunningham and Don Eisele on the test objectives for Apollo VII.

It's interesting to note that after the success of this flight, the last three flights of Mercury 10, 11 and 12 were canceled. NASA was ready for

Program Gemini.

MERCURY ATLAS -9

Try as we might, it is difficult to plan the birth of your children to coincide with the launch schedules. We were still going back and forth from Houston to Cape Canaveral. My son Kevin was due soon but we were scheduled to start preparations for MA-9. I knew that I would have to leave soon so I arranged for a maid to help my wife Jane. Sure enough, Kevin was born on May 1st and I left a day or two later. That really goes over well! To top it off, the maid was more of a hindrance than a help.

Gordon Cooper's "Faith 7" launched on May 15, 1963 was to be the longest and last Mercury flight. This required two shifts of flight controllers. John Hodge would relieve Chris Kraft as the Flight Director. John was the Bermuda Flight Director on earlier flights. The flight was fairly routine until things started to fail during the last couple of orbits. But all went well. My role for this flight both preflight and during the mission was fairly routine; mission rule development, communicate with the remote sites, keep up with the countdown interactions and basically help Gene.

PROGRAM GEMINI

As things progressed in the control center, it was becoming clear that some different displays were needed both on the "big screen" as well as on some consoles. We began to get some minor changes during the last couple of Mercury missions but would document what we needed for Gemini. This began a process of requirements analysis for the control center to be built in Houston.

Flight controllers provided input to this very complex process resulting in series of documents called, "Flight Control Requirements for the Development of the Integrated Mission Control Center." I was involved in the console layout and displays, the communications panels and the pneumatic tube system. The new Mission Control Center was back up to the Mercury Control Center on Gemini 4 and prime for Gemini 5.

By the end of Project Mercury in May of 1963 to the first unmanned launch of Gemini in April of 1964, we prepared for a new ballgame. We learned about the new spacecraft, a new Titan II launch vehicle, an Agena target vehicle for rendezvous, a new Manned Spacecraft Center in Clear Lake with a new Mission (versus Mercury) Control Center. 1963 was a year of learning and training for much different, longer and more challenging missions.

The Manned Space Flight Network was also being upgraded, but the number of sites that we would send flight controllers to, was reduced. The speed and quality of transmission of voice and data to the MCC was now improved.

While NASA didn't fly any Gemini flights in 1963, the Russians launched Valentina Terishekova on Vostok 6; the first women in space. The X-15 roared to an altitude of 67 miles, the X-20 Dyna Soar program was cancelled and Syncom became the first geosynchronous satellite.

While this was the year of the Beatles and the beginnings of our participation in the Vietnam War; this would be the year most remembered for the assassination of President Kennedy.

Kennedy was in Houston the day before. We all stood outside of the Stahl Myers building and watched and waved as his motorcade went by. The next day we heard the news. We couldn't believe it. To us, he was the man with the vision; the man who convinced us we could really go to the moon. We didn't quite believe him in May, 1961 when he gave his famous speech; but now we did. Now we were on our way.

CARNARVON

The new Carnarvon tracking station in Western Australia was built in the early 60's. It was built as part of the STADAN network and just added the Mercury equipment. In May of 1964, a team of flight controllers headed up by Dan Hunter, including Stu Davis, Bill Garvin, Jim Moser and I went to Carnarvon to develop the operational procedures for the team. This station is in, what we would call, the "outback." It is located near the Tropic of Cancer. This station would be the first to receive the spacecraft and be able to communicate with the astronauts after a long flight across the Indian Ocean.

To reach that station, we would first have to fly tourist class from Houston to LA, then to Hawaii, then to Fiji and then land in Sydney. We stayed there about a day or so. Then we would fly in a DC-3 from Sydney on the east coast of Australia to Perth on the west coast. Then you would drive 260 miles north on a two lane paved road to Geraldton which was a truck stop and then another 300 miles on lesser roads to Carnarvon. You would stop to 'pee' along the way because there were few gas stations. When you got out of the car, the flies would cover your sweaty back. This journey is so tiring that Dan Hunter wrote a complaint to the travel office to allow people to travel first class for extended long flights.

We stayed at the Gascoyne Hotel. It was made of corrugated sheet metal and had one bathroom on the second floor for all the guests. But, it did have three bars; one for men; one for women; and one for couples. If you saw the movie, "Crocodile Dundee", that bar scene pretty much captures the bar at the Gascoyne Hotel. The owner, Gordon Meiklejohn was a great host.

While I have a dozen stories to tell about this trip; I will only retell the one that relates to operations. (there are more to hear!).

During one simulation, we had our NASA team at the consoles and the Australian Maintenance and Operations (M&O) people were in the back room getting the tracking station ready. We had one of us playing the "System" guy, one playing the "Surgeon" and I was playing the "CapCom." One day, we were already for this one particular test and per the timeline, I called out on the communications link; "M&O, Capcom, ready to support test." No response. I checked to be sure I had punched up the right call button on the comm panel. "M&O, this is Cap-Com ready to support." Again, nothing. I tried again. Nothing. I took off my headset and walked into the back room. There were all the guys sitting down with a cup of tea. "What's going on, we're in a test." "It's time for tea" was the response. "Well I hope this doesn't happen during the flight." I was to learn a few more cultural shocks.

The result of a month's work with the new consoles and tracking station equipment was the writing of "The Gemini Remote Site Flight Controller's Handbook" which went to all of the tracking station remote site teams. There were also some hardware changes that had to be made to the consoles; for example the plastic covers on the communications panel would melt after being on too long.

GEMINI 3

A month or so prior to launch time, Gus Grissom invited me to go to the launch pad to see "Molly Brown" on top of the Titan II launch vehicle. We went up the elevator inside the gantry and I just stared at the monster up close. I thought to myself, "Boy, there is a lot to go wrong." I had never been up that close to a launch vehicle and spacecraft before. It added a lot to my feelings about the Mission Rule process.

On March 18, 1965 just a week prior to Gemini 3, the Russians launched

Voskhod 2 with Pavel Belyaev and Alexei Leonov. Leonov was the first to perform an extravehicular activity (EVA) or "Space Walk." Leonov's pressure suit inflated to a point that after his 12 minute spacewalk, he had ballooned bigger that the hatch; he couldn't get back in! He had to slowly deflate his suit and finally got back in. About two decades later, he was visiting Washington with Tom Stafford and I had the occasion to ask him about that situation. By this time I had already been an Apollo Pressure Suit Test Subject and had flown high altitude missions in full pressure suits and had about 500 hours in space suits. It was an interesting conversation for me as I had never talked with a cosmonaut before, especially about something with which I had some experience.

Gemini 3 was launched on March 23, 1965. It was just three orbits to check out everything and was the first successful manned Gemini mission. I was now 29 years old.

There was, however a flight control problem at the Carnarvon remote site. Dan Hunter and astronaut Pete Conrad got into an argument about who's in charge. This became a big deal and is well documented in Gene Kranz's book. This went up to Chris Kraft and Deke Slayton to resolve. It was ugly to say the least. Dan transferred to the Goddard Space Flight Center and eventually to the Madrid tracking station for Apollo.

Sometime after Gemini 3, Gordon Cooper was driving me around in his new 1965 Corvette Sting Ray. The astronauts had a deal with Jim Rathmann (1960 Indy Winner) Chevrolet in Melbourne, Fl. to get Corvettes at cost. My Network Controller friend Dick Holt was driving around in Gus Grissom's convertible Corvette. Gordo didn't like his because it was a coupe; not a convertible. Gus didn't like his for some other reason. Gordo said, "You can have it if you want it, I'm going to get a different one." So, I bought it for $4,400. The kids were still small enough that they could get in the back.

Coming back from the Cape after a mission, I got caught for speeding in the Florida pan-handle somewhere. The cop made me get out of the car and drove me to the police station to see the judge. My wife followed with the kids in the Corvette.

I gave the police the story of the Gemini launches and how important it was for me to get back to Houston to report on the mission. I think I kept talking until they finally left me go with a fine instead of locking me up. Dick Holt and Capt. "Pete" Clements drove back to Houston in what was Gus Grissom's blue Corvette.

GEMINI 4

Gemini 4 was Gene Kranz's first mission as a Flight Director and mine as Assistant Flight Director (AFD). This was also the first manned mission out of the new Mission Control Center in Houston although the Mercury Control Center was prime; Houston backup. Gene knew about the possibility of adding an EVA to the mission before most of us. But when I was advised of the plan, I attended what was my first SECRET meeting; complete with a guard outside the door. This particular meeting with Ed White and his Flight Crew Support guy John O'Neill, General Bolander from Headquarters and just a few others was to finalize the Mission Rules for this activity. This was a special set of rules just for that activity if management decided to do it.

The EVA was really exciting and we were all ears in the control center. Ed White was really having a ball and didn't want to come back in. After a while, Chris Kraft wanted him back in but Gus Grissom was going to let him stay out for a while. Kraft said, "I said, get him back in."

We had already beat Leonov's time and Ed had a device that allowed him to maneuver around the spacecraft; not just hang out on the umbilical. The spacecraft was about to enter the night side so why risk it anymore.

The new Houston Mission Control Center 1965- White Flight's Team

This is also the mission that Gene first wore the now famous "White Vest" that his wife Marta made for him. He was now "White Flight." Kraft was "Red Flight" and John Hodge was "Blue Flight."

This is also the mission that coined the word "Trench" for the front row of consoles. The Retro, John Llewellyn, first used the term because of all the pneumatic tube cylinders laying on the floor around him. They were used to send and receive hard-copy messages between the rooms and floors of the building. This reminded him of 105 mm howitzer shells around him during his days as a Marine in Korea. I had worked on the requirements for that system and would often be "teased" about it if anything went wrong. You wouldn't believe what people would put in those things.

GEMINI 5

Gemini 5, launched on August 21, 1965, was to be an eight day mission for Gordon Cooper and Pete Conrad. We had three teams again in the control center. This spacecraft had fuel cells for the first time. This presented pressure problems that caused me to send out more messages to the remote sites. There were also questions about where to bring them down if this presented a bigger problem. Gemini 5 set a new spaceflight duration record.

Also during this period, I was also involved with mission documentation such as the Mission Requirements Document, post flight documentation, and representing Flight Operations at the Cape for Gemini/Titan launch operations meetings. This all went on before and after the actual missions. We were now launching about every 2-3 months. We were all very busy. In 1965, I received the Manned Spacecraft Center Outstanding Performance Rating for work in control center planning and operations. By this time, I was Head of the Mission Operations Section under Gene Kranz.

GEMINI 6

It was time to try rendezvous; that is, bringing two spacecraft from different orbits together. This was the chosen method for Apollo. The Lunar Module would have to lift-off from the Moon and rendezvous with the lunar orbiting Command Module. An Agena target vehicle would be launched from the Cape on an Atlas launch vehicle, then the Gemini would be launched on the Titan II and the Gemini would rendezvous with the Agena.

The Atlas/Agena was launched on October 25, 1965. Upon separation of the Agena from the Atlas and the firing of the Agena, it apparently exploded. I remember calling down the Atlantic Missile range to see if anybody had any contact. The RSO reported tracking pieces falling.

Gemini 6 was in the final stages of its countdown, but was scrubbed. There was nothing to rendezvous with. Neither the Russians nor the Americans had yet rendezvoused, yet alone dock; both critical to going to the moon.

GEMINI 6/7

GENE KRANZ, GEORGE LOW & DUTCH VON EHRENFRIED
DURING GEMINI 7

A brilliant management decision was reached within two days of the Agena failure. Frank Borman and Jim Lovell would be launched first on Gemini 7 and Gemini 6 with Wally Schirra and Tom Stafford would be launched second and rendezvous with Gemini 7 as the target vehicle.

In November 1965, we deployed flight controllers again to support two spacecraft in orbit at the same time. There was of course, double documentation and planning. There was also a more complex launch countdown with two launch vehicles and two spacecraft. The remote sites had to scramble to support two different spacecraft coming at them at different times. We had many network simulations and data flow tests to get ready to support.

On December 4, 1965 Gemini 7 was launched and within hours, the Gemini 6 launch vehicle and spacecraft was being readied for its launch which occurred on December 15th. We now had two spacecraft in orbit at the same time. Prior to launch, Gene Kranz was set on getting the remote sites ready for anything. By this time I had a TTY machine built into my console. It was heavily insulated for sound. I would receive and send out messages to the remote sites concerning mission procedures and possible events that Gene wanted them to prepare for. The voice network was improved and it was now easier to talk to the sites.

The importance of performing rendezvous on this flight was well understood. It was key to proceeding with the Apollo Program. Of equal importance was to prove that the crew could endure a very long duration flight to the moon.

Only four orbits after launch, Wally Schirra and Tom Stafford aboard Gemini 6 rendezvoused with Frank Borman and Jim Lovell on Gemini 7. There was no docking capability, but Wally could hold a standoff position with the Gemini 7 target vehicle. The Russians were never able to do that.

Chris Kraft was Flight Director at the time. I was Assistant Flight Director and was standing with Gordon Cooper next to Chris when Jerry Bostick passed out American flags to everybody and we all waved them and celebrated this remarkable accomplishment. A photo of this event hangs on my office wall. It was a "really big deal" at the time and was to be my last Gemini mission.

Jim Lovell and Frank Borman went on to set an endurance record that lasted for many years.

A CAREER MOVE MISTAKE

During this period of time, I had met a lot of managers from the aerospace companies. I had met "Mr. Mac" McDonnell of McDonnell Aircraft, Donald Douglas, Jr. of Douglas Aircraft and others. The local Houston representatives lived and worked across from the Manned Spacecraft Center. I had worked closely with IBM and TRW engineers. These companies wanted to hire some experienced flight controllers and engineers from NASA as their businesses were also expanding.

"Red" Colin Harrison from Martin Company was a friend and he told me about their operation in Denver where they built the Titan launch vehicles. They were also big in spacecraft testing and wanted to win some Apollo contracts. He arranged for me to meet with Caleb Hurt (who later became President of Martin) and Dr. Karl Kober their chief scientist. Dr. Kober had worked on the Bismark over-the-horizon radar. While he could play the German scientist, privately he was pretty funny. These were very impressive people and they had a very impressive operation. They offered me a 50% raise! For a 29 year old guy with a family of four, that is hard to resist! Kranz and Kraft tried to talk me out of it. I moved to Denver in January, 1966 to work on the Apollo Experiment Package. Needless to say, it turned out to be a big mistake. I got homesick for flight operations; especially after hearing about Gemini 8. The Denver winter was horrible; my wife was very sick due to the low humidity and the cold. Her lungs couldn't take it. After only four months, I asked Gene Kranz to come back to NASA. Fortunately, Glynn Lunney was staffing up for Apollo and I was offered a job as a Guidance Officer in the Flight Dynamics Branch. Charlie Parker was my Section Head. I was happy to take the pay cut to get back to flight operations. I was also grateful that they took me back.

APOLLO I

From June, 1966 to the Apollo I accident on January 27, 1967, I trained to be a "Guido." This was a fascinating assignment and utilized my physics, astronomy and math education. Some of the Flight Dynamics people joined the Apollo astronauts Grissom, Chaffee and White and others for training at MIT. Inertial guidance and navigation is not generally something taught in schools at that time. But there was the MIT Lincoln Laboratories headed by Dr. Charles Stark Draper and his post graduate students who knew that subject well. The Guidos would be responsible for the Apollo spacecraft computer programs that would be used for maneuvers and to send command updates to the computer. The Guido section worked with IBM on the computer telemetry and the control center displays. We developed our console procedures and displays to support this function. We also joined the Apollo astronauts at the Griffith Observatory in LA to study the stars that would be used as backup to navigate to the moon. This first group of Guidos set the console procedures and displays that would be used for Apollo.

Others have described the technical details of this tragedy. I'll just relate my personal story as a Guido on the console when the fire broke out.

We had many simulations under our belts by January 27, 1967. Plenty of console and headset time in previous Mercury and Gemini missions and in Apollo data flow tests, program checkouts, command test, and much more. During those last several weeks before the accident there was a feeling of unreadiness in many a flight controller's mind. This was a new spacecraft, a new Apollo ground network, a new launch vehicle, new computer programs and new positions within the MCC for many of us. We still had a way to go before we would get that "flight ready" feeling we got in Gemini; the feeling you get when you are at home with your part of the system and with the job you have to do. We were confident that by launch day we all would be ready as we always had been in the past.

There were to be four Guidance Officers for Apollo I. Two Guido's were to be on the console for launch phase and two for orbit phase. Will Presley and I were to come on duty for the orbit phase. For this test, we were on with Chris Kraft, the Red Flight Director. We had worked with Gene Kranz and John Hodge and their teams during other simulations and tests. We had worked together efficiently; interpreting our data and passing critical bits of information to the correct person at the right time with the minimum amount of words and delay.

Most of the support for this "Plugs Out" (spacecraft on internal power) test consisted of command and telemetry. This consisted of formatting and transmitting several types of commands from MCC to the space- craft at the Cape and then checking the spacecraft and ground's systems response via telemetry.

Maurice Kennedy was the Fido to my left and Chuck Deiterich was the Retro to his left in the "trench." Will Presley was to my right. I forgot who else might have been there. We were all preparing for the test sup- port as well as the systems, network, surgeons, and everyone else in the control center. Will Presley and I checked the notes from the first shift and started checking our command procedures and equipment, our TV displays of telemetry, trajectory and general purpose data.

We were monitoring the various activities in the test that concerned or interested us and studying one problem or another during any holds, making pertinent notes in our mission logs. We had also sent some com- mands to the spacecraft.

The communications seemed poor most of the day. The blockhouse was having a little trouble reading the crew and a hold was called in order to remedy the problem. I remember thinking to myself after listening to one transmission from the crew, "This communication is so bad; their voices sound like they are changing frequency." But what I heard on the next transmission was clear enough, "Fire in the spacecraft!" I turned to Will and said, "Did you hear that?"

It seemed as though everyone was holding their earpiece into their ear so as not to miss a word. We couldn't see anything on our TVs since video was not transmitted to Houston. Several other conversations were being heard on our communications panel which had nothing to do with the blockhouse, so I punched them off. My first reaction was not so much for concern as to pay close attention to the conversations. As the conversation from the blockhouse became intense, I suddenly realized the extent of what was happening a thousand miles away. No one here could do anything about it.

All of us hoped and prayed silently but as the minutes slipped by, we knew the situation was bad. Top management was called in and advised of the situation or were called on the phone. I watched these same people that I was used to seeing "all smiles and cigars" after previous missions now take the shocking news of what had happened to the crew.

Chris Kraft was as stern and pale as I had ever seen him. The burden of his responsibility, even in hectic times, was always carried out with an air of confidence that would permeate the control center. This was a deep personal loss for everyone. My Guido partner, Will Presley, didn't seem to move for what seemed like hours. This was to be his first mission.

The accident happened at about 5:30 PM Houston time. By 7:30 PM there was nothing more I could do so I left the building. Fido, Jerry Bostick saw me as I came out of the building and I told him what had happened. Others were now coming into the MCC building to get the news.

Many thoughts went through my mind as I tried to sleep that night. We had other tense moments in the control center but this accident happened so fast we were just stunned. There was just nothing we could do. I could not help but to think about the guys on the launch pad and the valiant job they did. We all heard the voice communications between the Pad Leader and the Test Conductor. They struggled to open the hatch and couldn't do it in time. Later we heard that the crew probably died in 10-15 seconds.

I also remembered the time Gus Grissom took me to the pad to his Gemini/Titan III and the sobering feelings I had then. I had worked closely with Roger Chaffee on the Apollo on-board computer and navigation system. I worked with Ed White on his EVA mission rules and we talked about physical fitness. He had given me a tour of the astronaut's gym. We all had a lot of simulation time together and many a post flight celebration party. These were close friends.

What came out of this tragedy was a renewed dedication to the many difficult goals the country had set for us and the personal goals we had set for ourselves. These men were true pioneers into another dimension of human endeavor. If the ultimate meaning of life is to have purpose; to make a contribution; to have the admiration and respect of your fellow man; to have the love of your family; to enjoy life; then the Apollo I crew had it all!

APOLLO VII

In February 1967, with a two year stand down to redesign the Apollo spacecraft, I was assigned to the Apollo Program Office to be the Mission Staff Engineer on Apollo 7. This was now to be the first manned Apollo on a new and improved spacecraft. Wally Schirra, Walt Cunningham and Don Eisele were the crew. After the fire, Wally was a changed man. He was determined that things were going to change and he became much more stern and argumentative; not the cavalier test pilot he was before. Walt headed up a lot of the meetings on flight test objectives and Don focused on the navigation and guidance.

I was to be the lead Program Office engineer for the center-wide planning activities. This meant that I participated in the planning meetings, crew procedures to accomplish the engineering and scientific test objectives and supported the Apollo Program Office Manager at the Cape and in the MCC. I reported to Cal Perrine, Owen Maynard and Program Manager, George Low. During 1968, I also participated in the "planning and implementation" of my daughter Heidi's birth. This time, I didn't have to run off to Cape Canaveral.

**Apollo Pressure Suit
Test Subject
Crew Systems Division 1967-1970**

Also during this period, I obtained my pilot's license and became an Apollo Pressure Suit Test Subject.

Apollo VII was launched on October 11, 1968. I monitored the flight from the Program Office Support Staff Room and would go to the MOCR for questions about certain test objectives. This was a wonderful job and it culminated in a mission that was over 100% successful. We had proven the capabilities of the spacecraft that would eventually go to the moon. We even added additional tests after the intended ones were accomplished. While there were tests that caused a lot of frustration and eventually some arguments with the crew and the ground, the grand total of this mission was a resounding success and paved the way for the Apollo VIII mission to the moon. This was a great two years for me; I felt that I contributed a lot to the mission.

APOLLO VIII

Once the courageous decision was made to circumnavigate the moon on this mission, I assisted the prime Mission Staff Engineer, John Zarcaro. Essentially, I was backup and assistant to John for this flight. We often attended the mission planning missions together or I would take those that I was most familiar with. We would often be involved in the Mission Rules and crew procedures for the test objectives.

The big thrill for everyone was the flight around the moon on Christmas Eve, 1968. This event is described in Chris Kraft's book, "Flight" and in Gene Kranz's book, "Failure Is Not An Option." One must read these books to get a sense of what this mission accomplished and what the flight support and management teams felt during the reading of "Genesis" by Frank Borman, Jim Lovell and Bill Andres.

This mission also showed what great managers NASA had and their courage and genius to plan and approve this mission. To many, this mission was more courageous than the lunar landing.

During this period, I also worked part time for Jack Mays in the Crew

Earth Resources
High Altitude
Aircraft Flight Suit

Systems Division as a test subject. I was in excellent physical condition and performed nearly all the tests that the astronauts were subjected to. These included many rides at high G loads in the centrifuge, testing suits in the vacuum chamber to space altitudes, a ride on the Zero G "Vomit Comet", and hours on treadmills checking various medical parameters. There were also tests to see how fast and accurately you can throw switches given visual cues.

Space suits were evolving and new ones were being designed for later Apollo flights. In late 1969, I went to the International Latex company in Delaware where the Apollo suits were made to be fitted for my own suit. This suit was the first A7LB to be used on Skylab. By this time I had over 500 hours in various pressure suits including the ones I wore on the RB57F.

EARTH RESOURCES AIRCRAFT PROGRAM

In January 1969, after Apollo VIII, I transferred to the Earth Resources Division to become a Mission Manager and crew member on the RB57F. This was a unique and rare aircraft that could carry a 4,000 lb. payload of sensors to extremely high altitudes. That was ten times the payload of a U-2. The Earth Resources Aircraft Program was managed by Ole Smistad. Ben Hand managed the high altitude portion. This program started in 1964 with a Convair 240A but was later replaced with a Lockheed C-130B. A Lockheed P-3A was added and then in 1969, the RB57F was obtained from the Air Force. Our Air Force liaison officers were Major Bob Danielson and Major Ed Hull.

We would coordinate with the Earth scientists to determine how we could obtain their test objectives and then plan flights to obtain data for their studies. Often, there would be other lower flying aircraft and scientists on the ground as we took data at altitudes in the 60,000 to 65,000 feet range. On one flight to track a comet, we flew at 70,000 ft. On another flight, the deep submersible "Alvin" was taking ocean data. On another flight, the Severe Storm Institute in Norman Oklahoma had sensors and radars on the ground while we flew on top of the storm anvils. This added data to the "cell" theory of storms. I would work with our Air Force pilots to plan the flight paths and work with the scientists to determine when to turn on and off the sensors that were in a special pallet in what was originally the bomb bay. I flew on 46 high altitude missions as the Mission Manager and sensor operator. We were known as the "back seater." The Air Force crews fondly called us NASA guys, the "GIB"; the guy in the back! But they call their Air Force guys "Reconnaissance Systems Officers." It depends on your point of view.

The home base for this aircraft was the 57th Reconnaissance Squadron at Kirkland AFB in Albuquerque. This is where I started training for these missions. This squadron was known as the "F-Troop" because the F model of the RB57 was the high altitude reconnaissance version. They flew a lot of neat classified missions. Even today, NASA still uses two of the nearly 50 year old planes for research.

By October 1969, I had my pilot's license, had 500 hours of pressure suit experience, had many missions of Mercury, Gemini and Apollo flight operations experience and conducted a lot of the tests that the astronauts had to go thru as a test subject. So, with the encouragement of Deke Slayton, I took the long shot of applying for the astronaut program. I thought that Space Station would be just around the corner and I could be a Mission Specialist. Who said, "A man's reach should be farther than he's grasp." Isn't that what dreams are for?

SCIENCE REQUIREMENTS & OPERATIONS BRANCH

During my last year in Houston, I was the Chief of the Science Requirements and Operations Branch. This job was responsibility for the definition, coordination and documentation of the requirements for the science experiments assigned to Apollo and Skylab. This included the Apollo Lunar Science Experiment (ALSEP) packages left on the moon, and experiments in lunar and earth orbit. These were mounted in the Scientific Instruments Module in the orbiting Apollo Command and Service Module.

The ALSEPs were very sophisticated and designed to operate automatically once the astronauts deployed them. They transmitted millions of readings each day; some lasting for many years.

There were seismic sensors, magnetometers, spectrometers, ion detectors, heat flow sensors, charged particle and cosmic ray detectors, gravity measurements, and more and more. We now know more about the moon than ever before; and there were some surprises.

This required managing 25 engineers and contractors to coordinate and develop the required mission documentation. This provided experiment objectives input for the crews and procedures for deploying and conducting the experiments on the moon and in orbit. We developed the Earth Resources Applications Program (ERAP) Users Handbook. We coordinated with the various scientists who wanted their experiments flown on Apollo or Skylab. I thought of this as my contribution to lunar science.

While I was not in the MCC for the lunar landing, I feel my contribution was in the experiment packages left on the moon and all the mission support work I contributed up to that point. I am proud of my NASA Apollo Group Achievement Award for the Lunar Landing.

AFTER HOUSTON

I left Houston in 1971 for a contractor job at Goddard Space Flight Center in Maryland. I worked with my old Network Controller friend Dick Holt with EG&G Wolf Research on the Earth Resources Technology Satellite. This was later called Landsat. I continued to work with various Earth scientists and engineers as this was a continuation of my work on ERAP. This contract only lasted a year. I began to learn about the problems with government contracting.

This led me to a job with TRW in McLean, VA with another NASA friend, John Bryant. I was the Manager, Systems Engineering & Development Department with responsibility for work on various systems engineering projects including the World Wide Military Command and Control System (WWMCCS). This utilized my MCC user requirements and operations experience. This work was for the Secretary of Defense for Intelligence and for the Department of the Navy Fleet Command Centers. I spent two years in Hawaii working for the CINCPACFLT in Pearl Harbor. This led to Top Secret and Intelligence clearances. I continued this effort until 1975.

At the request of another old NASA friend and Retro, Tom Carter, I joined the newly created Nuclear Regulatory Commission in 1975. Later, Apollo VIII astronaut, Bill Anders was appointed the Commissioner. I was the Chief, Test & Evaluation Branch, Nuclear Safeguards Division. I had a team of USA "Green Berets" assigned to me to be the calibrated terrorist threat ("black hats") against uranium and plutonium fuel cycle facilities. We were so successful that I was awarded the NRC Sustained Superior Performance Award and a GS-16 rating. This led to becoming an independent consultant to the Nuclear Industry that was required to increase the protection of their facilities. Using my NASA and NRC experience, another NASA flight controller friend and colleague, Dick Sutton and I wrote contingency plans (much like mission rules) for both nuclear power and fuel cycle facilities up to 1979. Dick continued in the nuclear security field for many years.

I was then hired by International Energy Associates, Ltd. (IEAL) at the Watergate in Washington, DC. This company was heavily involved in the energy business; nuclear in particular. John Grey and others had worked with Admiral Rickover on submarine reactors and the first commercial nuclear power plant at Shippenport, PA. My work was primarily an extension of the nuclear safeguards work at the NRC.

At the time, a uranium/plutonium reprocessing facility was built in Barnwell, SC. We had a team that defined the security requirements but President Carter decided against reprocessing fuel. All of the spent fuel from the nuclear power plants could have been reprocessed to obtain plutonium for subsequent fuel use. However, the anti-nuke environmentalists convinced the administration to close the plant in 1983 after $500 million was spent. We also examined the Strategic Petroleum Reserve for similar threats.

It was at IEAL that I met my current wife of 29 years, Dayle Thompson. She was the office manager and we were married years later in 1982. Dayle and I thought we would make a good business team so we went out on our own to be contractors to the FAA Office of Aviation Safety and NASA Headquarters. Our big break came when NASA friends John Hodge and Clay Hicks started a task force for the Space Station Program.

Our first contract was a $10,000 purchase order for a requirements document. One thing led to another and when the Task Force became the official Space Station Program Office, we competed for and won a small support contract. We started the Technical & Administrative Services Corporation (TADCORPS). We grew into a company of over 30 people and supported the Program Office until 1994 and other NASA Headquarters offices until 2000.

TADCORPS won the NASA sponsored Small Business Administration (SBA) Administrator's Award for Excellence and the SBA Region V Award for Prime Contractors in 1995.

After our move to St. Petersburg, FL I went back to school and received my Chartered Financial Consultant (ChFC) and Chartered Life Underwriter (CLU) certifications to be a Financial Advisor. I've been licensed for the past 15 years and currently have a Raymond James office in Lago Vista, TX.

EPILOGUE

Looking back over one's life, what does one remember that is important? Its key people and events that actually make you who you are. Out of the thousands of people that I met as part of my professional career, here are the NASA ones that are etched in my now ancient mind:

Gene Kranz; not because he taught me everything and worked me to my utmost capacity and therefore expanded my capabilities but, because he was the best example of what a man, colleague, husband and father should be. He is my definition of a man's man.

Chris Kraft; not because he was my first Flight Director but, because he gave a young man an opportunity to achieve his utmost and taught me the importance of responsibility, recognition and reward. He also forgave me for most of my shortcomings (but I suspect, not all).

John Hodge because he trusted his people and gave them responsibility. He was always a gentleman even when he probably shouldn't have been.

Arnie Aldrich because he was so knowledgeable, cool under fire, a good systems engineer and a good person. He was one of the first people I met and learned from at Langley.

Glynn Lunney because he took me back after I left NASA and gave me a chance to be a "Guido."

John Llewellyn; my fellow 'judoka' because he is such a unique and unusual person. I have even forgiven him for ripping my shoulder out of its socket because I teased him. (We also drank of lot of beer together).

Wally Schirra because he actually spent time with a new 25 year old flight controller who was just learning how to do his job.

Many of my NASA colleagues were involved in my post JSC Houston life as well. People like Dick Sutton, Dick Holt, Pete Clements, Clay Hicks, Tom Carter, John Bryant, Ole Smistad and others. I could list another 100 but space doesn't allow it. Even today, three flight controllers live within 30 miles of me; Jerry Bostick, John Aaron and Chuck Deiterich.

At age 75, you just start to understand the meaning of what you were involved with so many years ago. I'm sure we all are proud of what we have contributed to manned spaceflight.

IX - William J. Boone, III

FROM LELAND, MS THROUGH APOLLO XVII

(with limited discourse post Apollo)
By Bill Boone

*This is written to document some of my life's experiences for Flight
Dynamics as well as for my children.*

How could a person from a small town in Mississippi, population 6000, end up participating in one of the most fascinating, best, unique, memorable events the world has ever seen…the Apollo Program, including the First Landing of Humans on the Moon and Apollo 13? The simple answer is that in 1967 I accepted a job with NASA in Houston, Texas at the then Manned Spacecraft Center (now Johnson Space Center) working in Flight Operations in a group called Flight Dynamics. With respect to the late Paul Harvey, however, this is the rest of the story. I hope to recall the many people, experiences and events in my life that influenced me to become a Flight Dynamics Officer (FIDO) during the Apollo Program and participate in Apollo. My story will be documented within 5 time segments: 1945-1959; 1960-1967; 1967-1972 (the Apollo years); 1972-1983 (the rest of my NASA career); and 1983-present (post NASA, a summary.) How some of the people, experiences and events got me to Houston and through Apollo may not be obvious. But they all influenced me somehow and helped mold me into whom I am. I also hope you see how important relationships have been in my life.

1945-1959

I was a product of World War II, born July 15, 1945, in Greenwood, Mississippi, but lived in Leland "all my life." My parents met in the early 1940s at Mississippi State (State) and married in 1943. My mother, Elsie Miller was from West Point, Mississippi, which is near State, in the rolling hills. She majored in Accounting at State. My dad, William Jack Boone, Jr. was from Leland, Mississippi, which is near the Mississippi River in the Delta, totally flat land formed from many years by the flooding of the Mississippi River and other smaller waterways. This is the part of Mississippi where most of the plantations were and some still are. Dad wanted to be a Doctor but WWII cut that short. He never finished his degree.

I know mom and dad loved me, but they were different people and showed their love in different ways. Mom would tuck me in at night and listen to my "problems." When I was sick, she would come home to check on me, bringing me the latest comics to read. She was the nurturer. Even though both were raised during the depression, dad was really influenced by it. He always kept some cash in a cigar box, just in case. His method of child raising was also influenced by his parents. He mainly called the shots. He was a strong disciplinarian who believed in spanking, often I thought needlessly. He would tell "everyone" how proud he was of me, but he never would tell me that until late in life. He did not hug or show much outward affection until later in life, but I knew he loved me. He often said his job as a parent was to raise me to "take care of myself." He did a good job.

I was fortunate to know my maternal grandparents and a maternal great grandmother. It took close to four hours to drive from Leland to West Point. Mother would go home several times a year. I would often go with her, riding in the back of the car, usually sleeping under the rear window. We didn't use seat belts then, so either mother was a good driver and/or we were lucky to not have an accident. My grandfather Miller had been a successful merchant and city councilman but was wiped out during the depression. Grandmother worked at the movie theater where I could see movies for 10 cents. My great grandmother, Mattie, was a sharp lady. She couldn't get around much due to old age, but she had a sharp mind and loved to play games. We would play Chinese checkers, card games and other board games for hours. Usually she won. To this day I love to play games, any kind, and usually play to win. A lot of visiting can be done playing games. I attribute my initial love of games and my desire to win to Mattie. I also now know that my "frugal" nature was influenced a lot by the depression lessons my maternal grandparents learned, as well as my dad.

I was also fortunate to know my paternal grandparents as well as one of my paternal great grandmothers. My great grandmother, Mamaw, lived in Boyle, Mississippi, about 20 miles north of Leland. My papaw Boone worked for the Illinois Central Railroad as a station master and was stationed away for many years. My grandmother, Mama, lived in Leland where she helped dad at the Funeral Home (more to come), was a nurse and rented part of her house to make ends meet. (Here is the frugal again). When papaw was in town, we would often hunt together, mostly squirrels and rabbits, and fish for crappie and bream with my dad. I would mimic their habits, but they were "always" more successful than I. It seems like the older folk just have more ability/luck than the younger ones. As a youngster, I often went fishing with Mama and Mamaw and was amazed that they could carry the fishing motor down a river bank. I thought they were old…guess I am that age now….but they were "tough" and survivors. Mamaw even went to the Oklahoma territory in a covered wagon to make her/their fortune, but returned because it did not "fit" their lifestyle. Since Mama lived in Leland, I spent many days and nights with her. She had a TV before we did and she had a window air conditioner, which was really needed in hot, humid Mississippi. All my grandparents meant a lot to me then, just like all my living family does today.

My mom was never a practicing accountant.   She was a bookkeeper for several businesses all of her life, which meant she wasn't home all that much during the day.   I was fortunate to have several black ladies who helped raise me.   They were good cooks who also were literate.   They encouraged me to read and do math way before my time.

Until I was five, my dad traveled and sold burial and life insurance.   We rented a small duplex.   Dad was frustrated since he had wanted to become a doctor.   His taking care of his family, however, was now more important than his dream.   Dad also worked part time at the local Funeral Home.   When it came on the market in 1950, somehow dad bought it.   At the same time we bought our first house.   The Funeral business is 24/7, so he was always on call.   Our time together was good but limited.   He coached little league, taught Sunday school and was my scout master, all of which gave us some good time together when he wasn't working.   But, I decided then that I did not want a life that made me a slave to the business.   Dad wanted me to go into the funeral business with him, but the 24/7 and being around sadness wasn't my cup of tea.

My parents were born in the early '20s.   Their lives were influenced by the depression and WWII.   My life was also influenced by their biases and experiences.   We didn't get a TV until I was 10 (thank goodness for Mama.)   We had one window air conditioning unit, in their room, and one in the bathroom, which gave the definition of sharing a new meaning.   To keep cool, we learned to use an attic fan and open/close windows as needed.   Dad believed if you couldn't pay cash for it, you didn't need it.   Being debt free is still an obsession of mine.   I loved my parents.   They sacrificed for me and provided all my needs and lots of my wants.   They did the best they could.   We stayed in that first house until I was 14.

On Christmas Day, Papaw would show up at our house by 4:00 AM.   I always got a silver dollar from him and still have them today.   One day when I was a pre teen, Papaw had the north bound train stop in Leland in the morning.   I climbed in the caboose.   It stopped in Boyle.   I got off, visited with Mamaw.   It stopped again in the afternoon on its way back south.   I climbed on and exited when it stopped in Leland.   No way could that happen today.   There was a vacant lot nearby where my friends and I would play pick up baseball and football.   We were all different ages, but we would play together.   We made and enforced our rules without adult intervention.   Sometimes being picked last hurt, but you dealt with it.   Life isn't always fair
.

I was able to ride my bike everywhere in Leland, a small town of 6000.

There was no fear, no locked doors. Mom and dad liked to play bridge on Sunday. When dad would get a "death call," I would play for him. My love for bridge began when I was eight, and continues today. My love for card games evolved into rook, canasta, solitaire and eventually poker. To this day I love card games, any kind. I play to have fun, but I play to win. I also had great fun with a chemistry set, often smelling up the house. Leland is a small town, which, every four years, has a reunion for anyone who went to Leland High School. These frequent gatherings are great to keep in touch with old friends. Leland's population is still 6000 today. I was a better baseball player than football, basketball, etc. but I played them all. Dad did a good job coaching me in little league baseball. He was able to convince me and everyone else that he was my coach who happened to be my dad; but, sometimes it seemed he went too far not showing favoritism. Even though he was my dad, I had to earn my playing time. Nothing was given to me. I loved scouting, eventually becoming an Eagle Scout. Loved camping out too, up to 30 nights/year. Learned to cook and take care of myself…important tools when you leave home.

During this time I developed a close bond with Bob Fratesi, who is still my best friend today. We were best friends, but we also competed against each other. Bob was my age and lived on a farm, so we had different experiences when we stayed at each other's houses. When I stayed with Bob, I would help "slop the pigs" and feed other farm animals. I hand picked cotton, putting it into a burlap sack. It was hard, back breaking work. We would hit baseballs in his front yard, with them occasionally rolling into the raw sewage ditches. Luckily his basketball goal was in the back yard, away from the ditches. We would also spend hours running around his house being chased by his collie. His dad had a country store where we "always" had lunch consisting of a slab of bologna, crackers, RC Cola and a Moon Pie. They still taste good. His Mom cooked Italian food, but her specialty, to me, was a Red Velvet Cake. It is still one of my favorites. We would water ski near his lake house just across the Mississippi River into Arkansas. Once we were across the lake, about ½ mile from his dock when the motor failed. We had to swim/push the boat across the lake, taking several hours. We double dated a lot, even switching dates during one outing. We played all high school sports together, vied to make better grades than the other, and even went to the same colleges. But, we didn't room together so we could get to know others. We drifted apart early on at Millsaps. Luckily we realized it and spent several hours on the balcony of a motel at a fraternity party discussing what had happened. We resolved any issues, becoming close again and remain best friends.

Another friend, Rodney Glover, and I created a game we called "baseball cards." We both had lots of baseball cards. I had practically all the Yankees…Mantle, Berra, Ford, etc. We made a proportional field with 1x12's as the fence, placed the cards on the field where players should be, drew circles around the players to indicate "outs," and used a marble as a ball and a stick as a bat. From centerfield, the marble would be "pitched." If the hit marble landed and stayed inside the "circles" or outside 12 inches beyond the fence, you were out. This was great fun, but competitive. Other friends would bring their "teams" over. Many, many games were played.

When I was eight, dad bought me a lawn mower and said I had the summer to pay him back. This started my work life which continues today. I scrambled, found yards to cut and paid him back that summer. I mowed yards with that mower for many years. I learned early on how to keep that mower running. I fished and hunted when I could. I was busy. We also would go to Starkville to see Mississippi State play football, although they weren't very good. At these games I would see and visit with two very influential people that went to State: Senator John Stennis and Representative Sonny Montgomery. Turns out, my maternal grandfather Miller had gone to State and roomed with John Stennis. Mom had even dated Sonny Montgomery for awhile. Much later in life I finally figured out how "powerful" they were. I began to learn the value of networking. During this time we had several vacations that were memorable…St. Louis to see the Cardinals play baseball…Stan Musial, etc. I flew to Chicago with Dad in 58 and saw the College All Star Football game and the Chicago Museum of Natural Science. We went to Biloxi, MS to the beach once where I lost my bathing suit after diving off the high dive…just a little embarrassed because there were girls in the pool also. But, time away was scarce…the Funeral business was and is very demanding. Papaw and mother's mom passed away… my first experience with family death.

In elementary school, I got good grades but flunked self control. I couldn't keep still and quiet. It is still hard today…guess I may be ADHD. Academically I was ready to skip second grade, but mom and dad wisely chose to let me progress slowly, to continue to mature. In junior high, I played all sports, finished my Eagle Badge, was President of the Methodist Youth Fellowship, made A's and B's and continued to mow yards and do other things to earn money. The Funeral Home grew so we were able to buy a larger house in 1959.

Leland was the old south. There was a caste system, but I didn't know it then. Leland had three social groups, I guess: the blacks, the whites and the "Italians." Dad's business didn't do black funerals, but he did the others. Occasionally my parents would have two parties back to back: one for the whites; one for the Italians. I enjoyed all groups, but I slowly became aware of "differences." Dad went by Billy; I went by Bill. Lots of dad's friends would call him Bill also. It was very confusing. I determined then that, if I had a son, he would not be called Bill or Billy. He would have his own identity. During this time period, the Korean War occurred. I was vaguely aware of it. Several ladies in Leland lost their husbands in the war, but I was not sensitive to their loss/ sadness. A Leland native, Hubert Lee, received the Medal of Honor but I did not know this until I was out of college. Guess I was too young. As you can tell, my interests during this period of my life were sports, friends, family and earning some spending money, probably typical of this age. Focused academic interests were TBD, but I knew I liked all subjects up to this stage, through the 8th grade. I liked girls, but I did not "like" girls yet.

1960-1967

Lots of interesting things happened to me during my teenage years. Guess lots are typical to most young men. I made many mistakes, but I learned from them and survived. I had lots of fun also. I was a young "human *doing*", not a "human *being*" as my future mentor Phil Shaffer would often say. I also learned a lot by doing.

In 1960 Kennedy was elected President. That would affect my life in several ways. During Thanksgiving, 1960, the phone rang with the adult wanting to talk with "young Bill." Dad handed me the phone with a quizzical look. On the line was Senator Stennis. He offered me the opportunity to become his page in the Senate, beginning in January 1961. I would go to school in the Library of Congress, stay in a boarding house, earn my keep and be "on my own" for the rest of high school, if I wanted to. Of course he wanted me to discuss this with my parents. I was honored, excited and confused. During the fall of 59, our football team went 9-1. I was an all star in baseball and was being looked at by the Detroit Tigers. Playing sports was big in my life. I discussed Senator Stennis's offer with mom and dad, along with my concerns about giving up what I liked, sports. Hoping a decision would be made for me gave way to the fact that this would be my decision. Mom and dad offered to discuss it with me, but it was my call. I was torn. After a couple of days of "agony," I decided to go to DC to be a page in the Senate. Doing so meant that, for one season at least, I would give up my love, baseball, and maybe the potential of playing in the Pros. Making hard decisions is tough at any age, but really difficult at 14. Life is full of priorities.

On January 2, 1960, mom and I drove to Birmingham, Alabama, and boarded the northbound City of New Orleans to DC. It was cool, experiencing my first overnight train ride. Arriving in DC, we found my new home, Mrs. Smith's boarding house where I would have a roommate and would share the house with a few other pages from around the country. My roommate was Al Jordan from Stone Mountain, Georgia. He was a page in the House, but only for one term. He was also a senior; I was a second semester freshman. We became close friends, experiencing lots of the District together. He was in love and married his sweetheart, Claudia, during spring break. We kept in touch for many years. He became a high school principal and is still married to Claudia. Mrs. Smith ran as tight a ship as she could for all of us teenage boys, but we were free to come and go and make our own decisions. She was a good cook, preparing great boarding house meals for supper M-F. Otherwise, I was on my own. I made ~$375/mo., a lot of money for a 14 year old. I was responsible for me…for paying my rent, washing clothes, cleaning my room, etc. I would rise ~ 4:00 AM, eat breakfast at a local greasy spoon, and arrive for school on the top floor of the Library of congress by 5:30. I was in class until 8:30 when I would walk across the street to the Senate side of the Capitol. My classes were taught by college profs who were demanding. The classes were hard, requiring homework most every night. Guess you could say they were really college prep. We had a basketball team that would play the local high school teams, but I did not have the time, or inclination. My duties were to prepare the Democratic Senators' desks for the day (Stennis was a Democrat) and run errands for the Senators until the day was over. Sometimes the days were long when there was an occasional filibuster which would go real late. I was often asked to tour visitors around the Capitol, so I learned all the neat stuff, trivia, like where Lincoln lied in State and where his viewing pall was, where the perfect echoes were, etc. I believe I met all the Senators, getting to know some, and some of the Representatives also. I became friends with the other pages but the friendships dissolved when we left. I also learned how Congress operates, how deals are cut, how the committees really work, the value of seniority, etc.

In January 1960, I was selected to participate in John Kennedy's inauguration. My function was to help the dignitaries find their seats on the rostrum and provide them with the program. I was able to see the inauguration from the rostrum. The really cool thing was shaking hands with the living Presidents…Hoover, Truman, Eisenhower, and of course JFK and later to be Presidents Johnson and Nixon. LBJ was the VP who also happened to have a teenage daughter, Lucy. I got to know her and was fortunate to attend some parties at LBJs. We had a Spring Formal where I invited a girl, Judy Pistotnik, from Arma Kansas, to be my date. Judy and I had met a couple of years earlier at Yellowstone where I was in route to the Boy Scout Jamboree in Colorado Springs. She and her mom flew to DC for several days. I gave them the grand tour. For the prom, we tripled dated. One of the pages from Wisconsin was older and able to drive. He borrowed his Representative's limo. We decided to park for awhile. After much nervous arm action and thoughts of rejection, I got my first real kiss. I had finally discovered girls! The bad news was the car battery died, so we had to call for assistance. But, it was a great experience! Judy and I kept up for several years, but Kansas and Mississippi were just too far apart. In late spring I contracted mono and flew home for awhile. I had been OK up to then, but that trip home started my being homesick. I finished the semester with A's and B's, was really enjoying all DC had to offer for a now 15 year old, but became aware of what I was giving up in Leland. Although I had the option to remain in DC for all my high school, the tug of sports, long time friends, and my family was too strong. With mixed emotion, I told Senator Stennis of my decision to return to Leland when the term ended (~ July). He understood. My relationship with him continued until he passed away. During my stay in DC, Mamaw passed away. I wasn't told until I returned home. I would not have been able to attend any way, but would have appreciated knowing.

I returned to Leland late in the summer of 1960, a lot wiser, but also as an outsider. My peers had started to seriously date, began driving, formed cliques, etc. I had missed all the fun they were experiencing, but I had matured in a different way, making me more serious than my peers. I also had missed a baseball season and was never able to regain the prowess I once had. But, I returned to enjoy a fantastic three years of high school, experiencing most/all I could. I continued to make good grades...mostly. In random classes, I would mess around for a six weeks session, then apply myself for the rest of the semester...always ending with at least a B. I enjoyed all my classes except physics. My instructor just couldn't make it interesting/relevant to me, so I just "got by." All the rest of the sciences, math, languages, English, history, etc. were interesting and easy. During the summers I worked at the USDA Experiment Station near Leland, checking the effect of different insecticides of cotton insects. Dad occasionally pulled me out of bed to go help him do an emergency ambulance call. I still remember a wreck where a lady died as we were loading her in the ambulance and another where a lady's water broke with me helping load her into the ambulance with the hospital a long way away, it seemed. Sports were still my thing though. I played three years of football, two on championship teams and three years of baseball, one on a championship team. In

May 1961, JFK gave his eloquent speech about "men going to the moon and returning them safely." I had no idea then how that speech would impact my life.

The Mississippi Delta was a great place to be a teenager. The Delta stretched from the Peabody in Memphis, south to Vicksburg, and from the rolling hills near Greenwood, west to the Mississippi River. Leland is ~ 8 miles from the river. The Mississippi River was a great place to watch the submarine races with a good looking girl. During the fall/winter, we would hunt; during the spring/summer we would fish. During the summer we would water ski; watch the moon come up with a good looking girl; occasionally skinny dip; etc. I was what you would classify as a "good" kid. Sometimes I had mixed emotion about being "good" and missing out on whatever. All year long there were dances all over the Delta. I hit as many as I could, meeting as many girls as I could. I knew lots of the guys from sports. After I earned my Eagle Badge, I became inactive in scouting; but I remained close to two scout-masters, and great men, who spent a lot of time with me: "Doc" Manning and Mr. Head. Both had sons my age, and both were good teachers of skills by letting me try to do something, but being there to assist if needed. They were also very active in the Methodist Church. During my last two years in high school, I was selected to lead youth Sunday and give the sermons. They, along with the pastor, often mentioned that I should consider becoming a minister.

As my senior year began in earnest, I started to think about colleges. Since "all" of my relatives had gone to State, I applied and was accepted there, and avoided any consideration of Ole Miss like the plague. I would have been disowned if I even thought about going to Ole Miss, because the previous two generations were State people. I applied to and was also accepted to smaller Liberal Arts schools Vanderbilt, Tulane and Millsaps. I liked the idea of a smaller, academic school and decided on Millsaps, a Methodist school in Jackson, Mississippi. With the end of the baseball season, I felt free to act my age, 17. I knew all the bootleggers in town, since most were dad's friends. (Mississippi was a dry state.) I remember driving to the back of the building to buy scotch only to be told that dad bought some yesterday...with a wink. Somehow, dad knew everything about what I was doing, often right after I did it. As I left for college he told me to keep my nose clean, which really "torqued" this now 18 year old off; but, with that statement, he put on me the choice of deciding what was right and whether to do something. I did get away with one major screw up though before I left for college. The family had just bought a new Ford, and I was allowed to use it for an end of senior year dance. It had ~100 miles on it. With a friend, we went to a remote place to drink a few beers...sports training was over.

After putting the ice chest back in the trunk, I realized the keys were in there also. All I could see was my dad killing me. Luckily initiative won out. We took the back seat out, climbed into the trunk, got the keys and lived happily ever after…and a lot smarter. I believe dad died never knowing this story. As I prepared to leave for Millsaps my wise math teacher and guidance counselor, Mr. Worsham, told me that I would be encouraged to jump into advanced math classes. Although he thought I could handle them, he advised me to start with the basics to get a good foundation…great advice in any circumstance.

At Millsaps, I was an honor student who was also active in intramural sports, fraternity life, school activities, etc. I was an officer in my pledge class, KA. I often would head to the Natchez Trace for a "woodsie", where I would have some beer and food and discuss life with a lady friend. Watching Combat was fun and seemed mandatory, but the Roadrunner was more of an obsession. In November, 1963, I was heading for a woodsie when JFK was assassinated. I couldn't understand that or why Oswald was murdered. It seemed like my childhood bubble burst, and I was really an adult. College life changed for awhile, but we quickly readjusted to the way it was. I thought I could pitch on the baseball team, but I wiped out the ligaments in my right ankle doing figure eights on our KA basketball team. This ended my baseball career, and the injury still affects me today. I had heeded Mr. Worsham's advice and resisted being put into advanced math classes. And, I started to really enjoy math because it came easy to me. I was elected VP of the math honorary as a second semester freshman. In the fall of my sophomore year, I ran for VP of the sophomore class. I lost be 7 votes. 10 of my fraternity brothers "forgot" to vote.

But, I began thinking about what I wanted to do after college, concluding that, if I stayed at Millsaps, I would probably end up in grad school. Vietnam was gearing up which convinced me to get a terminal degree somewhere to hopefully avoid Nam with a deferment. So, I transferred to State in 1965, thinking I would get an Engineering degree and, in the back of my mind, to keep the family tradition alive. Knowing physics was my short suit, I had taken an "elementary" physics class at Millsaps to prepare me for engineering or so I thought.

During the summer between Millsap and State, I went to a local golf course to practice. While there, I ran into a friend, Jack Ingram, who used to live down the street from me when I was a pre-teen. Jack was 3 years older than I was. We played sandlot baseball and football for years until Jack moved to a neighboring town where I lost touch with him. He was in the Army, stationed in Louisiana and home for a short visit with his parents. We spent a long time catching up on our lives and said farewell. Two days later I read where he had been killed in a car wreck returning to his duty station. I was devastated. But, I was thankful for the opportunity to reconnect and to say goodbye. This was a huge life message to leave someone on good terms because you never know if you will see each other again.

When I stepped into nuclear physics at State, I knew engineering was not my field. I still liked math, so I opted to major in math. Transferring to State turned out to be the right decision for me for many reasons. I occasionally would see Senator Stennis and Representative Montgomery when they would come for an event. I was rush chairman of KA and helped organize many events. I was elected to the Student Senate. I dated a lot and went to many football games. I continued to play bridge, winning the campus duplicate championship twice with my partner and KA fraternity brother, John Frazier. I renewed my acquaintance with Dr. Giles, the President of State, who at one time had lived in Leland. West Point was close to State, so I got to see Grandfather Miller a lot. Dad's brother, Uncle Tommy, lived in Starkville, so I had the opportunity to become closer to him. I had never owned a car before, always hitchhiking or bumming a ride. When I transferred to State, Dad let me take an old ambulance called the "Jitterbug." I rigged the back up with a recliner and an ice chest. Many of my friends wanted to double date. My social life was great, but I wasn't ready to get serious.

In the Delta, there was a formal social life, highlighted by the Debutantes, an organization that introduced post high school ladies to "society." I was fortunate to escort several ladies to the Debutante Ball over those college years, even buying a tuxedo and learning how to act "proper." Off and on for many years I had dated a great lady, Allegra Cope. While I was at State we reconnected with thoughts of getting serious, but I wasn't ready. Her Dad, who I still correspond with, and Phil Shaffer, who I was to meet at the Johnson Spacecraft Center (JSC discussed later), are the 2 smartest men I ever knew.

Toward the end of my junior year, I began to think in earnest about what I would do after graduation. Vietnam continued to convince me to not join the military and get my butt shot off for an undeclared war. I had worked one summer for NCR who wanted me for their embryonic computing world; IBM was interested in me for technical sales; Pan-American Petroleum wanted me as a geophysicist; Oak Ridge wanted me in their Software area; University of Florida offered me a free ride to get a Masters in math; Met Life wanted me to be an actuary. The offers were many and quite varied in the scope of jobs. And the money being offered was huge. As I was plodding along, evaluating these options, Space appeared. Ford Aerospace wanted me to move to Houston to work with NASA. Then, a NASA recruiter came to campus. He was from Houston, not Huntsville which was lots closer to State. His syllabus sounded interesting, so I scheduled an interview. We hit it off well, with him saying that I seemed to fit in several areas, including Mission Planning and Analysis (MPAD) and Flight Dynamics. I was not a Space Cadet. I was aware of our Space Program and of JFK's speech on May 25, 1961 about landing a man on the moon. I would watch the launches, but my interest was not yet great. Shortly after the recruiter's visit, I was contacted by Jerry Bostick who discussed Flight Dynamics. He was and is a good salesman. We had a lot of parallels: he was from Mississippi; had gone to State; and had been a page in the House. He described the job and presented the case that there would be just a handful of us who would be a Flight Dynamics Officer (FIDO). Landing guys on the moon sounded "out of this world." The pay was much less than the other offers, but the opportunity sounded too good to be true. Jerry knew I was just a math major, not an engineer, and a BA at that, but that was OK. It didn't take long for me to say "YES." I drove home to tell my parents my decision. They were happy for me, but there was sadness also…they were divorcing after 24 years of marriage. I was shocked, but accepted it. I never took sides and hope they both knew that I loved them throughout their lives.

Coming back from a party in Jackson, I was pulled over for speeding on the Natchez Trace, a Federal highway. My future was vanishing before it ever started. With a Federal offense, NASA would not want me or so I thought. So, I wrote a letter to the judge to explain my case. Either I did a good job and/or he had mercy on me, because he dropped the charges. After graduation and with apparently no major obstacles in view, I began to prepare for my "forever job" with NASA and landing guys on the moon.

The Apollo Days, 1967-1972

1967 was a most unusual time. We had the war in Vietnam and the protests (think Berkley) on the war and practically everything else. We had Motown (The Supremes, Temptations, Four Tops, etc.) competing against the British invasion (Beatles, Rolling Stones, etc.) and the "mainstream" American music. And we had the Apollo Program readying to send the Apollo Astronauts into orbit. The fatal fire of Apollo I occurred before I arrived, setting back the first manned launch. The fire, however, allowed me to participate in Apollo VII, the first manned Apollo flight. Often in life something good comes from something bad.

I left Leland in mid June 1967 with my car loaded with "essentials." Since my parents were divorcing and selling the house, I was fortunate to inherit some furniture, etc. that would, to some degree, fit very well in my apartment and it was free. My parents realized I needed transportation so they had bought me a Chevrolet. I was very thankful, and it was free also. But, the movers would move the furniture only when they had enough other stuff to fill a van. So, I slept on the floor for a few weeks. I had to really stretch my dollars since it would be several weeks until I got paid. My first apartment was in Pasadena, Texas. It was inexpensive and close to Hobby Airport. Hobby was the only airport in Houston and lots of stewardesses stayed in the area. My car was yellow and was parked uncovered. Daily it would be covered with "ash" from the local oil refineries. We were breathing all that stuff also. Denny Holt was a new hire into Landing and Recovery (LRD) who showed up when I did and resided at the same complex. Denny and I became good friends. Denny played bridge, so, with two of his LRD friends, we would often have bridge marathons. He had played tennis at Tennessee Tech. My playing frequently with him really pushed my tennis game to a new level. We went to church together, sometimes, and would see the Astros (Hosuton baseball team) and Oilers at the Astrodome. We learned to get around Houston without using the freeways by getting a city map and driving the streets. That knowledge saved me countless hours when the freeways, especially the Gulf Freeway, would back up...which was frequently. Another FIDO, Bill Stoval (Stump), arrived about the same time I did, but stayed at a different complex. A Guido, Jerry Mill, came a little later that summer. Even though Bill, Jerry and I worked in FDB, we never became as close as Denny and I were during the Apollo years.

I found a duplicate bridge game at Ellington Air Force Base and paired up with Jim Rainey, another NASA person. Jim and I would frequently play in the "big" games in downtown Houston and hold our own against the masters of the game...John Gerber, etc. I played a lot of bridge at night before I began to get serious about dating. Since I loved to play poker, I helped start a nickel, dime, quarter game. In the early years, Frank van Rensselaer played for awhile. Ken Young started playing with us also. We continued to play in the Monday night game for many years. (We even had an occasional FDB game at Dave Reed's with people from the trench playing and others like Ed Lineberry and Ken Young from MPAD.) As the years progressed, the Monday night poker games continued, the stakes increased, and players came and went. Astronaut P. J. Weitz would occasionally play as would several JSC higher ups like Pete Clements, Jim Correale, etc. The competition at these games was intense and the stakes were high, but it also provided the opportunity to create relationships and sometimes discuss Space stuff.

I loved to play golf with Phil Shaffer, Bill Stoval, Bob Regelbrugge, and Ken Young. But these guys were much better than I was. We would usually play the 9 hole course twice at Ellington or at Dickinson Country Club. Regelbrugge had been good enough at one time to play professionally if he desired. Shaffer, being ~6-6, 330 was very imposing. With his size, he knew he could really powder the golf ball, but he also knew that he could not always control the trajectory. So, he was always saying the mantra, "baby golf." This would help him to not over swing, to swing easy and find the fairway more often.Stoval had a huge, sweeping hook that, when controlled, went a long way. We would walk the course and visit. Charley Parker, Maurice Kennedy, Pete Williams (FSD) and others were playing partners and Gary Renick, Gran Paules, and Steve Bales would occasionally play as well.

One of the favorite pastimes at night was shooting pool wherever, playing shuffleboard at the Singing Wheel and drinking beer, usually lots of beer, all over. Some FDBers, like Llewellyn, Massaro and Bales would randomly join the "hard, single core" of Shaffer, Stoval and me shooting pool and drinking beer. At the end of my first week, Shaffer, Llewellyn and Massaro convinced me to go to the 'Wheel' for a few beers. Being fresh out of college, I could keep up with anyone, or so I thought. That first Friday night was a "rude" introduction into FDB. After many beers, Llewellyn left and Shaffer, Massaro and I piled into Shaffer's convertible. Phil thought it was "appropriate" for me to see the gulf coast, at night, as part of my education. We went to Galveston where they ate at 'Gaidos'. I stayed in the back seat, unable to get out. I remember ending up at Shaffer's stilt house in Friendswood that night where I fertilized lots of trees. I may have drunk lots of beer many times later, but I learned my lesson. I didn't compete against the veterans in beer drinking again, especially anyone in the Trench. Eventually Phil became my mentor and best friend from my days at NASA. My separate tribute to his memory (pp388) elaborates on our relationship and experiences.

When I graduated from State, President Giles gave me the info on two alumni to look up: Mancill Allen and Richard Bradley. They lived in the Memorial area, no where close to the Bay Area. Regardless, I took the initiative, called them and initiated a great friendship with them and their families until they passed away. Mr. Allen was a landscape architect, owned land to grow his plants and was a real estate investor, knowing Houston well. He also became my surrogate dad. I began investing with him in Houston land and made a few dollars. He would take me dove and deer hunting as well as fishing in his ponds. We even went to Zapata, Mexico to buy fish for his ponds. Mr. Bradley was a stock broker. He gave me wise advice to build my credit by borrowing money and paying it back early. He advised me on stocks where I made some money also. All this investing and making money was good. Mr. Bradley had a daughter, Anne, a senior at Ole Miss. Anne and I became great friends. She introduced me to many of her friends who lived across Houston also. Anne also introduced me to Beverly Scoble who later became my wife. Many nights were spent with Anne and her friends learning the good restaurants and night spots in downtown and southwest Houston. All these people became a large part of my life, but they were not connected to NASA nor did they live close to me. They did, however, give me access to the world outside of Space.

Prior to Apollo VIII, I purchased my first of three convertibles, a red, Super Sport Impala. I kept it until I reluctantly sold it in 1981. We moved to Denver in 1983. One day I was shopping near my home and saw, once again, my red convertible. I knew it was mine, since I had made a mod to it. I left a note for the owner to contact me, but never got a response. I purchased my second convertible in 1999, a white Sebring, when my kids were in high school at Clear Lake. Today I drive my third convertible, a red Solara. Shaffer must have passed onto me the freedom you feel when driving with the top down.

Looking back, I think those of us in the Trench thought and knew we were someone special. We had an esprit de corps that the systems positions and others did not seem to have. We were competitive in all areas. We worked hard and we partied hard. The three sections of the Trench... Flight Dyanmics Officer (FIDO), Guidance Officer (Guido), and Retrofire Officer (Retro)...had unique jobs, but our success depended on each position working well with each other and communicating effectively and frequently. Prior to the various missions, we learned our jobs through discussions, reading, meetings, simulations and training in the mockups. Any time the Real Time Computer Complex (RTCC) was being checked out was an opportunity to "play" with the maneuver processors. Other than the simulations and playing with the processors, the learning was mostly independent of each other. During the flights, though, we were very dependent on each other. I thought it interesting that "most" of the systems people could not understand what we did or how we did it. I believe that the "non trench" Flight Directors had the same lack of understanding of the Trench, but they all were aware of the critical job we did and knew we had to do it well.

Prior to one of the missions, a PhD showed up to program how the flight controllers did their job. He started with the systems people and quickly saw that monitoring of several of the systems could be "automated." He came down to the trench to watch a launch with Shaffer as the launch FIDO. Seeing the limit lines on our displays, he had concluded the FIDO job could be automated also. On this particular sim, there were failures that caused the trajectory to veer off nominal and head "directly" for a limit (abort) line. Prior to hitting the limit line, we lost data. Shaffer then called for an abort with no data. During the debriefing, it was noted that Shaffer had made the correct call. The PhD could not understand how Shaffer knew to abort with no data and prior to hitting the limit. When Phil explained that he "knew" the trajectory was incapable of recovering, the PhD mumbled to himself that the Trench was in a class by itself and ceased trying to automate our functions.

When I arrived in June '67, the Trench was comprised of Mercury and Gemini veterans, 3 new hires that summer, and others who had been there ~ 3 years. Everyone except us 3 newbies (me, Stoval and Mill) seemed way older than we were. In fact, we were all very young. Jim I'Anson was the oldest, with the rest of the Trench seemingly 35 or less. All the veterans were busy building displays, going to meetings, etc. and all were way smarter than I. I was given a desk in a separate office with Jay Greene. Shaffer gave me some CSM handbooks to study. I did not have the foggiest idea what I needed to know to do my job nor how to do my job nor exactly what my job was, and my pride, I guess, was preventing my asking for much help. My desk was not in the large bullpen room with many others, so I was isolated from the "air wave" discussions to learn and bond. It seemed obvious that everyone else knew what their job was and how to do it, so I started to question my abilities. I'm sure my not being an engineer didn't help the learning process. Luckily Shaffer and Dave Reed would often give me guidance and answer my, probably, many simple questions, but their help wasn't enough. I felt I was floundering and questioned why I was here. Thoughts of quitting surfaced. Then I would think about my draft status and being deferred for a critical job. I seemed to be heading into a downward spiral.

Assignments were being made and I was fortunate to be assigned to Apollo VII. This assignment went a long way to bring me out of that spiral. I soon started watching and participating in sims and would often be in the RTCC at night with Shaffer, Jay and/or Reed, running our various processors and "learning" our job. I had a lot to learn, but I now saw how the job was done and I also was able to ask my many questions to the other Apollo VII FIDOs. Prior to Apollo VII, I was summoned to Dr. Kraft's office. After the pleasantries were completed, he asked me a technical question. I don't remember Dr. Kraft's question, but I had been forewarned that the question he asked was one of his techniques to determine who would man a console and who would not. He wanted to feel comfortable that his flight controllers could be believed by the Flight Directors and other controllers. Thus, there were only a couple of acceptable answers to his question: the correct answer, or I don't know but will get back with you. I answered one of the acceptable answers. I was later told that others had not provided an acceptable answer and never flew a mission. With the jobs we had, it was extremely important to be believed by your bosses and your peers. We Flight Controllers could not afford to be labeled a 'Bull S...er'.

There was lots of fun to be had also. Jerry Mill showed up later on in the summer of '67 and went through orientation just as the rest of us newbies, had done early on. We convinced Jerry that they forgot to have him do the NASA Pledge (non-existing); so, being led by an authoritative voice on the phone, he rose, faced the flagpole, placed his right hand over his heart and repeated the Pledge. I still smile.

While we worked hard during the day, we continued to play hard at night and on weekends. The real debriefs after sims were often held at the Wheel over many beers. Pavelka would frequently have all of us to his house for food, drink and to watch our and the Russian satellites pass over. All this team building was invaluable. Golf occurred "every" weekend. I joined the MSC fast pitch softball team. We would travel downtown to play the industrial teams, often losing, but competing. Stump and I played flag football and basketball and, eventually, slow pitch softball. I suffered a concussion playing football in '68, ending up in Pasadena Bayshore Hospital not knowing much. Those that knew me well before the concussion said that my personality changed. Dad flew out to check on me and informed me he was remarrying during Thanksgiving '68. I was happy for him as I wanted both of my parents to be happy. His new wife, Mary, became a great step-mother and we have grown very close over the years. My Mom never remarried and passed away too early in 1978. Since Apollo VIII was approaching, Cliff Charlesworth, the Apollo VIII Prime Flight Director, issued a ban on our playing flag football. He needed all the flight controllers healthy.

Apollo VII was the first flight not only of the manned CSM but also of me. I had gained lots of confidence during the sims, but most of the real training went to the Launch and Reentry teams, the high activity phases. I was one of the on-orbit Fidos. I don't remember having to execute any burns, so my role must have been planning and monitoring. Looking back, I am glad for my role on Apollo VII, because it gave me some much needed confidence. On VII I created solid relationships with the great FSD people we needed to run the RTCC (like Johnny Cools, etc), to massage the Doppler (like Gerry Devezin, Bill Wollenhaupt, etc.) and to load our maneuver requests into the various processors (like Pete Williams, Bob Arndt, etc.). Dr. Quentin Holmes and Bob Davis really knew the ins/outs of the various processors like LOI/DOI and midcourse. We would spend many hours together in the sims as well as at night or whenever the computers were available. The many night operations were necessary to not only checkout the various processors but also so us FIDOs could generate and constantly update our procedures, checklists, etc. All the support people were invaluable to helping me learn as much as possible prior to sims and the real missions.

Apollo VIII was during Christmas 1968. It was the first time I was not in Leland for Christmas. Apollo VIII was the first time to leave Low Earth Orbit (LEO). There were lots of other firsts also. One was the first time for us to use the Deep Space Network (DSN) for manned communications and tracking at lunar distances. My role on VIII was to understand the various nuances of the DSN. The big dishes were mandatory for trajectory determination outside of LEO.

I was fortunate to be assigned to Apollo IX and to be given more responsibility. Dave Reed was prime and really taught me a lot during the sims as well as the many nightly RTCC checkouts. Dave became known for his lengthy and detailed debriefings. He also wanted to drop some weight, going to two meals/day, a late breakfast and dinner. His discipline was contagious.

On one of the sims I had my first major screw up. The crew was late in setting up to do a burn just before apogee and LOS (loss of signal) was approaching. I flagged for them to maintain burn attitude and execute it just after apogee. When we got AOS (acquisition of signal) and confirmed the burn, they were now on a reentry path; so, we did an emergency burn to maintain orbit. I was embarrassed to admit I screwed up during the debrief, but that was why we did the sims, to learn.

I skipped Apollo X and was assigned to Apollo XI. Everyone wanted to be involved in XI, the First Lunar Landing. I was excited, but I also knew that there would be at least two FIDOs on every shift. I learned a lot watching the sims and again at night checking out the lunar processors which were new to me. My role was secondary, supporting Pavelka. While the LM was on the surface, every orbit we would recompute the "next" ascent/rendezvous", just in case. I remember watching the

Doppler react to the mascons on the moon. You could "see" the CSM pick up speed and slow down as it flew over certain mascons. Today I have a hard time when I think I may not live to see the next Apollo program. After XI, personnel changes seemed to begin. Promotions were given to the veterans, freeing up slots for us youngsters.

I was a FIDO on the rest of the Lunar flights, but never flew the "real" high activity events like Launch, Descent and Ascent. My assignments were typically a subset of SIVB Lunar Impact, LOI/DOI, LM Lunar impact, the various midcourse maneuvers, TEI, and entry. These would vary from mission to mission. I had more confidence in my abilities and wanted to be trained to fly one of the high activity phases, but I never had the opportunity to fly one. The flight teams were becoming fixed by roles and by the assignments of the Flight Directors. Each Flight Director wanted the personnel on his team constant from mission to mission, phase to phase, if possible. I understood the logic, but this seemed to fit the systems people more. The Flight Dynamics team of FIDO, Guido and Retro was a team within the larger team. To me, we were phase independent, and all of us wanted to fly the high activity phases.

When the Apollo XIII assignments came out, I hit the roof. My team would fly the sleep shift the entire mission, which meant all this Fido would do is monitor the trajectory and plan. I felt punished and relegated to menial tasks below my ability. I wanted more. I fleetingly thought about hanging it up but reconsidered with the mind-set of making the best of the situation. My training was not as intense for my role on XIII as the others were for the high activity phases. Little did I know that I was being prepared for what was to be a significant life lesson.

The Apollo XIII accident occurred just prior to shift handover. When I arrived, Stump's (Bill Stoval's nickname) team was already looking at return to earth alternatives, but we did not know for sure what the problem was. Glynn Lunney was my Flight Director and urged the teams to make the handover as quickly as we could. Listening to all that was going on, however, really convinced me that we had a huge problem and would be heading home ASAP. Apollo XIII reinforced the discipline of listening to the other Flight Controller problems to understand how they would affect me and my job; that is, to look at the big picture. Apollo XIII was on a "non free return" trajectory when the explosion occurred, so something had to be done to get the crew back to earth. Quentin and Bob were in the Staff Support Room (SSR) helping to optimize the various processors as we began to fine tune several options that Stump had started. Options considered were turning around "now", doing nothing until the systems guys knew more, and the eventual winner which was do a midcourse to get back to free return with the option to speed up a day at LOI plus 2 (hours). The midcourse that used less fuel put us just off the coast of Madagascar, not in the Pacific. The Doppler was all over the place, reacting to the consumables coming from the Service Module. We also thought that the explosion had put some unplanned Delta V on the vehicles, but it would take us awhile to figure all this out. Since we didn't really believe the vector due to the Delta V and the "out gassing" from the tanks, Madagascar was "good enough" for Flight. I also asked the crew to store the urine rather than dump it to avoid perturbing the Doppler any more than it already was. The rest, as they say, is history. The saga of Apollo XIII has been covered well many times. I learned a huge life lesson about being prepared regardless of the job given to me. I "KNEW" that my assignment of the sleep shift would be boring and uneventful. How wrong I was. For me, it was my 15 minutes of fame and the highlight of my career with NASA and Flight Dynamics. Apollo XII was significant in that it was the first landing on the moon. Helping to successfully bring the XIII crew home was what we were trained to do but hoped we would never have to, and gave me personal satisfaction that is immeasurable and a great sense of pride. After XIII, the remaining CSMs were modified, and we flew Apollos XIV through XVII. I finally was trained for all phases of a mission. However, my teams were typically scheduled for the midcourse corrections, Lunar Orbit Insertion/Descent Orbit Insertion (LOI/DOI), Trans Earth Injection (TEI) and Reentry. I never was able to experience the excitement and satisfaction of flying the high activity phase of Launch or Ascent/Rendezvous.

During the Apollo missions, a lot of interesting "non-technical" things occurred. Ed Pavelka became our section head, replacing Jerry Bostick who became our branch chief. Ed was also an artist who drew cartoons of Captain Refsmat and his arch enemy, Victor Vector. These two caricatures were where we would write down "space truisms", wise and/or dumb sayings by flight controllers, and other items for posterity. John Llewellyn had many events happen to him. He had so many tickets that NASA Security took away his car pass. So, during a mission he rode his horse to the Mission Control Center (MCC). John was late for a shift handover once when he was "kidnapped" at a bar by 2 ladies. Luckily he escaped and arrived for his shift only 4 hours late. Then there was the running joke about Gary Renick's bald spot requiring powder to reduce the glare for the TV cameras. It was rumored that, for any given mission, Jay Greene did not wash his coffee cup from the beginning of simulations through splash down. The Flight Directors would pass out cigars during reentry, but they weren't lit until the crew was safely extracted from the CM. During one of the lunar missions, the world's atomic clock was updated by a second. Retro then did a Ground Elapsed Time (GET) update to synch the clocks. My Flight Director, Gerry Griffin, gave me the dubious honor of trying to explain to the press what we did and why. Then, on another flight, when the CSM/LM entered the Lunar Sphere of gravitational Influence, the crew jokingly reported they felt a "bump." Thanks to Gerry I got to explain this "non event" to the press as well. And finally there were the many splash down parties after each flight. It is a wonder we survived the unlimited free beer and booze.

MSFC had the responsibility to actually prepare the SIVB burn for lunar impact. After TLI, as a challenge, I would manually compute the burn also. It was fun trying to compute the burn faster than MSFC. It turns out that by doing so I actually found an error in their burn during one of the missions. It is always good to have multiple sets of eyes look at the answers. For many different reasons, all the rest of the Apollo missions were fun. We continued to train and learn during the sims but, fortunately, there was not another Apollo XIII. Although we still had Skylab and ASTP, to me the Apollo era ended with Apollo XVII. Another era began during Apollo though, when I was married in 1971. I felt honored to have many FBDers attend the ceremony and with Stump, Bales and Denny helping me down the aisle.

Looking back, I see that everything associated with being a Fido required me to be cognizant of what was going on around me, to see the big picture. I also became aware that I would never know it all, so, I learned the valuable lesson of finding the experts to use when needed, but to know enough and to ask questions to make sure I wasn't being fed BS.

1972-1983 (the rest of my NASA career)

Post Apollo, I transferred into Experiments and was no longer "close" to anyone in the Trench. Phil Shaffer was now a Flight Director. He still was my mentor and close friend. We remained close until he passed away, often visiting during my travels back to Houston or on his trips to Huntsville. On Skylab, I was responsible for interacting with the ATM Pi's (principle investigators) at their daily planning session and helping them translate their requirements into activities the crew could perform. Being around these PhDs in Solar Physics was stimulating and educational. I learned a lot about the Sun, and what the various experiments would, hopefully, teach us. After Skylab, I transferred into the Aircraft Engineering Division, becoming a Project Engineer on the WB57Fs. I also became very close to a Bill Molnar. We would have many poker weekends at his cabin on Lake Mary near Palestine, TX.

During this "down time" between Programs, I got my MBA from the University of Houston at Clear Lake, specializing in business, not Operations Research. I was able to convince JSC to pay for my MBA, including lots of accounting courses. It was a sign of the times as many of my peers left NASA or got Law Degrees, MBAs, etc. We were not used to the down time. (Seems like déjà vu as the end of the Shuttle era approaches.)

With the Shuttle program gearing up, I transferred into Payloads where I was a Payload Officer (PLO) on the STS (Space Shuttle Transport System) 1, 3 (lead), and 5 and in Span on STS 7. Prior to STS 1, we decided that Payloads needed some esprit de corps. So, we adopted the Kangaroo as our mascot and became known as the Roo team. We even had a Roo on our console. Apparently that torqued off several flight controllers for it would frequently vanish when the PLO (Payload Officer) had to vacate the console for Mother Nature calls. The Fido training was put to great use on STS 3 where I was the lead PLO for over 12 different experiments, including the first time to use the RMS (Remote Manipulator System) with the IECM and PDP (Plasma Diagnostics Package). The IECM (Induced Environmental Collection Monitor) was to be picked up first by the RMS. Since the IECM was aft in the bay, both TV cameras were mandatory for the crew to properly see the grapple fixture, etc. I had a camera fail during a major simulation to wring out that particular mission rule…both aft TV cameras were mandatory to pick up the IECM. That rule was then scrutinized by many elephants, but all agreed it was correct. During the flight, Murphy decided to really test us and failed one of the cameras. I enforced the Mission Rule to the chagrin of many, but I and they knew that the rule was correct. In a separate event, one of the PIs had a rule to not turn his high voltage on until a vacuum had been verified. Going through the procedures, he commanded the apparatus to be evacuated, but the telemetry still indicated high pressure. Despite my insisting we redo the procedure, he insisted we turn the high voltage on. This was a new era…this was his experiment. Of course the telemetry was correct and the experiment became useless due to arcing. He had violated his own Mission Rule.

Another era began in September 1982 when my fraternal twins, William Cameron and Kathryn Elizabeth, were born. There was a lot of skill involved in having fraternal twins. We did take "awhile" in naming them, having expected 2 girls. We had lots of help, though, with the Payloads Branch keeping a running list of "suggestions." And, as I had promised years earlier, my son goes by Cameron.

1983-present (Post NASA, a summary)

Prior to my twins birth, I had felt it was time to do something else, to move on. Everything after Apollo seemed anticlimactic. I was proud of what I had done with NASA, but I also knew I needed to continue to grow and use my MBA. So, in July 1983, after STS 7 and with 11 month old twins in tow, I left NASA with mixed emotions and moved to Denver to join Martin Marietta. I was able to create my own job and soon became a Manager of Payload Integration as well as a New Business person. I was in Denver from the summer of 1983 until I was asked to transfer to Corporate staff and move to Huntsville. There I was responsible for Business Development for the NASA field centers of MSFC, JSC, KSC and Stennis. It took 2 years to convince some of the MSFC higher ups that I wasn't a spy for JSC. In 1990, with a sad heart, I left Martin to move to Boulder with Ball Aerospace. Boulder was a great place to live, but Ball was falling on some hard times. Anticipating a cut in personnel, I moved back to Huntsville in 1992 as Director of Corporate Development with Nichols Research. In 1994 I became disenchanted with Aerospace and purchased Supreme Floral, a wholesale florist. In 1996, I was approached by Loral Corp. to move back to Houston. So, in the summer of 1996, I returned to Houston with Lockheed Martin (LM) which had purchased Loral. Since I had great employees at Supreme, I kept the business and let them run it without me present. I still have Supreme today and they continue to run it well with minimal involvement from me.

In 2000, I transferred to LM in Sunnyvale, Ca. as Director of Business Development for Strategic Systems. My customer base was now the Navy and Air Force. Since I was on a plane every week to somewhere, I never moved from Houston. My time in Sunnyvale was rewarding, but it took a toll on my health and marriage. I decided to retire in hopes of getting my health and marriage back in order. My health improved when I retired from full time employment in 2006. But, Beverly and I divorced, and I again moved back to Huntsville.

As I write this it is now December 2010. I am a trustee in my church; I still own Supreme; I am helping a small Aerospace company, Wavelink, grow; I own 1/3 of an import/export company that moves food products from the Ukraine and other countries into Ghana/Africa; and I try to play golf at least twice/week. I have adapted to the single scene and have been seriously dating Rebecca Sconyers for several years. I am thankful to be very close to my twins who are now 28. Cameron is married to the former Angie Cates, living in Houston, and anxiously expecting their first child in June 2011. Kathryn married Rees Arnim in September 2010 and immediately moved to Denver.

X - William Stoval

APOLLO MEMOIRS

Copyright © 2010

By William Stoval
1910 Rustic Drive
Casper, WY 82609

H. David Reed

When I first met Dave Reed in 1963, we were both engineering majors at the University of Wyo. He was a senior and I was a freshman. I had pledged Sigma Nu fraternity and for some reason Dave took great delight in testing the resolve of this cocky young pledge. Apparently I passed the various tests with flying colors as he was very instrumental in my eventual employment by NASA. After he graduated, Dave went to work for NASA in Houston and I didn't see him for a couple of years. I recall a visit from him the spring of 1966. Dave spoke at length about his great job and the Apollo program. I was quite captivated by the whole discussion but it really didn't re-enter my mind until the winter of 1967. It was then that I realized that many of my fellow engineering seniors were making job interview trips around the country while I was drinking beer and enjoying being a BMOC (big man on campus). I did a few interviews on campus and decided to send an application to NASA in Houston. About the same time that I received a job offer from Boeing, I got a call from Dave asking if I had any interest in coming to work at the space center. He told me that the Flight Dynamics Branch (FDB) was looking for two more "Flight Dynamics Officers" (FDO or FIDO) to fill out their manning requirements for Apollo. They had decided to pursue people that were somewhat of a known quantity rather than just grab a body out of the NASA applicant pool. The two people that they went after were myself and another engineering senior from Mississippi named Bill Boone. I told Dave that I was very interested and already had an application somewhere in the NASA system. Within a couple of weeks he called and offered me a job...I was blown away. I had the opportunity to be one of only nine men who would man the FDO console in Mission Control (MCC) for the Apollo program. I made an excited call to my high school math teacher and told him of my two job offers, seeking his opinion on which job would be better suited to my personality. His comment was succinct: "People will be designing wings for airplanes for a long time...we are only going to the moon once. Go to Houston." That was all I needed to hear. I called Dave and told him to process the paperwork and get me signed! After graduation, I took a couple of weeks for R&R and headed to Clear Lake City, TX, for what was to be the greatest 9 years of my life.

The Apollo I Fire

In January of 1967, the Apollo program was rolling along fast, too fast. The race to the moon was in full swing and NASA was rocking with the success of Gemini and the promise of Apollo. The terrible fire on the pad that claimed the Apollo I crew was a startling and sobering wake-up call to the Apollo team that the challenges and dangers involved in a program of this magnitude demanded a special attention to detail. I arrived in Houston a scant 5 months after the fire and began my training immediately. At the time I did not realize it but, had it not been for that fire, my role in Apollo would have been significantly different. Basically, that tragedy delayed our lunar landing by about 2 years and it was during that period of time that my initial training took place. During those training years I began to realize the all-encompassing nature of the FDO job. We of course had to understand trajectory stuff, rendezvous theory, orbital mechanics, etc. But then we had to understand how the various guidance systems worked to insure proper maneuver execution, how the onboard navigation systems worked, a complete knowledge of the various propulsion systems for all vehicles, and much, much more. When the going got tough, the FDO was charged with making maneuvers happen, correctly, regardless of what was happening to the onboard systems. This was never more obvious than on Apollo XIII when most everything was broken or frozen and we still had to execute maneuvers to get the crew home safely. I quickly came to the realization that the FDO was indeed the second-most responsible position in Mission Control, just behind the Flight Director(of course this conclusion of mine was somewhat biased).

The Flight Dynamics Section – July 1967

When I arrived in Houston on the July 4th weekend in 1967, Dave began introducing me to the whole environment. We inevitably ran into the Lunney's and thus began a lifetime friendship. Not only was Glynn my boss but he and Marilyn and the kids became a huge part of my life. I would begin meeting my fellow-Fido's that next week. Jerry Bostick was my section head and it would turn out that he was my boss for almost my entire career. Ed Pavelka would soon become my new section head and became a tremendous friend. Jay Greene became a great friend and was one of the finest flight controllers that we had, eventually becoming a Flight Director. Phil Shaffer was to become the greatest of my friends, my mentor, my biggest fan and my harshest critic. We would stay connected as he moved from the Fido console to branch management to the Flight Director office to Data Priority chair and finally to a Shuttle software operations manager. Of course there was Dave, moving me in the directions he knew were important and always there to help. I truly think he felt I would become his protege with similar console operating techniques, mission preparation (he was the master), and overall outlook as to what the job of the Fido really was. In my view, I eventually became a blend of Dave, Jay and Phil with Phil having the biggest impact. The rest of the troops (Maurice Kennedy, Bill Boone, George Guthrie and Stu Davis) had little impact on my career although they were fine friends and co-worker.

Training Overview

My training to become console ready consisted of three main pieces: (1) classroom training conducted by Flight Control Division (FCD) (2) Observing simulations in the control center (MCC) and (3) hours of office time with the guys going over mission rules, console operations, etc. The A-I fire had slowed the pace of manned Apollo flights but there were still some unmanned missions scheduled and I spent every possible hour I could watching the various simulations. We launched two Saturn Vs and flew an unmanned lunar module (LM) flight. In 1968 the first manned Apollo, Apollo VII, finally flew with the new improved CSM and I got my first taste of manned flight from our back room position. When NASA scheduled a third unmanned Saturn V launch, Jerry Bostick called me into his office and said I was to be the launch Fido for that flight....I was thrilled beyond explanation at the thought of that challenge. Unfortunately, as I was learning everything there was to know about the Saturn V, its guidance and navigation systems, its engines, and the various abort modes, NASA reversed its decision and instead created A-8 which was to use "my" vehicle to conduct a manned lunar flyby mission. I was certainly not ready for that challenge but I felt proud that my bosses had been ready to put me in the MCC even if it was for an unmanned flight. The simulations for Apollo VIII and many hours spent with Ed Pavelka gave me an opportunity to become an expert in the mid-course correction processor which was used to compute small trans-lunar trajectory changes to keep the spacecraft on its proper path for entry into lunar orbit.

The Early Missions

Apollo IX was an earth orbit mission in which both the CSM and the LM would be inserted into space and the planned separation and rendezvous would simulate a lunar landing profile, at least from a propulsion standpoint. I eagerly waded into the details of rendezvous and all its options and that particular part of mission operations would eventually become my passion. Hours and hours of simulation watching, mission rule sessions, and mission reviews via the Data Priority group were beginning to elevate my awareness and my visibility. It was shortly after Apollo IX that Jerry once again called me into his office and told me that not only was I to have a front room assignment on Apollo X but I was designated as the "lead" Fido! Being lead meant little else than being the guy who was responsible for the mission rule process as well as integrated meeting attendance at Data Priority and other multi-discipline meetings. It would however prove to be invaluable personal exposure and a huge acceleration in my learning curve. While my console work on Apollo

X was almost totally that of the set-up guy, that role was instrumental in a dramatic acceleration in my knowledge of our various processors. As the pre-launch Fido, I worked with many outside agencies such as the tracking network, Range Safety at the Cape, and many others. Dave was the launch Fido and I sat beside him for the dozens of launch simulations that he went through. Similarly, my shift preceded the execution shift for the two lunar orbit insertion burns(called LOI and DOI) that Phil would execute and I learned that processor inside and out. I also set up the Ascent/Rendezvous sequence for Phil and spent many hours with him in those simulations. Indeed, after Apollo X I was knowledgeable about all of our many tasks and confident in my ability to handle off-nominal situations. The proximity of Apollo X and Apollo XI meant that many of us who worked on Apollo X would not see assignments on Apollo XI. For the most part, Apollo XI was manned by the old-timers who had spent years waiting for the lunar landing. We new kids had to wait our turn...and mine came fast. I was assigned to be the Ascent/Rendezvous Fido on Apollo XII and was back-up for launch!

The Job

In order to understand the significance of being named the Fido for a major mission phase one needs to know just how few men actually performed that task. Of the 9 Fido's in our section, only two (Jay & Dave) ever flew the Descent (lunar landing phase), only four ever flew launch phase(Jay, Dave, Phil, myself) and only 3 ever flew Ascent/Rendezvous (Dave, Phil, myself). These high speed and potentially dangerous sequences required not only diligent training and off-console preparation but also demanded an ability to wing it, fly by the seat of your pants, and an intuitive understanding of how to recover from a severe anomaly. Being the Fido required that you had to overcome the consequences of engine malfunctions, guidance system failures, etc and still get the maneuver executed and keep the crew safe. Simulations continually pounded us with failures not only to test our mettle but also to condition us to think quickly and correctly as onboard systems went south. No other position in Mission Control, other than the Flight Director, was required to have the multi-discipline knowledge that the Fido needed. We needed a working knowledge of all of the various propulsions systems that we would use over the course of a nominal mission. That included the three stages of the Saturn-V, the CSM SPS (main) engine as well as the small reaction control (RCS) thrusters, both the LM Descent and Ascent engines and its RCS system. We had to understand what the engines could and couldn't do and their characteristics such as thrust profile, build-up and tail-off properties and ullage requirements. We needed a working knowledge of the three guidance systems (Saturn-V,

CSM, LM) that we would use during the course of a mission as well as the back-up systems in the CSM and LM. Indeed, it turned out that I would call upon the LM back-up guidance system (the Abort Guidance System or AGS) twice in my career.

About ullage: spacecraft engines are typically designed with the "fuel pumps" (e.g., impellers, injectors, etc) located at the "bottom" of the tank nearest the engine bell. When a spacecraft is thrusting the fuel is forced to the bottom of the tank where the "pump" can access it in a continuous, uninterrupted fashion which is mandatory to achieve steady, stable thrust. In zero G however, the fuel floats around in the tank which represents an unacceptable situation which must be rectified before the engine is ignited. Ullage is simply the act of accelerating the vehicle forward to force the fuel to the back (bottom) of the tank. It is usually achieved by using the +X-axis RCS thrusters which burn for approximately 8-10 seconds. Ullage was standard fair for all maneuvers performed in space.

My First MCC "Biggie"

Apollo XII was a virtual replay of Apollo XI but with a new crew and new flight controllers. My role as Ascent Fido brought me in fairly constant contact with the flight crew as well as the back-up and support crews. Thus would begin my many friendships within the astronaut office several of which are still in place 35 years later. The astronauts, from attending mission rule meetings, simulations, and their roles as capsule communicators (CapCom) in Mission Control, quickly realized the roles/importance of the various flight controllers. For those mission phases, such as launch, powered descent and ascent/rendezvous, where it could be critical that we understood exactly what each other was thinking and doing, there were many hours spent debriefing simulations, refining mission rules, and visiting each others offices for casual chats. So it was on Apollo XII and my learning curve was getting steep. Phil was at my side for many of the rendezvous simulations to maximize the benefit I would get out of those sometimes torturous days. I learned well and the real Ascent/Rendezvous went superbly and I had my first "major" under my belt.

Apollo XIII

Because of my role as back-up launch Fido on Apollo XII, I had sort of assumed that I would get my shot at launch on Apollo XIII. Initially Jerry confirmed that I was going to get the assignment but it wasn't long before he called me into his office and said that he and Dave had decided I wasn't quite ready to handle that role and would again be the back-up, this time to Jay. Initially I felt betrayed by Dave but soon decided that if he didn't think I was ready for launch, then I probably wasn't. So I rededicated myself to improving my overall knowledge of that highly complex mission phase. I was however assigned as the Fido for the redesigned and potentially dangerous single burn lunar orbit insertion (LOI/DOI) sequence which would break the spacecraft out of it's trans lunar coast trajectory into a lunar orbit with a fairly low perilune. Again, the new and controversial sequence increased my visibility and credibility as we developed new mission rules and procedures. Of course, all of that was for naught as Apollo XIII was to write it's own script. My team was on the console when the Apollo XIII explosion occurred. In those first few hectic hours we accomplished little from a trajectory standpoint other than to realize that a major event had occurred which, although it probably hadn't changed the trajectory significantly, was trashing our tracking data making it impossible to get a good post-event state vector. I did have the sense that the lunar mission may be in peril and computed a minimum burn that would take the spacecraft from its current non-free-return trajectory to one that would theoretically return it to earth if all else failed. Executing that maneuver would of course signal the end of the Apollo XIII lunar mission and we were not ready to go there yet when we handed over to the black team.

After our team handed over, Flight Director Gene Kranz directed us all into a conference room where we spent several hours brainstorming the problem as we knew it and developing possible scenarios. I informed the team that we would have an opportunity shortly after the vehicle appeared from behind the moon to utilize the descent engine and LM guidance system to execute a large maneuver which would bring the crew home 24 hrs faster. Other than that, the trajectory issues were minimal. Indeed, we did execute such a maneuver on my next shift and it turned out to be a lifesaver.

On my final A-XIII shift we determined that a small mid-course correction was needed to keep the vehicle in the center of the reentry corridor. While that all sounded simple enough I was informed that there was insufficient power remaining in the LM batteries to bring up the guidance system so the maneuver would have to be done manually based on time or something equally inaccurate. Return to earth mid courses were somewhat forgiving in that they were extremely non-time-sensitive and were generally radial (perpendicular to the velocity vector). However, proper execution was critical as the corridor was quite small and fractions of feet/second mattered. My problems seemed to compound as the shift wore on. The first problem was to place the spacecraft in the proper attitude so that the descent engine could be used to perform the burn. The good folks in the planning division (MPAD) had created a computer simulation, complete with a model of the two LM body-mounted telescopes(the alignment optical telescope ot AOT) and the COAS (crew optical alignment telescope) whereby they could place the stack in the proper attitude(perpendicular to the velocity vector) and slowly rotate it. The simulation then showed the views thru the two telescopes. Eventually they found an attitude where the earth appeared in the COAS and the sun in the AOT. If the crew could manually hold the vehicle in that attitude using the LM RCS thrusters for the few seconds required to execute the maneuver, then we had a chance of pulling it off. With the attitude issue resolved adequately, the larger question of how to execute the maneuver loomed. Using burn time as the only criteria was extremely inaccurate primarily because we had little data on how the descent engine would perform in zero G. Without accurate information on thrust build up and tail-off, the maneuver that we modeled in the MCC computers may be considerably different than what actually occurred. However, when I started trying to pin down the LM propulsion guys on precisely how the engine would perform, they just sort of threw up their hands and said "we don't know." So much for that help. With an "iffy" knowledge of how the engine would perform we desperately needed something that could measure the velocity change (Delta V) that we actually got. With the primary guidance system shut down there was only one alternative and it was a wild card. The LM was equipped with a body-mounted strap-down set of accelerometers called the AGS (Abort Guidance System). The AGS had only one role and that was to assist the LM crew in achieving some sort of lunar orbit in the event that the primary guidance system failed during the descent phase, on the lunar surface, or during ascent. However, even with the LM shut down to almost no electrical power being used, the AGS would still measure the Delta V accrued during the burn. The question was how good that data would be...the poor old AGS was being exposed to -250 degree cold, was always accumulating some sort of numbers in its readout register, and was never intended to support this kind of a burn. Again I was unable to get anyone in the LM world to step up and tell Flight that the AGS would be acceptable to use as a maneuver monitoring device so myself and the guidance officer just sort of winged a plan. As I explained to Flight Director Gerry Griffin, we could have the crew zero out the AGS register just prior to starting the burn, and we could watch the AGS accumulate Delta V as the burn proceeded. We knew what we expected the descent engine to do at 10% thrust and that the burn would last about 14 seconds if all went as advertised. We had to under burn a bit on purpose so as to insure that we could finish the burn with the LM +X thrusters. (The -X thrusters caused issues with the CM windows.) So, we would have the crew ullage for 10 seconds, then manually ignite the descent engine at 10% for 13 seconds and shut it down at which time we would check the AGS to see if it had measured the 7 or so fps (Delta V) that we were looking for. If it appeared that the AGS had a handle on the burn, then I would give them an AGS reading to trim to. (The AGS actually accumulated 0.2 fps after they zeroed the register so that had to be subtracted from the value we were after.) I did the math and the CapCom read them my number and they used the +X for a few seconds to achieve the desired reading(e.g., 7.6). As it turned out, the maneuver was nearly perfect (a tiny MCC was executed just prior to jettisoning the LM using the LM +X thrusters and the same attitude alignment technique). To my knowledge those two mid course corrections were the only completely unguided maneuvers ever done in our space program. It must be stressed that entire process of computing and executing a 14 second burn consumed nearly the entire 8 hour shift and it was without a doubt the most frustrating day I ever spent in the MCC.

Things Get Interesting

The Challenge of M=1 Rendezvous

The immediate result of the Apollo XIII explosion was the postponement of Apollo 14 while the agency regrouped. It was over a year before we flew again. Many of my fellow flight controllers began moving on to other programs such as Skylab and the Shuttle. Phil moved on to the Flight Director Office and Jay was working advanced mission things. That left Dave and I doing most of the Apollo chores. The folks over in the planning world had gotten together with the flight crew people and were proposing a new, faster lunar rendezvous which they had designated as the M=1 sequence. All of the Apollo rendezvous' so far had been long, laborious and pretty forgiving sequences, not much different than what we flew in Gemini. The M=1 rendezvous was quite ambitious...the orbit that resulted from ascent would put the LM on a course where one single maneuver, TPI (terminal phase initiate), would initiate the closing sequence. The final closing and docking would occur on the front side of the moon only 2 hours after ascent. However, the M=1 sequence was quite demanding and we had to develop new mission rules for what equipment had to be working 100% in order to commit to that rendezvous. Further, we had to rethink the actions that the crew took immediately after the ascent engine shut down.

Maneuvers in space are fairly tricky. The simple version is that we (Fido/Retro) would compute the upcoming maneuver which would then be transformed into a set of external delta V targets (X,Y, & Z axes). Those targets would be up-linked to the guidance computer and a backup set voiced up to the crew for manual loading if need be. The computer would then place the vehicle in an attitude such that whichever engine we were using was pretty much aligned with the vector that the targets created. Involved in all of this were things like burn arc, engine buildup and tail-off characteristics, etc. In order to execute the maneuver, the guidance system went into a high speed mode called Average G wherein the accelerometers on the guidance system platform began measuring the velocity change that occurred as the engine burned. The guidance system would shutdown the engine when it sensed the remaining delta V would be achieved as the engine tailed-off. Of course this was never quite perfect and there would always be some small "residual" of the desired delta V change left. Usually the small RCS thrusters on the vehicle would then be used to "trim" the residuals thus completing the maneuver. Unfortunately, due mostly to the myriad of opinions that would be voiced during Data Priority meetings, the act of trimming became onerous and often a subject of heated discussions. In the end Mission Rules were written which defined the acceptable residuals to nearly every maneuver. Lunar ascent however was one maneuver where "trimming" was not only unnecessary but often the wrong thing to do. This situation occurred because once the ascent engine shut down, we were now in a rendezvous sequence and the residuals from the just completed ascent burn meant nothing. What really mattered was that the lunar module was in the correct orbit from which to execute the necessary rendezvous burns. We slowly convinced the world that the correct thing to do after insertion into lunar orbit was for the Fido to compute a quick "tweak" maneuver that would change the LM velocity by whatever small amount needed to set up the rendezvous sequence. The resulting "trim vs. tweak" debate seemed to have a life of its own... primarily driven by the flight crew people who never wanted the crew in a situation where the ground (Mission Control) was the sole controller of their destiny.

In the early Apollo rendezvous, the profile was so forgiving that it generally wasn't a big deal and we often just trimmed out the X-axis residual after insertion and called it good. In the M=1 sequence however, the "tweak" maneuver was incredibly important since there were no other maneuvers left to establish the proper phasing at TPI. So it evolved that after the ascent engine shutdown , we would compute the necessary delta V change to put the LM on an acceptable M= 1 trajectory and then examine the 3 options at hand. Option 1 was to compare the necessary "tweak" to the X-axis residual that the LM guidance computer was showing and, if it was compatible (i.e., same direction..like posigrade) have the crew trim however much of the residual was needed to do the "tweak." Option 2, which I actually called on Apollo XVI was to make the same comparison to the AGS read-out and see if the AGS accidentally had stumbled on the correct delta V. The final option was to quickly voice up to the crew the proper delta V to put them on the needed trajectory and have them burn that amount using the onboard guidance system. Although this is what we almost always did, the crew never really liked it because they had no onboard back-up to my calculation. Eventually however, this too became a normal part of the mission and the furor died down. All of the "tweaks" on the last four Apollo missions were small and uneventful.

The Later Apollo Flights

Things were changing fast in and around Apollo XIV. Glynn & Cliff had moved on to the Flight Directors Office, Jerry and Phil were the branch bosses, and Ed Pavelka was the section head. While we were on shift during one of the moon walks (EVA's), Dave told me that he was leaving NASA and headed to Boston to work for the DOT. More surprisingly (to me) he told me he was going alone. His wife Vicky was not following and a divorce was in the works. While divorces and affairs were pretty common in Houston, FDB had been pretty removed from that. I was sad on both counts. When Apollo XIV was done and over, the rate of change seemed to accelerate. Many of the old troops were moving on, some chasing Skylab, others working on advanced missions, and others retiring. Gene Kranz was now head of Flight Control and he 'edicted' that for the remaining three Apollo flights, the flight control teams would be kept as intact as possible and they would fly the same mission phases as they had on Apollo XIV. With Dave out of the picture, it was no great surprise to me when Jerry told me I would finally be flying launch for the rest of Apollo. That was tremendously exciting to me and gave me a massive work load. Being the back-up for the last two flights had allowed me to watch a million simulations and to run a few myself but now I was going to be the man! Clearly I had arrived and was now pretty much the face of Flight Dynamics. So it came to pass that I was the launch Fido as well as the Ascent/Rendezvous Fido for Apollo XV, Apollo XVI, and Apollo XVII. Those flights while all different, had many similarities from a trajectory standpoint. They were incredibly complicated with many experiments, the new lunar rover, and hectic timelines, far removed from the relatively simple early Apollo's. We did crazy things such as after the TLI (transluar injection) burn (the large maneuver using the 3rd stage of the Saturn-V that placed on a lunar intercept trajectory). Once the crew had extracted the LM from the nose of the S-IVB (Saturn V third stage) and separated from that vehicle, the pressure in the empty S-IVB fuel tank was used to execute a maneuver which put the S-IVB on a trajectory that would result in it's crashing into the moon. This was done primarily to test the seismographs that earlier flights had left on the lunar surface. In much the same fashion, we also started crashing the LM ascent stage into the moon after the rendezvous had been completed and the crew was safely aboard the CSM.

Likewise, the CSM had become filled with all sorts of experiment packages, some of which had moving parts like booms that stuck out of certain bays. On Apollo XVI one of those booms would not retract and we had to jettison that guy before we could come home. Jettisoning things in space can be dicey because they tend to end up in an orbit very similar to that of the vehicle that did the jettisoning and those objects are moving fast. The preferred technique was to jettison things in a posigrade fashion so they would end up drifting above and behind you over time. Non-nominal things like that became routine and we got awfully good at "winging it."

The New Guys

By late Apollo, we had added a couple of guys to the branch, transferees from the defunct Landing & Recovery Division. Ron Epps joined the Fido ranks and Mike Collins became a Retro. Ron became my "boy" and we spent many many hours together over the next few years. I was pretty brutal on him at times but he became quite the Fido during Shuttle and eventually the Division Chief, retiring in 2008 as I recall. Mike too lasted many years and was Ron's assistant finally taking over the division when Ron left. Mike stepped down in 2009. They both got lots of training time in Apollo and would work the front room in Skylab and ASTP (Apollo Soyuz Test Project).

Boy, Did We Have Fun

In case I have painted a picture here of all work and no play, that was certainly not the environment in Houston. Flight Control was known for its parties, especially the post-mission "splash parties" and the "post-flight debriefing" parties with the flight crews shortly after each mission. We were a very tight, some would say exclusive, group. FCD had an intra-mural football team that I played on for years and our basketball team became known as "F-Troop", a take-off on a popular TV show. I even recruited an astronaut for the team, Bob Overmeyer, so we could practice in the astronaut gym. Eventually softball became the sport of sports and we had a dandy team for a number of years. While all this was going on, I fell in love with golf and played constantly with many

Ruth Scarlett and Bill

fellow FCD'ers. I married my college sweetheart Ruth Scarlett during the summer of 1968 and we eventually had two Texas-born sons, Bill and Shawn. We spent many hours with Glynn and Marilyn and their four kids, including most holidays that we didn't sneak home to Wyoming.

Post-Apollo & The Routine of Skylab

The post-Apollo era was way different,,,the glamour was gone, many of the guys were leaving or retiring, and the Skylab program didn't offer too much excitement from a flight dynamics standpoint. Our role would basically be confined to getting the crew to the Skylab, baby-sitting the trajectory data over the course of the 30 to 60 day mission, and finally bringing them back to earth when their stay was over. I was chosen to fly all 4 of the launches and the three rendez-vous' that would occur over the course of that year (1973). Ron would be my helper and set-up man. Phil was now a Flight Director, Ed would eventually move on and Jay became the section head. Even Jerry Bostick finally left and Flight Director Don Puddy became the branch chief. Of course each launch and rendezvous would entail a new crew and the associated hours of simulations. Skylab was a year out of our lives but it was all about science and experiments and rep-resented little challenge from a trajectory standpoint.

ASTP

The joint operation with the Russians, called Apollo Soyuz Test Proj-ect (ASTP), was supposed to be a symbol of a new, cooperative era with the USSR, which had of course propelled us into the space busi-ness and the race to the moon. Again, it was pretty simple for us. The Soyuz would launch first and establish its orbit. We would follow with our launch hours later and then rendezvous with the Russians. The crew was great and I had shared many hours of work with all of them...Tom Stafford from Apollo X, Deke Slayton who was the boss of the astronauts and a frequent visitor to Mission Control, and Vance Brand who had come up through the astronaut ranks and had also spent many hours in the control center. It was a fun mission but we all knew it was the end of the line for manned flights as we knew them. The Shuttle was on the way! ASTP was to be my last time in the control center. When it was over, I had flown more launches (7) and executed more rendezvous' (8) than any Fido in the history of the space program! I had loved my job and its challenges and rewards.

My Brief Encounter With Shuttle

After ASTP I began working full time on the Shuttle. Phil, as head of Data Priority, had made me the lead flight controller in the development of an Ascent Baseline Operations Plan(BOP) which was supposed to tell the world how we envisioned flying Shuttle launches. Unfortunately, while our document ended up being pretty accurate, it was inconsistent with the early Shuttle operations philosophy of having the vehicle perform autonomously from the ground. This experience was consistent with most of my brief Shuttle exposure.....Flight Controllers were considered a necessary but semi-obsolete carry-over from earlier programs and the Shuttle was going to perform so flawlessly that we were almost extraneous. Of course the various companies and committees that were developing these new visions had no clue and, in the end, Mission Control was just as necessary and important to the Shuttle flights as we had been to all previous manned missions.

Fate Takes a Twist

My father died suddenly in the spring of 1976 shortly after I returned from the Shuttle Ascent Design Review at North American-Rockwell. It was at that meeting that I became the whipping boy who had to tell the world how "we" expected to fly the ascent phase and the powers that be who were there told me that we were way off base. Fortunately, I was surrounded by several of my astronaut pals who patted me on the back and told me to hang in there. I was an accomplished veteran of multiple space flights and was being blasted by people who had not, and would, never see the inside of Mission Control. It was a humiliating and

Receiving NASA Superior Achievement Award from Dr. Christopher Kraft

frustrating experience.

My father's passing gave Ruth and me the opportunity to return to Wyoming, go into the family business, and raise our kids where we had been raised. It was an easy decision. I returned from the funeral and spent two hard months trying to finish my main task which was to help design the launch phase processor which the Fido would use to determine Shuttle abort modes. I left Houston in June of 1976.

Reflections

Over the past 35 years I have returned to Houston many times to see old friends and attend reunions. I have given talks about my part in Apollo, Skylab, and ASTP at schools, service clubs, colleges, country clubs, etc. Every time it appeared that interest in the space program was waning, something would happen to renew that interest. Sometimes it was a catastrophe like the loss of Challenger or Columbia, sometimes it was a movie like "Apollo 13." Whatever the case, people never seem to tire of hearing about that piece of American history.

In 2007 I was inducted into the University of Wyoming Engineering Hall of Fame, thanks in large part to letters written on my behalf by Dave Reed, Jerry Bostick, Glynn Lunney, Phil Shaffer, Chris Kraft, Mike Collins, and astronauts Charlie Duke and Al Worden.

We were all so lucky to be part of something so rewarding and exciting. I was maybe the luckiest of all to have grown up in Wyoming, find my way into the best section of the best branch of the best division, not only in Houston but quite possibly in all of NASA, and to have become a pretty darn good Fido. I wouldn't have missed it for the world!

About me

Being born and raised in Wyoming tends to develop certain characteristics in people. We tend to be fiercely independent, have strong family values, and some would say develop a stubborn streak. I attended Catholic schools through 8th grade in Cheyenne and Casper. I guess that good old Natrona County High School (NCHS) is where I started to make the change from a pretty 'geeky' kid to more well-rounded individual. I loved sports and was a good baseball player, playing through my 15th summer and being part if the State Championship All-Star team. I took all of the Honors courses that NCHS offered and was a good student, graduating in the top 15 in my large (555 kids) class. My first love was wrestling and I excelled it winning 27 matches my Jr. year and 20 in my injury-shortened Sr. year. I finished 2nd in the State that last year in my 138 lb. class. I was a debater when I wasn't wrestling and that skill stayed with me. Phil used to say that I was the only guy he knew that could argue either side of an issue and win both arguments!

Although I was accepted at several colleges and had a couple of wrestling scholarship offers, I decide on the University of Wyoming probably due more to the fact that my girlfriend was going there than the academic challenges presented in Laramie, WY. It was in college that I really "blossomed" and became highly social, involved in student government and all of the honorary societies. I was very active in my fraternity and soon expanded that interest to inter-fraternity council (IFC) work which expanded into a position in the Western Regional IFC and a couple of national conventions. My two years on the Student Senate provided me with exposure, challenges and a couple of years in the Who's Who in American Colleges and Universities annuals. I was the quintessential BMOC!

Unfortunately, something has to suffer when your extracurricular activities are that extreme and my suffering came in my grades. My first two years were basically spent on the Dean's Honor Roll and my last two were a maze of failed classes, D's, class re-takes and general poor performance. My GPA (grade point average) was being carried by those first two years and it was truly by the grace of God that I made it out of school with my BS in Aeronautical Engineering (an option of Mechanical) in 4 years.

I had very little interest in science as a kid and not a whole lot more in college. I decide to major in engineering primarily because I was so damn good at math. It was about the middle of my Junior year when I figured out that I wasn't probably going to be a great engineer unless something special came along. I did enjoy the Orbital Mechanics course that I took as a Junior but in the grand scheme of things, I think the only reason that I ended up in Houston was because Dave Reed gave the job such a huge buildup that I couldn't resist the adventure. That opportunity allowed me to continue on my chosen path of being the biggest non-engineer that an engineer could be.

Two Special Friends

We have lost two Fido's from that original group and both were very special guys. Ed Pavelka, or Fast Eddie as I dubbed him, was my section head for most of my time in Houston. He was a great friend and we had many a party at his house in Friendswood (suburb of Houston). Early on in Apollo I would make trips to the MIT labs in Boston where the LM software was being developed. On my way back to Houston I would go to Boston Harbor and buy 5 to 7 large live lobsters which were then packed in seaweed in boxes that I carried onto the plane. When the plane touched down in Clear Lake, we would head straight to Ed's place and the party was on. A mixture of Fidos, Guidos, and Retros would be there and we had spirited lobster races to determine the order that those bad boys went into the pot of boiling water!

Ed was a car nut and we spent many an hour working on my various cars, changing plugs and the like. I bought a spiffy new orange Corvette in 1973 and drove it until I left Houston. I sold it to Ed and he drove it for many years. He was pretty much done with console work when I got there and as I remember it, Apollo VIII was his last mission. However, he spent many hundreds of hours watching our simulations in order to evaluate our individual progress as front room operators. No return visit to Houston was complete without a trip to "Ferndale" and a beer with Fast Eddie.

As I have mentioned before, Phil Shaffer was probably my closest friend from the section. He was a giant of a man with very short reddish hair and he was known to his friends as "Jolly Red"or JR. He was a bachelor until late in his life, loved big white Chrysler convertibles, and lived for many years on the water (Houston Bay) in Baycliffe. He was truly a genius and loved spirited debates. At his insistence I took a few IQ tests and qualified for the Mensa Society to which he belonged. I attended some of their local lunches for about a year and decided I really didn't enjoy the group. Shortly thereafter, I dropped my membership and he eventually followed my lead.

We were virtually inseparable during the months leading up to Apollo X and he made sure that I understood the how's and whys for every mission rule, every console procedure, and the proper way to conduct business on the console. As Phil moved on from the section to the branch office to the flight directors office and eventually head of the omnipotent Data Priority group we stayed in constant contact both professionally and socially. Ruth and I spent many an evening with him, eating seafood in Kemah (suburb of Houston on Clear Lake Bay) and then adjourning to Baycliffe to sip scotch and enjoy the view. JR once decided to build a sailboat and I was his right hand carpenter. He left me alone with the project one afternoon and I apparently built a slight warp into one of the pontoons. He always claimed that my warp was why the boat didn't sail well...but it made a heck of a fire when we finally burned it up on his beach! We played a lot of golf together and he was a pretty good player for a guy that size but he eventually lost interest in the game probably because he didn't have special pals to play with. Phil was eventually assigned the almost impossible task of single-handedly representing flight control in the development of the shuttle software. He struggled mightily with the job but it eventually got the best of him and he had the equivalent of a mental breakdown. He was in a sanitarium for few months and became very reclusive not wanting to see anyone. This was all happening as I was in the process of packing up for the trek back to Wyoming. JR heard I was going and showed up at our house one Saturday morning for a visit and a good-bye. He was awfully quiet and eventually teared up and had to leave. It was a traumatic moment for all of us. He eventually recovered and had many roles in the shuttle world but I don't believe that he was ever quite the same. He visited us in Wyoming a couple of times and we always got together on our Houston visits. With the exception of the Lunney family, no one has ever impacted my life like Phil did.

XI - Remembrances

Thomas Carter

MEMORIES OF TOM CARTER

By Jerry Bostick

 Tom and I met in our freshman year at Mississippi State. We both were majoring in Civil Engineering and had several courses together. We studied together some and played pool and ping-pong together a lot. By the time we were seniors, we had become obsessed with playing pool and were great friends and competitors.

Upon graduation, Tom went to work for the Tennessee Valley Authority in Knoxville, Tennessee, and I went to the NASA Langley Research Center. He became dissatisfied with his job at TVA about the same time I switched from Langley to the new Manned Spacecraft Center. Within a few months, he asked if I could help him get a job with NASA in Houston. He sent in an application and I recommended to my Branch Chief, Carl Huss, that he hire Tom. Carl, in his usual manner, said okay. My recommendation was all he needed.

Shortly thereafter, my college friend was now my office mate in the Houston Petroleum Center, the temporary office space for the Mission Planning and Analysis Division. Tom was a very quick study at mission planning, especially launch abort and entry planning. Carl and I soon agreed that Tom should start training to be the third RETRO for Gemini, behind John Llewellyn and me. By the time he worked his first mission, I had switched to FDO and for several missions I enjoyed being his console mate. It was always my request in those days, that Tom and I be on the same shift.

At the conclusion of the Gemini program, Tom left NASA and went to work in California for TRW. Always looking for a challenge, he helped design an underwater control center for nuclear submarines.

In the early '70s, when I was at NASA headquarters in the Office of Energy Programs, he called again, looking for another challenge. Jack Schmitt, the Assistant Administrator for Energy Programs, remembered Tom from his RETRO days and had no problem in offering him a job. We worked together again for over a year, when I decided to go back to

Houston, Jack decided to go to New Mexico to run for the U.S. Senate, and Tom went to the newly formed Department of Energy. For several years there, he was in charge of transporting nuclear waste material across the country. I used to kid him about feeling uneasy about that, but in reality, with Tom in charge, I felt perfectly safe.

* * *

By "Dutch" von Ehrenfried

I knew Tom while he was a RETRO in Houston but got to know him better when he moved to the Washington, DC area. He lived in the Potomac area near John Hodge. Tom was a pilot and so was I and we flew a few times together. He joined the Nuclear Regulatory Commission in about 1975 and encouraged me to join, which I did. We were both Branch Chiefs in the Nuclear Safeguards Division so we worked together closely. When my sister Georgie was dying, he flew me up to the Philadelphia area to see her for the last time, waited for me and flew me back home. Later, he and I worked at International Energy Associates, Ltd. (IEAL) at the Watergate in the nuclear safety and safeguards area.

* * *

Clifford Charlesworth

MEMORIES OF CLIFF CHARLESWORTH

By Glynn Lunney

In the first acquisition for what became the Flight Dynamics Branch two years later, I hired Cliff Charlesworth into the emerging Mission Logic Section in March 1962. If I had written a specification for my first hire and canvassed the country, I could not have selected better. Cliff was the first achiever in a long line of young men who joined the Flight Dynamics Team at the new Manned Spacecraft Center during the 60's. The solid majority of these young men, like Cliff, were exceptional and the work we were about to do offered them the opportunity to demonstrate their true potential.

Cliff was the start of that process and he helped to frame what we were doing in so many ways, big and small. I don't credit any magical interviewing skill on my part. Cliff, and the rest, came because they wanted to participate and contribute to this historic program. They selected themselves.

Cliff brought a demeanor of calm, thoughtful competence with a no-nonsense attitude towards people's behavior, probably developed in his upbringing in Jackson, Mississippi and his couple of years service in the US Army. He had nicknames like Mississippi Fats and the River-boat Gambler – all of which conveyed a man of reflection and action, an ability to assess situations and to handle them. That was also the job description for a Flight Dynamics Officer, Flight Director, Program Manager, Head of a Directorate, Deputy Center Director – all of which were positions Cliff served in with distinction over his career.

Cliff had various quirks, like: be on time; you are responsible for your work; take care of your hygiene duties before you come to work; get to the point and be clear in what you are saying and recommending. He also believed in supporting people, providing encouragement when folks screwed up, and helping them grow in their assignments. When visiting Cliff at home, I often found him in a lawn chair, having a beer and watering his lawn by hand. He claimed that he did his best thinking while watering.

He was a major contributor to the formation and leadership of the Flight Dynamics team and in all his subsequent positions. Cliff was five years older than me, and although I was nominally the boss, he was always like the older brother I never had. He was always a good friend to me and a trustworthy partner, in whatever we were doing. He tried to re-strain my enthusiasm when appropriate by observing " Lunney, you will never get an ulcer, you just give them to other people. You are a carrier." And, he did it occasionally with just the codeword 'ulcer'.

Cliff recommended and we hired Bobby Spencer a few months later. Bobby was a friend and colleague of Cliff's at his last job. Bobby joined the section in June 1962 and was assigned to the Apollo group in the July 1964 organization of FDB. Bobby served as a RETRO throughout his FDB career and was the technical point man for the FDB command function of the Little Joe abort test at White Sands Missile Range, north of El Paso. Bobby sent the destruct command to the solid rocket when it got to the desired test conditions and that started the spacecraft abort sequence. We shared that project out at White Sands. When I was named as a Flight Director in August 1964, I was assigned as the over-all lead for the post-liftoff activities associated with these test flights, just like the handover between the MCC and the Launch Control Center. The White Sands Little Joe project was also my first opportunity to work with George Page of the Kennedy Space Center launch team. George went on to work Apollo, Skylab and Shuttle at KSC in various capaci-ties, as did I.

* * *

By Jerry Bostick

We called him "Mississippi Fats" after the famous pool player, "Minnesota Fats." It fit, because Cliff was born in Minnesota, but was raised in Mississippi. It fit also because Cliff was a very steady hand. Of all the people in the Trench and at the Flight Director position that I had the privilege of working with, Cliff was definitely one of the most steady, unflappable guys I ever saw. He didn't draw a lot of attention to himself, but he certainly set the standard for competence on the console.

Most will remember Cliff for his dedication to being on time. He was never late to anything. Linda and I usually had a New Years Eve party at our house each year during the late '60s. If the announced start time was 8:00 pm, the door bell would ring at 8:00 and there would be Cliff and Jewel. If you were late to a meeting that Cliff had called, he would most likely tell you that if you had a slow horse, you should get an earlier start. He was obsessed with starting meetings on time and ending them as soon as the business was concluded. We all learned a lot from Cliff, and time management was definitely one of them.

As a FDO understudy to Cliff, I remember him as thorough, steady, a quick learner, and patient. There were many times when I made mistakes, but Cliff never raised his voice and always patiently explained what I had done wrong. He was a great teacher. As a Flight Director, he was one of my favorites even though I was aware that he knew as much about the FDO position as I did. But he never tried to second guess any of my decisions or recommendations. His knowledge of the FDO position really made it easier for me because Cliff, like Glynn, understood what we were saying and usually left us alone.

* * *

By Bill Boone

Cliff was the Assistant Branch Chief and a Flight Director when I was hired in 1967. We both had gone to small, liberal arts colleges in Mississippi, 15 miles apart. He went to college at Mississippi College in Clinton, while I had attended Millsaps College in Jackson (for 2 years).

Cliff was the Green Flight and lead Flight Director on Apollo VIII. As a result of my stay at Pasadena Bayshore Hospital for a concussion during a NASA flag football game at Ellington Field, Cliff decided that his flight controllers would not participate in NASA's flag football league until at least after the December mission.

* * *

Carl Huss

MEMORIES OF CARL HUSS

By Jerry Bostick

I have always felt very fortunate that Carl was my first supervisor at the Manned Spacecraft Center. He was my Branch Chief in the Mission Planning and Analysis Division (MPAD). At the time (early Mercury Program) he also served as the Retrofire Controller at Cape Canaveral. Carl gave me ultimate freedom, encouragement and trust. He preached that in mission planning and flight control, we had to "think operationally." I wasn't smart enough at the time to know that what he was saying was that we had to practice systems integration. By thinking operationally, Carl meant that we could not ignore the impact of whatever we planned or did on everyone else and the complete system. He continually was upset with people in the Program Office and Engineering Directorate because, according to him, they didn't think "operationally." For me, it was a great thing to learn at such an early age, and served me well throughout my career.

He must have thought that I got his message, because when he had his heart attack and couldn't serve as a RETRO anymore, he recommended me for training to become a RETRO. John Llewellyn replaced Carl as the prime RETRO and I became John's understudy. As I think back on it now, there were several people in Carl's Branch who had many more years of experience than I, who he could have chosen. Maybe he did ask others before me, and he probably did, but I would like to think I was his first choice. At any rate, I felt tremendously honored at the time, and still do now, that I was even in the running to one day step into Carl's shoes as a RETRO.

I will forever feel indebted to Carl for his leadership, his guidance, his inspiration, and his trust. At the onset of my career, I don't think I could have had a better supervisor.

* * *

By "Dutch" von Ehrenfried

I liked Carl; he was smart, knowledgeable and a pleasant person to work with. But what I remember most was a trip to the Mercury Control Center one very early morning. We left the hotel on Cocoa Beach and drove to Cape Canaveral. It was about 4 a.m. As we approached the launch area, the pad was all lit up. I forget what mission it was, but it definitely was a Mercury/Atlas. It is a sight that you don't forget. The launch vehicle just shines with all the search and flood lights focused on it in contrast to the dark night. Carl was driving and as we approached, he turned to me and said, "Someday you'll look back and remember this." I have looked back some 50 years and I remember! Thanks Carl.

* * *

Jim I'anson

MEMORIES OF JIM I'ANSON

By Jerry Bostick

The first thing I think of about Jim is his maturity. He was the oldest member of the flight dynamics group and was somewhat a father figure to a lot of us. He used to say, "The only reason I'm here is so that Llewellyn can't claim to be the oldest."

Jim flew B-17s in WWII and used to say "All those bombs I dropped on the Japs are now coming back over here as Toyotas." He especially gave Jerry Elliott a hard time when Jerry bought a Toyota.

I can't recall a single shift change in the MOCR when Jim didn't come to me and tell me how appreciative he was just to be there. He was convinced that he had the best job in the world and thanked God every day for being able to participate in such an endeavor. He would tell me that he couldn't believe he was getting paid to participate in history.

With the life experiences Jim had, I felt humbled and very fortunate to be one his co-workers. We all took our job seriously, but I dare say none more serious than he did. He knew how fortunate we all were, while we just imagined it.

* * *

By Jerry Mill

I don't remember exactly when I first met Jim, but I remember his wisdom, which he unsuccessfully tried to impart to me. He was definitely a Southern boy, both in dialect and manners. He was very spiritual, kind

and gentle. I especially remember his laugh...definitely unique. Since I was both young and dumb, Jim took me under his wing and occasionally offered some "fatherly" advice. I remember in particular, his comments about marriage and how to treat one's wife. (If only I had learned and listened!)

My best memory of Jim was when I had been a bit too cocky in the office one day and Jim called my bluff. Jim was a "Colonel" in the Confederate Air Force, flying a rebuilt WWII AT-6 2-seater trainer aircraft that had been modified and painted to look like a Jap Zero. It had a "big-assed" 600 hp radial engine that was incredibly loud and powerful.

Jim invited me to meet him at the airport in Galveston where the plane was based...It was a beautiful day and Jim stuck me in the back seat (as I recall), explaining a few of the gauges to me and warning me NOT TO THROW-UP IN THE PLANE! We took off and I spent the next hour experiencing +3 Gs and -2 Gs, along with stalls, flying inverted and other maneuvers deliberately chosen to make me throw up. Jim kept watching my face in his rear view mirror. Just when my face was green enough we landed, I climbed out and kissed the ground. I was sufficiently humbled and never bragged in front of Jim again.

* * *

By William Boone

Jim was a World War II pilot who was still participating in the Confederate Air Force on weekends. Jim was older and his experiences were unique to the rest of us. He also had wisdom that came with his age. I believe we used to call him "Fossil." His moustache went with his demeanor, a little rough around the edges.

I would often complain about paying too much Income Tax. This would set him off with replies like, "quit working and you will pay less;" "aren't you glad you earn so much that you can gripe;" "do you realize how fortunate you are to have a job and earn enough to be able to pay taxes."

He had a pair of white bucks (shoes). I remember him wearing a white shirt, tie, belt and pants with those bucks earning the moniker "Ice Cream Man."

* * *

John S. Llewellyn

MEMORIES OF JOHN LLEWELLYN

By Glynn Lunney

John and I have been friends since we first met in the Space Task Group, sometime in 1959. It is strange because we were very different people-- different by upbringing, faith, being raised in the North versus the traditions of the South, physical size and strength, style of interaction with others and, generally more differences than similarities. These were topped off by the fact of John's life-defining experiences as a Marine in the Korean War before we met. John never talked about it, but it profoundly marked him for life. I had nothing to compare to that. With all those differences, our passion for what became the MCC flight operations work bound us together.

We were only together in that cause for a little more than a dozen years. And then our careers separated and we never worked together again. But they were the best of years. We were entrusted to invent and write the how-to books for manned space operations. And then to execute those ideas and decisions in the MCC for the Mercury, Gemini and Apollo programs. What a time—what an opportunity for young men to serve in this first burst of space exploration, taking humans off the planet and as far as landing on our moon. We did something that humans had been dreaming about since they first began to observe their surroundings—looking at the moon over a primitive campfire.

John found many other interests and adventures, but none to surpass the ones he had already experienced. And, now, we find ourselves celebrating our fallen comrade. It is a time to recall and re-live the many unbelievable stories about John.

The bigger story is about a man, courageously grappling with the many challenges of life and doing his very best. I am proud to call John my friend. Until we debrief this long and event-filled journey again, good-bye, my friend.

May God bless you and welcome you home.

* * *

By Jerry Bostick

John was definitely one of a kind. When God made him, he broke the mold. There will never be another like him.

When most people first met John they assumed he was a native born Texan, because he was a caricature of a cowboy. He actually was born and raised in Virginia but was truly a cowboy even there. Like Gerry Griffin once said "John was just born 100 years too late. He would have been the best sidekick Butch Cassidy ever had!" I first met John in Houston in 1962 when I was working for Carl Huss. Carl was the original RETRO and John was his understudy/backup. What I observed quickly was that John became an entirely different person when he entered the Control Center (then at Cape Canaveral). He instantly shed his "wild-man" persona and became very serious and single-minded to the task at hand.

When Carl had a heart attack, John replaced him as prime RETRO and I became his understudy. He was a hard taskmaster. He expected perfection in himself and anyone who had ambitions to sit at the RETRO console. He taught me a lot and I will forever be grateful.

Away from work, to say that he was a lot of fun would be an understatement! He could party like no one I have ever met. It was always a treat to be around him and all that you could expect was the unexpected! All of us who worked and partied with John could talk all day about "John Llewellyn stories." There are a million of them. All unbelievable, but most are actually true.

John gave the "Trench" its name, saying that the pneumatic tubes which covered the floor (he didn't have time to return the empty ones) near his console in Houston reminded him of the artillery shells in the trenches in Korea. He also gave us a "swagger" which we all will carry for the rest of our lives. He once said "It ain't bragging if it's true!"

I never met anyone who didn't like John. I feel very fortunate to have known and worked with him for many years at NASA, and to have our friendship continue up until his departure from planet Earth.

GOD SPEED JOHN LLEWELLYN!!

* * *

By Dave Reed

John was a unique individual to say the least. He was a 3sigma personality...or maybe 6 sigma. He was quick with his characteriztion of a situation and you had to hear him out as he was no fool.

I recall a simulation that the sim people had devised a problem so that a Flight Dynamics solution was the determined outcome. The way we worked would have the three (RETRO, FIDO, GUIDO) TRENCH positions discuss and then finalize a solution. In this case I had to make the call and it didn't sit all that well with John. But I distinctly recall him saying: "I don't agree with you FIDO but I'll back you all the way!"

As John became more incapacitated in his last months I spoke to him quite often on his book that we were assembling. The original plan was to fold his story into this main book. But as it was still in progress, we decided that the we should produce John's book as a standalone so that he could see the finished product. When he received it he was elated. So much so that he called me and told me how much he liked it, commenting that this would be a first for a RETRO to thank a FIDO!

John 'THE LEGEND' will live on forever.

* * *

By Stephen Bales

From the first day I met John I sensed a loyalty; to the Flight Dynamics Branch, to the crews, to NASA and to the United States. He never talked about it and probably would have loudly denied it if I'd brought it up; but it was always there.

When I was just a grade school student John was fighting for our country in Korea and his sense of loyalty may have started there. Or it may have begun earlier; I don't know. I just know he was loyal.

I also remember something Phil Shaffer said more than once: "John is always there with that one piece of data when you need it." He was referring to the times John had helped him in the early Apollo simulations where three words at the right time can mean all the difference. But I think many of us were the beneficiaries of this help in other situations; I know I was.

So to John : "Thank you –we'll see you later".

* * *

By Neil Hutchinson

On a personal note, I was always impressed with John's passion for the work he did and the panache with which he accomplished it. After his Retro tour he took on the Earth Resources Experiment Package (EREP) Officer job in Skylab; his perseverance (EREP was often in conflict with other Skylab payloads) turned that instrument into a great performer on all three missions.

He represented so much that was the way we were at NASA in the 60's and 70's...or wanted to be, because NO ONE could emulate him. John gave the Trench a personality that allowed us to pull off impossible tasks while never taking ourselves too seriously. He was truly a unique manned spaceflight pioneer.

* * *

By Dutch von Ehrenfried

I first met John at Langley Research Center in 1961. We both were in the new Space Task Group. We first got together because of our interest in Judo. We used to go to Fort Monroe to work out as they let the NASA people use the facility. Our families used to go to the beach together. Our kids were small then. As we got to work together I realized how unique a man he was. I didn't know much about his Korean War experiences but he was still very much a young Marine in looks and action.

During the early Mercury days at Cape Canaveral we worked and played together. He could work and play harder than anyone. As the years and decades went by, one would realize that God made a "One Off" with John. I have never met a man so unique. We could verbally joust with one another in fun. You could bait him with a line and he would come back with the most extraordinary flourish of comments.

Talking to John you would never know that this was a man with a Masters in Physics who could plan and execute the reentry of a spacecraft.

When he was in the Control Center he was a different man than he was outside that environment. We had a lot of fun together and I always enjoyed our company even thought I sometimes would have to take a ration of his comments. You never got the last word in.

There are enough stories about John that you could write a book.
A few months prior to his passing a few of us spent some quality time with John and his wife Sandy and heard some more stories. If you knew John, you could never forget him.

"What a guy!"

* * *

By William Gravett

"GOTCHA!....and a Farewell"

John Llewellyn (aka Super Retro) was one of the most intense people I have ever known, especially when it came to the RETRO job; but he also had an amazing sense of humor that could absolutely double you over with laughter. He used to pay off-hand compliments like, "You really look good in cheap clothes!" or "Is that a London Fog or Japanese Mist overcoat you're wearing?" or "I don't care WHAT Kraft (or Kranz or Lunney or whoever) says about you, I think you're a great guy!" And on and on. But one bright spring day back in 1967 we really got him! MPAD (Mission Planning and Analysis Division) used to provide lunar landing mission planning data for us including projected EOM (end of mission) spacecraft landing points. For one particular mission (AS-504 I believe), the landing points looked pretty marginal as far as earth reentry tracking coverage, recovery ship logistics, lighting, etc. Since mission liftoff time was dictated by the sun angle constraints at the lunar landing site, there wasn't too much that could be done to fix the end-of-mission landing point situation due to the required earth-moon geometry.

As we looked at the data, Jim Payne I think it was, mused that what we really needed to fix the situation was some way to vary the earth's rotation rate. That cranked up Super Retro, and he told Jim to write up a design for a potentiometer on the console that could be used to vary earth's rotation rate. Everybody had a big laugh over that, and a few days later Jim produced a masterful multi-paged memo addressed to the powers-that-be including copies to NASA upper management (Dr. Kraft, Kranz, Lunney, etc.). Jim used all the formal Latin and scientific names, semi-latus rectum, earth nutation, etc., etc., and showed it to John and all of us – all typed up on formal NASA letterhead stationery and ready for FCD (Flight Control Division) upper management signatures. Again, we all chuckled at our "cleverness." John even laughingly signed it as a joke, but warned us not to let it be seen.

John took off for some well-deserved vacation time the next week. As the old adage goes, "while the cat's away, the mice will play!" Through "creative" use of the copy machine and copies of old signed memos, we were able to "forge" signatures, making it look like the memo had gotten into the signature mill and that management had signed off on it and sent it out to the NASA world to have the concept implemented. The section secretary made an author's "comeback-copy" with all those bogus forged signatures and placed it in John's in-box.

When John came back, he was all smiles, looked tan and rested, and was his old wise-cracking self again. He went into his office and we all waited in agonized anticipation as he dug through the mountain of mail which had accumulated in his in-box. Suddenly, the paper-shuffling noises coming from John's office stopped, and it became very, very quiet. Then a long, loud, thunderous string of expletives burst from his office, and he came running out into our office area. His eyes were huge, his face was beet red; and in his shaking hand was the dastardly, cleverly-conceived author's comeback copy of the bogus formal memo telling all of NASA that the RETRO's wanted an earth rotation rate potentiometer installed on the RETRO console!

I know that all of us were bloody in the lips from biting them to keep from laughing. We had all promised each other that we wouldn't laugh, as we planned to milk this one for all it was worth...and Super Retro had taken it hook, line, and sinker! "I've got to call Kraft and apologize!" "I've got to call Flight Support Division, the astronaut office, the directorate office, all those people, and tell them the truth about this thing!" "How did this ever get out?!??" John implored. Of course we all looked at each other with puzzled, "beats-the-heck-out-of-me!" looks (carefully rehearsed, naturally). We also meekly commented our ideas of how this memo EVER got out as a formal requirement. My, my, what a disaster!

Super Retro paced back and forth mumbling to himself something to the effect, "How the Hell am I ever going to get out of this one?" All the while we continued to look shocked and most sympathetic.

Finally, crest fallen, his voice barely audible, he said, "I'd better start making the necessary phone calls." We let him go so far as to actually pick up the phone before we all said, "GOTCHA!" and laughed until the tears were rolling down our cheeks. He was embarrassed at first, a little angry, then he started laughing too and joined in the hilarity.

We will miss you, John "STAR" Llewellyn, as you used to call yourself. You were unique, no doubt about it: a brave battle-tested Marine, a Virginian, a Sun Dance Kid, a wild cowboy all rolled into one.

You inspired us with your knowledge and dedication. You made us think deeply about our jobs. You knew how to get to the right people to help us solve the complexities of manned spaceflight operations. Your "buffoonery" could release the pressure we all felt. You could jump right into the middle of a serious mission situation; and although you might not know all the details, you could help with that sharp mind of yours. And somehow, just your being there was a comfort to us.

With all the power and consummate skill you possessed, you carefully guarded the lives of astronaut crews, ready to get them safely home. We admired the way you could "save the day" with knowledge and gut feel.

To you, John Llewellyn, we say thank you, goodbye, and God-Speed! You will be missed!

And you will never be forgotten!
* * *

By Sandy Llewellyn

John and I have been married 35 years and it has truly been a hell of a ride. We married in 1977 but I knew him from 1964, he was a friend of the family. I always explained our marriage that we were two wild horses put in traces and had to learn to pull together which we did after many trial and errors with many years to get it right. I'm not sure what astronaut said it but I can see his face at the bay house party in Baytown after we got married. He said something to the effect: "John is a great guy but why would you marry him"? I told him because I was crazy too.

John was to me so full of life, always did exciting things, had such energy for the projects he tackled. He was like a bulldog that tackled, bit and wouldn't let go which sometimes was great and other times you hated it. He WAS someone you wanted on your side when things got tough because you knew he would do everything he could to get you through it.

He was unorthodox; who else could have done mission control, while being a cowboy herding cows in Matagorda Island, trail rides, ranching in Belize, whooping it up at the Singing Wheel, running down Highway 3 in only his cowboy hat and boots and riding his horse into work at NASA when he his parking pass was cancelled for too many tickets?

His energy was boundless. People would come to our house in the country and tell us they got tired just watching all of our activity. Vacations with John and the family were exciting too. One was most interesting in a land rover from Merida to Belize and on to Guatemala to see Tikal the Mayan ruin on mostly gravel rutted roads, with 3 children, wife/husband, a new mother-in-law and no a/c in July.

Finally he retired to the country but still he prepared a garden for me, put in the irrigation system, had his cows and his beloved tractor. I hated to see him go mow and would always ask him please don't mow under the trees. He always said OK and then would come back with blood and scratches everywhere, hat eaten by the mower, shirt torn. Several times grape vines would get around his neck and literally almost pull him off the tractor before he could detach himself. But no relaxing for him like reading a novel, he studied and learned new things up until the end. Our library is full of books and DVD's on physics, math, quantum theory, quarks, astronomy, history, the mind, etc.

The world just got a little less interesting on May 8, 2012 at 1:56pm. I know people wondered how or why our marriage worked but I truly loved him and he ALWAYS told me I was wonderful, beautiful and thanked me for loving him.

What more could you ask?

* * *

By Ken Young
Big John The Legend

Every morning at the Trench, you could see him arrive.
Sometimes by horse, but usually he'd drive;
Kind of broad in the mind, but narrow in his views.
And everybody knew you shouldn't give no booze to Big John… Big John..
    …Big Bad John

Nobody seemed to know what planet John came from
He just showed up at NASA and he sure wasn't dumb.
He didn't say much, kind of quiet and shy
And if you believe that, then you never knew the guy--not John.
Somebody said he came from the US Marines,
Where he got into fights with the North Koreens.
And a Browning Automatic Rifle in his huge hands,
Sent a whole lotta [NKPA] to the promise land…. Big John…
    …Big Bad John

Then came that fateful night on Apollo Thirteen,
When a O2 tank burst and the spacecraft careened.
Controllers were scrambling, and hearts beat fast
And everybody thought the crew had breathed their last
                         ...cept' John.

Through the alarm and confusion of this period so black,
Came Black Retro with a plan to get our brave men back .
With the help of M-PAD he started planning Free Returns,
And he and FIDO computed the necessary burns, Big John... Big John...
                    ...Big Bad John

And with all of his smarts he helped with the rescue plan.
Til'at last the whole world watched the weary crew land.
And three men were saved from that tragic 'eternal void'
And NASA bosses were glad that they had employed...
                    ...Big John

With that close-call behind them the Moon Missions went on,
And before John knew it, four more had perfectly flown,
Then Tricky Dick cancelled our Nation's glorious endeavor
And the challenge and the joy of Apollo went out of him forever, Big John....
                ... Big Sad John

So Congress gutted NASA's budget because of Vietnam,
And Big John decided it was time for him to move on.
John told Chris Kraft as they listened to Apollo's swan song:
"We lost the best job we ever had and we didn't do anything wrong!" Big John...
                    ...Big Sad John

Now they finally retired that Control Room as a historic site;
They should place a marker in the front row—it only seems right.
These few special words should be written on that stand,
"In the Trench of this Room worked - one Hell of a man, Big John"...
            ....Big John.......Big John Llewellyn... BIG JOHN........

THE LEGEND

"Semper Fi, Big John"

* * *

Granville E. Paules

MEMORIES OF GRANVILLE PAULES

By Jerry Bostick

When I think of Gran and his days in the Trench, the word "steady" comes to mind. As a co-worker during missions and during mission preparation, he was always steady and un-flappable. Under even the most trying situations, he never got "excited" and remained as cool as a cucumber. He also was a very devoted husband and father, always talking about his family in a very loving way. We remained good friends after he left the Johnson Space Center to pursue new challenges and I will miss him a lot!

* * *

By William Boone

I don't remember working any flights with Gran, but I do remember occasionally playing golf with him. The following story did occur and it was a GUIDO, and I believe the culprit was Gran; however, the years have dulled the faces...

At least four "FDBer's" were playing golf in Houston at Glenbrook on the Gulf Freeway in the late 60's. We were walking the course, either pulling a cart or carrying our clubs. I believe in my foursome was Gran, Renick, Bales and myself. One of the holes required a shot to carry over a lake. Gran had not been having a great round when we came to the water hole. He proceeded to hit 10 or so balls into the lake. As he walked back to the clubhouse he muttered a few words of disgust including the words..."never again." I don't think he ever played another round of golf.

* * *

By Chuck Deiterich

On Monday, August 31, 1964, I started my career at MSC in the Apollo Section of the Flight Dynamics Branch. Gran, George Guthrie and I shared an office over the lobby of building 30. Grady Meyer was the section head, Dave Reed, Bobby Spencer and Phil Shaffer rounded out the section. At that time, the Little Joe II project was in full swing with support from Bobby, Grady and Phil. Gran, George and I were assigned to the first two Apollo missions (both unmanned) designated AS-201 and AS-202. Gran and I supported these flights as GUIDO and RETRO, respectively. George coordinated the FDO support for these. Gran and I were prime for mission real time support with Grady as FDO and George as 'Yaw' on AS-201. George was also the Carnarvon FDO for AS-202.

I was always impressed by Gran's Navy duty aboard a missile frigate. He was extremely professional and never had a derogatory word about anyone, even when they clearly deserved it.

Gran had a 3 speed Sears bicycle that he would ride from his home in Nassau Bay to work. At times, he would let me borrow his bike to go to Building 2 (now called building 1). My kids were amazed at the fort Gran had built in his back yard for his son, Skipper.

After he moved to the Boston area, several of us had dinner at Gran and Diane's while we were on TDY to MIT (including Gary Renick, I can't remember the others). Skipper practically insisted we check out a pond behind their home where he would ice skate.

June of 2009 found the Trench Family on a tour of Canada following a GALA celebration of the 40th Anniversary of Apollo XI held in Seattle. Couples paired up for the trip sharing transportation and accommodations. Diane, Gran, Betty and I comprised one of the groups. Gran arranged for the vehicle while I set up the hotels. Of particular note was the Victoria Regent, obviously, in Victoria, BC. When we arrived they were running short of suites, so they assigned us to the top floor penthouse, WOW! Like kids at Christmas, we scampered about to take in the sunroom, sitting room, living room, 2 fireplaces, kitchen, huge bedrooms. We were especially impressed with the balconies that overlooked the harbor with its water taxis, cruise ships, seaplanes, and ferry rides. We traveled to Victoria to tour Butchart Gardens and then on to Vancouver, Stanley Park, and lunch at the Teahouse followed by the Sea-to-Sky Highway, Shannon Falls, and Granville Island.

Our time with Gran and Diane will be forever an outstanding period of Betty's and my lives.

Victoria Regent Balcony

Victoria Regent Sunroom

Victoria Regent Breakfast

Stanley Park Teahouse Lunch

Granville Island

$$* * *$$

By Glynn Lunney

When I first met Gran after his tour in the Navy, he certainly impressed me in our first interview. He was truly an 'officer and a gentleman', in the best traditions of that noble description. It was always easy to imagine Gran in his dress whites as a defender of our country. He went from a US Navy officer to a NASA Guidance officer and the gentleman part of him carried over for a lifetime. He was probably the most genuine gentleman of our entire team. As others have noted, Gran never had a harsh word about anyone and was always positive and constructive in his behavior.

Upon arrival, he was assigned a lead role on the Apollo side while Charley Parker steered the Guidance officers grappling with the Gemini project. He made a point of following and absorbing the Gemini development of the Guidance officer role and bridging that experience into the new and broader specifics of Apollo. There was new, major software to influence and learn for both the Command Service Module (CSM) and the Lunar Module (LM). There were also brand new mission phases to master and, for which to invent the flight concepts, techniques, and the Guidance officer console operator manual. Gran was always upbeat and most dependable and was tested quickly on the early unmanned Apollo flights.

The early unmanned missions were more difficult for the entire MCC team because we did not have a crew to discern the onboard situation and perform the necessary monitoring and commanding of the onboard guidance system. His role was like an astronaut on the ground manipulating the guidance system controls to perform the necessary moding and selection of options. This was especially true for AS-201 and AS-202 in 1966, which were unmanned tests of much of the Apollo system, especially the heat shield. He participated in AS-203, primarily a launch vehicle test, and he skipped the Apollo V unmanned test of the LM to allow the LM specific Guidance officers to get their opportunity. Gran was on console for the first and second unmanned Saturn V flight tests, which were designed to duplicate the lunar return entry conditions. I was the Flight Director for AS-201 and AS-501, also designated Apollo V. Gran always made me feel comfortable that his end of the business was entirely under control. He had a real test of nerves on the second Saturn V mission.

Cliff Charlesworth was the Flight Director for this launch, designated AS-502 and, also, Apollo VI. This second launch was to be a repeat of the first Saturn V mission. It was anything but when the Saturn V experienced major failures on each of the three stages. Afterwards, Cliff expressed his complete admiration for how Gran and the Trench professionally responded to the very different launch trajectory and the extreme lengths the guidance system had to exercise in order to get into orbit at all. The failure of the third Saturn stage to re-ignite, as planned on orbit, required Gran and the Trench team to prepare and use the CSM guidance and propulsion system to set up as severe an entry test as they could. I watched Cliff, Gran and the entire team handle these unprecedented problems and salvage a respectable re-entry test.

Gran went on to support Apollo flights VII through XIII with all the excitement that those missions brought to the MCC team. In 6 years, Gran contributed to all of the core flights leading to the lunar landing and then to the challenge of rescuing Apollo XIII. In that short span of years, Gran always stepped up to any challenges and provided the self control and expertise to solve any problem in his area.

Gran was a devoted husband and father and, to me, truly represented the best of his lifetime title of an 'officer and a gentleman'.

* * *

By Dave Reed

Gran and I worked many missions as a team. In the TRENCH the RETRO, FIDO and GUIDO were 'joined at the hip' in all we did on the console. I learned a valuable life lesson from this close relationship. Whenever the RETRO, FIDO and GUIDO worked together it could only go as smoothly as it should when all three thought and interfaced as one. Gran had that knack as most did that I had the pleasure of working with. No words needed to be exchanged over the loop. When something happened that would affect the trajectory, these men of the TRENCH knew it and would only forward the critical/essential items to their team mates. Gran was superb at this. A nod of the head, a raising of a pen, a glance at a plot board and you knew exactly what he was "telling" you. Only once again in my life's careers would I ever see this interpersonal understanding take place in a professional environment. Hard to describe it, but to know Gran was to know the beauty of his insight.

* * *

By Bill Stoval

We have recently lost one of our finest...Guidance Officer Gran Paules. Gran was an accomplished console veteran by the time I arrived in Houston but he always went out of his way to instruct and aid a fledgling FIDO. While the majority of my console time was spent with GUIDO's Ken Russell, Will Fenner, Will Presley and Gary Renick, I was always in awe of Gran's presence in the control center.

Away from our work environment he was one of those few individuals who never had a bad word to say about anyone nor did anyone have anything negative to say about Gran. In our tightly wound world his ever-present smile and infectious optimism made him incredibly unique.

I last saw Gran and Diane at the 35th anniversary gala of Apollo XIII at the Boeing Air and Space museum. Although we hadn't seen one another in 30 years, it was almost eerie how easily we reconnected. I consider myself lucky to have met a significant number of very special people in my life and Gran is certainly included in that group.

* * *

By "Dutch" von Ehrenfried

While I worked with Gran as a GUIDO, I remember him most for our trip to Europe together in 1986. My wife Dayle, his Gran's wife Diane, Gran and I rode the trains in Germany, Switzerland and Italy together. Our destination was the International Space Conference in Venice, Italy. We toured together, went to the Venice Opera and walked around St. Mark's square and had a great time. We were very compatible travelers and had a lot of fun.

* * *

Edward L. Pavelka

MEMORIES OF ED PAVELKA

By Jerry Bostick

Most people remember Ed as the creator of Captain Refsmmat, the ideal Flight Controller. In truth, Ed *was* Captain Refsmmat. Ed was the perfect example of people who just routinely go about doing their job as good as or better than anyone else without expecting or wanting any accolades. Ed never went to a post-shift press conference and that was fine with him. He got his satisfaction from knowing that he had done a good job on the console.

When I think of Ed, three things immediately come to mind. First, as a co-worker and as a supervisor, I was always comfortable in know that he was on duty. There just was no question in my mind that he would do the right thing. Secondly, he wias a truly funny guy! He always brought some levity to any situation. He was a terrific artist and was always drawing funny cartoons. We would usually discuss the popular TV shows of the '60s, Laugh-In, Batman, The Smothers Brothers, Glenn Campbell, etc. Ed could have been a writer for any of those shows. Lastly, he was an excellent auto mechanic. I loved cars but Ed knew how to fix them! He was always the first person I went to when I had a car problem and he was always correct in his diagnosis of the problem and how to fix it.

* * *

By William Boone

Ed was the artist for Captain Refsmat and Victor Vector. Once a week we would head to the Monterey House for some "good," inexpensive TexMex food and free pralines. He and Joyce would host all of us at his house in Friendswood where he would have lots of beer and a great cheese/rotel/hamburger fondue. We would be outside hoping to see any satellites streak by and discuss which were Russian and which were ours.

Ed became our section head during Apollo. No matter how good a year you had, during the annual performance evaluation, he would always find something for you to improve upon. On my early flights, he was sometimes there with me, but he allowed me to be in charge. I will always remember him as the consummate gentleman, always smiling.

* * *

By Dave Reed

Numerous stories could be told about Ed and his many talents. He was truly an artist in every sense of the word. He was artful in his approach to all he accomplished. His various car restorations and oil paintings were a sight to behold.

Ed and I put our combined artistic thoughts together following splashdown of Apollo XI. The crew was receiving such accolades Ed and

I were convinced that we controllers would never see an award for what we had done. So he and I sketched up a placque that we would have engraved and mounted for ourselves. At least we knew we'd have that to hang on the wall. The engraving read simply: "Be it known that [name] was a Flight Dynamics Officer for man's First Moon Landing, July 16-24, 1969.

Of course we would later receive many awards and forms of recognition, but hanging proudly among them remains our *very first award*.

* * *

By Bill Stoval

We have lost two FIDO's from that original group and both were very special guys. Ed Pavelka, or 'Fast Eddie' as I called him, was my section head for most of my time in Houston. He was a great friend and we had many a party at his house in Friendswood. Early on in Apollo I would make trips to the MIT labs in Boston where the LM software was being developed. On my way back to Houston I would go to Boston Harbor and buy 5 to 7 large live lobsters which were then packed with seaweed in boxes that I carried onto the plane. When the plane touched down in Clear Lake, I would head straight to Ed's place and the party was on.. A mixture of FIDO's, GUIDO's, and RETRO's would be there and we had spirited lobster races to determine the order that those bad boys went into the pot of boiling water!

Ed was a car nut and we spent many an hour working on my various cars, changing plugs and the like. I bought a spiffy new orange Corvette in 1973 and drove it until I left Houston. I sold it to Ed and he drove it for many years. He was pretty much done with console work when I got there and as I remember it, Apollo-VIII was his last mission. However, he spent many hundreds of hours watching our simulations in order to evaluate our individual progress as front room operators. No return visit to Houston was complete without a trip to "Ferndale" and a beer with 'Fast Eddie'.

* * *

Philip C. Shaffer

MEMORIES OF PHIL SHAFFER

By Jerry Bostick

Phil was one of the most exceptional people I ever met. Very modest, very thorough, very dedicated, and very smart. We called him "Jolly Red" because, physically, he was a giant and he had a red complexion and red hair, so instead of the "Jolly Green Giant" of TV ad fame, he was the "Jolly Red Giant."

When Phil came to the Flight Dynamics Branch he was assigned to the Apollo FIDO group under Grady Meyer. We were pretty busy with Gemini, so initially I had little interface with him. He soon came to see me however, to ask questions about rendezvous. He was the first of the Apollo guys to do so, and as I recall, the only one. He came into my office and said "Tell me everything you know about rendezvous." I attempted to explain that it really was pretty simple. All you had to do was achieve a position and velocity match. Once the target vehicle is in place, you launch the chase vehicle in a lower orbit, which gives it a faster velocity, and just gradually decrease the altitude difference until you catch up. Along the way, you may need to include some orbital plane changes, but that is minimized by the launch window. Of course, it was somewhat complicated by the limited ground radar coverage which dictated how much tracking you could get on the two vehicles and where you could pass up the required maneuvers to the flight crew. He was a quick study. He immediately grasped the concept and the execution techniques we were using. When he left the meeting, I had a strong feeling that this guy is going to make a great FIDO.

When Glynn and Cliff left the Flight Dynamics Branch to become full time Flight Directors, I was offered the job as Branch Chief. My first job would be to select a Deputy. It was an easy job because there were so many qualified people, but a complicated one for the same reason. I asked Phil if he would rather be my Deputy Branch Chief or take over the FIDO Section Head job. He said he would refuse to be a Section Head but would be my Deputy if I wanted him. He explained that he did not want to be saddled with all the paperwork associated with a supervisory position. So, he became my Deputy and it was a great match.

He handled most of the technical work and I did the paperwork. He was a great instructor for the younger, less experienced guys in the Branch. When it came to assigning people to upcoming missions, he was an invaluable source. Not only did he understand the mission requirements, phase by phase, but he clearly pointed out the strengths and weaknesses of all the potential assignees.

When it was time to name the positions for the first manned Apollo flight, Phil was the obvious choice for the lead FIDO. I told him I wanted him to be the lead and that he could choose the other FIDOs to work with him. It became clear very quickly that he had gained the respect of all the other flight controllers and the flight crew. He also was respected by the Program Office, Flight Ops management and MPAD.

I will always feel privileged to have known Phil and to have had the honor of working with him. He truly was a giant in more ways than his physical size! 　　　　* * *

By Jerry Mill

My memories of Phil include some at work at NASA, including night shifts on console and others during personal interactions at night or on weekends at his place in Seabrook. I still see visions of him threateningly leaning over his console towards Stoval. He was such a giant of a man that he was physically intimidating to me. Being extremely bright, one couldn't put anything over on him. He was a good friend and tried to help me professionally as much as he could.

He used to tell me stories of his childhood growing up in Oklahoma, and to this day anytime Oklahoma comes up in conversations, I think of Phil. I once deliberately drove through the panhandle of Oklahoma because I think that was where Phil grew up. It was also the location of the following story he told me. I assume it to be true, although I don't really know. All I know is that Phil never lied.

The story he told me is that he learned to fly while still in Oklahoma, and owned a small high-wing single engine airplane (probably a Cessna). He took the doors off and used it to hunt wolves and coyotes from the air, using a shotgun. He flew alone most of the time, and did it just for the "sport" and the love of flying. Obviously, he flew at very low altitude. Apparently, for some reason, he landed on the prairie in the middle of nowhere, bouncing along on what he had thought was a level area. Rolling to a stop, he dipped down into a hidden ditch or depression, resulting in the plane going in nose first, with the prop still turning. Needless to say, the propeller was badly bent and, in theory, was unusable. Miles from anywhere, Phil said he WAS ABLE TO BEND THE PROP BACK INTO SHAPE ACROSS HIS KNEE, which seems reasonable since he was a giant of a man. After fixing the prop, he turned the plane around and flew it home. He said it "shook a lot" but kept flying! Only Phil would have the strength and the guts to do something so out of the box. I totally believe him.

After I left NASA, I would visit Phil occasionally at his Seabrook home. Once he lost his weight, he never seemed the same. I valued his friendship very much and still miss him. Whereever he is, I'm sure he's busy intimidating all around him!

* * *

By William Boone

This is hard to write because Phil became my closest friend and mentor from my time in Houston. We shared a lot from 1967-2007. I still miss him. I first met Phil on Wednesday, June 15, 1967, when I hired into NASA. He had a window office, but had to pass through my and Jay Greene's office to get to his. He was imposing with his short, red hair and size, 6ft 6in and 320 lbs, give or take a little. He didn't say much as was his custom, but he visually assessed me. He gave me some CSM hand-books with instructions to read and study as part of my education. On Friday two days after meeting Phil, he invited me to have a beer after work at the Singing Wheel to officially welcome me to the Flight Dynamics Branch (FDB). It was me, Dave Massaro, John Llewellyn, and Phil, also known as Jolly Red (JR). Llewellyn left after a couple of brews. Jolly Red and Dave proceeded to initiate me by ordering many more beers for all of us. Being a new grad, though, I had no doubt I could drink them under the table. After awhile, JR piled me into the back seat of his convertible, Moby, put the top down and proceeded to show me the Gulf Coast, at night,...part of my education. I spent that night in his stilt house by the creek, hugging many trees, throwing up, etc. Welcome to FDB and to a long, great friendship and continuing education with JR.

Jolly Red often would get several of us single guys (Bill Stoval, Steve Bales, etc.) on weekend nights to go have some beer (or the hard stuff), shoot pool, etc. Somehow we all survived trying to keep up with him. Phil and I, and others (Stoval, Bob Regelbrugge, Charley Parker (Fox), etc.), played lots of golf on Saturdays, walking, mostly at Ellington AFB. His mantra was "Baby Golf." He knew that with his size he could powder the ball, but the trajectory would be suspect. So, he was always telling himself to swing easy, to play "Baby Golf."

He didn't just hang around with us golfers, though. He loved to fish with Don Puddy and took occasional road trips with Massaro to Mexico, always with the top down. He told the tale of Massaro jerking his chain by shifting into reverse just to see what would happen while he was going 90 MPH.

Phil had assessed me well. I would often go to him with "problems," thinking I needed his help to solve them. He would help me by asking enough questions so that I would solve my own problems. What a trait! Many years later, he would do this with my son, Cameron.

I remember a couple of simulations where JR demonstrated his decision making capabilities. During one sim, the launch trajectory was nominal. During second stage, sim failed his console. With no more data, he was "go" through burnout. He explained "why should he assume a failure would occur." The second was another launch sim when a failure was causing the trajectory to approach a limit line "head on." He aborted prior to hitting the limit. He explained "there was no way the trajectory would correct itself, so why wait." Both were correct calls.

After Apollo, Phil was assigned to develop the Shuttle software. He thought he was to do this "by himself." After awhile, he realized he could not perform this huge task solo. For lots of different reasons, he checked himself into a hospital in Galveston. His reasoning ability soon became obvious and he was soon counseling the staff. He retired from NASA with a medical disability then went to school to get a MS in Psychology. He was always learning. He later took an interest in oil and gas and got another degree in Geology. Through Phil, I participated in drilling several oil and gas wells and was fortunate to participate when he helped take an oil and gas company public. Until he died, he was the general partner for Polyventure, a compilation of many oil and gas wells. Along with other friends, I was a participant and continued to financially benefit from Phil's ability to make good decisions.

Phil and I often discussed our different investing philosophies. He tended to speculate much more than I. Through the years, his medium of investing changed several times. Finally, in the early 2000s, he concluded that he would have had more money if he had just put his money in a 5 percent CD rather than stocks. He eventually found a value Money Manager, finally becoming convinced he could not beat the pros. However, he still had his "play" money where he would invest in small companies he found through his many readings.

Phil went through many stages while I knew him. He went from drinking a whole lot to zero when he realized his short term memory was going. He became a "non meat" eater for awhile and had a large garden by the house on the Bay. He was always learning new "stuff," experimenting. He was into "experiences", such as swimming with the dolphins, looking for Bigfoot, etc. He championed being a human "doing", not a human "being." As he aged, he saw some of his allergies vanish and others appear. He would walk many miles daily until his knees started hurting from supporting his weight. This eventually led to a knee replacement and a drop in his height. His weight also dropped from 330 to ~220 lbs, which really changed his looks. He "visited" the Indians for a while to study the Shamans. He then found the Monroe Institute in Virginia which he frequented a lot, even teaching there. Like the Shamans using drums, Monroe was designed to help the brain's two hemispheres communicate with each other using diurnal sound which enabled Phil to become even more cerebral. I remember many nights at his house on the Bay where we would listen to the surf crash on his bulkhead and talk about "things/ideas." Being the insatiable reader, he had "data" on most any subject broached.

One night in the early '80s, with a storm approaching and waves crashing on the bulkhead, he had a fire going in his fireplace (this is important because during a party years earlier, he had a fire in his landlocked boat.). He put on a tape containing oriental music…a flute, harp, etc. My instructions were to stare at the fire without "seeing" it. I soon had an out of body experience, which really scared me. He observed the event as my body "relaxed." When I recovered, he discussed my experience relative to his observations and experiences at the Monroe Institute and recommended that I should go there someday. I finally made it in 2005, before he passed away. After my trip to Monroe, many hours were later spent comparing our different experiences.

When I was living in Huntsville, Alabama, in the '80s, he would drop by on his way to/from Monroe. He would always have some new, exciting experiences to pass on as well as what he had learned. He would do the same after his trips to the woods in New Jersey where he would fast for many days for the positive effects he felt in his body and brain. During one of his visits in Huntsville, I had hurt my hip. On a clear spring night, on a wooden deck, he had me stand, hold my hands out -- and passed a huge jolt of energy from him to me. The effect was so powerful, I cried. Putting my hands on my aching hip, the pain subsided. My wife, Beverly, saw it all, including the jolt when the energy passed into me.

I remember how happy he was to find and marry Sue later in his life. They were very different people with different friends and experiences, but they made it work. Even after his marriage, we continued to visit in Houston (I had moved back in 1996) and communicated frequently. He seemed to not have as much free time as in his single days, especially since he had moved from Clear Lake. He now had residences in Oklahoma and Lubbock. As he aged, he concluded that he should live within 30 minutes of good emergency care. Phil frequently drove back to Clear Lake to tend to business matters and, while there, to visit with some of his many friends. It became necessary for him to generate an hourly schedule so he would have time to visit with his many, many close friends. Somehow he was able to nurture many close friendships even while living remote. This was one of his many gifts.

Into his later years, we continued to compare our theories and successes in investing and other things. He also continued to enable me to work through any problems I would have. Phil was to attend Cameron's wedding in 2007, but noticed he wasn't feeling up to par and cancelled. He was having trouble getting a good diagnosis of his ailment. Finally, he checked into the hospital with an eventual diagnosis of Creutzfeldt–Jakob disease. He died in the hospital. Knowing Phil, he had a computer in the room with him, researched his disease and found out his brain would slowly "turn to mush." The tragedy is that here he was, the smartest man I ever knew, sitting around while his cognitive thoughts were ebbing away, probably being aware of it and being powerless to stop it. I miss my great friend and mentor and will always remember our experiences and the education he provided me.

* * *

By Bill Stoval

As I have mentioned before, Phil Shaffer was probably my closest friend from the section. He was a giant of a man with very short redish hair and he was known to his friends as "Jolly Red"or JR. He was a bachelor until late in his life. He loved big white Chrysler convertibles, and lived for many years on the water (Galveston Bay) in Baycliffe. He was truly a genius and loved our spirited debates. At his insistence I took a few IQ tests and qualified for the Mensa Society to which he belonged. I attended some of their local lunches for about a year and decided I really didn't enjoy the group. Shortly thereafter, I dropped my membership as he too teventually did.

We were virtually inseparable during the months leading up to Apollo-X and he made sure that I understood the how's and why's for every mission rule, every console procedure, and the proper way to conduct business on the console. As Phil moved on from the section to the branch office to the flight directors office and eventually head of the omnipotent Data Priority group we stayed in constant contact both professionally and socially. Ruth and I spent many an evening with him, eating seafood in Kemah and then adjourning to Baycliff to sip scotch and enjoy the view.

JR once decided to build a sailboat and I was his right hand carpenter. He left me alone with the project one afternoon and I apparently built a slight warp into one of the pontoons. He always claimed that my warp was why the boat didn't sail well...but it made a heck of a fire when we finally burned it up on his beach!

We played a lot of golf together and he was a pretty good player for a guy that size but he eventually lost interest in the game probably because he didn't have special pals to play with.

Phil was eventually assigned the almost impossible task of single-handedly representing flight control in the development of the shuttle software. He struggled mightily with the job but it eventually got the best of him and he had the equivalent of a mental breakdown. He was in a sanitarium for few months and became very reclusive not wanting to see anyone. This was all happening as I was in the process of packing up for the trek back to Wyoming. JR heard I was going and showed up at our house one Saturday morning for a visit and a good-bye. He was awfully quiet and eventually teared up and had to leave...it was a traumatic moment for all of us. He eventually recovered and had many roles in the shuttle world but I don't believe tha he was ever quite the same. He visited us in Wyoming a couple of times and we always got together on our Houston visits. With the exception of the Lunney family, no one has ever impacted my life like Phil did.

In order that readers might get a feel for the genius of Phil I am including the letter that he wrote supporting my nomination to the UW Engineering Hall of Fame. I am hopeful that these words, penned by his own hand, can give insight into his unbelievable grasp of what our job was all about. No one ever did it better.....

Dean Ovid Augustus Plumb
University of Wyoming
College of Engineering
1000 East University Avenue Laramie, Wyoming 82071

Dear Dean Plumb:

I am pleased and, privileged to add my support to the nomination of William M. "Bill" Stoval as the Outstanding Engineer for 2007 for the University of Wyoming College of Engineering Hall of Fame.

To begin I wish to provide background for the reasons I believe Bill Stoval to be an outstanding engineer. Manned space flight is a very complex technical undertaking. The tasks range widely from designing and building launch vehicles and spacecraft to providing worldwide tracking, communication and data networks. Many of the NASA centers are involved with Kennedy Space Center for launch and landing responsibilities, Goddard Space Flight Center for worldwide tracking, data, and communications network, Marshall Space Flight Center for launch vehicle design and development. These tasks bring with them equally important activities such as interfacing, integration cooperation and communication. All of these tasks and activities must be well performed at each organization level; locally at each center, nationally between the NASA centers and their supporting contractors, and internationally in missions such as Apollo-Soyuz with Russia. To be truly effective in this environment one must have and practice all the skills. Being technically competent is required but is not sufficient. High levels of competence are also required in the other activities. From the University of Wyoming Bill Stoval brought with him not only a sound technical foundation but also the ability to perform the other activities necessary for effectiveness. Bill Stoval arrived at the Johnson Space Center in July of 1967 and reflecting his apparent abilities quickly was assigned and began training as a Flight Dynamics Officer.

For multi-day missions multiple teams of flight controllers were established to provide around the clock support. Approximate two dozen controllers in the Mission Operations Control Room constituted the primary controllers of each team. These represented the on-¬ board and ground based disciplines requiring real-time support. The most complex of the disciplines was arguably that of trajectory management which required three of the two dozen primary flight controllers. These three were the Flight Dynamics Officer for trajectory determination and on-orbit maneuver calculations, the RETRO-fire Officer for normal and contingency end of mission planning, coordination, and maneuver calculation, and the Guidance Officer who prepared and maintained the on-board computers guidance and control functions. In May of 1969 Bill Stoval was certified as a Flight Dynamics Officer and moved to the Mission Operations Control Room for Apollo 10, the dress rehearsal of the first lunar landing mission the following July.

The Flight Dynamics Officer was the leader of the trajectory management team. In the preflight planning and preparations the Lead Flight Dynamics Officer was the lead for all the teams of trajectory management controllers and so was the principal interface for trajectory management planning with the rest of the organizations involved in preflight activities leading to real-time operations. These organizations included his trajectory management teams, the flight control team, multiple Johnson Space Center organizations ranging from spacecraft hardware oriented engineering and design to flight crew, flight crew support, and flight software development, multiple NASA centers and contractors, and the U.S. Air Force for Range Safety operations and for orbital debris avoidance monitoring, and the international participants. The Lead Flight Dynamics Officer was also an active participant in inter-disciplinary organizations such as "Data Priority" where the primary sources for real-time data and information were established and complex mission techniques were considered or developed and approved. All of these roles required. high levels of activity and competence in interfacing, integration, cooperation, and communication. Bill's performance in these areas during preflight planning, during mission operations, and in abnormal operations such as Apollo 13 was extraordinary.

Bill demonstrated the ability to innovatively address very complex problems. The following examples illustrate this ability. On Apollo 13 Bill led an effort to execute transearth mid-course corrective maneuvers without a guidance system using the lunar module propulsion systems. This effort included the development of the flight crew procedures and the validation of those procedures with backup flight crewmembers in the mission simulators. This technique was used, twice during transearth coast and was essential for the survival of the Apollo 13 crew.

On the later Apollo missions Bill was instrumental in the development and implementation of the M=l rendezvous sequence. Contrary to earlier rendezvous techniques taking multiple orbits to accomplish this sequence took one orbit after achieving orbit to dock. The efficacy of this innovation is best demonstrated by its successful use on the last four Apollo missions and on the Apollo-Soyuz mission.

As a part of the preflight interface planning activities far the Apollo-Soyuz mission Bill conducted extensive interface and integration activity with his Russian counterparts for rendezvous and docking. The level of integration was profound considering the sequence included a very different rendezvous sequence for the Russians, very different docking mechanisms for both the Apollo and Soyuz spacecrafts, and many issues including which crew would perform which actions. This integration activity was successfully executed as shown by the successful rendezvous and docking of the two spacecrafts.

Bill's consistently extraordinary performance was recognized and commended by NASA awarding him the NASA Superior Achievement Award for his outstanding Apollo 13 work, and the NASA Certificate of Commendation for his outstanding Apollo-Soyuz work.

Bill also brought personal characteristics that were primary contributors to his ex-

traordinary performance. He did not compete in the sense that his idea or proposal for an approach or solution was the best. This attitude was extended to his juniors, his cohorts, his seniors, and his supervision. His primary objective was to get it right irrespective of who originated the solution or proposal. His clarity in both verbal and written communications was very well developed which was unexpected and generally exceeded that of his peers and seniors. He typically was able to get to the heart of a matter quickly and so provide a solution, recommendation or decision void of extraneous data. These characteristics combined with his outstanding skills in engineering, interfacing, integration and communication greatly enhanced his effectiveness as both a leader and as an engineer. As a NASA flight controller he had the "right stuff". He is outstanding!

With enthusiasm and without reservation I restate my support and recommendation for the recognition of Bill Stoval as the Outstanding Engineer for 2007.

Sincerely,
Philip C. Shaffer
NASA Johnson Space Center
Flight Dynamics Officer: Apollo 7, 8, 10, 11, 12
Deputy Chief, Flight Dynamics Branch
Chief, Apollo Data Priority
Chief, Skylab Data Priority
Chief, Shuttle Data Priority
Flight Director: Apollo 16
Flight Director: Skylab 2, 3, 4

* * *

Bobby Spencer

MEMORIES OF BOBBY SPENCER

By William Boone

Bobby was from Rosedale, Mississippi which is in the Mississippi Delta, approximately 30 miles from my home, Leland. We had several missions where we were on the same team. I remember him talking about his exploits at White Sands Missile Range (WSMR) in New Mexico, and the crazy trajectories he observed during testing.

Bobby was known for his ability to buy/sell used cars. He was able to assess the condition, buy below market, drive it awhile, and then usually sell it for more than he paid.

* * *

Tecwyn Roberts

MEMORIES OF TEC ROBERTS

By Glynn Lunney

We had adult leadership role models all around us. Another of those was Tecwyn (Tec) Roberts. Tec came by way of Canada and the AVRO windfall to STG. Originally from the country of Wales, he was raised in the small town of Trefnant Bach, Llanddaniel. He was the branch chief and leader of the Mission Control Center branch. He was about 10 years older than the rest of us in the unit. But he patiently required our boisterous opinions to be backed up and reinforced by well studied background, compelling logic and reasoning to support any positions we took. It was a maturity lesson that we all internalized very well and enjoyed using to the fullest with our other colleagues who did not have the benefit of Tec's coaching. He was a quiet spoken man, but did not shy away from pushing a discussion to what he thought was the correct conclusion. And he did it with grace, charm and a kind of impish style with which one could not be angry.

All twenty-two year olds should have an engaging, talented role model like Tec to start their career with. We would all be better off. When I went to meet with Tec at my request, he often started with "Well, Mr. Lunney what are you trying to sell to me today?" Guilty as charged. To whatever extent I was successful at the art of framing and selling ideas, Tec was the teacher who got me started. I sometimes am unhappy or disagree with what I say or write, but looking back on my oral history interviews, I was happy with these comments about Tec, only slightly edited for clarity.

"So for a number of years, Tec was our leader and mentor and kind of a –not quite a father, but maybe an uncle figure- to a lot of us young fellows in the flight dynamics discipline and he was a tremendous help to Chris in putting together the Control Center concept in both of its locations. Tec was the original Flight dynamics officer at the Cape when they operated out of the Mercury Control Center. But he was such a gentle and yet demanding kind of guy—those two words don't go together, but he was that. He was kind of gentle with people and also demanding of their performance, and because of his talents, he evoked a tremendous amount of confidence that people had in him, management had in him, and it was like he was a perfect match for us."

"We were a random group of young engineers that arrived from all over America and a little brash and a little hasty at times and sometimes a little emotional and he would kind of counsel us along. After Tec died a few years ago, I wrote a note to his wife Doris expressing my appreciation for all that Tec had meant to me personally, and I told her how much I and the rest of the men who worked for him had learned from him and how I felt that I used a lot of what I learned from Tec in raising our family. So I wanted her to know that there was some of Tec Roberts floating around here in Houston in the next generation of Lunneys. Tec was one of a kind and I felt blessed because Tec was such a jewel and he got to be our boss. We had a wonderful time learning from him, and he had a hell of a time dealing with us, I'm sure."

* * *

By "Dutch" von Ehrenfried

Tec was much older (maybe 35) than the younger flight controllers. He was also much wiser and experienced. He also spoke with his English/Welsh accent which always made him appear even more polished and smarter than the rest of us. But I think the funniest thing that happen to Tec is when President Kennedy came into the Mercury Control Center following John Glenn's flight.

As Kennedy moved along the consoles, Chris Kraft would introduce him to some people. Tec was all the way over to the end of the consoles where the Flight Dynamics consoles are located (The first TRENCH). Tec sees that the President of the United States is coming in his direction stopping along the way and talking. He's coming closer and closer to Tec. Being from the United Kingdom, Tec is getting more excited...and nervous? As Kraft brings Kennedy over to Tec, Tec jumps up and greets the President saying, "Your Highness."

Now Tec denied this happened, but I think it did. It's a great story even if it didn't happen.

* * *

Epilogue

We all went on to many more exciting challenges in the space program and other endeavors. And yet, when we reflect on our careers, we are always drawn to our time together in the first decade plus of the Mercury, Gemini and Apollo years and what we were privileged to do. The events of those times always emerge with a warm, golden glow around them. The lessons from these experiences are legion. Most of them can be captured with more universal or general categories.

Leadership - The value of leadership cannot be overrated. It is the talent of clarity that keeps a team moving confidently and on the correct path. It is about the direction rather than the mechanics. Lack of it ends up in muddling, loss of 'follow-ship' and poorer decisions on the path to follow. It is not simply the province of the bosses. It is necessary at all levels in a team. Without doubt, the best example we had was Chris Kraft. He was uncanny in his ability to assess a complicated set of circumstances, reduce it to workable options and decide the best course. It was clarity of thought, underpinning his leadership ability. And, we saw his example reflected in the actions of so many of his followers. They say leadership can be taught but the first step is the need to recognize and value it, then to strive to live up to it. Learn from the examples of those around you, when you see it in action. Leadership is trust *of* the leader and *by* the leader- and we had a grand abundance on both sides of the trust compact.

In our NASA time, the best examples of leadership were: John Mayer- from early days in mission planning. Bill Tindall - for his enthusiastic synthesis of possibilities into realities. Tec Roberts - for his grace in teaching us to marshal facts and logic to persuade. Chris Kraft - for everything he did for us then and for over five decades of shaping the NASA human space flight program. George Low - for his profound contributions to the policy beginnings of human space flight and to the success of Apollo. There are so many examples of leadership in the flight operations area that it is not helpful to select just a few. They selected themselves. They answered the call and they prevailed.

Teamwork- This is so obvious that it hardly needs discussion. Our operations were a beautiful orchestration where the performance of the team far exceeded the sum of its individual parts. It reached new levels, beyond the ability of any of us as single contributors. We had so many examples of unselfish help being given to bring new people up to speed, to remove some problem or impediment and to explain the reasons behind some of our approaches. This transfer of comprehension and trust accelerated the learning process and made the execution stage much more reliable and dependable. We salute the mentoring contributions of at least these few of the early Trench pioneers- Carl Huss, Glynn Lunney, Cliff Charlesworth, Jerry Bostick, John Llewellyn, Charley Parker, Phil Shaffer, H. David Reed and Chuck Deiterich.

Preparation - In any endeavor, dues must be paid and a certain level of basic understanding and skills must be attained before even starting. This is a ticket to the show and gets you in the door. Then you will likely discover that several more levels of preparation are necessary which must be personally identified and then achieved. Activities have a way of looking simple from the outside. They usually are more complex than they appear. And, at least in our 'real- time' world, they show up at unexpected times.

Attitude - This may be the underlying prerequisite to all of the three above. It enables performance and provides confidence that, even without knowing "how" at the start, the problem will be resolved. It is not so much asking, "How should I do this?" but rather, "When do you need the answers?" Attitude can overcome many drawbacks or disadvantages. It is as simple as how one chooses to look at the world — half empty or almost full.

For the men of the Trench, may we forever treasure our friendships and contributions in opening the frontier of space.

Glynn

AEC	Atomic Energy Commission
AFB	Air Force Base
AFD	Assistant Flight Director
AGS	Abort Guidance System
ALSEP	Apollo Lunar Science Experiment Packages
AMR	Atlantic Missile Range (Later ETR)
AMU	Auxiliary Maneuvering Unit
AOS	Acquisition of Signal
AOT	Alignment Optical Telescope
ARIA	Advanced Range Instrumentation Aircraft
AS	Apollo (spacecraft) Saturn (launch vehicle)
ATDA	Augmented Target Docking Adapter
AVRO	A.V. Roe and Company
BAR	Browning Automatic Rifle
BS	Bachelor of Science
BSE	Bosster Sytems Engineer
CAPCOM	Capsule Communicator
CD	Compact Disk
CDH	Constant Delta Height (rendezvous maneuver)
CDR	Commander
CINCPACFLT	Commander in Chief Pacific Fleet
CLU	Chartered Life Underwriter
CPDS	Crew Procedures Dynamics Simulator
CM	Command Module
CSI	Coelliptic Sequence Initiate (maneuver)
CSM	Command and Service Module
CSQ	Coastal Sentry Quebec (tracking ship)
CYI	Canary Island Tracking station
DoD	Department of Defense
DOI	Descent Orbit Insertion
DOT	Department of Transportation
DSN	Deep Space Network
ECG	Electro Cardiogram
EECOM	Electrical Environmental & Communications
EG&G	Edgerton, Germeshausen & Grier
EOR	Earth Orbit Rendezvous
ERAP	Earth Resources Applications Program
EREP	Earth Resources Experiment Package
ETR	Eastern Test Range
EVA	Extra Vehicular Activity

FAA	Federal Aviation Administration
FD	Flight Director
FDB	Flight Dynamics Branch
FIDO	Flight Dynamics Officer
FSD	Flight Support Division
GE/B	General Electric/Burroughs
GET	Ground Elapsed Time
GLV	Gemini Launch Vehicle
GNC	Guidance Navigation and Control
GPO	Government Printing Office
GS	General Schedule (gov't pay grades)
GSFC	Goddard Spaceflight Center
GUIDO	Guidance Officer
GT	Gemini (spacecraft) Titan (launch vehicle)
HF	High Frequency
I/O	Input/Output
IBM	International Business Machines
ICBM	Intercontinental Ballistic Missile
IEAL	International Energy Associates, Ltd.
ISS	International Space Station
IT	Information Technology
LCC	Launch Control Complex
LLTV	Lunar Landing Training Vehicle
LOI	Lunar Orbit Insertion
LOR	Lunar Orbit Rendezvous
LOS	Loss of Signal
LRD	Landing and Recovery Division
M&O	Maintenance and Operations
MA	Mercury (spacecraft) Atlas (launch vehicle)
MAP	Message Acceptance Pulse
MBA	Masters of Business Administration
MCC	Mercury Control Center
MIT	Massachusetts Institute of Technology
MOS	Military Operations Specialty
MOCR	Mission Operations Control Center
MPAD	Mission Planning and Analysis Division
MR	Mercury (Spacecraft) Redstone (launch vehicle)
MSC	Manned Spacecraft Center
MSFC	Marshall Spaceflight Center
MSFN	Manned Space Flight Network
MVP	Most Valuable Person

NAA	National Aeronautical Association
NACA	National Advisory Committee for Aeronautics
NASA	National Aeronautics and Space Administration
NASCOM	NASA Communications Network
NRC	Nuclear Regulatory Commission
PAD	Pre Burn Advisory
P-tube	Pneumatic tube
PCS	Personal Communication System
PDP	Programmable Data Processor
PI	Principle Investigator
RB	Reconnaissance Bomber
RCS	Reaction Control System
REFSMMAT	Reference Stable Member Matrix
REFSMAT	(same)
RETRO	Retrofire Officer
RFO	(same)
RMS	Remote Manipulator System
RPI	Rensselaer Polytechnic Institute
	Richmond Professional Institute
RSO	Range Safety officer
RSOC	Rockwell Space Operations Center
RTCC	Real Time Computer Complex
RTG	Radioisotope Thermoelectric Generators
SBA	Small Business Administration
S/C	Spacecraft
STG	Space Task Group
SPS	Service Propulsion System
STADAN	Satellite Tracking and Data Acquisition Network
TADCORPS	Technical & Administrative Services Corp.
TDY	Temporary Duty (travel)
TEI	Trans Earth Injection
TPI	Terminal Phase Initiate (rendezvous maneuver)
TRW	Thompson, Ramo, Wooldridge
TTY	Teletype
Ullage	Use of Reaction Control System to settle fuel
VIP	Very Important Person/People
VP	Vice President
WSMR	White Sands Missile Range
WWII	World War II
WWMCCS	World Wide Military Command & Control System

U, V, W, Y, Z _____

Made in the USA
Charleston, SC
24 August 2012